The Binding of Isaac and Messiah

SUNY Series in Judaica: *Hermeneutics, Mysticism and Religion*

Michael Fishbane, Robert Goldenberg, and Arthur Green, Editors

The Binding of Isaac and Messiah

Law, Martyrdom and Deliverance in Early Rabbinic Religiosity

Aharon (Ronald E.) Agus

State University of New York Press

Published by
State University of New York Press, Albany

© 1988 State University of New York

For information, address State University of New York
Press, State University Plaza, Albany, N.Y., 12246

Library of Congress Cataloging in Publication Data

Agus, Aharon, 1943–
    The binding of Isaac and Messiah : law, martyrdom, and deliverance
in early rabbinic religiosity / by Aharon Agus.
      p. cm. -- (SUNY series in Judaica)
    Bibliography: p.
    Includes index.
    ISBN 0-88706-735-2. ISBN 0-88706-736-0 (pbk.)
    1. Martyrdom (Judaism) 2. Rabbinical literature--History and
criticism. 3. Isaac (Biblical patriarch)--Sacrifice. 4. Messiah.
BM645.M34A38 1988
296'.09'015--dc19   87-24496
                                                              CIP

10 9 8 7 6 5 4 3 2 1

This work is dedicated to the memory of my father
and teacher,
Irving A. Agus,
a pioneer in Jewish historiography.

Contents

Partial List of Abbreviations

A.Z.	Tractate *Avodah Zarah*
B.B.	Tractate *Bava Batra*
Ber.	Tractate *Berakhot*
B.K.	Tractate *Bava Kamma*
B.M.	Tractate *Bava Mezia*
BT	Babylonian Talmud
DDS	*Dikdukei Soferim*
G.R.	*Genesis Rabbah*
L.R.	*Leviticus Rabbah*
M	Mishnah
Pes.	Tractate *Pesahim*
PT	Palestinian Talmud
San.	Tractate *Sanhedrin*
Yad	*Yad ha-Hazakah*

Preface

W ere I to write of all those who have helped I would have to engage in something akin to autobiography. Instead I shall only mention a few of the people who are directly connected with this work.

My father and teacher, Irving A. Agus, of blessed memory, started me along the way, and his example has always inspired me. I pray to be worthy of being his *talmid muvhak*.

Ms. Esther Seligson was the first to read this book and to suggest corrections. Professor Georg Fohrer encouraged me in a time of crisis. Ms. Sarah Lerner typed and corrected the manuscript. Ms. Esther Beatrice Cameron edited the manuscript with sensitivity. Professor Raphael Posner made some corrections and saw the manuscript through its second typing. Ms. Eveline Goodman-Thau suggested the publisher to me.

I also wish to thank the editors of the SUNY Series in Judaica for including this volume in the series, as well as the staff of the SUNY press for their work and help.

I must give the warmest thanks to my dear mother, Tema Agus. She has stood by me as she stood by my father. Her love and generosity are a pillar of strength for me.

I owe an inexpressible debt to my very dear friend Jacob Taubes of blessed memory. It was together with him that the inner and outer worlds in which this work happens came into focus for me.

Jerusalem, October 1987

Introduction

One dusty day in the heat of early June, while I was reviewing the year's lectures, a student suddenly asked me: "Why did you talk so much about the Rabbis' attitudes toward suffering? People don't suffer so much nowadays, at least not in the West. So why did you harp so much on the subject?" This question, posed by a serious young officer in the regular Israeli army, brought home to me that the awareness that being involves suffering is a religious sensibility. This is not only because religious man, by nature, is claustrophobic in the confinement of the here and now and thus prone to a sense of suffering. It is also because the precariousness of his being in the world is in danger of collapsing when confronted with pain and evil that bewilder and threaten to tear him apart. Religious man, perhaps, can convince himself that his own suffering is bearable, but he is infinitely perturbed by that of others.

> Rava said: When they bring a man in for Judgement they say to him: Did you deal honestly? Did you set aside fixed times for the study of the Law? Did you make an effort to have children? Did you await deliverance? Did you discuss (the Law) wisely? Did you understand the implication of things? And, even so, if "the fear of the Lord is his treasure" (Isaiah 33:6)[1] then yes (all is well), if not, then no. (BT *Shabbat,* 31a)

At Judgment man is asked if he acted in accordance with the order ordained by Heaven even while being aware, paradoxically, of the need for deliverance. If he does not know that the heaven-ordained order is not something given but a desperate prayer, if the suffering caused by the Exile

1

of Israel and God does not shake his feeling of well being, then his religiosity is sorely lacking.

Human experience cannot be described in terms of 'I' only; neither can it be described in terms only of 'we' or 'it'. There can be no knowledge of a world without the 'I'; any statement we make about the world presupposes 'knowing' or 'believing' or 'perceiving' or 'feeling' and so on, all of which make the 'I' part of the statement. But neither does it have any meaning to speak of an 'I' existing as a thing-in-itself: The experience of 'I'-ness is one of being in the world. Being, for man, is not elemental; it can be grasped only as an event, an event that involves an 'I', an 'other', and the dynamism of time. Nor is this less true of religiosity in the mainstreams of Judaism and Christianity, where religiousity must involve some stance, be it positive or negative, within the world—a world whose meaning, to be 'true', must be perceived by a 'we'. Thus, religiosity has always to do with the 'I' *and* the 'we', and it subsists always in the continuum of tradition.

Because suffering is an intensely lonely experience of I in the world it stretches to the limit man's grasp on sanity, threatens both the understandability of the world and the self's sense of integration. We should never be surprised, therefore, by religious man's preoccupation with suffering. Reality for the religious soul, in any case, is always a becoming, an effort.

The present work does not deal, however, with the problematics of suffering. I have chosen to begin by dwelling on the subject of the Binding of Isaac. The hearer of the biblical story is expected already to be well on the way in the exhausting journey of suffering and its confrontation. The story does not, for even a moment, raise the question of why man suffers or of what the essential meaning of suffering is. For Abraham, the call to give Isaac up causes no surprise, though it does inflict infinite pain. Abraham is wise enough in his old age to know that pain is reality and that the ability to forego is the mark of religious man; Abraham's strength is being tested, not his belief. It would be trivial to suppose that we are being told how Israel, in its "spiritual infancy," came to the realization that human sacrifice is abhorrent. Rather, we must see the command to sacrifice Isaac in a cultural-religious thought-context, where the religiosity of human sacrifice is so far removed from expectability that the listener is no longer concerned with the theological polemic against it. The frightening demand made of Abraham is the demand to give up everything. It has nothing to do with the pagan custom of child-sacrifice (which is man's passionate participation in the brutal fertility of nature, a fertility in which life and death, giving up and gaining, dance back and forth in the single purpose of struggling through to the survival dictated by that very brutality), and it is the deaf listener to biblical tradition who hears that dissonant chord in the straightforward story. In the same way, the storyteller would cease the telling of his tale if asked, "Why must man suffer?" The listener already knows the sadness and weariness of religiosity and is straining to hear of the massive strength with which Abraham raised the knife in trembling hands.

In order to hear the story of Abraham, one must listen carefully from beginning to end. Our story begins where the everyday story ends. When Terah's way abruptly ends at Haran, Abraham is called upon to continue the journey into Canaan, but his continuation is to be a starting anew on a different and altogether strange journey. He reaches the Land, passes through its hostile inhabitants, and is promised the realization of a dream in the course of history. His wanderings are fraught with danger but sustained by his vision of the future. When confronted with the might of the four kings, he unhesitatingly plans and executes his midnight strategy, spurning any thought of partnership with the forces of evil. Abraham does not doubt for a moment that redemption will come in the very unfolding of the events. It is only Melchizedek who finds it necessary to pause in wonderment at the divine intervention and to gather up its tithe. Again Abraham is assured of the future. He foresees the exhausting enslavement of his children and just as clearly foresees their redemption in the inexorable direction of the divinely written history. Nor does he miss any chance at the implementation of his vision, even in the person of Ishmael and his offspring, though he does not always succeed. No aspect of life is unworthy of the vision, no demand too tedious or difficult, no people incapable of merit. And finally, after so long a way, Sarah is with child and the future is assured. Here the story should end and begin again with Isaac. But, instead, the stage has only been set for the real story of Abraham. Until now, it has been a tale of history; now begins the tale of Abraham. Until now, it has been the drama of one of the Fathers; now begins the story of the religious man Abraham and his only beloved son.

> ". . . after these things . . " (Genesis 22:1): These were meditations upon things. Who meditated? Abraham did. He said: I rejoiced and I gladdened everyone, and I did not set aside for the Holy One, Blessed is He, either a single bull or a single ram. The Holy One, Blessed is He, said to him: In order that I should tell you to sacrifice unto me your son without any hesitation on your part. (*Genesis Rabbah* Chap. 55 [Genesis 22:1], p. 587)[2]

The story has been hollow, impersonal, it could have been told about a man without a name, Abraham was not a part of it. Now, it suddenly becomes a drama of such intimacy and loneliness that all the earlier tales about Abraham are both left behind and given their climax.

Because the Binding of Isaac is told to those who are far along the road of religious sensibility, very far indeed, it has stood before its many hearers as a powerful, almost and perhaps even, ungraspable picture of religious being. I shall begin this work by dealing with the way in which the story was heard by some. The purpose of this essay is to follow that road that draws into *Akedah*, to follow its inexorable, divinely commanded attraction, to follow it to an end no less extravagant than that of Abraham's first command to leave his country and his kindred and his father's house and to go to the land that he was to be shown.

II

> Our Rabbis repeated [i.e., Tannaitic text]: Three sounds reverberate from one end of the world to the other, they are: the sound of the wheel of the sun and the sound of the multitudes of Rome and the sound of the soul when she leaves the body. And some say, [the sound of] birth as well.[3] And some say, (the sound of) Ridya[4] as well. And the Rabbis pleaded on behalf of the soul when she leaves the body and it ceased. (BT *Yoma* 20b–21a))[5]

One point, at least, of this wondrous vision is best heard against the background of the following exhortation of Epicurus in the "Letter to Menoeceus":

> Accustom thyself to believe that death is nothing to us, for good and evil imply sentience, and death is the privation of all sentience; therefore a right understanding that death is nothing to us makes the mortality of life enjoyable, not by adding to life an illimitable time, but by taking away the yearning after immortality. For life has no terrors for him who has thoroughly apprehended that there are no terrors for him in ceasing to live. Foolish, therefore, is the man who says that he fears death, not because it will pain when it comes, but because it pains in the prospect. Whatsoever causes no annoyance when it is present, causes only groundless pain in the expectation. Death, therefore, the most awful of evils, is nothing to us, seeing that, when we are, death is not come, and, when death is come, we are not. It is nothing, then either to the living or to the dead, for with the living it is not and the dead exist no longer. But in the world, at one time men shun death as the greatest of evils, and at another time choose it as a respite from the evils in life. The wise man does not deprecate life nor does he fear the cessation of life regarded as an evil. And even as men choose of food not merely and simply the larger portion, but the more pleasant, so the wise seek to enjoy the time which is

most pleasant and not merely that which is longest. And he who admonishes the young to live well and the old to make a good end speaks foolishly, not merely because of the desirableness of life, but because the same exercise at once teaches to live well and to die well. Much worse is he who says that it were good not to be born, but when once one is born to pass with all speed through the gates of Hades. For if he truly believes this, why does he not depart from life? It were easy for him to do so, if once he were firmly convinced. If he speaks only in mockery, his words are foolishness, for those who hear believe him not. (Diogenes Laertius, vol. 10, 124–127, Loeb translation, pp. 651–653)

Despite the exaggerated jauntiness, one cannot but be moved by this ancient statement of what must be the conviction of men who believe in the absolute autonomy of our "even by reason of strength fourscore years." It is particularly appealing because it entails, no doubt, a powerful air of bravery. And one cannot accuse Epicurus of callousness, since he at least recognizes that man's mortality is liable to make him despair of this life; the fact that man pushes on is the final statement of the meaningfulness of life for him. How different are the views sung in the Psalms:

> I love that the Lord should hear
> My voice and my supplication.
> Because He hath inclined His ear unto me,
> Therefore will I call upon Him all my days.
>
> The cords of death compassed me,
> And the straits of the nether-world got hold upon me;
> I found trouble and sorrow.
> But I called upon the name of the Lord:
> 'I beseech Thee, O Lord, deliver my soul.' (Psalms 116:1–4)

The cords of death are smothering and the straits of the netherworld oppressive. The encroachment of death is presaged in tribulation and sorrow. The prospect of death is so frightening, and as such so real, that only the vision of a dismal netherworld can express the poet's emotion. The poet cries out with all his being, "Please, Oh God, spare my spirit!" Death is not merely a fearful prospect; it is the antithesis of man's essence and the very fact of his being cries out against death. But neither is death a conquering nothingness that changes our being not even into a 'becoming' but into an 'unbecoming' or a 'becoming naught', at least not for religious man. The intenseness of the poet's being conquers, in the end, the dread of nothingness. His being prevails, "I love that God hears my voice and my supplications."

> Gracious is the Lord, and righteous;
> Yea, Our God is compassionate.
> The Lord preserveth the simple;
> I was brought low, and He saved me. (Ibid. 116:5–6)

His God, for whom death is also abhorrent,

> Say unto them: As I live, saith the Lord God, I have no pleasure in the
> death of the wicked, but that the wicked turn from his way and live; turn
> ye, turn ye from your evil ways; for why will ye die, O house of Israel?

> For I have no pleasure in the death of him that dieth, saith the Lord God;
> wherefore turn yourselves, and live. (Ezekiel 33:11 and 18:32)

hears his prayer. The poet's being remains, finally, complete and serene:

> Return, O my soul, unto thy rest;
> For the Lord hath dealt bountifully with thee.
> For Thou hast delivered my soul from death,
> Mine eyes from tears,
> And my feet from stumbling.
> I shall walk before the Lord
> In the lands of the living. (Psalms 116:7–9)

In this view, as I have said, "Death is not merely a fearful prospect; it is the antithesis of man's essence."

> For in death there is no remembrance of Thee;
> In the nether-world who will give Thee thanks? (Psalms 6:6)

> The dead praise not the Lord,
> Neither any that go down into silence;
> But we will bless the Lord
> From this time forth and for ever. (Psalms 115:17–18)

Man is to praise God. The experience of being for man is not a passive acceptance of a dumb necessity. At his never-ending escape from the clutches of death, man celebrates the fact of being and praises the source of being, his Creator. The essence of man's being, as religious man sees it, involves thanksgiving for it, and death thus is the more terrible because it is a going "down into silence" before God.

> What profit is there in my blood, when I go down to the pit? Shall the
> dust praise Thee? Shall it declare Thy truth? (Psalms 30:10)

Not only does man praise God, he says the "truth" of God, the essence of God, as well. Man in his passionate need to be, to overcome nothingness, is saying the essence of his God, the Creator, and this is expressed in his thanksgiving for salvation.

Hear, O Lord, and be gracious unto me;
Lord, be Thou my helper.
Thou didst turn for me my mourning into dancing;
Thou didst loose my sackcloth, and gird me with gladness;
So that my glory may sing praise to Thee, and not be silent;
O Lord my God, I will give thanks unto Thee for ever. (Ibid. 30:11–13)

Indeed, for religious man the fact of being is such an intense affair that he is unable to cope with nothingness:

I shall not die, but live,
and declare the works of the Lord. (Psalms 118:17)

Thus, for him, true being is always eternal in one way or another:

The dead praise not the Lord,
Neither any that go down into silence;
But we will bless the Lord
From this time forth and for ever. (Ibid. 115:17–18)

So that my glory may sing praise to Thee, and not be silent;
O Lord my God, I will give thanks unto Thee for ever. (Ibid. 30:13)

For Thou hast delivered my soul from death,
Mine eyes from tears,
And my feet from stumbling.
I shall walk before the Lord
In the lands of the living. (Ibid. 116:8–9)

Although, in these verses, there is no more than a hint at a developed personal eschatology, they say a primal religious perception: The experience of being is totally incongruous with nonbeing and excludes it. The poet sees himself as praising God "for ever," but he carefully refrains from overstepping the bounds of that praise giving as it is rooted in the fact of living as we experience it. The experience of living is a sense of being that allows no other reality than that of 'to be'. Though we see death in others and contemplate it in ourselves, we live an immortal being—a being without nonbeing in the present. For the self, death is always a fantasy of the future and never a knowledge of the present in the sense that 'I am' *is* a knowledge for the self—now. Therefore, the self in the assertion of being experiences immortality; the poet surrenders himself to the self-experience and declares his intention to praise God forever. In the ecstasy of thanksgiving to God for the escape from death now, the self is overwhelmed by the joy of living, of being the self, and admits no death. This is the primal religious perception that combines with a passionate awe before death to form a foundation for later structured notions of being after death or despite death.

A similarly primal religious perception is the vision of the resonant thundering of the soul as it leaves the body, as in the *Baraitha* quoted earlier. In order to take in the force of the vision we must first pay attention to the breadth of the tanna's painting.

> The heavens declare the glory of God,
> And the firmament showeth His handiwork;
> Day unto day uttereth speech,
> And night unto night revealeth knowledge;
> There is no speech, there are no words,
> Neither is their voice heard.
> Their line is gone out through all the earth,
> And their words to the end of the world.
> In them hath he set a tent for the sun,
> Which is as a bridegroom coming out of his chamber,
> And rejoiceth as a strong man to run his course.
> His going forth is from the end of the heaven,
> And his circuit unto the ends of it;
> And there is nothing hid from the heat thereof. (Psalms 19:1–7)

The notion of the "sound" made by the "wheel of the sun," as our *Baraitha* has it, is an overwhelming one and conjures up, no doubt, a great deal more than even the sense of power associated with the light and heat of the sun as in this psalm:

> R. Hanin in the name of R. Samuel b. R. Isaac. . . . "But his younger brother shall surpass him, and his offspring shall suffice for nations." (Genesis 48:19)[6]. . . . "His firstling bullock, majesty is his; and his horns are the horns of the wild-ox; with them he shall gore the peoples all of them, even the ends of the earth" (Deuteronomy 33:17). Is that at all possible? But [what the verses are really referring to] is Joshua, who is his [Ephraim's] offspring, that he stops the sun and moon,[7] both of which

rule from one end of the world to the other.[8] (*Genesis Rabbah* Chap. 6 [Genesis 1:18], p. 49)

So, too, the *Baraitha*'s notion of the "sound of the multitudes of Rome": "R. Joshua ben Levi said: If someone should say to you: where is your God! Answer him: In the metropolis of Rome"[9] (PT *Ta'aniot* 1:1 64a). And that of Ridya, "the angel whose charge is the watering of the earth from the rains of the heavens above and from the waters of the deep" (Rashi):

> R. Hama ben R. Hanina said: The day it rains is as great as[10] the day the heaven and earth were created. . . . R. Oshaiah said: The day it rains is so great that even salvation multiplies on it. . . . (BT *Ta'anit* 7b)

> R. Johanan said: The day it rains is as great as the day on which the Diaspora is gathered in. . . . (Ibid. 8b)

The contrast between the deafeningness of these sounds, though inaudible, and the terrible stillness of death is striking. It is precisely the intention of the tanna to play up this cacophony and to thus tarry in awe before death. In this context, the noise made by the soul at the moment of death or, correlatedly, at the moment of birth, is microcosmic.

This dramatic religious sensibility of what dying is changes the very perception of dying as a phenomenon in time. It is not merely a line marking the passage from a state of living to a state of death; rather, dying is a moment in itself and a moment that cannot be measured by duration but only by its momentousness. The primal religious perception focuses first on the intense beingness of death; only later are the various superstructures of life after death crystallized. How different are the words of Epicurus: "Death is nothing to us; for the body, when it has been resolved into its elements, has no feeling, and that which has no feeling is nothing to us" (The Sovran Maxims, 2; Diogenes Laertius, vol. 10, 139, Loeb translation, p. 665.) The perception of Epicurus is soothing, and one can well understand why "the Rabbis pleaded on behalf of the soul when she leaves the body and it ceased (its ululation)."

Religious man's sense of tragedy, his very tears, then, are not the knell of despair and breakdown but rather an expression of the very intenseness of his religiosity and a restatement of his basic religious perceptions. The way that we are following in this essay, the inexorable way that knows martyrdom, will make sense to us only if we allow ourselves some sense of the religious soul's perception of things.

III

Rabbi Israel of Ruzhin (died 1850) said:

> If a pregnant woman goes into labor in the eighth month when her time
> is not yet come, they try to stop her labor. But not so in the ninth month.
> If the woman goes into labor then, they try to hasten it, so that she may
> soon give birth. That is why formerly when people called to Heaven
> begging God to free the earth of some misery, their prayer was granted,
> for the time was not yet come. But now that redemption is near, no
> prayer which ascends in behalf of the sorrowful world is of avail, but
> sorrow is heaped upon sorrow so that the birth may soon be accom-
> plished.[11] (Buber, *Tales of the Hasidim,* vol. 2, p. 67)

Chapter One

The Mother of the Sons

I set out by examining a particular configuration of the event of martyrdom as told in an ancient story. In Jewish tradition, the story is known as Hannah and her Seven Sons.[1] It is far from a complete story; little is told about the background of the protagonists. We have mainly their act of martyrdom. But because of its function as a typological story (myth) in the life of the people, it can illuminate beyond the information it contains.

The story has come down to us in different versions, and I am not going to discuss or even list them all.[2] My goal is a comparative study of the story's configuration in several versions with an eye to understanding its early rabbinic manifestation. I shall begin with the version appearing in the second book of Maccabees.

> 1   It happened also that seven brothers, with their mother, were arrested and tortured with whips and scorpions by the king to compel them to partake of swine meat forbidden by the Law. 2   One of them made himself their spokesman, and said: "What do you intend to ask and to learn from us? It is certain that we are ready to die rather than transgress the laws of our fathers."
>
> 5   . . . the children with their mother encouraged each other to die nobly, saying:
> 6   "The Lord God is watching, and in very truth will have compassion on us, just as Moses declared in his Song, which bears testimony against them to their face, saying: 'And He will have compassion upon His servants.'"
> 7   When the first one had died in this way, they brought the second to be mocked . . . and asked him: "Will you eat, or else have your body dismembered limb from limb?"

8   He however replied in the mother tongue and said: "Never." . . .

9   But with his last breath, he said: "You accursed wretch, you may release us from our present existence, but the King of the Universe will raise us up to everlasting life because we have died for His laws."

10   After him the third one was brought. . . . He courageously stretched forth his hands, 11   then nobly said: "From heaven have I had these, yet because of God's laws I count them as nothing, for from Him I hope to have them back again."

13   . . . the fourth one. . . . 14   As he was dying he said, "Better is it for people to be done to death by men if they have the hopeful expectation that they will again be raised up by God, but as for you, there will be no resurrection to life."

15   Next they brought up the fifth. . . . 16   . . . he said: "Because you, a finite mortal, have authority among men, you may work your will; but do not think that God has abandoned our people. 17   You will see how His overwhelming power will torment you and your offspring."

18   After him they brought on the sixth. As he was about to die, he said, "Do not vainly deceive yourself. We suffer these things because of ourselves, because we sinned against our own God. That is why these astounding things have come upon us. 19   But do not think that you will go free in thus daring to wage war against God."

20   Their mother was truly wonderful, and is worthy of blessed memory. Though she saw her seven sons die in the space of a a single day, she bore it bravely because of her faith in the Lord. 21   She encouraged each one of them . . . and said to them,

22   "How you ever appeared in my womb, I do not know. It was not I who graced you with breath and life, nor was it I who arranged in order within each of you the combination of elements. 23   It was the Creator of the world, who formed the generation of man and devised the origin of all things, and He will give life back to you in mercy, even as you now take no thought for yourselves on account of His laws."

29   "Do not be afraid of this executioner, but show yourself worthy of your brothers. Accept death, that in God's mercy I may receive you back again along with your brothers."

30   . . . the young man said, "What are you waiting for? I will not obey the king's command, but I will obey the command of the Law that was given to our fathers through Moses. 31   But you, who have shown yourself to be the contriver of every evil against the Hebrews, shall not escape the hands of God. 32   We are really suffering for our own sins. Although our living God, in order to punish and discipline us, is angry at us for a little while, He will again be reconciled with His servants. 34   You profane wretch, vilest of all men, be not vainly buoyed up by your insolent, uncertain hopes, raising your hand against His servants. 35   You have not yet escaped the judgement of the Almighty, all-seeing God. 36   Indeed, our brothers, after enduring brief trouble, are under

God's covenant for everlasting life; while you under God's judgement will receive just punishment for your arrogance. 37 I, like my brothers, surrender body and soul for our paternal laws, invoking God speedily to be merciful to our nation, and to make you acknowledge through affliction and torment that He alone is God, 38 while it has devolved upon me and my brothers to stay the wrath of the Almighty which has justly been brought against the whole of our nation." (II Maccabees 7: 1–41)[3]

In telling a story of martyrdom of this kind, the storyteller undertakes two different tasks. The first is to convey the marytrs' heroism. The notes of this motif already are adumbrated in the second passage, where the "spokesman" implies that any attempt to convince the group is useless— there is no room for discussion. The story is not a suspenseful one: From the very beginning we share the teller's conviction that no hesitation on the part of these martyrs is conceivable. The blood-curdling description of some of the tortures used (I have not quoted them here) leaves no doubt whatsoever as to the inner strength of the sons. And the author is almost tempted to be carried away with this motif and to describe the martyrdom in something like the following manner:

> And . . . even reached such a pitch of nobility that none of them groaned or wailed, showing to all of us that at that hour of their torture the noble martyrs of Christ were absent from the flesh, or rather that the Lord was standing by and talking with them. And paying heed to the grace of Christ they despised worldly tortures, by a single hour purchasing everlasting life. And the fire of their cruel torturers had no heat for them. . . . (*The Martyrdom of St. Polycarp, Bishop of Smyrna* [occurring in the year 155 or 156 C.E.], II, 2–4)[4]

He shows this temptation with remarks such as: "He courageously stretched forth his hands"(10), "the young man said, 'What are you waiting for?'" (30), and "'Indeed, our brothers, after enduring brief trouble (!)'" (36). But he reveals what is really on his mind with statements with pathos, such as "it has devolved upon me and my brothers to stay the wrath of the Almighty" (38). The suffering of the martyrs, finally, is very troubling, and the author's temptation is short-lived. And this brings us to the second task that must be carried out by the teller of each version.

If the aim of the storyteller were only to amaze us with the greatness of a particular martyrdom, his task would have been merely a matter of proper literary technique—a technique of which he shows himself capable by revealing just enough frightening detail to let our imagination spin with every mention of words like *suffering* and *mutilation*. But the writer has a far more difficult task, one in which he himself is not merely the teller but a tense audience as well, since he must convince himself as well as others. This is the task of "rationalization," of making the personality of the martyrs in their act of martyrdom believable. If their action is unreal, then the listener cannot be moved by their heroism. If the listener cannot picture to himself the actuality of "real" people doing such a thing, then it remains a legend for him. It is a "true" story and not a legend only when the action he hears is "rational"; that is, when he himself is capable of following the heroes through their anguish and terrible decision—at least in thought—even if his courage fails him when he entertains any notion of actually enduring it himself. If the being acted out by the martyrs thus is rational to him, then and only then might he be moved to similar heroism at the proper time by the impressive example to which he listens, absorbed. With Pascal:

> Example of noble deaths of Spartans and others hardly affects us, for what good does it do us?
>
> But the example of the deaths of martyrs affect us for they are our members, we have a common bond with them, their resolution can inspire ours, not only by example, but because it has perhaps deserved ours.
>
> There is none of this in heathen examples. We have no connection with them, just as we do not become rich through seeing a rich stranger, but through seeing a father or husband rich. (*Pensées*, no. 359)[5]

We can feel the effort of the author of the passages in II Maccabees to find the "connection" with the mother and her seven sons, and we sense that his need to find that "connection" is one grounded deeply in his own religiosity. He presents us with a threefold "rationalization":

1. Resurrection. The second, third, fourth, and seventh sons, as well as their mother, proclaim a conviction that they will be resurrected to life after death. This proclamation arises out of the awareness that the martyrs are wronged deeply and suffering profoundly. In other words, it is not merely a proclamation of an article of faith, it is an intrinsic part of the event of martyrdom. The martyr, in the intensity of his suffering, and because of it, transforms his dying from a meaningless "whimper" into an act of becoming: "the King of the Universe will raise us up to everlasting life because we have died for His laws" (9). "Accept death, that in God's mercy I may receive you back again along with your brothers" (29). The yearning for resurrection arises out of the love for living and is not a negation of it. Precisely because these martyrs do *not* want to die, they dream of resurrection while dying. This is the tone of most of the story. It is in keeping with the notion of bodily resurrection rather than that of immortality of the soul. "From heaven have I had these (hands), yet because of God's laws I count them as nothing, for from Him I hope to have them back again" (11). It is not his hands that he "counts as nothing," rather, it is the "illusion" of losing them that he counts as nothing! The thought of bodily negation is bearable only because it is viewed as temporary. Belief in the immortality of the soul can be a negation of living; not so the belief in bodily resurrection, and certainly not in our story. Its proclamation here, therefore, is an essential part of the being in the world of the mother and her sons. It is a "rationalization" of their actions because it proclaims a personality that, in the fullness of its being, is understandable to the storyteller and his audience. The 'I' of the martyrs has been validated and is 'real'.

2. *Punishment of the Oppressor.* Anyone who is sensitive to the evil that abounds in the world cannot but be very uneasy indeed at the sight of the easy impudence of its perpetrators. Perhaps humanity's greatest sin is its indifference to the lot of oppressor and oppressed. For religious man the evident lack of discrimination between the two, or the preference that reality seems to foster for the former, shakes the reality he knows to its foundations. How much more grotesque is suffering when it is malignantly inflicted by one who considers himself superior in one way or another to his victim, particularly when the oppressor's behavior is only evidence of the beastiality of man! The mother and her seven sons knew only too well the arrogance of their malefactors, and the martyrs' sanity is upheld by the conviction that there is a saner reality than the immediate one. "Because you, a finite mortal, have authority among men, you may work your will; but do not think that God has abandoned our people" (16). Even the thoughts of the oppressor are unbearable! Or perhaps, for religious man, the thoughts of the oppressor are the most unbearable aspect of the nightmare, because for religious man the world of thinking is the world in which the reality of holiness is rooted. "You will see how His overwhelming power will torment you and your offspring" (17). Reality for the Jew is grounded in the continuity of generations and retribution must be manifested in the fullness of reality. "You profane wretch, vilest of all men, be not vainly buoyed up by your insolent, uncertain hopes, raising your hand against His servants (34). You have not yet escaped the judgment of the Almighty, all-seeing God" (35). Those who told and listened to the story felt an unhappy identification with its heroes and must have felt the cry for divine justice well up in their own throats.

3. *Martyrdom as Punishment for Sin.* "We suffer these things because of ourselves, because we sinned against our own God. That is why these astounding things have come upon us (18). But do not think that you will go free in thus daring to wage war against God" (19). These sentences are surprising because the martyr thereby includes himself in one category

with his tormentor. I think that this is one of the most heroic facets of the story. Rather than disassociating himself from the evildoers, the sufferer ties himself ever more firmly to the reality of being as part of the dark world. Both oppressor and oppressed are intimately part of a history in which a divine immanence unfolds. Both their lives are ineluctably part of the weave of the same Divine fabric, different as their end ultimately will be. This notion is evidence of the profound acceptance of historical reality in Jewish thinking. It also is evidence of the intertwining of personal piety and history. The martyr acknowledges his own sins as a necessary part of the rationalization of his suffering—"We suffer these things because of *ourselves*, because *we* sinned against our God." The martyr needs to rationalize not only his act of martyrdom but his being in the world with all the circumstances that led him to this terrible confrontation. It underscores the immensity of the task of the storyteller as well as the inner pain with which the story is told and listened to.

The essence of our story thus indeed is twofold. It is both a tale of heroism *and* a "rationalization" of martyrdom. This is true of all the story's versions, which I intend to discuss.

The rationalizing elements in the version of Maccabees IV are the main point of that book and are the frame into which our story fits. The author points this out at the very beginning:

> 1:1 Thoroughly philosophical is the subject I propose to discuss, namely whether religous reason is sovereign over the emotions; and I may properly advise you to attend earnestly to my philosophical exposition. 2 The theme is essential to everyone as a branch of knowledge, but in addition it embraces a eulogy of the highes virtue—I mean, of course, prudence.
>
> 7 Many and diverse sources would enable me to demonstrate to you that reason is sovereign over emotions, 8 but I could far best prove it from the heroism of those who died for virtue's sake—Eleazar, and the seven brothers, and their mother.
> 9 All these despised suffering even unto death, and so proved that reason is sovereign over emotions. (IV Maccabees 1:1–2, 7–9)[6]

The various themes of rationalization are summed up toward the end of the book as follows:

> 17:11 Divine indeed was the contest of which they were the issue. 12 Of that contest virtue was the umpire; and its score was for constancy. Victory was incorruptibility in a life of long duration. 13 Eleazar was the prime contestant; but the mother of the seven sons entered

the competition, and the brothers too vied for the prize. 14   The tyrant was the adversary, and the world and humanity were the spectators. 15   Reverence for God was the winner, and crowned her own champions. 16   Who did not marvel at the athletes of the divine legislation, who were not astonished by them?

17   The tyrant himself, and his whole council, were amazed at the constancy 18   whereby they now have their stand before the throne of God, and live the life of eternal blessedness.

20   These, then, having been sanctified by God, are honored not only with this distinction, but also by the fact that because of them our enemies did not prevail over our nation; 21   and the tyrant was chastised, and our land purified—they having become as it were a ransom for the sin of the nation. 22   It was through the blood of these righteous ones, and through the expiation of their death, that divine Providence preserved Israel, which had been ill used. (Ibid. 17:11–18, 20–22)[7]

I have chosen these sentences from Maccabees IV although their philosophical self-assuredness, in contrast to the authenticity of the martyrs, is the opposite of moving, because they show clearly what its author saw as the "rationalization" of martyrdom. The repetition of these themes throughout the book and the very form of the book itself are evidence of the seriousness with which its author felt the need for "rationalization." Perhaps, he has exaggerated this aspect of our story, but he undoubtedly is correct in his initial recognition of its centrality. I stress this point that is also apparent in the longer of the rabbinic versions as it will shed light on the shorter of the rabbinic versions. Let us turn now to the former.

There is a story about Miriam bat Tanhum who was seized together with her seven sons. They were taken by Caesar and placed in seven cells. He brought forth the first and said to him, "Bow down to the icon." He answered him, "I dare not bow down to the icon." He said to him, "Why?" He answered, "Because it is written in our Law, 'I am the Lord thy God' (Exodus 20:2)." He was at once taken out and executed. He brought out the second and said to him, "Bow down to the icon." He answered him, "I dare not, my brother did not bow down and I shall not bow down." He said to him, "Why?" He answered; "For it is written in the Law, 'Thou shalt have no other gods before Me' (Ibid. 20:3)." He at once sentenced him and he was executed. He brought out the third and said to him, "Bow down to the icon." He answered him, "I shall not bow down." He said to him, "Why?" He answered, "For it is written in the Law, 'For thou shalt bow down to no other god' (Ibid. 34:14)." He at once sentenced him and he was executed. He brought out the fourth and the son said his verse, "'He that sacrificeth unto the gods, save unto the Lord only, shall be utterly destroyed' (Ibid. 22:19)." He sentenced him and he was executed. He brought out the fifth and he, too, said his verse, "'Here, O Israel: The Lord our God, the Lord is one' (Deuteronomy 6:4)." He at once sentenced him and he was executed. He brought out the sixth and he, too, said his verse, "'. . . for the Lord thy God is in the midst of thee, a God great and awful' (Ibid. 7:21)." He sentenced him and he was executed. He brought out the seventh and he was the youngest of them all. He said, "My son, bow down to the icon." He answered him, "I dare not." He said to him, "Why?" He answered, "For it is written in our Law, 'Know this day, and lay it to thy heart, that the Lord, He is God in heaven above and upon the earth beneath; there is none else' (Ibid. 4:39). And furthermore, for we have sworn to our God that we shall not exchange Him for another god, as it is written, 'Thou hast avouched the Lord this day to be thy God' (Ibid. 26:17). And just as we have sworn to Him, so He has sworn to us that He will not exchange us for another nation, as it is written, 'And the Lord hath avouched thee this day to be His own treasure' (Ibid. 26:18)." He said to him, "Your brothers had their fill of years and of life, and they tasted goodness; while you are young, you have not had your fill of years and you have not tasted the goodness of the world. Bow down to the icon and I will do goodness for you." He answered, "It is written in our Law; 'The Lord shall reign for ever and ever' (Psalms 115:18), and it is written, 'The Lord is King for ever and ever; The nations are perished out of His land' (Psalms 10:16). And all of you and your empire are to be nullified. Man, who is flesh and blood, today he is alive and on the morrow—dead, today he is rich, and on the morrow—poor. But the Holy One, Blessed is He, lives and endures for ever and ever." He said to him, "Look at your brothers who are lying dead before you; and I will throw my ring on the ground before the icon, and you pick it up, so that everyone may see that you heed my command." He answered him, "You are pitiful; and if you are intimidated by humans like yourself, shall I not fear the Ruler of Kings of Kings, the Holy One Blessed is He, the Lord of the world?" He said to him, "But is there a God to the world?" He answered, "You poor thing, and do you perceive a world in anarchy?" He said to him, "But does your God have a mouth?" He answered, "Concerning your gods it is written, 'They have mouths but they speak not' (Ibid. 115:5); while concerning our God it is written, 'By the word of the Lord were the heavens made' (Psalm 33:6)." He said to him, "But does you God have eyes?" He answered, "Concerning your gods it is written 'Eyes have they, but they see not' (Ibid. 115:5); while concerning our God it is written, '. . . the eyes of the Lord, that run to and fro through the whole earth' (Zechariah 4:10)." He said to him, "But does your God have ears?" He answered, "Concerning your gods it is written, 'They have ears, but they hear not' (Psalms 115:6); while concerning our God it is written, 'then they that feared the Lord spoke one with another; and the

Lord hearkened, and heard, and a book of remembrance was written before Him' (Malachi 3:16)." He said to him, "But does your God have a nose?" He answered, "Concerning your gods it is written, 'Noses have they, but they smell not' (Psalms 115:6); while concerning our God it is written, 'And the Lord smelled the sweet savor' (Genesis 8:21)." He said to him, "But does your God have hands?" He answered, "Concerning your gods it is written, 'They have hands, but they handle not' (Psalm 115:7); while concerning our God it is written , 'My hand hath laid the foundation of the earth' (Isaiah 48:13)." He said to him, "But does your God have legs?" He answered, "Concerning your gods it is written, 'Feet have they, but they walk not' (Psalms 115:7); while concerning our God it is written, 'And his feet shall stand in that day upon the Mount of Olives' (Zechariah 14:4)." He said to him, "But does your God have a throat?" He answered, "Concerning your gods it is written, 'Neither speak they with their throat' (Psalms 115:7); while concerning our God it is written, 'And the sound that goeth out of His mouth' (Job 27:2)." He said to him, "If all these attributes are found in Him who is your God, why does He not save you from me as He saved Hananiah, Mishael and Azariah from the hands of Nebuchadnezzar?" He answered, "Hananiah, Mishael and Azariah were upstanding and Nebuchadnezzar was a worthy king for the purpose of a miracle being accomplished through him as an instrument. But you are not worthy. And we have been condemned to death by heaven. Were you not to kill us, the Divine has many other executors; there are many bears, many wolves, and lions and snakes and leopards and scorpions who would assail and kill us. But in the future the Holy One Blessed is He will finally bring retribution on you for our blood." He at once sentenced him to be killed. The boy's mother said to the ruler, "By your very life! Give me my son and I will hug him and kiss him." They gave him to her and she drew out her breasts and suckled the child. Then she said to the ruler, "By your very life! Kill him only after your have killed me first!" He answered her, "I shall not heed you because it is written in your Law, 'And whether it be cow or ewe, ye shall not kill it and its young both in one day' (Leviticus 22:28)." She said to him, "The world's fool! You have already upheld all the commandments so that there is none left wanting for you except this one alone!" He at once commanded that the boy be killed. The mother fell upon her son and while hugging him and kissing him she said to him, "My son, go to Abraham your father and say to him, 'My mother has said as follows: Let not your spirits soar[8] with the thought that "I have built an altar and I have offered up my son Isaac." Behold our mother has built seven altars and has offered up seven sons, in one day! Yours was a test, but mine an actuality!'" While she was kissing him and hugging him the ruler instructed that the boy be killed upon her. After his death the Sages figured the age of the child to be all of two years and six months and six and a half hours. It was then that all the nations of the world cried out saying, "What is the God of these people doing to them that they are

killed for Him thusly all the time!" And about them it is written, "Nay,
but for thy sake are we killed all the day" (Psalms 44:23). Some days later
that woman went mad and fell off a roof and died in fulfillment of the
verse, "She that hath borne seven languisheth" (Jeremiah 15:9). And an
Echo goes forth saying, "A joyful mother of children" (Psalms 113:9).
But the Spirit of Holiness cries out shrilly, saying, "For these things I
weep" (Lamentations 1:16). (*Lamentations Rabbah* 53 [to Lamentations
1:16])[9]

This rabbinic version blends the elements of rationalization in its own
special way thus underscoring the paradox of martyrdom. Let us examine
some of its aspects.

"Caesar" calls upon the youngest of the sons to consider the fullness
of living that the martyr gives up. "Your brothers had their fill of years and
of life, and they tasted goodness; while you are young, you have not had
your fill of years nor of life and you have not tasted the goodness of the
world. Bow down to the icon and I will do goodness for you." Living has
for us that quality of reality that even when it is past we can look upon it as
part of the 'I am'. An old man can feel that he has lived in the world and is
now one with it, without hunger or malice. What "was" was real and fills,
therefore, the present with a sense of contentment. The old man may be
readier, perhaps, for death than the young because his long past gives him
a sense of not being deprived of what could have been. This, at least, is
mighty Caesar's plea to the child. The child is not to give up what he has
not yet had.

The child answers, however, that being is not exhausted in the
fleetingness of the here and now: "Man, who is flesh and blood, today he
is alive and on the morrow—dead, today he is rich and on the morrow—
poor. But the Holy One, Blessed is He, lives and endures for ever and
ever." At this juncture we are no doubt tempted to see the boy's power in
his ability to repudiate the physical world in favor of a spiritual one. But
listen to the continuation of the subtle Rabbi's words: "He answered him:
You are pitiful; and if you are intimidated by humans like yourself, shall I
not fear the Ruler of Kings of Kings, the Holy One Blessed is He, the
Lord of the world?" The boy fears his God as he fears the Roman, only
infinitely more so. His God has a mouth whose words created the world;
his God's eyes scan the entire world; his God listens to the words of the
righteous in conversation with one another, "Then they that feared the
Lord spoke one with another; and the Lord hearkened, and heard, and a
book of remembrance was written before Him." His God smells the sweet
incense of the sacrifices of man; his God's hands forged the earth and his
feet will be planted firmly on the mount of Olives, even when he redeems

man "in that day." And he is a God who speaks to man. In short, the boy knows the being of God in the being of the world, in the words of the righteous and in the turning of God toward living man. The reality of God is a reality of being in the world, a physical world and not a spiritual one. Or, more correctly, a world of here and now and not merely one of "the end of the days" or of an eternal heavenliness. "If all these attributes are found in Him who is your God, why does He not save you from me as He saved Hananiah, Mishael and Azariah from the hands of Nebuchadnezzar?" asks the Roman, who is as sharp as he is cruel. To this the boy answers, "Hananiah, Mishael and Azariah were upstanding and Nebuchadnezzar was a worthy king for the purpose of a miracle being accomplished through him as an instrument. But you are not worthy. And we have been condemned to death by heaven." It is precisely the immanent nature of God that prevents divine redemption at this moment in history. God in his immanence works redemption through an indwelling in man. The requisites of that redemption, therefore, are grounded in the lives of the men involved—sufferer and antagonist. Since neither the sons (so says the boy) nor the Roman are worthy, wherein can the divine drama unfold to its climax? The divine drama will undoubtedly unfold in the world of here and now, but it must proceed through the agonies of time. No doubt the dying of the martyr is part of the creation of a here and now in which the divine immanence unfolds: "Were you not to kill us, the Divine has many other executors, there are many bears, many wolves and lions and snakes and leopards and scorpions who would assail and kill us." Numberless are the means through which God can work his ways and no doubt does. The death of the martyr is a witness of divine justice unfolding. But that rich expression of divine immanence, which man can recognize as revelation, namely redemption, can take place only when the proper configuration of being in the world is an actuality. "But in the future the Holy One, Blessed is He, will finally bring retribution on you for our blood."

Nor does the mother of the seven sons give up even a few seconds of life with her youngest boy: "The boy's mother said to the ruler: By your very life! Give me my son and I will hug him and kiss him. They gave him to her and she drew out her breasts and suckled the child." This is certainly the most tragic moment in this rabbinic version and it bears the stamp of the rabbinic sensibility. The mother caresses the trembling softness of the child and slips for a moment, albeit the last one, back into the warmth of living. To her onlookers, she is mad; to her and to her son, this is the last moment of complete sanity. After the boy's death the woman falls silent. She lingers on for a few days in the twilight of waning lucidity. Finally, she is insane indeed and plunges to death.[10]

So the rabbinic storyteller weaves together the seemingly unrelated threads of what we have called *rationalization*. Divine Law and retribution, the promise of redemption, an eternal yet immanent God are parts of an all-too-human drama where the wail of the committed martyr is the highlight of reality.

Yet, for all his mastery, the homilist, or the editor of the earlier text, has left us with some sense of confusion. "My son, go to Abraham your father and say to him, 'My mother has said as follows: let not your spirits soar with the thought that "I have built an altar and I have offered up my son Isaac." Behold our mother has built seven altars and has offered up seven sons, in one day! Yours was a test, but mine an actuality!'" It must be admitted that the motif of the Binding of Isaac, as it appears here, is not altogether harmonious with the tone of the story as a whole. One could, perhaps, conclude that the mother's almost blasphemous denial of partnership in meaning to the passion of Abraham and Isaac is a realistic description of her anguish. But to me the incongruity of the *Akedah* motif with the skillful theological structure of the homily as a whole is rather a result of the literary archeology of that homily.[11] This conjecture becomes reasonable when we examine the talmudic version of our story where the *Akedah* motif is central:

"Nay, but for Thy sake are we killed all the day; we are accounted as sheep for the slaughter" (Psalms 44:23). And Rav Judah said: This refers to the Woman and Her Seven Sons. The first son was brought before Caesar.[12] He was told, "Worship the heathen god!" He answered, "It is written in the Law,[13] 'I am the Lord thy God!'" (Exodus 20:2). He was taken out and killed, and the next son was brought before Caesar. He was told, "Worship the heathen god!" He answered, "It is written in the Law, 'Thou shalt have no other gods before Me' (ibid. 20:3)." He was taken out and killed. The next son was brought forth. He was told, "Worship the heathen god!" He answered, "It is written in the Law, 'He that sacrificeth unto the gods, save unto the Lord only, shall be utterly destroyed'" (ibid. 22:19). He was taken out and killed. The next son was brought forth. He was told, "Worship the heathen god!" He answered, "It is written in the Law, 'Thou shalt bow down to no other god!'" (ibid. 34:14). He was taken out and killed. The next son was brought forth. He was told, "Worship the heathen god!" He answered, "It is written in the Law, 'Hear, O Israel: the Lord our God, the Lord is one' (Deuteronomy 6:4)." He was taken out and killed. The next son was brought forth. He was told, "Worship the heathen god!" He answered, "It is written in the Law, 'Know this day, and lay it to thy heart, that the Lord, He is God in heaven alone and upon the earth beneath; there is none else'" (ibid. 4:39). He was taken out and killed. The next son was brought forth. He was told, "Worship the heathen god!" He answered, "It is written in the Law, 'Thou hast avouched the Lord this day to be thy God, and that thou wouldst walk in His ways, and keep His statutes, and His commandments, and His ordinances, and hearken unto His voice. And the Lord hath avouched thee this day' (ibid. 26:17–18). We have already sworn to the Holy One Blessed is He that we dare not exchange Him for another God; and He too has sworn to us that He dare not exchange us for another people." Caesar said to him, "I will throw my signet before you and you will bend down and pick it up in order that it may be said, 'He has recognized the authority of the king'." The boy answered, "You are pitiful Caesar, you are pitiful Caesar! For the sake of your honor it is so, for the honor of the Holy One Blessed is He how much more so!" He was taken out in order to be killed. His mother said to the ruler, "Let him be given to me so I may kiss him for just a little while." She said to him, "My sons, go and say to Abraham your father, 'You bound one altar while I have bound seven altars.'" She, too, went up on the roof and fell to her death. An Echo went forth saying, "A joyful mother of children" (Psalms 113:9). (BT *Gittin* 57b)

This is not merely a shorter version. Here, the theme is the starkness of the martyrdom as resulting inevitably from the sons' adherence to the Law. In the words of the last son, there is only one embellishment added to the stern, uncompromising commandments of God. Not only have we "sworn to the Holy One blessed is He that we dare not exchange him for another god," but He also has "sworn to us that He dare not exchange us for another people." This underlines the centrality of the Binding of Isaac motif for this version. The present martyrs, like Abraham and Isaac, have been assured by the Lord of History that they and only they are the chosen; there is no possibility of Covenant with Ishmael ("for in Isaac shall seed be called to thee" [Genesis 21:12]) or with Esau—Rome.[14] Though the death of the sons need not necessarily spell the demise of Israel, the sons surely must have felt the imminent crumbling of the Covenant itself; they and their mother surely must have felt the breakdown of all Promise, just as Abraham and Isaac before them did. And this is the intent of the talmudic storyteller, to paint a tragedy of *Akedah* in the present. The description of the Roman's attempt to find a way out for the boy by telling him merely to bend down in order to pick up the ring, and the boy's refusal to do so, serves to heighten the martyr's absolute loyalty to the word of God, loyalty like that of Abraham and Isaac.

The intentional absence in the talmudic version of the theological and eschatological structures, which dominate the other versions, is underlined if we pay attention to the contextual meaning of the verse that sets the stage for the homily here:

2 O God, we have heard with our ears, our fathers have told us;
　　A work thou didst in their day, in the day of old.

3 Thou with Thy hand didst drive out the nations, and didst plant them in;
　　Thou didst break the peoples, and didst spread them abroad.

4 For not by their own sword did they get the land in possession,
　　Neither did their own arm save them,
　　But Thy right hand, and Thine arm, and the light of Thy countenance,
　　Because Thou wast favorable unto them.

5 Thou art my king, O god;
　　Command the salvation of Jacob.

6 Through Thee do we push down our adversaries;
　　Through Thy name do we tread them under that rise up against us.

7 For I trust not in my bow,
　　Neither can my sword save me.

8 But thou hast saved us from our adversaries,
　　And hast put them to shame that hate us.

9 In God have we gloried all the day,
　　And we will give thanks unto Thy name for ever. Selah.

10 Yet Thou hast cast off, and brought us to confusion;
　　And goest not forth with our hosts.

11 Thou makest us to turn back from the adversary;
　　And they that hate us spoil at their will.

12 Thou hast given us like sheep to be eaten.
　　And hast scattered us among the nations.

13 Thou sellest Thy people for small gain,
　　And hast not set their prices high.

14 Thou makest us a taunt to our neighbors,
　　A scorn and a derision to them that are round about us.

15 Thou makest us a byword among the nations,
　　A shaking of the head among the peoples.

16 All the day is my confusion before me,
　　And the shame of my face hath covered me,

17 For the voice of him that taunteth and blasphemeth;
　　By reason of the enemy and the revengeful.

18 All this is come upon us; yet have we not forgotten Thee,
　　Neither have we been false to Thy covenant.

19 Our heart is not turned back,
　　Neither have our steps declined from Thy path;

20 Though Thou hast crushed us into a place of jackals,
　　And covered us with the shadow of death.

21 If we had forgotten the name of our God;
　　And spread forth our hands to a strange god;

22 Would not God search this out?
　　For He knoweth the secrets of the heart.

23 *Nay, but for Thy sake are we killed all the day;*
　　We are accounted as sheep for the slaughter.

24 Awake, why sleepest Thou, O Lord?
   Arouse Thyself, cast not off for ever.
25 Wherefore hidest Thou Thy face,
   And forgettest our affliction and our oppression?
26 For our soul is bowed down to the dust;
   Our belly cleaveth unto the earth.
27 Arise for our help,
   And redeem us for Thy mercy's sake. (Psalms 44)[15]

If we pay careful attention we catch a subtle note at the very beginning of the Psalm: "Our fathers have told us." In the present state of affairs the notion of the Lord of History who saves his people is a tale passed on to us by our forebears. "A work Thou didst in their days, in the days of old." The old memories linger on in tradition, memories of His right hand and the light of his countenance. God is the poet's king, who can, if he will, "Command the salvation of Jacob." The poet doubts not that only through God can Israel "push down" their adversaries; and only through his name can they "tread them under that rise up against us." The poet knows only too well that he cannot trust in his bow, nor is his sword able to save him. "But thou hast saved us from our adversaries, And hast put them to shame that hate us." Even in the present despair, we remember that "In God have we gloried all the day" and despite all "we will give thanks unto Thy name for ever."

But memories cannot dim the realities of the present. As great as the people's faith is their disappointment. Though they waver not in their praise of the Lord, he has cast them off and brought them to "confusion." The enemy advances and the most hated prevail. The chosen people are "like sheep to be eaten"—as if their death were not a horrible enough mockery of the covenant. Nor is anything whatsoever to be gained by this madness in history; God himself seems to partake in the delirious dealings where humans become chattel, albeit worthless, and the oppressed are shamefaced and the power of the oppressors is a blasphemy.

And "yet have we not forgotten Thee." A stubborn memory indeed must a people have so as not to forget! Theirs is not only a knowledge of God, they have discerned him in history and their memory draws the reality of history into the present. The Jews are not the conscience of the world, they are its memory. They remember suffering—how the world loathes them for that—they remember redemption, and above all they stubbornly remember the covenant; may one say that for this, too, they are hated? They are the people of the covenant and their fate is the proof of that. Does God himself forget the covenant? Or, does he mercilessly pursue them for some unforgivable stain? But surely, "He knoweth the secrets of the heart," the innermost fears and hates and loves of the oppressor and oppressed. Surely, God must know the truth that we ourselves know in the deep and secret chambers of our being! No, never can it be! There is no justification or explanation for the suffering of Israel. "Nay, but for Thy sake are we killed all the day; We are accounted as sheep for the slaughter." We know, as no other people can know, that we are the people of covenant and precisely because of that we are murdered. Covenant and martyrdom are eternal partners in a world made uneasy by a Chosen People who always remember, just as the only beloved Isaac had to be bound on the altar—Isaac who was loved because he was the child in whom the covenant was to be incarnate. "Awake, why sleepest Thou, O Lord?" Had not the psalmist himself uttered such words, who would dare say that in the night of holocaust God himself sleeps, the ringing and the clanging of church bells notwithstanding.

Thus, the verse and its context that open the talmudic homily mark that homily's mood. Theology and eschatology recede into a background of dimness. In their place stand, in the starkness of immediacy, Law, martyrdom, and *Akedah*. The centrality of the Law is evident in the sheer space given to the sons' answers. All the answers imply that, in the face of God's commandments, there is no room whatsoever for the mind-boggling power of the Roman Empire. The individual Jew is grasped, body and soul, by the divine commandments. All other structuring realities, be they political, social, or economic, are simply pale and limp in comparison—even when their power is felt in the sword of some Roman lackey. The grandeur of Rome was in the structuring of their vast empire. But when the Jew is called upon by God Almighty to lay down his life for the Law, his lonely self becomes a kingdom of humanity and a dimension where the only empire is the I before God. Had the Romans understood that their own power was as much psychological as physical in nature, they would not have been unable to understand why their might was not visible to the Jewish and Christian martyrs. Those whose self was totally taken up by the personally commanded Law of God did not really live in the Roman world. They were impervious to that world and, instead, flourished in an inner world of self and community: of self sustained by a personal communion with God through the Law and the actuality of personal martyrdom; of community sustained also by the Law and by the covenant between Israel and God.

In the talmudic homily before us, the Law leads to martyrdom. The heroic mother, by identifying her own personal tragedy with that of Abraham, is expressing a sense of community, albeit a historical one, which means a communion including covenant and martyrdom (martyrdom is *Akedah* only when the very covenant is seen to be sacrificed, as it was in the Trial of Abraham). The most intense of personal piety—martyrdom as drawing-out of devotion to the Law—thus inextricably is a part of the sense of 'we', of Jewish peoplehood. But in order to have some insight into what is going on both in the talmudic homily and in the structured concept hinted at, let us linger for a moment on the story of Abraham and Isaac.

The Abrahamic stories, to the attuned listener, are a biography of a religious man. The biography begins when Abraham is wrenched from his country, his kindred, and even his father's home. The divine call that demands this of him sets him off on a journey the nature of which we cannot, at this point in the story, fathom. The dream of a "land that I will show thee" (Genesis 12:1) says uncerainty, a destiny known only to God and not revealed to Abraham in any concrete or specific way. It is a land of promise, and with that knowledge of its essence alone, the man must set out. But, together with the unfathomable divine command comes the assurance that, come what may, the man will be blessed. Thus, though Abraham knows neither his goal nor the nature of the promised greatness, he sets out with that strange, perhaps irrational, confidence exuding from his faith in himself as divinely called. How many times has the old man experienced doubt and failure in the past? No matter, in his faith he is young; and though our biography begins when Abraham is already seventy-five years old, it begins at a beginning, it will tell a complete story of a religious man.

So Abram took his wife Sarai, "and Lot his brother's son, and all their substance that they had gathered, and the souls that they had gotten in Haran. . . . And Abram passed through the Land unto the place of Shechem, . . . And the Canaanite was then in the land" (ibid. 12:5–6). Now, Abraham knows already where the land is and what it looks like; but the divine call is still a dream as the land is inhabited by the morally depraved Canaanites. Upon seeing those depraved people Abraham must have been even more confused as to where the divine call was leading him. But, again he is assured, "Unto thy seed will I give this land"(Ibid. 12:7). He is not sure of the ends of the divine call, he knows only that he is indeed being called and has a sense that things will work out.

And Abraham continued his wandering. And he experienced bad times and good times and wandered to places where he scarcely understood the people or their customs. Through all, God was with him and he "was very rich in cattle, in silver and in gold" (ibid. 13:2). After his dazzling success against the four monarchs and the freeing of Lot, his brother's son, Abraham pays his tithe to Melchizedek without a word and curtly disdains any thought of dealings, however trivial, with the king of the evil city of Sodom.

But something is deeply troubling the father of Israel. And though

God assures him, "Fear not, Abram, I am thy shield, thy reward shall be exceeding great" (ibid. 15:1), Abraham is not calmed: "O Lord God, what wilt Thou give me, seeing I go hence childless, and he that shall be possessor of my house is Eliezer of Damascus? . . . Behold, to me Thou hast given no seed, and, lo, one born in my house is to be mine heir" (ibid. 15:2–3).

Here, we begin to glimpse the religiosity of Abraham. The wanderer has not yet come to his journey's end, not at all. He is a dreamer who gazes into the vast expanse of future history stretching out uncertainly before him and sees the actuality of divine call and promise in the generations of his seed, long long after his own death. And, with this revelation begins the long dialogue between man and God, the covenant, a dialogue whose real meaning, at this point, Abraham has yet to learn. Abraham is brought to know that, indeed, there is a working-out of divine ways through the labyrinth of long, patient history. And, again, he is assured that all will end well. But the biography of religious man is not yet finished, not at all.

Abraham knows the promise, but he does not yet know the way. He wants to think that in Ishmael he has found the way. But knowledge of the way belongs more to Sarai, whose name was changed to Sarah, than to Abraham. Abraham performs, indeed, the covenant of circumcision on his son Ishmael but his story is far from over.

And the Lord appears to Abraham again. He is told that his journey is not yet ended. A son, Isaac, will be born yet to the old couple. Sarah laughed, though she, too, undoubtedly experienced the divine revelation. Sarah was torn between vision and self-knowledge, and the great mother laughed, what else could she do? Even Abraham himself had laughed at the thought, "Then Abraham fell upon his face, and laughed, and said in his heart: Shall a child be born unto him that is a hundred years old? and shall Sarah that is ninety years old, bear?" (Ibid. 17:17). And yet, both had the vision.

And so we have Abraham at the height of his faith. He has Ishmael and is promised Isaac. "Abraham shall surely become a great and mighty nation, and all the nations of the earth shall be blessed in him" (ibid. 18:18). And when he is told of the imminent doom of Sodom, he cannot contain himself: "That be far from Thee to do after this manner, to slay the righteous with the wicked, that so the righteous should be as the wicked; that be far from Thee; shall not the Judge of all the earth do justly?"(ibid. 18:25) Abraham's faith had reached the point of complete confidence in the prevalence of divine order, even in the present. "Shall not the Judge of all the earth do justly?" And, indeed, Lot, his brother's son, is saved. And even Abraham's misadventure with Abimelech ends well; the vision of the promise is kept bright.

"And the Lord remembered Sarah as He had said, and the Lord did unto Sarah as He had spoken. And Sarah conceived, and bore Abraham a son in his old age, at the set time of which God had spoken to him. And Abraham called the name of his son that was born unto him who Sarah bore to him, Isaac" (ibid. 21:1–3). Knowledge of the way of the promise was with Sarah the mother, and Abraham was told to follow her will, "for in Isaac shall seed be called to thee" (ibid. 21:12). "And Abraham arose early in the morning, and took bread and a bottle of water, and gave it unto Hagar, putting it on her shoulder, and the child, and sent her away" (ibid. 21:14). Abraham, "the father of a multitude of nations" (ibid. 17:5), now saw the promise clearly, "And also of the son of the bondwoman will I make a nation, because he is thy seed" (ibid. 21:13), but "In Isaac shall seed be called to thee." Abraham's success continued. "And Abraham planted a tamarisk-tree in Beer-sheba, and called there on the name of the Lord, the Everlasting God. And Abraham sojourned in the land of the Philistines many days" (ibid. 21:33–34). And the promise remained bright and sure.

But now begins another story of Abraham, the religious man. "And it came to pass after these things, that God did prove Abraham, and said unto him: 'Abraham'; and he said: 'Here am I'. And He said: 'Take now thy son, thine only son, whom thou lovest, even Isaac, and get thee into the land of Moriah; and offer him there for a burnt-offering upon one of the mountains which I will tell thee of'" (ibid. 22:1–2).

Imagine what must have been the drama of Abraham's being at that terrible, terrible moment. The same Abraham who journeyed through Canaan and sustained all kinds of trials and tribulations, who was the epitome of faith in divine order on earth and in promise through history by covenant—this same Abraham is witness to the sudden crumbling of his world, a disaster far greater than that of Job. I address this demand for imagination to the religious listener only, to he who waits with bated breath to hear the end of the story of the Binding of Isaac. For he alone knows what happened to that father. Religious man knows that Abraham had to discover the terrible truth that he had not confronted until that moment when the voice of God called him to Moriah. Finally, theology breaks down in the reality of living. Finally, the world turns out to be not a divinely ordained cosmos (κόσμος) but rather an existence in which the most divine of promises is wrenched away and suddenly dissolved, as if a mere vision. Finally, even our children, as great as their promise may have been, are snatched away from us in the cruelty of chaos that is the real world. God calls upon Abraham to sacrifice his beloved Isaac in order to test Abraham, to see whether he can continue in the world as it really is. That is, after all, the real test for religious man, and only the religious listener knows that this is the essence of the trial of Abraham. Like all the biblical stories, the one told of the Binding of Isaac is not meant for heathen ears.

And how, indeed, does Abraham go through that terrible ordeal? How is he able to continue living when all that which his own life has shown to be so just crumbles in an instant? Is not Abraham's very sanity threatened? Is there anything but chaos to a world where the Creator himself sanctions—nay, demands—martyrdom? Is it not madness that the vision of covenant turns into a vision of doom?

For the answer, I turn again to religious man, for surely the answer is not philosophical, the answer is given at the very outset of the story. The *Akedah* is the trial of Abraham. When all that makes sense breaks down, the divine turns toward man. The final place, and perhaps the only one, for the divine order is in man himself. When the religious personality hero- ically preserves its own inner integrity despite the massive confrontation with an outside absurdity, then the truth of godliness has been proven. Let us take the mother of the seven sons as our example. To her, the outside world, with its grandiose incarnation of Roman power and empire and its incarnate malignancy in the person of the Roman executioner before her, must have been an unbelievable confrontation with the satanic evil. The warmth of home and children suddenly must have seemed pitifully unreal in the face of reality. Or rather, her very sense of what is real must have been sorely tried at the sight of the slaughtering of her children, for whose lives she would have spared nothing, nothing at all. Surely, her very sanity must have been threatened at the sight of the coarse and arrogant Roman destroying that which, to her, being itself was subservient to. But this is the heroism of that woman. She does not loosen her grip on that which is holy and real for her. Even in the final minutes she asks to be allowed to kiss her remaining son. She is not crazy, but the Roman is. She is not pitiful or unreal, until the end she knows very well what is real. Her love for her children is real, for that is inside her truest being. And, as for the mighty Roman Caesar and all that he stands for, her son had expressed, no doubt, her very feelings: "You are pitiful Caesar, you are pitiful Caesar!"

So we learn from that woman about the trial of Abraham. The person of Abraham, his psyche, preserves its inner integrity when all reason breaks down, when he is called upon to give up all. Abraham survives the ordeal because he proves that he is able to go on living, even when he is to lose Isaac. He is the paradigm of religious man who continues in his faith though that very faith has brought him to the most terrible of sacrifices, to martyrdom. From Abraham, religious man learns that he must be ready to pay the most dreaded of prices for his faith and that it is possible to linger in the midst of hell and emerge sane and human. For those who can hear,

the lessons of the Binding of Isaac are the possibility of retaining faith in a
mad world where faith leads to martyrdom, and the ability of man to
suffer that martyrdom.

We have learned from the mother of the seven sons something about
Abraham. And we can now have some intimation of the meaning of the
woman's anguished reference to Abraham. In her terrible ordeal, the
woman is all alone. Her sons cannot comfort her, she is an onlooker to
their death. Like Abraham's, her world has crumbled. But she sees herself
as an Abraham binding his son. This means that she finds in herself the
strength to pass through this ordeal without regretting her faith or relinquishing her conviction as to what is sacred, namely life and love, because
she knows that Abraham before her found that strength in himself.
Whether the mother really finds in herself the strength to continue living,
we do not know. The woman falls to her death from a rooftop and we
cannot be sure whether she does this in anticipation of her own fate at the
hands of the Romans or whether she finally succumbs to the reality of
absurdity. Perhaps, this is the talmudic storyteller's way of hinting that
martyrdom is so terrible that no one really can be expected to make it a full
Akedah. In any case, up to her death the woman sees herself as Abraham,
and the talmudic version has thus expressed a certain religious understanding of the ungraspable Binding of Isaac.

If we recall now the other versions of our story, perhaps we can
understand what the talmudic storyteller is saying. In crises of suffering
and martyrdom the coherency of the world is called in question by the
individual. This can be countered by belief in a world structure that either
transcends the here and now or else prevails by way of the patient unfolding of history. In both otherworldliness and eschatology the immediate
here and now shrinks in importance either before the "other" reality or
before the "lasting" reality. In the first three versions we analyzed, the
martyrs maintain the coherency of their world in the face of martyrdom by
allowing that event either to recede in starkness before the overwhelming
theological structures or at least to become part of those structures. I have
called this *rationalization*, meaning that the storytellers thereby make the
lives of the martyrs understandable and enable the listener to identify—to
varying degrees, of course—with the actions of the story's tragic heroes.
Comparison with the fourth version shows that here rationalization is
achieved by the *Akedah* motif alone. For the talmudic storyteller, the
mother retains her sense of coherency through an inner strength that she
finds by identifying herself with Abraham.

As I have pointed out, the talmudic version is unique in its starkness
not merely its brevity; the latter could have been achieved in many different ways. The martyrdom of the seven sons stands plainly, even austerely,

before us, and the theology richly accompanying the other versions has retreated to a dim background. But this does not mean that there is less rationalization of the heroes' behavior. On the contrary, if structural analysis of the different versions convinces us that the *Akedah* motif serves the same function that the complex theological statements serve in the other versions, then the very starkness of the description of the martyrdom here implies that the concomitant rationalization must be equally to the point.

In the father Abraham, the heroic mother sees herself. She knows firsthand his ascent to Mount Moriah in order to bind his son there, because his faith had led him on a way where he must be ready to give up all. Like her, he gladly would die himself in his son's stead, but that cannot be. Despite the incoherence of the circumstances crushing in upon him, Abraham, like the mother, perseveres. He continues to love Isaac yet does not draw back from the altar: These are her tears. His world is in chaos, but inside he is strong and retains faith and love, knowing that in the absurd world the two have been split apart: This is her agony. The mother of the sons does not ask why God should demand from the father the life of his son when he has promised the future through that very son, nor does she question the behavior of the father. She knows only too well that this is the price the faithful must pay if they are not to succumb to the barbarism of the forces of darkness. She understands full well what is demanded of Abraham, for she herself is experiencing the same thing. She marvels at the father's unshaking hands. "To what fearful heroism the man aspires!" But he passes through the ordeal, he has indeed done it! It is possible, it is real! She herself is not insane, her consciousness is coherent, for she is like Abraham. Through him, she has learned that religiosity does not disintegrate before the absurdity of the world. Through him, she knows that the test of the woof of reality is the being of the religious, not in the order of things. And so, she finds that she, too, can follow that fearful path to holocaust; and she binds seven sons not one!

Thus, in the talmudic version of the Mother of the Sons, the recognition of religious man's inner strength takes the place of eschatology and theology as rationalization of the martyrs' behavior.[16] For the listener to this story, the martyr is believable because the listener knows of the inner strength of some men. Thus, the tale of the Binding of Isaac conjures up for the religiously attuned a heroism that they might find in their own holiest depth; and it therefore frightens them as well. This tragic chapter in the biography of Abraham is properly told only when it is heard by martyrs, for only they grasp the tragedy and the power of the trial. They alone know Abraham.

Chapter Two

Martyrdom and the Law

W e have seen that the martyr hears the story of the Binding of Isaac through the sharp reality that he himself is living out; and in turn, he is able to act out his own grim drama because the *Akedah* "really was." I have called this a sense of community, albeit a historical one.

The Mother of the Sons knows about Abraham through the reading of the Law, the Torah, in the public of the community, or at least through contact with tradition. Let us stop for a moment in order to crystallize some notion of the "whatness" of Holy Scripture in Jewish tradition, and thus of "tradition."

> Rav Judah said in the name of Samuel: [The book of] Esther does not render the hands unclean [for the purpose of eating *terumah*: contact of the hands with Holy Writ is said to render them unclean[1]]. Is that to say that Samuel thinks that [the book of] Esther was not said through the Spirit of Holiness? But Samuel[2] did say: [The book of] Esther was said through the Spirit of Holiness! It was said [through the Spirit of Holiness] in order to be read, but it was not said in order to be written. (BT *Megillah* 7a)[3]

The third century Babylonian amora Samuel follows two apparently old traditions[4] that seemingly are contradictory. An anonymous talmudic scholar has succinctly distilled the real meaning of the amora's words: "It was said in order to be read, but it was not said in order to be written." The book of Esther is divine revelation indeed, but only to be read publicly in the community. However, as a written book by itself, it is not divine revelation. The book does not state fully the revelation of providence in the clarity of a real historical dynamics. It lacks the usual historical verisimilitude found in the Bible and the name of God is never mentioned in it. Or, to state the case historically, the literary telling of the miracle of Esther has not been refined sufficiently by the hermeneutics of tradition. The process of the canonization of the book is completed when it is read in the specific context of the holiday of Purim, which says fully the real meaning of the miracle. The religious Jew who celebrates Purim (listens to the reading of *Megillat Esther*, gives to the poor, sends tasty dishes of cooked food to friends, sets a festive table, and rejoices to the point of drunkenness) knows well the significance of a story that speaks of the hidden indwelling of God in a world that reels in unknowingness like a drunk who "knows not the difference between 'Haman be cursed and Mordecai be blessed'."[5] The celebration of Purim removes the story from the sterility of a historical past—and a not clearly placeable past at that—and makes it into a tale of overcoming evil, which is palpably contemporary at least in its aspiration. This changes the story from "fable" to "Scripture." The knowledgeable community listening to the communal reading is a structure in which, tradition says, the story of the miracle of Purim becomes divine revelation to the point where it can be canonized.

We may take this as a paradigm case for the "whatness" of all Holy Scripture. Even those books canonized in their literary form are never complete except when read by a minimally knowledgeable member of the community. To an outsider, the books are a far cry from a description of a common-sense universe; without the community we cannot ascribe any real meaning to notions like the word of God or holiness. Canonization of Holy Scripture takes place only in the context of the understanding of those scriptures by a community. Nor can scripture be holy for an individual alone without a community. The holiness of writ depends upon a meaning that is "really there" in the text. Only the communal reading-understanding of the texts makes their meaning, the meaning that is capable of being called holy, as real as the community itself. Thus, the intensity of the sense of community is the intensity of the holiness of the Scripture. And a true member of the community sees the "proper" meaning of the holy text as the real meaning. It is *peshat*, the evident meaning for him as an individual. And this is true not only of Scripture but of all verbal tradition.

The Mother of the Sons, too, heard the story of the Binding of Isaac as tradition. So, she is a true member of a religious community, which is not limited to the contemporary community. She identifies with Abraham in her own martyrdom. She can "realistically" do so, because she is a daughter of Abraham. At the moment of her life told to us as this story, she feels a stronger sense of community with Abraham than with any contemporary. It is clear, then, that when she hears the public reading of the Law in the community she is partaking of a communion both contemporary and historical. She is able to understand Abraham the father in terms of herself the mother *and* vice versa with a sense of utter reality, because they are both part of a community whose being spans the dimension of history. One who would understand the Jewish religious sense of community, therefore, must know the experience of the public reading of the Law in its profoundest moments.

This sense of community that is evident at moments of the reading of the Law and in the general happening of tradition, and palpable at a moment of martyrdom, is the continuum through which Tradition subsists and is to be interpreted. Armed with some sense of that continuum, we now may attempt to perceive the meaning of the Binding of Isaac more intensely through an analysis of tradition. This will be our procedure throughout the book.

> What is the Order of the Fast-Days? The Ark is brought out into the town's street. And burnt ashes are put upon the Ark and on the head of the *Nasi* and on the head of the *Av bet-Din*, and each and every man takes [the ashes] and puts some on his own head. The eldest one among them preaches a sermon of admonition [such as]:[6] Our brothers! It is not said about the people of Nineveh, "And God saw their sackcloth and their fasting"; but rather, "And God saw their works, that they turned from their evil way" (Jonah 3:10). And in Tradition it is said, "And rend your heart, and not your garments, And turn unto the Lord your God; For He is gracious and compassionate, Long-suffering, and abundant in mercy, And repenteth Him of the evil" (Joel 2:13).[7] (M *Ta'anit* 2:1)

The Mishnah is referring to the order of fasting and prayers when the community is faced with grave danger or calamity.

The causes for such dramas were various:

> If the first of Kislev arrives and there is yet no rainfall, then the *Bet Din* imposes three fasts upon the community. (M *Ta'anit* 1:5)

> Because of the following, the cry of the ram's-horn is sounded [calling the community to prayer and fasting] everywhere: Because of blight and mildew and locust and caterpillar and predators. And the cry of the ram's-horn is sounded immediately [everywhere] because of the sword,[8] for it is a wandering scourge.[9] It happened that elders went down from Jerusalem to their towns and imposed a fast because a blight covering an extent of the mouth[10] of an oven was spotted in Ashkelon. And another time[11] a fast was imposed because wolves devoured two small children in Transjordan. R. Yose says: Not because they devoured but because they were seen. Because of the following, the cry of the ram's-horn is sounded

[even] on the Sabbath: Because of a town that was surrounded by heathens or a river and because of a ship which is floundering at sea.[12] . . .
Because of any calamity—may it not happen—for the community, the
cry of the ram's-horn is sounded. (M *Ta'anit* 3:5–8)

The seriousness of the situation, and its implication for those gathered there may be sensed from the following:

> [The Mishnah says:] "And burnt ashes are put upon the Ark", for
> the verse: "'I will be with him in trouble'" (Psalm 91:15). R. Ze'eira
> said: Whenever I used to see them doing so my body would tremble.
>   R. Judah bar Manasseh and R. Samuel bar Nahman, one of them
> said: In order to recall the merit of Abraham. And the other one said: In
> order to recall the merit of Isaac. . . . for the verse, "[I, Abraham,] am but
> dust and ashes" (Genesis 18:27). . . . it is as if the ashes of Isaac were
> gathered up upon the altar. (PT *Ta'aniot* 2:2 (65a)[13]

The praying of those days is described in detail. We shall dwell only
on part of it:

> When they stand in [the *Amidah*] prayer, an old man is sent down before
> the Ark; he should be used to praying [before the public], he should have
> children and his house should be empty in order that he pray whole-
> heartedly. And he says before the public [an *Amidah* prayer of] twenty-
> four blessings: The eighteen daily ones, and adding another six.

> To the first blessing he adds:[14] He who answered Abraham on the
> mountain of Moriah, may He answer you and hearken this day to the
> voice of your pleading, [And he closes that blessing:] Blessed art Thou,
> God, the Redeemer of Israel. (M *Ta'anit* 2:2, 4)[15]

Here we are presented with a seemingly fantastic notion. Abraham sets
out on his frightening journey because he is impelled to sacrifice by the
voice of God himself. Abraham's outwardly quiet acquiescence to the
divine command states clearly that however painful the *Akedah* may be for
the father, whatever his inner struggles may have been, he has no doubt
whatsoever—at least on the existential level—that his God is demanding
of him the supreme sacrifice, that of life itself. And yet the tanna sees the
voice that says, "Abraham, Abraham. Lay not thy hand upon the lad,
neither do thou any thing unto him" (Genesis 22:11–12), as coming from
God in his role as redeemer of Israel in history from the clutches of evil. Is
God redeeming Isaac from Himself, as he redeems man from the terribleness of evil?

The Palestinian Talmud underscores this reading of the Mishnah by using the very words we apprehend in this context:

> But was it not Isaac who was redeemed [from the need to be sacrificed on the mount of Moriah, and what, then, is the connection of the *Akedah* with the "first blessing" which closes with "the Redeemer of Israel"]? Since Isaac was redeemed it is as if all Israel were redeemed. (PT *Ta'aniot* 2:4 (65c–d))

Isaac redeemed indeed! From God himself?

The structure in which such a redemptive dynamics takes place is implicit in the careful strokes of the midrashic painters found in the Palestinian *sugya* as a whole:[16]

> But was it not Isaac who was redeemed? Since Isaac was redeemed it is as if all Israel were redeemed. R. Bibi [bar R.] Abba[17] [said] in the name of R. Johanan [third century]: Abraham said before the Holy One Blessed is He: "Master of the Worlds, it is eminently clear to You that when You told me to offer up my son Isaac I had what to say before you. Yesterday You said to me 'for in Isaac shall seed be called to thee' (Genesis 21:12), and now You say 'offer him there for a burnt-offering' (ibid. 22:2)! I dared not do so but rather I overcame my nature and did Your will. In the same way may it be desirable before You, Lord my God, that when the sons of Isaac my son become troubled and there is no one to speak in their defense, You shall speak in their defense. 'God will see' (ibid. 22:8),[18] You will remember for them the Binding of Isaac their father and You will be filled with compassion for them." What is written after that? "And Abraham lifted up his eyes, and looked [literally, and saw], and behold behind him a ram [literally, a ram after] caught in the thicket by his horns" (verse 13). What does "after" [in the literal text] mean? R. Judah son of R. Simeon [late third to early fourth century] said: "After" all the generations your sons will inevitably be "caught" up in sin and ensnared in troubles, and finally they will be redeemed with the horns[19] of the ram;[20] as it is said, "And *the Lord shall be seen* over them, and His arrow shall go forth as the lightning;[21] And the Lord God will blow the [ram's] horn, And will go with whirlwinds of the south" (Zechariah 9:14). R. Huna [said] in the name of R. Hinena bar Isaac [around the turn of the fourth century]: Throughout that whole day Abraham saw the ram get caught in a tree, and be released, and then caught in another shrubbery and released, and then caught in yet another thicket and released. The Holy One Blessed is He said to him, "Abraham, so shall your sons inevitably be caught up in sin and ensnared in empires: From Babylonia to Media, from Media to Greece, and from Greece to Edom (Rome)." [Abraham] said before Him, "Master of the Worlds, shall it be

so for ever?" He answered, "And finally they will be redeemed with the horns of the ram,"[20] ". . . And the Lord God will blow the [ram's] horn, And will go with whirlwinds of the south". (PT *Ta'aniot* 2:4 [65c–d])

The meaning of our texts becomes transparent if we realize that the *Akedah* and martyrdom are herein related to one another, as they are in the talmudic version of the Mother of the Sons.

"And thou shalt love the Lord thy God with all thy heart, and with all thy soul" (Deuteronomy 6:5), even if He takes your soul,[22] and so Scripture says, "Nay, but for Thy sake are we killed all the day; We are accounted as sheep for the slaughter" (Psalms 44:23). R. Simeon ben Menasya [second half of the second century] says [on the above verse]: But how is it possible for a man to be killed daily? [The verse means,] rather, that the Holy One Blessed is He considers the righteous as if they were killed daily. Simeon ben Azzai [first part of the second century] says: ". . . with all thy soul", love Him even to the fatal exhaustion of the soul.

R. Meir [second century] says: Note that Scripture says, "And thou shalt love the Lord thy God with all thy heart", love Him with all your heart as Abraham your father did, in the manner of which the verse says, "But thou, Israel, My servant, Jacob whom I have chosen, the seed of Abraham My friend" [literally, "Abraham My lover", or "who loved Me"][23] (Isaiah 41:8). ". . . And with all thy soul!", like Isaac who bound himself upon the altar, in the manner of which the verse says, "And Abraham stretched forth his hand, and took the knife to slay his son" (Genesis 22:10).[24] ". . . and with all your might" (continuation of Deuteronomy 6:5), be thankful to Him like Jacob your father, as the verse says, "I am not worthy of all the mercies, and of all the truth, which Thou hast shown unto Thy servant; for with my staff I passed over this Jordan; and now I am become two camps" (Genesis 32:11).[25] (*Sifre* to Deuteronomy 6:5 [32, p. 55])

The comparison of martyrdom to the *Akedah* is not meant to soften the starkness of martyrdom by referring it to a prototype experience whose intensity is always conceived of as greater (in the way that, for Christians, the cross of Jesus casts all future sufferings in the shade). On the contrary, the experience of the sons is no less intense than that of the fathers, and indeed in the tannaitic tradition, Abraham's experience acquires meaning as an anticipation of the future experience of Israel. Martyrdom partakes of *Akedah* in that they both result from divine necessity; and *Akedah* partakes of martyrdom because, as we shall see, it results from the nature of religiosity itself and is not a capricious or transient divine command peculiar to the trial of Abraham. Let us follow this through in our reading of the texts from the Palestinian Talmud.

What does "after" ["a ram after" in the literal text] mean? R. Judah son of R. Simeon said: "After" all the generations your sons will inevitably be "caught" up in sin and ensnared in troubles, and finally they will be redeemed with the horns of the ram.

The ram that Abraham sacrifices in place of Isaac represents the future martyrdoms of Israel. Unlike Isaac, the ram is not spared from death, because martyrdom is real *Akedah*, actual holocaust. And because the martyrdom of Israel and not the Binding of Isaac is the complete and therefore paradigmatic act, the ram's horn, rather than Isaac, became the symbol of *Akedah*:

> "And Abraham took the wood of the burnt-offering, and laid it upon Isaac his son [and they went both of them together]" (Genesis 22:6): Like him who bears his cross on his shoulder. (*Genesis Rabbah* to Genesis 22:6 [56, p. 598])[26]

The image of a Jew dragging his cross illuminates the Binding of Isaac, rather than vice versa!

> R. Abbahu [Palestine, around the turn of the fourth century] said: Why is a horn of a ram[27] sounded?[28] The Holy One Blessed is He says, "Sound before Me the horn of a ram so that I remember, for you, the Binding of Isaac the son of Abraham, and I shall consider you as if you had bound yourselves before Me." (BT *Rosh Ha-Shanah* 16a)

Sometimes, as an alternative to placing the ram at the center of the story, the retellings speak of the Binding of Isaac as a complete martyrdom:

> "[And the blood (of the pascal lamb) shall be to you for a token upon the houses where ye are;] and when I see the blood, [I will pass over you, and there shall no plague be upon you to destroy you]" (Exodus 12:13)—" I see the blood of the Binding of Isaac", as the verse says, "And Abraham called the name of that place 'The Lord will see' [literal translation]"[29] (Genesis 22:14); and later on Scripture says, "[And God sent an angel unto Jersalem to destroy it]; and as he was about to destroy, the Lord beheld, and He repented Him of the evil, and said to the destroying angel: 'It is enough; now stay thy hand'" (I Chronicles 21:15): What is it that He "beheld"? He "beheld" the blood of the Binding of Isaac, as the verse says, "God will see for Himself the lamb for a burnt-offering" (Genesis 22:8, literal translation).[30] (*Mekhilta* to Exodus 12:13 [pp. 24–25])[31]

And so the midrashic perception becomes manifest.

> May it be desirable before You, Lord my God, that when the sons of
> Isaac my son become troubled. . . . "God will see" (Genesis 22:8), You
> will remember for them the Binding of Isaac their father and You will be
> filled with compassion for them. What is written after that? "And Abra-
> ham lifted up his eyes, and looked [literally, and *saw*], and behold behind
> him a ram [literally, a ram after] caught in the thicket by his horns" (verse
> 13). What does "after" [in the literal text] mean? R. Judah son of R.
> Simeon said: "After" all the generations your sons will inevitably be
> "caught" up in sin and ensnared in troubles, and finally they will be
> redeemed with the horns of the ram . . .

When Isaac asked his father "Behold the fire and the wood; but where is
the lamb for a burnt-offering?" (Genesis 22:7), Abraham replied, "God
will see for Himself the lamb for a burnt-offering, my son" (literal translation). Likewise, in verse 14, a strange explanation was given for the name
for Mount Moriah:

> And Abraham called the name of that place "the Lord will see"; as it is
> said to this day: "In the mount where the Lord will be seen." [Literal
> translation[32]][33]

To the midrashic perception God did indeed "see for Himself the lamb for
a burnt-offering": He saw the ram, he saw the future martyrdoms of
Israel—each a complete *Akedah*, as the first was complete in the immolation of the ram. And God in his mercy will continue to see all that. Such is
the essence of the theophany of "the Lord will see"—"the Lord will be
seen" (God will be seen through the fact that he will see the "Ram").[34]
Paradoxically, Israel's suffering of martyrdom ensures its covenantal survival. Abraham realized this truth when he saw the ram irrevocably
trapped and fated for sacrifice in place of Isaac.

That martyrdom somehow counteracts the menace of sin and, therefore, has a redemptive quality is decidedly an early rabbinic theme, though
not necessarily a central one, as we shall see later.

> "[Sing aloud, O ye nations, of His people; For He doth avenge the blood
> of His servants, And doth render vengeance to His adversaries,] And
> doth make expiation for the land of His people" (Deuteronomy 32:43).
> From whence can it be learned that the death of Israel at the hands of the
> nations of the world is an expiation for them for the Coming World? For
> the verse says, "A Psalm of Asaph. O God, the heathen are come into
> Thine inheritance; . . . They have given the dead bodies of Thy servants
> [to be food unto the fowls of the heaven, The flesh of Thy saints unto the
> beasts of of the earth]. They have shed their blood like water [For they
> have devoured Jacob, and laid waste his habitation. Remember not

against us the iniquities of our forefathers; Let Thy compassions speedily come to meet us; For we are brought very low. Help us, O God of our salvation, for the sake of the glory of Thy name; And deliver us, and forgive our sins, for Thy name's sake.[35]" (Psalms 79:1–3, 7–9).[36] (*Sifre* to Deuteronomy 32:43 [333, p. 383])

"Expiation for the coming world" underlines the significance of the notion for the martyrs themselves. But, the rabbinic conception is not limited to penance for sin. This may be seen in comments on the classic biblical martyrs Hananiah, Mishael, and Azariah (Shadrach, Meshach, and Abed-Nego, Daniel, Chapter 3). In the midrashic tradition, they are compared as martyrs to Isaac and their story sheds light on the *Akedah* story:

"So Abraham returned unto his young men [after the Binding of Isaac], [and they rose up and went together to Beersheba; and Abraham dwelt at Beersheba]" (Genesis 22:19). Where is Isaac? R. Berechiah [Palestine, fourth century], in the name of Babylonian Rabbis, said: He [Abraham] sent him to Shem in order to study the Law. . . . R. Yose ben R. Hanina [Palestine, second half of the third century] said: He sent him in the dark of night because of the [evil] eye,[37] for from the time that Hananiah, Mishael and Azariah left the fiery furnace they are no longer mentioned [by Scripture], and to where did they go? R. Lazar [R. Elazar ben Pedat, a Babylonian who settled in Palestine, the third century] said: They died by spit [they were spat at].[38] R. Yose ben R. Hanina said: They died by the [evil] eye.[39] R. Joshua ben Levi [Palestine, first half of the third century] said: They moved away and went to Joshua the son of Jehozadak in order to study the Law. (*Genesis Rabbah* to Genesis 22:19 [56, pp. 611–12])

The three are said to have viewed martyrdom as an expression of the very nature of the divine call to man and not merely as a quirk of the times:

Todos of Rome [Rome, the latter part of the first century] taught the public the following as well: What thoughts brought Hananiah, Mishael and Azariah to give themselves over for the sanctification of the Name, to the fiery furnace? They drew for themselves a conclusion, *a minori ad majus*, from the frogs [of the second plague wrought on the Egyptians]: If the frogs, who are not commanded concerning the sanctification of the Name, are said by Scripture to "go up and come into thy house . . . and into thine ovens, and into thy kneading-troughs" (Exodus 7:28); [and] when are "kneading-troughs" together with the oven? Manifestly, when the oven is hot! Then we, who are commanded concerning the sanctification of the Name, how much more so [are we to submit to the flames]! (BT *Pesahim* 53b)

And the three martyrs eventually even were raised by some to a level of significance comparable to that of the Fathers:

> It is [for] this [because Hananiah, Mishael and Azariah submitted uncon-
> ditionally to the flames and did not await the intervention of God, as the
> story is told before by the homilist] that people swear, saying, "Upon
> Him Who stood the world on three pillars": some say that they (the
> pillars) are Abraham, Isaac and Jacob, and some say they are Hananiah,
> Mishael and Azariah [the latter opinion being as reasonable as the former
> in view of the homilist's preceeding discourse].[40] (*Song of Songs Rabbah*
> to Song of Songs 7:8 [13, 60c])

At the beginning of the third century, a sage could publicly expound a biblical verse by juxtaposing Daniel's three friends, Daniel himself, who was also a martyr (Daniel 6), King David, and the Messiah:

> R. Tanhum [Palestine, the latter half of the third century][41] said: Bar
> Kappara [Palestine, first part of the third century], when in Sepphoris [in
> Galilee], publicly taught the following: What is the meaning of the verse,
> "And she [Ruth] said: 'These six measures of barley gave he [Boaz] me'"
> (Ruth 3:17)? . . . It was hinted to her that six sons were to be descended
> from her, each one of which was to be blessed with six blessings. And
> these are they: David and the Messiah, Daniel, Hananiah, Mishael and
> Azariah . . . (BT *Sanhedrin* 93a–b)

It was even considered legitimate to attribute the exodus from Egypt to the efficacy of the three martyrs, thus giving sharp expression to the connection between martyrdom and redemption:

> By what merit did the Children of Israel go out of Egypt? . . . R. Eliezer
> ben Jacob [the second century][42] says: By the merit of Hananiah, Mish-
> ael and Azariah, as the verse says, "And God saw the children of Israel"
> (Exodus 2:25); and concerning them [Hananiah etc.] the verse says,
> "[Therefore thus saith the Lord, Who redeemed Abraham, concerning
> the house of Jacob: Jacob shall not now be ashamed, Neither shall his
> face now wax pale;] When he seeth his children, the work of My hands,
> in the midst of him, That they sanctify My name; Yea, they shall sanctify
> the Holy One of Jacob, [And shall stand in awe of the God of Israel]"
> (Isaiah 29:22–23): What does "When he seeth his children" mean? ". . .
> Youths[43] in whom was no blemish" [Daniel 1:4, concerning the youths
> among whom were Hananiah etc.],[44] who sanctified My Name in the
> fiery furnace.[45] (*Midrash Shoher Tov—Tehillim* to Psalms 114:1 [5, pp.
> 472–73]

The three are seen as affecting a deliverance of proto-messianic proportions:

> R. Johanan [Palestine, third century] said: What is the meaning of the verse, "I saw in the night, and behold a man riding upon a red horse, and he stood among the myrtle-trees that were in the bottom; and behind him there were horses, red, sorrel, and white" (Zecharia 1:8)? What does "I saw in the night" mean? The Holy One Blessed is He wanted to transform the whole world into the darkness of night. ". . . and behold a man riding", "a man" is no other than the Holy One Blessed is He, as the verse says, "The Lord is a man of war, The Lord is His name" (Exodus 15:13). ". . . upon a red horse", the Holy One Blessed is He wanted to transform the whole world into blood. Upon heeding Hananiah, Mishael and Azariah He was appeased, as the verse says, "and he stood among the myrtle-trees that were in the bottom"; and "myrtle-trees" are none other than the righteous, as the verse says, "And he brought up Hadassah [Myrtle], that is, Esther" (Esther 2:7);[46] and "bottom" [or "depths"] is no place other than Babylon, as the verse says, "That saith to the deep:[47] 'Be dry, And I will dry up thy rivers'; [That saith of Cyrus: 'He is My shepherd, And shall perform all My pleasure'; Even saying of Jerusalem: 'She shall be built'; And to the temple: 'Thy foundation shall be laid']" (Isaiah 44:27–28). At once those ["horses"] which, when angry, become "sorrel" and "red", now become "white".[48] (BT *Sanhedrin* 93a)

And the martyrdom of the three is connected to resurrection of the dead:

> Our Rabbis repeated: When the evil Nebuchadnezzar threw Hananiah, Mishael and Azariah into the fiery furnace the Holy One Blessed is He said to Ezekiel, "Go and revive the dead who are in the valley of Dura".[49] Once he had revived them, the skeletons came out and slapped that evil man on the face. He [Nebuchadnezzar] said, "What kind of men are these [the three friends]?" He was answered, "The friend of these [men] is the one who revived the dead in the valley of Dura." [It was then that] he [Nebuchadnezzar] held forth and said, "How great are His signs! And how mighty are His wonders! His kingdom is an everlasting kingdom, And His dominion is from generation to generation" (Daniel 3:33).[50]
> Our Rabbis repeated: Six miracles were wrought on that same day, and these are they: The furnace floated [up to the surface of the ground in order that it should be seen publicly—Rashi]; and the furnace was split open [so that the wondrous events inside be public—Rashi]; and it [finally] crumbled; and the idol was turned over on its face; and four kingdoms were burned;[51] and Ezekiel revived the dead in the valley of Dura. (BT *Sanhedrin* 92b)

Thus, we discern a structure of *Akedah*—martyrdom—redemption, and a redemption of eschatological import at that. But, our first interest is the relationship between *Akedah*-martyrdom and atonement, atonement not as mere penance but as a jolt in the awesomeness of the Law, a happening that can connect up with the ultimate redemption—salvation. Later on, we shall follow out the thread as it draws to a yet grander drama.

The relationship between *Akedah*-martyrdom and the convenantal survival is expressed effectively in our Palestinian text, as

> "When You told me to offer up my son Isaac I had what to say in answer before You: Yesterday You said to me 'for in Isaac shall seed be called to thee', and now You say 'offer him there for a burnt-offering'! I dared not do so but rather I overcame my nature and did Your will. In the same way may it be desirable before You, Lord my God, that when the sons of Isaac my son become troubled . . . You shall speak in their defense (סניגוריא)", . . . You will remember for them the Binding of Isaac their father.

The term סניגוריא, συνηγορια, means "legal defence" and we appreciate its force here only when we read it parallel to כבשתי את יצרי, "I overcame my nature." Abraham has no illusions as to the importance of his son to himself. He does not relinquish his this-wordliness as being evil or meaningless and thus embrace a mystic release for himself and for his son. The physical well being and future of Isaac are, for Abraham, a theophany in their own right. And yet, Abraham is able to overcome the nightmare of death and acquiesce to the divine will. He "conquers" himself. He breaks from the inertia of his very living into the knowledge of a terrible truth. So, too, we must understand God's "speaking in defence" of man. God is, as it were, defending man against God himself. Divine justice is making way for divine mercy; God himself in his awesomeness is drawing back before the defence made for man. It is as if God were "conquering" himself, Abraham imploring God to follow his lead. This theme comes out even more clearly in later versions of our text:

> Rava said in the name of R. Johanan: Abraham our father said before the Holy One Blessed is He, "Master of the World, When You told me 'Take now thy son' (Genesis 22:2) I had what to answer: Yesterday You said to me, 'for in Isaac shall seed be called to thee' (Genesis 21:12), now You say, 'Take now thy son'; and I overcame my compassion in order to do Your will. In the same way may it be desirable before You, Lord my God, that Your compassion shall overcome Your anger towards the sons of Isaac[52] and You will remember for them that Binding and You will be

filled with compassion for them". (*Midrash Lekah Tov*[53] to Genesis 22:14 [51a])

And in liturgical crystallization:

> And may there appear before You the Binding wherein Abraham our father bound Isaac his son on the altar and overcame his compassion in order to do Your will with all his heart. In the same way may Your compassion overcome Your anger toward us and in Your great benevolence may Your wrath toward Your People and Your city and Your country and Your portion be abated. (From the *"Zikhronot"* portion of the *Musaf* prayer of the New Year festival)

> As Abraham our father overcame his compassion for his only son, and wanted to slaughter him in order to do Your will, in the same way may Your compassion overcome Your anger toward us, and may Your compassion overtake Your principles, and may You deal with us without recourse to the letter of Your law, and may You deal with us, Lord our God, with the measure of beneficence and the measure of compassion, and in Your benevolence may Your wrath toward Your People and Your city and Your country and Your portion be abated. (From the prayer recited after the daily reading of the Binding of Isaac, at the beginning of morning prayers)[54]

Thus martyrdom-*Akedah* saves Israel from God's anger for their transgression of the Law, for their being "caught up in sin." But our texts still remain opaque, for after all their deepest concern is the redemption of Israel in this world and not its martyrdom. We still are missing the point entirely unless we grasp the implicit dynamic structure as a whole: In martyrdom the demands of the divine law recede in awesomeness as God draws back before the heroism of man, but man may step back at the last moment from martyrdom by bearing the yoke of the Law, because the Law obviates the terrible need for martyrdom. Israel finds its peace in a dialectic of Law and martyrdom, and so finally is redeemed.

Law and martyrdom play such a central role in western religiosity that an attempt to understand them fully is far beyond the scope of this book. Here, we will concentrate on their meaning as dialectical counterparts. Why is there refuge from Law in martyrdom and how does man draw back from martyrdom through Law? Why should religiosity be caught up in a dialectic where death may become a divine imperative? Why should religious man be drawn under the yoke of Law, especially if this involves him in a drama where death stalks?

The answer to these questions lies in what perhaps is the most important aspect of the religious soul, its sensitivity. At this point, we shall allow
overselves a digression on the religious psyche's perception of self and
world, as the ground of the meaning of the Law. Our aim will not be
analysis but rather a search for a sense, a feeling of seriousness, an appreciation of which will be a sine qua non for the continuation of our argument.

Our discussion will begin in the book of Psalms because we are
speaking of a consciousness whose roots are deep in Israel's ancient traditions.

[A Psalm] of David

1   Bless the Lord, O my soul;
    And all that is within me, bless His holy name.
2   Bless the Lord, O my soul,
    And forget not all His benefits;
3   Who forgiveth all thine iniquity;
    Who healeth all thy diseases;
4   Who redeemeth thy life from the pit;
    Who encompasseth thee with loving-kindness and tender mercies;
5   Who satisfieth thine old age with good things;
    So that thy youth is renewed like the eagle.
6   The Lord executeth righteousness,
    And acts of justice for all that are oppressed. (Psalms 103)[55]

The poet is speaking to himself as a man, not as spirit and body. "O
my soul,"[56] in the first half of the first verse, is parallel to "all that is within
me"[57] in the latter half of that verse.[58] He is speaking of man in all his
humanity, beginning with his innermost sensitivity and vulnerability. To
this, the poet addresses the command: "Bless the Lord!" and we are immediately confronted with the paradox of frailty and godliness. This play on
duality continues in the following verses: "Thou, O myself, hast sinned,
But God has forgiven thee; Thou art diseased with iniquity, but surely He
healeth thee; Thy very living [thy "being in the world"] is in the pit, but
He redeemeth thee; He crowns thee[59] with loving-kindness and tender
mercies." Man is a lowly creature, a creature of the pit, because he sins.
Man's self-image as a humble being does not stem from a conviction that
his very essence is unworthy but rather from his awareness that he has
sinned. This is why man is redeemable. Redemption is seen as a 'healing',
that is, a return to his natural condition. The awareness of sin and the
possibility of redemption go together, the two are expressed by the poet in

one breath. Man's very appreciation of his lowliness in sin, his self-disgust, enables him to be raised to what he really is. And, finally, he is crowned with "loving-kindness and tender mercies,"—these being the fitting crowns for man's real nature. Man in redemption returns to his youth like an eagle. God executes the demands of righteousness, he returns to man what rightfully belongs to him. What greater injustice to man than to see his sinfulness as a stain on his essence; God redeems man from such an oppression by making redemption from sin pursuant to the true recognition of guilt. The poet concludes in the seventh, and as we shall see, key verse:

> He make known His ways unto Moses,
> His doings unto the children of Israel.

God has made redemption, man's return to himself, pursuant to man's awareness of his terrible lowliness in sin, by giving man the knowledge of the ways of God. Man can discover the godly in himself and return to it, because he has the faculty of knowledge *and* the ability to follow the ways of God.

The first part of this psalm may thus be summed up as follows: The poet sees his sinfulness as a terrible lowliness, as a "being in the pit"; redemption from sin is a return to man's real nature; that return is possible because man can know the ways of God and fulfill himself by following those ways. Thus, man's sense of painful inadequacy is a suffering from the contrast between his present smallness and his wonderful potential. Man's sense of sickness in the present is a claustrophobia brought about by an intimation of profound self- knowledge, a self-knowledge that, as we shall see, demonstrates godliness.

This interpretation is borne out as we continue through the psalm:

> 8   The Lord is full of compassion and gracious,
>   Slow to anger, and plenteous in mercy.
> 9   He will not always contend;
>   Neither will He keep His anger for ever.
> 10   He hath not dealt with us after our sins,
>   Nor requited us according to our iniquities.
> 11   For as the heaven is high above the earth,
>   So great is His mercy toward them that fear Him.
> 12   As far as the east is from the west,
>   So far hath He removed our transgressions from us.
> 13   Like as a father hath compassion upon his children,
>   So hath the Lord compassion upon them that fear Him.

So cosmically lost is man in sin that he can see redemption only in a God of cosmic proportions. Perhaps, the very notion of an omnipotent God is rooted in man's notion of sin and not vice versa. The gods of nature and society were sufficient for man as long as his needs were sustenance, fertility, and order. But when man began to sense failure and guilt, when he saw a cosmic vision of his potential and suffered the resulting disappointment with himself in the present, only the concomitant vision of a cosmic God could save him. God's mercy toward men "that fear Him" is as great "as the heaven is high above the earth" and, therefore, man can return to himself. How vast must be the abyss between what man is and what he can be, if so great must be the divine mercy! How sure must man be of the possibility of crossing that abyss, if he accords that potential to the essence of the divine! How seriously must man view his fall and redemption if he perceives them as cosmic!

> 14 For He knoweth our frame;
>   He remembereth that we are dust.

Evil abides deep in man, and God knows our smallness and frailty. So the poet brings the sense of the vastness of redemption to its height. In the following two verses, the awareness of the human condition is intensified for the purpose of emphasizing the irony of the climactic end of the poet's message.

> 15 As for man, his days are as grass;
>   As a flower of the field, so he flourishes.
> 16 For the wind passeth over it, and it is gone;
>   And the place thereof knoweth it no more.
> 17 But the mercy of the Lord is from everlasting to
>   everlasting upon them that fear Him,
>   And His righteousness unto children's children;
> 18 To such as keep His covenant,
>   And to those that remember His precepts to do them.

Man is not irrevocably doomed to the despair of sin, and his redemption is not merely a matter of grace. Man can know God's will and follow in his ways because that is the essential expression of the existence of a merciful God. (God makes Law known to man not through grace but because His knowledge and Law "is" only through man's knowing and doing. Indeed, God himself "is" through man standing before him. And man's awareness that he stands in utter humility before God tears open the vast spiritual potential that is his.) By choosing to follow God's precepts, which He in his essential mercy makes known to the people of the covenant, man raises himself up from being a fading and placeless creature to one who fears him who is everlasting and "hath established His throne in the heavens."

> 19 The Lord hath established His throne in the heavens;
> And His kingdom ruleth over all.
> 20 Bless the Lord, ye angels of His,
> Ye mighty in strength, that fulfil His word,
> Hearkening unto the voice of His word,
> 21 Bless the Lord, all ye His hosts;
> Ye ministers of His, that do His pleasure.
> 22 Bless the Lord, all ye His works
> In all places of His dominion;
> Bless the Lord, O my soul.

These final verses are carefully structured as the climax of the psalm. God reigns on high and his kingdom is omnipresent. The angels are called upon to praise him because they are "mighty in strength." But, in the same breath, there is a subtle intimation, they "fulfil his word." This is a faint but clear direction, and it is carefully amplified in the continuation, "Hearkening unto the voice of His word." In the next verse, this lead is taken up, and the words "angels of His" are replaced by the words "His hosts", "mighty in strength" by "ministers of His", and "fulfil His word, Hearkening unto the voice of His word" is paralleled by "that do His pleasure." The final verse completes the descent to man, "all ye His works," and thus raises man to the exalted state of the angels, for he, too, is to "bless the Lord" like them. Nor are we surprised by this exaltation; we already know that man is capable of being "those that remember His precepts *to do them* (לעשותם)" (verse 18) just as the angels "*fulfil* His word (עֹשֵׂי דברו)."

The final verse, the twenty-second—the "extra" verse outside the cycle of three times seven—brings us back to the beginning of the psalm with the words "Bless the Lord, O my soul." The meaning of the psalm is pressed home. "Bless the Lord, all ye His works," even the loneliest of them, man's innermost self, the "O my soul" of the first verse. "In all places of His dominion", even in the innermost humanity and frailty of man, the "all that is within me" of the first verse. For it is precisely man's awareness of his utter humanity that enables him, finally, to "bless the Lord" with his soul. This meaning of the psalm also may be perceived in another way—by noting the careful repetition of certain key verbs.

In the second verse the poet admonishes his soul to "forget not all His benefits." Even in his most despairing moments deep in man's consciousness there lingers a memory, often vague but always disconcerting, of what is beyond the blackness of the present moment. The poet awakens his soul to an ecstasy of praising the Lord by shaking it out of its forgetfulness. God, on the other hand, is presented in verse 6 as an actuality of righteousness, "The Lord executeth righteousness." In verse 7, God is not only an actuality, he also is a giver of knowledge, "He made known His ways unto Moses, His doing unto the children of Israel." Consequently, man, or Israel, becomes not only one who *remembers* God's mercy but also one who *knows* the ways of God. In verse 10, God is one who *refrains* from doing, "He hath not dealt with us after our sins, Nor requited us according to our iniquities." At the right moment, the arrest of divine grandeur, the relief of man's fear of standing before that which is too awesome, enables redemption! And in verses 11 and 12, the staggering dialectic of God's awesomeness and man's need for a relief from that awareness is brought home in the irony of "For as the heaven is high above the earth, So great is His mercy toward them that fear Him. As far as the east is from the west, so far hath He removed our transgressions from us." The second seventh verse, verse 14, is like verse 7, a key verse. Here the divine knowledge is contrasted to the knowledge given to man, as in verse 7, and repeated in verse 18. Divine knowledge is knowledge of man's frailty, "For He knoweth our frame; He remembereth that we are dust." The notion of divinity, of godly awesomeness, is most intimately bound up with the notion of the smallness of man. The existence of the former is the knowledge of the latter, it is man who is standing before God that is small. And that is precisely why man is a "knower" when the divine ways are made known to him (verse 7, also verse 18, "those that remember his precepts to do them"). By "knowing God's ways," man is able, through awareness of his humbleness, to contemplate, to reach out toward, and to achieve a far greater potential. God's knowledge of man is a merciful recognition of inadequacy, and man's knowledge of God is a recognition of potential and the possibility of its actualization. And both are rooted in the dialectic of humility and godliness.

Verse 18 thus sets the stage for the psalm's climax. "To such as keep His covenant, And to those that remember His precepts to do them." Man is a knower, or "rememberer," and doer of the divine precepts. The divine awesomeness has "established His throne in the heavens; And His kingdom ruleth over all" (verse 19). It is angelic to bless the Lord, and they that "fulfil His word" are "mighty in strength" (verse 20). In both verse 18 and verse 20 the verb "to do" (עשה) is used, and this is followed in verse 21 as well, "Ye ministers of His, that do His pleasure." In the final verse, the subtle use of the verb "to do" in the form "His works" (מעשיו) draws the various directions of the psalm together. Man, too, is one of "all His works" and as such is humble; but, by virtue of the peculiar way in which he is a work of God, he is also capable of being a doer of God's words and being godly. In that case, "His dominion" is "in all places," even in the innermostness of a man. "Bless the Lord all ye His works, In all the places of His dominion; Bless the Lord, O my soul." Even "all that is within me, bless His holy name" (verse 1). So the poet reveals the profoundest self knowledge, and in the intimacy of this knowledge, he cannot but bid his innermost self to praise God.

The notion of man's diminution through sin is not merely a floating fantasy. It is a matter of self-blame, a perception of man as the center of being and as therefore responsible for it. The concept of sin is rooted in religious man's sense of the imperfection of the world, an imperfection painfully manifest in the proliferation of suffering. Since evil as a reality in the world centers upon man, who is responsible for the meaning of the world, redemption must be accomplished through and in the domain of man. The Law, then, is not merely a salvation from the smallness of sinning. It is the Jew's way of embracing the knowledge of suffering and imperfection, and the intense conviction that through him the world can and must be redeemed; and that redemption (involving the social–historical axis), not merely salvation (which is personal and ahistorical), is possible and necessary. Evil subsists because of man's insensitivity, ignorance, and uninformed behavior; therefore, redemption is through the knowledge, action, and sensitivity of man himself.

This becomes more manifest through the rabbinic sensibility:

It was repeated: R. Yose [ben Halafta, the middle of the second century] said: I was once walking along the way and I went into a certain ruined house, one of those ruins of Jerusalem, in order to pray [the *Amidah*]. Elijah, of good remembrance, came and waited for me until I finished my prayer.[60] After I finished my prayer he said to me, "Peace on you my master [רבי]." And I said to him, "Peace on you my master and my teacher [מורי].[61] And he said to me, "My son, why did you go into this ruin?" I said to him, "In order to pray." And he said to me, "You should have prayed on the way." And I said to him, "I was afraid lest passers-by interrupt me." And he said to me, "You should have prayed a short prayer." At that time I learned from him three things. I learned that one does not enter a ruin, and I learned that when on the way one nevertheless prays, and I learned that when one prays on the way he prays a short prayer. And he said to me, "My son, what voice did you hear in this ruin?" And I said to him, "I heard an echo [*Bat Kol*] cooing like a dove and saying, 'Woe for Me[62] that I have destroyed My house and have burnt My temple[63] and have exiled my sons among the nations'." And he said to me, "By your life and limb, it does not say so at this time alone but rather day by day, thrice daily, it says so. And not only that, but when

> Israel enter the synagogues and the houses of learning and call out in
> response, 'Let His great Name be blessed,'[64] the Holy One Blessed is He
> nods His head and says, 'Happy is the King Who is so praised in His
> house. Woe[65] for the Father Who exiled His sons, and woe for the sons
> who were exiled from their Father's table'."(BT *Berakhot* 3a)

Here the rabbinic storyteller employs irony and surprise. Rabbi Yose prays
amidst the ruins of Jerusalem. While this scene sets the stage for the
halakhic context of the story, it also is meant to conjure in our mind's eye a
far wider scenery. In fact, it is probable that even the very halakhic content
is chosen so as to tell the story and not vice versa. We see not merely the
lonely tanna in a ravaged domicile; rather, we see the lonely tanna who is,
or shall be, a remnant of the terrible Hadrianic persecutions and the
devastating destruction hurled upon Judea by the downfall of Simeon Ben
Kozeva, or Bar Kokhba. The quietness of the ruin, a setting for praying,
and the anticipation of people passing by, going about on their business
and liable to interrupt the prayer on the way, add up to a picture not of
struggle but of aftermath and despair—the despair that set in after the
destruction of the temple or after the final spasms of the Bar Kokhba
uprising. This is borne out by the reference to the despair of God himself.
It paints a picture of barrenness and futility, a picture in which the appearance of Elijah, of good remembrance, is evidence of messianic yearning
and even of gnostic temptation, a temptation to shake off the reality of
this-worldliness altogether.

> Elijah was wont to visit the study-group of Rabbi [Judah *ha-Nasi*]. One
> day, when it was the first of the month, evening came before he arrived.
> He [Rabbi] said to him, "Why has the master been delayed until eve-
> ning?" He said to him, "[It takes time] until I help Abraham to get up
> and I wash his hands and he prays and I help him to lie down; and so to
> Isaac and so to Jacob."[66] "Why not help them to get up together?" "They
> are liable, in the intensity of their compassionate plea, to bring the Mes-
> siah before his time." He [Rabbi] said to him, "And is there anyone like
> them in this world?" He said to him, "There is R. Hiyya and his sons."
> Rabbi decreed a fast-day; he sent R. Hiyya, with his sons, to pray before
> the congregation.[67] He [R. Hiyya] said [in the *Amidah* prayer], "[You]
> cause the wind to blow", and a wind blew up, he said, "[You] bring
> down the rain", and the rain came.[68] When he came to say, "[You]
> quicken the dead", the world became frenzied. In heaven they said, "Who
> revealed the secret in the world?" They said, "Elijah!" They summoned
> Elijah and flogged him sixty fiery lashes.[69] He [Elijah], appearing as a
> fiery[70] bear, came and mingled among them [these engaged in prayer]
> and distracted them. (BT *Bava Mezia* 85b)

Elijah, who was jealous for God,[71] who rose to heaven in a fiery chariot,[72] is the embodiment of almost uncontrollable yearning for deliverance and is the bearer, or potential bearer, of the secret knowledge that will force the hand of history, or perhaps transcend it. This is the suspenseful expectation created by his apperance in R. Yose's tale. But, the suspense is momentary; we are not allowed to indulge the dream of quick deliverance. Elijah here is patient; he waits humbly by the door for the tanna to complete his prayer. He then greets him respectfully, but the subtly more respectful return of greeting by the sage again raises a tension of expectation, subdued as it is. So, too, Elijah's addressing R. Yose as "my son" and the gentle questioning of the man's behavior. R. Yose answers, laconically, "to pray." Here, Elijah neither hesitates nor is diffident. His answer is cutting, "You should have prayed on the way!" R. Yose must excuse his behavior but again he is told off, "You should have prayed a short prayer!" And here the tanna teaches us the meaning of the encounter. Elijah, contrary to expectation, does not reveal a secret gnosis but rather teaches the Law. Ironically, he is diffident in his initial appearance as Elijah the prophet but confident and authoritarian in his appearance as Elijah the sage! And, make no mistake, his information up to this point is halakhic; Rabbi Yose could have gained it from tradition:

> Our Rabbis repeated: For three reasons one refrains from entering a ruin: Because it arouses suspicion; because it is liable to cave in; and because of bogeys. (BT *Berakhot* 3a)

> Raban Gamaliel [the *nasi* at Jabneh from c. 80] says: One prays the "Eighteen" [benedictions, the *Amidah* prayer] every day. R. Joshua says: [One prays only] the highlights of the "Eighteen". R. Akiva says: If he easily remembers his prayer then let him pray the "Eighteen"; and if not, then the highlights of the "Eighteen".
> R. Eliezer [ben Hyrcanus] says: If one prays merely out of habit then his prayer is not supplication. R. Joshuah says: When one is going in a place of danger, he prays a short prayer. He says: "Save, O Lord, Your people, the remnants of Israel. In every crisis may their needs be before You. Blessed are You, O Lord Who hears prayer."[73] If he was riding on a donkey he should get down in order to pray. And if he cannot get down then he should turn his face [toward Jerusalem, if possible, toward the Holy of Holies in the Temple]. And if he cannot turn his face he should orient his heart toward the place of the Holy of Holies. (M *Berakhot* 4:3–5)[74]

Elijah's teaching is within the perimeters of Jabneh *Halakhah* (all the scholars just mentioned are from that period) and R. Yose is a pupil of that great assemblage. If the expectation of deliverance through Gnosis is alluded to, it is replaced by the redemption through the Law.[75]

The first half of the story expresses the rabbinic conception of the Law as redeeming. The second half expresses the rabbinic conception of the relationship between man and God or, more correctly, what that relationship says about the nature of God and man. And it thus explains how the Jew, though conscious of his plight, could entertain the hope of redemption by means of the seriousness with which he plods through the business of living in the world.

Elijah now turns to the sage and is told of a particular manifestation of what the prophet knows to be a constant truth. There is a divine sigh of anguish, a divine suffering for having wrought destruction on the world in which He dwells and exiled his people. "Know you," says the prophet, that the divine anguish is "day in and day out, and thrice daily!" Here, indeed, is a redeeming knowledge, one that only the prophet can reveal in its fullness. The suffering of God is as incessant as the prayers of Israel. But even here, where Elijah is revealing to the tanna something beyond what he already had known, there is nothing gnostic about his revelation. He does not teach a knowledge of which man in his humanness is incapable without revelation. He, rather, is teaching that man's own awareness of suffering is divine, for his sigh is like God's. Man knows only too well what is the sighing of God, not as revealed knowledge but from his own innermost experience of anguish. Paradoxically, the prophet is telling man something that he knows in the most personal sense of knowledge, but of which, for that very reason, he is unsure. Perhaps he is oversensitive, perhaps he lacks the strength to accept reality in all its uncouthness, perhaps he is masochistically exaggerating the meaning of history and peoplehood? No, says Elijah, your perception is divine, it is precisely the sensitivity to the suffering of Israel that you have in common with God. R. Yose himself was capable of the vision of the *Bat Kol*, the Echo, but he could grasp the togetherness of man and God in sensitivity to suffering only as a momentary flight. It is the prophet who reveals to him the essentialness of that sensitivity to godliness and, thus, to humanness.

Thus, we are speaking neither of man as an 'I' before the divine 'Thou' nor of an anthropomorphic description of a transcendent fantasy. We are speaking about the divineness of that which is most human in man, we are speaking of the sensitivity that religiosity sees as strength and not as weakness, as an attribute of real being and not as momentary or ignorable. We are speaking of man *with* God.

Man's recognition of his own strength is truly redeeming, for it enables him to realize the praiseworthiness of an imperfect reality. Only when man has learned to see his own utmost humanity as godly can he say of the God of so imperfect a world, "Let His great Name be blessed." In this sense, true religiosity is the ability to see the divine, at least potentially, in the darkest corners of living; and one can begin to understand a people for whom the most desolate of spaces and the smallest of moments become enchanted with divinity through the omnipresent working out of the Law. In Christianity, God became man, because otherwise man is lost. In Judaism, man is redeemable only if he can find it in himself to be godly. In both religions, deliverance is achieved not by God but with God. In both, the awareness of the need for, and the price of, deliverance is breathtaking. But, how vast the difference in their conception of what is divine. Paul could not imagine redemption with the divine persevering in the very midst of living: Jesus must be crucified in order for salvation to be achieved. Nor could the rabbis understand deliverance as the reascent of the Divine from the labyrinth of living.

> Rabban Simeon ben Gamliel says in the name of R. Joshua: From the day the Temple was destroyed, never a day goes by but it is cursed . . . (M *Sotah* 9:12)

> [Following upon this Mishnah] Rava said: The curse of each and every today is greater than the last, as the verse says, "In the morning thou shalt say: 'Would it were even!' and at even thou shalt say, 'Would it were morning!' [for the fear of thy heart which thou shalt fear, and for the sight of thine eyes which thou shalt see]" (Deuteronomy 28:67). Which morning [is longed for]? Can it be the following morning, not knowing what it will bring? It is rather the preceding morning [that one wishes would return, each present being experienced as far worse than what is only a memory]. But what, then, sustains the world? The *Kedushah De-Sidra* [the repetition of the doxology accompanied, this time, by its targumic translation, as the completion of the morning prayer] and the public response, "Let His great Name be blessed" [of the *Kaddish*] which is said at the lectures given by the Rabbis to the public.[76] (BT *Sotah* 49a)

Man redeems being by praising God in the midst of the imperfection and turmoil of living. The prayers in the synagogue declare it out loud:

> "Holy, holy, holy, is the Lord of hosts; the whole earth is full of His glory". (Isaiah 6:3)

> "Blessed be the glory of the Lord from His place". (Ezekiel 3:12)

> The Lord shall reign for ever and ever. (Exodus 15:18)

These three verses, which constitute the *Kedushah* (recited twice daily in the repetition of the *Amidah* prayer, the third verse being replaced by Psalm 146:10), are repeated again, together with their Targumic translation, in the *Kedushah De-Sidra.* The Aramaic Targum to the first verse underlines the significance of man's declaring, like the angels (*seraphim*), these verses:

> Holy in the transcendent heaven, where His dwelling is; holy upon the earth, the work of His greatness; holy always and eternally is the Lord of hosts: The whole earth is flushed with the glow of His glory. (*Targum Jonathan* to Isaiah 6:3)

God is holy in his awesome transcendence. But man praises Him amidst his smallness and God is holy in the midst of earthliness that, in its imperfection, is a work of divine power. God is holy always, whether in the celestial heights or in the darkness of the here and now. So, man redeems the world because it is only through him that the lowly is godly, flushed with the unseen glow of His glory.

> May His great Name be magnified and sanctified, in the world which He has created according to His will;[77] and may He ordain His kingdom during your lives and years and during the lifetimes of all the House of Israel, swiftly and soon. And say now: Amen! may His great Name be blessed always and eternally![78] (The first part of the *Kaddish* that is recited, among many other occasions, after the lectures given by the Rabbis to the public)

May the awesome divine Name be enhanced in this world that he has created according to his will; and may his kingdom be realized in our lives, despite their smallness, and not beyond us nor beyond history. This is the real celebration of the awesome divine Name, and not as a transience alone, but "always and eternally."

It is when the aforementioned passages are recited by the simple crowds, and in the Aramaic vernacular,[79] that humanity and mundaneness are redeemed. Man redeems the world because he—and this is his humanity—can see in its wretchedness the divine. It is the conviction that redemption is a working out of the divine through the most human, which underlies the seriousness of God's Law for man; and Elijah himself, in his capacity as sage of the Law, confirms this conviction.

It is when one is to understand the religious psyche, one must beware of misinterpreting what we have said. On the one hand, religious man's consciousness of suffering is not an infatuation with it. In fact, it would probably be better to describe religious man as overly sensitive to suffering, thus implying the very opposite of an infatuation with pain. The accusation of masochism aimed at religion must often stem from minds too used to the acceptance of brutality and even cataclysm. One may say that religious man is quixotic in his relentless underscoring of suffering. But, there probably would be a great deal less suffering in the world if religious people would stick closer to the primal religious shuddering at pain and engage less in "explanations" and "rationalizations" for evil. How much easier has the myth of satanic hypostasis made the acceptance of evil. And man has done altogether too much in conjuring up the reality of Satan by acting out in ghastly atrocities the myth of that malignant being.

On the other hand, one must be careful not to exaggerate the note of self-realization and resultant self-confidence that accompany the notion of redemption. We shall see later that self-confidence comes to religious man only at a frightening price. And, in any case, the sources under consideration have little to do with the orgies of self-congratulation that some religious thinkers see as the ultimate statement of the "greatness of man." Man is "great," religiously speaking, first of all when he recognizes his smallness. That is not an easy task for modern man and the idea itself does not have too much hope of being the most popular idea of our age. But Jews have memories of legendary length.

> "But if ye will not hear it, My soul shall weep in secret for your pride; And mine eye shall weep some, and run down with tears, Because the Lord's flock is carried away captive." (Jeremiah 13:17). Samuel bar Inya said in the name of Rav [Palestine-Babylonia, third century]: The Holy One Blessed is He has a a place called "secret". (BT *Hagigah* 5b)

God is not crying, says the homilist, *secretly* but in a hidden *place*. What is the difference between the two interpretations? The answer lies in the obvious fact that God's crying is not hidden from the people of Israel, for the prophet makes it known to them. There is nothing secret about his crying, though he "hides" himself. According to this interpretation the prophet wants us to imagine someone hiding his face and weeping. It is the image of a man who dare not reveal his tears to those around him. One behaves so when he knows that to the onlookers his crying is ridiculous. For them, all is well, or bearable, or at least they think that their "strength" is in never allowing a tear to wet their eyes. Were they to catch one crying they would no doubt laugh at him, scorn him for being weak and childish. And so when he does cry he hides himself, and these are the bitterest of tears! One's tragedy becomes nightmarish. He may think for moments that his suffering is a being smothered by cobwebs, that he has only to tear them aside and to breathe again the cool fresh air. But, to the original pain is added the fact of being an unwanted stranger among the serene whose tranquillity is disturbed by his sighing. How they hate him for questioning happiness! And how painful it is to know that they cannot even understand his crying! This is the sadness of Israel's Exile. And God himself cries the tears of that lonely people.

When we say that God cries like man, or that man's crying is divine, we do not intend to speak from that feeling of superiority resulting from a knowledge of "the truth." There is nothing "true" about tragedy—it depends on one's sensitivities. The divine sensitivity to tragedy is subtle; it always remains knowable only to the one that perceives it. And it remains a divine sensitivity only so long as it is so intensely personal, even if it is the sensitivity of a people. Lonely and tragic is a people for whom even God's knowledge of their suffering remains a personal experience of the sufferer and not a trumpet blast of revealed truth.

Man is surrounded by the hollow knell of absurdity and nothingness. How tenuous is the order or understandability of the world around us, how dreamlike are our aspirations, how imminent is the possibility of chaos! And that encroaching chaos is dreaded not only out of the intelligence-imparting nature of the psyche, a nature that is forever interpreting and ordering, but out of the awareness of the sharpness of suffering for oneself and others, an awareness marking the religious soul.

The religious soul in whose womb the Law is first conceived is musical to a passion. She hears cacophony where others hear symphony. She cringes at discord where others hum. She shudders with horror where others goggle at beauty. And she hears heavenly music where others are deaf, deaf. Her eyes are blinded where others strain for light. Her fingers are torn on what is satin to others. Her legs fail where brave men trample. She is frail so that she desires virginity; yet she is passionate and easily seduced to love.

Religious man is forever restless with fear of a threatening chaos, unlike his secular brother who faces life with the serenity of utter insensitivity, or so it seems to his religious peer. The cowering terror in the confrontation with nonbeing is the mirror image of the virility of the drive to be. The more unbounded the latter, the more unbridled the former. And, in religious man, that drive is a Divine hand that thrusts him into becoming; nothingness is countered precisely by the terror it inspires. Religious man withstands encroaching absurdity and nothingness with a sense of the overwhelming necessity of his being. Living becomes an acquiescence to the most irresistible and demanding of all divine calls, the call to be. To the certainty of death and the fear of nothingness, religious man answers with a compulsion to be. The augury of absurdity strikes upon his acute sensitivity, and in proportion to that sensitivity is the intensity of his reaction, which springs from the very wells of his drive to be. Life is a very serious matter indeed, and not a moment of living is to be taken lightly.

In the Law, the awesomeness of being that man finds in himself becomes the stance of truth for all the events of living. In the community, working through the ever-so-long patience of tradition, the many selves work out a structure of the I-we world in which the being of self reveals being before which each man stands. This is the nonecstatic revelation of developing tradition, and through it, man discovers God. The profound seriousness of man standing before God is very real because in Law it is a structure that includes all of experience.

> R. Eliezer [or Eleazar] Ha-Kappar [late second century] says: . . . And let not your [evil] nature assure you that the underworld affords you an escape: For you are driven into being; and you are driven from the womb; and you are driven to live; and you are driven unto death; and you are driven to give an accounting before the King of the Kings of Kings, the Holy One Blessed is He. (M *Avot* 4:22)

The compulsion of being is overwhelming and even death holds out no escape for religious man. And, the epitome of that seriousness is man standing before God in judgment. The vision of God is life compelling yet awesome and frightening.

We may now appreciate that this awesomeness of being well may become far too much to bear in day to day piety. And then, religious man dares to long for a dramatic, heroic moment of action, in which he can act out all the godliness of being and thus save himself from the pressing burden of the day-to-day compulsion. This moment of action is martyrdom; thus religiosity ultimately may entail a yearning for martyrdom.

> Rabbi [Judah the *Nasi*] wept and said: It takes some men years to make[80] their world[81] while others make their world in a moment![82] (BT *Avodah Zarah* 10b, 17a and 18a)

This statement, made about martyrdom,[83] focuses in on the meaning of *this-worldly martyrdom*.[84] Martyrdom is "making" one's "world" in a moment of ultimate action.

> Our Rabbis repeated: . . . When R. Akiva [martyred during the Bar Kokhba revolt, c. 132–135] was taken out to be killed[85] it was the time of day for the reading of "*Shema*" (Deuteronomy 6:4 etc.); and while his

flesh was being torn by iron combs, he accepted upon himself the yoke of the Kingdom of Heaven [as the essence of the "*Shema*"]. His students said to him, "Our teacher, so far?" He said to them, "All my life I was distressed by the verse '[And thou shalt love the Lord thy God with all thy heart,] and with all thy soul' (Ibid.: 5) which means 'even if he takes your soul';[86] I said to myself, 'When will it be possible for me to act that out?' And now that it has has become possible, should I not act it out?"[87] He drew out the word "[the Lord is] one" and his soul withdrew on that note. An Echo broke out saying, "You are happy, R. Akiva, for your soul has withdrawn on the note of 'one'."[88] (BT *Berakhot* 61b)

For R. Akiva, the act of martyrdom is an epitomization of all his life. He, therefore, acts out, even in his most terrible moments, what he has tediously (so it seems to him now) acted out all his life.[89] But how condensed and complete is his bearing of the yoke of heaven in the moment of dying! It is a liberation, a total salvation, the realization of a vastly long yearning. The unity of God is in the completeness and thus unity of the moment of martyrdom.

Thus, martyrdom may even become a temptation. However, we must remember that we are speaking of a dialectic of Law and martyrdom. Let us return to our texts and retrace the outlines of the entire implicit dynamic structure.

The Mishnah has already set the stage by identifying the sparing of Isaac as a redemption. Now, we understand from what he is redeemed. *Akedah* is a drive to martyrdom inherent in the very nature of man's religiosity and the divine command to bind Isaac is called out to Abraham through his innermost being. The second call to Abraham, telling him to desist from the terrible sacrifice, therefore, is a drawing back of the divine necessity, and thus a true moment of redemption. "He Who answered Abraham on the mountain of Moriah, may He answer you and hearken this day to the voice of your pleading. Blessed art Thou, God, the Redeemer of Israel." But the redemption is dialectical. Just as man may be redeemed from *Akedah*, so *Akedah* may save him from the divine anger over transgression of the Law. "When the sons of Isaac my son become troubled and there is no one to speak in their defence, You shall speak in their defence. 'God will see': You will remember for them the Binding of Isaac their father and You will be filled with compassion for them." Nor is the terribleness of the dialectical deliverance vicariously played out for Israel by Abraham and Isaac. Finally, the Binding of Isaac is complete only in the sacrificing of the Ram. The readiness of Abraham to sacrifice Isaac becomes meaningful only when viewed as part of the drama of the ram-Israel, who hesitates through history between escape from the yoke of the

Law into martyrdom and a drawing back from total holocaust into the day to dayness of Law. "After all the generations your sons will inevitably be *caught up in sin* and ensnared in troubles." It is Israel's shrugging off the yoke of the Law that leads to martyrdom, and the piety of Law always is an alternative to the need for martyrdom.

"And finally they will be redeemed with the horns of the ram." The ever-readiness of Israel to martyrdom saves them from the awesomeness of God and his Law, and that very Law enables redemption without total holocaust. Israel is delivered through the horn of the ram that symbolizes martyrdom *and* survival, a readiness to ultimate heroism yet an ability to draw back before the final moment of total destruction.

So it is that man's enormous vision of his godly potential erupts into a subterranean energy, which is religious man's sense of having sinned; and this becomes a yearning of cosmic proportions for the redemption of a world that centers around man as the one who endows it with meaning; and it is a weeping of God Almighty himself, who weeps as man does in the terrible and lonely knowledge of each man's suffering. And, in the grip of that tense energy of seriousness which informs the Law, the religious soul surges forward, her sense of strength inflamed by the immensity of her vision and her task, reaching out beyond her reach to the hard-bought knowledge of the horizon of deliverance; toward the perfection and freedom that martyrdom is, a salvation that is ultimate because it coincides essentially with religious man's self-immolation. And the redemption of Isaac from the holocaustal *Akedah* is a reshouldering of that huge burden of working out redemption through the Law; but now it is a soothing, embracing day to dayness that draws back from the abyss.

In short, martyrdom is not always a result of the cruelty of history alone—something deep in the nature of religious man drives toward the heroic, the final, and the complete; martyrdom is *Akedah*. The fact that more often than not history seals the terrible fate of man does not hide his partnership in seeking that fate. And the Law can be at once redemptive and oppressive. The beauty of the notion imbedded in our texts is that Israel finds its true deliverance in precariously hesitating between the absolute embrace of the Law and the daring yet freeing heroism of martyrdom.

Accordingly, the story of the Binding of Isaac is told in the dimensions of the individual, the community, and history. The psychological aspect of the dialectic between Law and *Akedah* is a personal religious experience, even though one person cannot act out both roles to the end. They are acted out by different members of the community of Israel in the stories of history. Both absolute adherence to the Law and actual martyrdom may subsist in the biography of an individual, but it cannot then be a true dialectic—actual martyrdom cuts the drama short. Martyrdom and Law are concretely real and yet dialectical in the dimension of community, and usually in the diachronics of history. But the individual who knows the history of his people and the reality of both poles may experience in the intimacy of his own religious life the drawing back from each pole toward the other.[90]

Chapter Three

The Binding of Isaac

W e have seen that the story of the Binding of Isaac is not merely a source out of which variegated meanings spring exegetically. It is rather the telling of a drama that unfolds fully for the listeners only in the history of Israel and the inner experiences of the truly religious. It is a tale told by religious man, full of life and awe, signifying an implicit dynamic structure that is not necessarily at the level of awareness even for its heroes and tellers, let alone its audience. We may now dare, perhaps, to listen again to the biblical recital of the story with some hope of insight.

Abraham sets out with Isaac on their journey to Moriah. In the beginning, the journey is routine enough. Abraham rises early in the morning in order to travel as far as possible before night falls. He takes two of his young men with him, the long journey requires assistance. He cleaves wood for the burnt offering, and they start for the place marked out by God. On the third day, Abraham finally sees the place far off in the distance. They still have some way to go, but Abraham prefers to go alone with Isaac. The two young men are not surprised by this. "We will worship and come back to you" is enough of an explanation for them; they sense nothing unusual. Even Isaac, walking along with his father and sharing in the chores, feels the routineness of the journey so far. He is puzzled only by the absence of the sacrificial animal from the present routine: "Behold the fire and the wood; but where is the lamb for a burnt-offering?" (Genesis 22:7).

Abraham alone is aware of tragedy. He turns to his son and answers gently, "God will provide Himself the lamb for a burnt-offering, my son" (ibid. 22:8). The son will know very soon what is happening, Abraham has no illusions on that score. But at this moment, looking into his son's questioning eyes, his heart trembles with love and he postpones the terrible revelation of truth. He savors the moment, the love between father and son, and wants to walk like this, arm in arm, for yet awhile, short as the fleeting minutes are. Refusing to spoil the present with the shadow of the future doom, he gently brushes aside Isaac's question. Perhaps, even Abraham himself forgets in the togetherness of the present the sorrow of reality. There is a quality of bated breath in that scene, a sense of time standing still: "So they went both of them together" (ibid.). Certainly, Abraham's love for Isaac embraces the whole of the waning present, and the gentleness of the father to the son at that moment is a blotting out of that which is yet to be.

During that last walk before the *Akedah*, Abraham loves Isaac not as the child of promise—for the promise has been denied—but as a future-less child with only the naked being of the present. This is true and selfless love, it is a love in which only the completely free man can indulge. Abraham knows that there is no longer any future, yet he clings heroically to the disappearing present; he is totally free in the isolation of the present, the future is not and the past is too painful to remember. He loves Isaac as a pure 'thou', a love in which the being of its object is the culmination of that love. The suspension of being in the limbo of a now reveals and concretizes a love that is otherwise indiscernible because it cannot be touched by yearning.

Abraham, in those final moments, thus is experiencing a complete love, an attainment. There are no expectations, no unfinished plans. He loves without yearning. Abraham is well on his way into the dark night of martyrdom.

The total withdrawal into the present frees man and enables total attainment. But the drive for total achievement in the present is also ominous, and its culmination is awesome. Abraham is approaching an absolute attainment, an obliteration of even the possiblity of incompleteness. He wants perfection, in scope and intensity, in the claustrophobic confines of a present moment. He is heroic and frightening. His gentle answer to his son is an indication of his mood. The epitome of that mood and its culmination is martyrdom.

"And they came to the place which God had told him of; and Abraham built the altar there, and laid the wood in order, and bound Isaac his son, and laid him on the altar, upon the wood" (ibid. 22:9). Did the father's hands tremble? We are aware only of a singleness of purpose. "And Abraham stretched forth his hand, and took the knife to slay his son" (Ibid. 22:10) Abraham is now to actualize heartrending yearnings of a lifetime in one heroic and terrifying act. He will attain absolute perfection and freedom. Nothing will be left undone, all smallness and frustration will be gone. What terror does the vision of God Almighty strike in man's heart that he is driven to this?

But, finally, God loves the father and the son. The same God who has driven Abraham to the pinnacle of Moriah draws the striking hand back at the last moment. "And the angel of the Lord called unto him out of heaven, and said: 'Abraham, Abraham.' And he said: 'Here am I.' And he said: 'Lay not thy hand upon the lad, neither do thou anything unto him; for now I know that thou art a God-fearing man, seeing thou hast not withheld thy son, thine only son, from Me'" (Ibid. 22:11–12). Finally, the loving God tells man not to go the way of martyrdom, not willingly at least. "And Abraham lifted up his eyes, and looked, and behold behind him a ram caught in the thicket by his horns. And Abraham went and took the ram, and offered him up for a burnt-offering in the stead of his son (Ibid. 22:13). Despite the infinitely relieving vision, the religious man could not altogether forego sacrifice.

> "And Abraham went and took the ram, and offered him up for a burnt-offering in the stead of his son." (Genesis 22:13) R. Yudan said in the name of R. Benaiah: He said before Him, "Master of All the Worlds, see the blood of this ram as if it were the blood of Isaac my son, the sacrificed portions of this ram as if they were the sacrificed portions of Isaac my son". . . (*Genesis Rabbah* to 22:13 [56, p. 606])

"And Abraham called the name of that place The Lord Seeth; as it is said to this day; 'In the mount where the Lord is seen'" (Ibid. 22:14). God sees and is seen in the pain of man.

After the heroic ordeal, Abraham again finds a placid peace with God. He returns to the assurance of faith in the future.

> And the angel of the Lord called unto Abraham a second time out of heaven, and said: "By Myself have I sworn, saith the Lord, because thou hast done this thing, and hast not withheld thy son, thine only son, that in blessing I will bless thee, and in multiplying I will multiply thy seed as the stars of the heaven, and as the sand which is upon the seashore; and thy seed shall possess the gate of his enemies; and in thy seed shall all the nations of the earth be blessed; because thou hast hearkened to My voice."(Ibid. 22:15–18)

The drama and immediacy of martyrdom is to be replaced by an ever-so-long patience. Abraham will be blessed: over the generations his offspring will multiply as the stars of the heaven, they shall possess the gate of their enemies and in the end all the nations of the earth shall also be blessed—in Abraham's seed.

"So Abraham returned unto his young men, and they rose up and went together to Beersheba; and Abraham dwelt at Beersheba" (Ibid. 22:19). Abraham slowly descends from the mountain, sighing with the thought of the long return journey lying before him. The heat and dust of the remaining day were heavy, the stink of the donkey unbearable, and the company of the young servants oppressive. Abraham returns to the tediousness of the patient, long way that leads through years and generations. He has narrowly escaped the awesomeness of total being in the present by accepting God's loving assurance of the rightness of the much longer journey through day to dayness. Now, he thinks of the way back, of life in Beersheba, of a wife for Isaac.[1]

> And it came to pass after these things, that it was told Abraham, saying: "Behold, Milcah, she also hath borne children unto thy brother Nahor: Uz his first-born, and Buz his brother, and Kemuel the father of Aram; and Chesed, and Hazo, and Pildash, and Jidlaph, and Bethuel." And Bethuel begot Rebekah; These eight did Milcah bear to Nahor, Abraham's brother. And his concubine, whose name was Reumah, she also bore Tekah, and Gaham, and Tachash, and Maacah. (Ibid. 22:20–24)

Tedious and pedantic after the drama of the *Akedah*! In the immediacy of those terrible moments there was room only for the important: Abraham and Isaac, the intense love between father and son, and martyrdom. Now, on the way back, Abraham's mind is crowded with wearisome thoughts and plans.

"So Abraham returned." "Isaac, where is he?" (*Genesis Rabbah* to 22:19 [56, p. 611]).

Love recedes together with heroism as the sharpness of the now dims, and Abraham descends the mountain lost in thought. "Isaac, where is he? R. Berekhiah said in the name of the Rabbis who are there [in Babylonia]: He [Abraham] sent him to learn the Law from Shem." (Ibid.).

Finally, God saves man from the terror of the total now by allowing him the placid way of the Law.

So, the remaining episodes in the patriarch's life are of a very different order from the Binding of Isaac. Abraham buys the cave of Machpelah from Ephron the Hittite, the son of Zohar, a cumbersome story of subtle negotiations, sale and possession. He buries Sarah and mourns her. Then, he sends his devoted servant with careful instructions to find a wife for Isaac. Here follows a long story full of hints concerning the nature of the future actors in the history of Israel. The *Akedah* becomes a memory, albeit a frightening one for Isaac, who will always wonder what drove his father to that terrifying scene on the mountain. For Isaac, God will remain always fearful and awesome, "And Jacob swore by the Fear of his father Isaac" (Genesis 32:53). But, for the time being, religiosity is saved from the totally heroic.

Thus, the story of the journey of Abraham and Isaac to Moriah and back is a story of the dialectic of martyrdom and Law (day to dayness). Abraham is able to give up the promise "for in Isaac shall seed be called to thee" (Ibid. 21:12) because martyrdom is an absolute compression of salvation into the now. Martyrdom is liberation. It frees one from the past and the future; it frees one from Law. It is the ultimate love of man for God, it is man escaping to God from God. But God loves man, too; gently, but firmly, He urges him back away from awesomeness onto the long and patient road of time and history.

For many people, the essence of religiosity is the striving for the future, for immortality, for children, for others. This, then, is the trial of the *Akedah*. Can Abraham act out the drama of his religiosity completely in the present? Abraham is a religious man because he finds the call to martyrdom irresistible. But, he is the father of Israel no less because of his drawing back at the last moment. All men who have had their dreams shattered, who remain with the loneliness of lost hopes may understand the difficulty of Abraham's trial. Who is heroic enough to remain with the present alone? But how many understand the strength needed to stay the patriarch's hand from delivering the fatal blow? Abraham's trial is not only in the call to climb the mountain of Moriah but in his return to Beersheba as well, and more so.

Here is, perhaps, a meaningful warning for modern man. Man today, both because of the smallness of his faith and the horrendousness of history, sees his God dying in the chaos of flux and doubt. Modern man's faith is to be tested by his ability to live intensely and meaningfully in the limbo of the present. We want to forget history—how dearly we want to forget history!—and we dare not be sure of the future. Though religious man's beliefs continually lose their clarity, though they gray and shrivel up in the winter of today, religious man today is called upon to gather up what is left of his faith and plunge into the now of action. Or rather, he is called to replace his transcendental faith with a heroic readiness for action in the present, regardless of its price. Modern religious man stands dangerously before the temptation of the heroic, the temptation of martyrdom. Modern man often has little left but the present—all else may recede like the stars blinking blindly from afar. Then, the present is to be the vehicle of faith, and unhappy will be he who cannot heroically face the loneliness of the now.

Let us recall for a moment the story of the Mother and Her Seven Sons as told in the Babylonian Talmud. For the martyrs in that story, all has receded into the night of suffering, even life, life after death, and divine order. But those martyrs are truly religious in the intensity with which they live their dying, the intensity with which they endow the final moment of life, the absolute now. Theirs is a greater religiosity than any "I believe," and it is one that even modern man, if he has the strength, may embrace. Thus, we may benefit from a rabbinic insight. Martyrdom is not vicariously acted out in one meta-historical act. It always may tempt us. Will modern man, too, find that God loves him and be spared the terrible need for heroism?

Chapter Four

Honi ha-Me'aggel

In order to understand a little better the phenomenology of what has been said, let us examine the "biographies" of some of the figures known in early rabbinic tradition as martyrs or as having martyrial tendencies. The stories will be interesting both for their own sake and as frames for the individual's statements, rather than the statements by themselves, because we are discussing an act of living-out and that takes place in the dimension of biography. For this purpose biographical traditions must be taken seriously. This means straining to glimpse an individual's biography as an organic whole, even though it is pieced together from different sources, different in the historical as well as the literary sense. Our aim is existential coherence rather than historical truth. If we uncover a coherent existential structure in the scattered biographical references chosen, then we legitimately may conclude that tradition is telling us an organic message, organic in the wholeness of the man's personality as presented in those sources. We shall begin with Honi ha-Me'aggel.

Josephus (*Antiquities* 14, 2, 1) relates that Honi was a righteous man, loved by God, who once in time of drought prayed for rain and his prayer was answered. This Honi, continues Josephus, was caught unwittingly in the fighting between the camps of Hyrcanus II and Aristobulus II (65 B.C.E.), and Hyrcanus' followers demanded that he pray for the downfall of Aristobulus' forces. When their pressure became unbearable, Honi stood up among them and cried: "Our Lord, king of the world, since these who are with me are Your people and the besieged are Your priests, I beg of You that You should neither hearken to these against the others nor perform what the others pray for against these." Whereupon the riffraff surrounded him and stoned him to death. Honi's death here is a truly heroic martyrdom. He could have saved himself easily by acquiescing to the people's demands. Instead, he not only refused to do as they wish but offered a dramatic prayer that seems calculated to inflame the masses against him and indeed results in his death. He was driven to embrace his ideals in the present, dramatically and totally, at whatever cost, rather than slip through the present somehow until happier days should enable different behavior. Honi chose the dangerous and heroic way where death lurks because he demanded of himself total realization in the immediate, ominously public present, rather than the much longer way of quietude and patience.

This story of Honi may contain a further implication that is less obvious. Honi seems to be saying that it is a priori impossible that one of the two parties locked in combat could be more in the right than the other, at least not sufficiently to justify war. Did Honi take this stance because both sides had supporters who were sons of Israel, or do his words imply a deprecation of struggle in the historical context of war in general? We shall see later the common matrix of martyrdom and pacifism.

The story of Honi's prayer for rain is told in the Mishnah as follows:

Because of any calamity—may it not materialize—for the community, the cry of the ram's horn is sounded [calling the community to prayer and fasting] except for overabundance of rain. It happened that Honi ha-Me'aggel was approached, saying: "Pray that it should rain!" He said to them, "Go out and bring in the Passover ovens so that they shouldn't crumble [from the rain]." He prayed, but no rain fell. What did he do? He drew a circle and stood inside it and said before Him, "Master of the World, Your children have turned to me as one initiated before you.[1] I swear by Your great Name that I shall not move from here until You have mercy on Your children." The rain started to drizzle. He said, "Not so have I asked, but rather a rain that will fill cisterns, ditches and caves." It began to pour angrily. He said, "Not so have I asked, but rather rain that is of goodwill, a blessing and a gift." It rained as it should; until the people of Israel in Jerusalem went up to the Temple Mount because of the flooding. He was approached, saying, "Just as you prayed that they should come, so pray that they should be gone!" He said to them, "Go out and see whether the sign-pillar has been submerged."[2] Simeon ben Shetah [the first century B.C.E.] sent him a message saying, "You should be excommunicated![3] But what am I to do when you luxuriate[4] before the Divine and He does your will for you,[5] like a child who luxuriates[4] with[6] his father and has him do his will.[7] And concerning you the verse says, 'Let thy father and they mother be glad, And let her that bore thee rejoice' (Proverbs 23:25)." (M *Ta'anit* 3:8)[8]

Honi's martyrial tendency comes out here as well. He swears in the name of God that he will not move from within his circle until the rain comes, despite the consequences that this may have. We may be assured of Honi's faith in his ability to bring rain, but we must be equally certain of the sincerity of his threat. He is convinced that his willingness to sacrifice himself will bring God to answer his prayer, and he is prepared to go the whole way. Honi is not merely a theatrical miracle worker; he understands the pain of those who have little faith, and he assumes the heroism for his people's sake.

In the Mishnah, it appears that the story of Honi is brought in order to illustrate the law that "Because of any calamity . . . the cry of the ram's-horn is sounded except for an overabundance of rain." Honi answers laconically that if the "sign-pillar," an impressive affair no doubt, is still visible then there is no call for prayer to halt the rain. This leaves open the theoretical possibility of begging for an end to the downpour if a destructive flood is imminent. Indeed, in the version of the *Baraitha* in the Babylonian Talmud, Honi does pray for the end of the deluge. But the words ascribed to him there are revealing:

> He said to them, "According to my tradition, one does not plead [to be spared] from too much bountifulness. Nevertheless,[9] bring me a thanksgiving bullock." A thanksgiving bullock was brought to him. He placed both his hands on it and said before Him, "Master of the World, Israel Your People, whom You brought out of Egypt, cannot cope[10] with either too much bountifulness or with too much tribulation: You were angry with them, they were not able to cope; You were bountiful towards them, they were not able to cope. May it be desirable before You that the rain should cease and there should be easiness[11] in the world."
> (BT *Ta'anit* 23a)

Honi's tradition speaks not of an "overabundance of rain" but rather of too much "bountifulness."[12] Dire as the consequences may be, the rain is divine bountifulness and therefore good. "Israel Your People" are not capable of standing extreme suffering where death lurks. But, Honi himself knows that the embrace of the divine fullness in the present very well may be complete only in the act of dying.

But, beyond that, we uncover a fascinating facet of the man's religious psyche. In his view salvation cannot be tardy, it is "now or never." His prayer is not one for a patient but merciful working out of things through the course of events. He is asking for—he is demanding—an immediate and perfect reality, an immediate and total dissolution of any intrusion of evil. For him the present is capable of such perfection, the reality of an almighty God means the concretization of divine fullness in the immediate, without the barrier of delay. The martyr's vision of total salvation in the present is real because he himself holds its achievement in his hands. Honi knows that the now is capable of complete fulfillment, and he achieves it finally in the act of martyrdom described by Josephus. It is not surprising that Honi takes no sides in the struggle between Hyrcanus and Aristobulus; there must be a dimension more immediate than history in which wrongs are to be righted.

Honi in a certain sense is a messianic figure, or rather his story is one of messianism. His story says that man may achieve immediate salvation. In Honi's world the Messiah has, as it were, already arrived; there is no need for messianism along the historical axis. The Babylonian Talmud (ibid.) records:

> Rav Nahman bar Rav Hisda taught:[13] What message did the Sanhedrin[14] send Honi ha-Me'aggel [after the incident of rain making]? "Thou shalt also decree a thing, and it shall be established unto thee, And light shall shine upon thy ways. When they cast thee down, thou shalt say: 'There is lifting up'; For the humble person He saveth. He delivereth him that is innocent, Yea, thou shalt be delivered through the cleanness of thy hands" (Job 22:28–30).
>
> "Thou shalt also decree a thing, and it shall be established unto thee"[15]—You decreed from below and the Holy One Blessed is He followed[16] your words from on high.
>
> "And light shall shine upon thy ways"—A darkened generation, you lit up through your prayer.
>
> "When they cast thee down, thou shalt say: 'There is lifting up'"—A generation that was lowly, you raised up through your prayer.
>
> "For the humble person He saveth"—A generation that was ashamed in its sinfulness,[17] you saved through your prayer.
>
> "He delivereth him that is innocent"—A generation that was not innocent,[18] you delivered through your prayer.
> "Yea, thou shalt be delivered through the cleanness of thy hands"— Through your perspicuous[19] actions.[20]

By making the last verse refer to the definiteness and drama of Honi's action in bringing about the rainfall, the homilist carefully avoids the notion of Honi's righteousness atoning vicariously for the sins of the people. One may question the exegesis of the biblical verses, but in the Honi story, it is Honi's heroic readiness for self-sacrifice, not his righteousness, that makes salvation immediate. Nor is the auspiciousness of the hero's readiness for self-sacrifice vicarious; the rainfall demonstrates an immediacy of salvation for Honi and the people benefit from the result of his heroism and do not vicariously partake of the heroism itself.[21] Honi's story demonstrates the potential of immediate salvation for every heroic individual. An actualized messianism based on such a notion would ensure the immediacy of such salvation for each person capable of it. We shall see the significance of this later on.

Simeon ben Shetah's displeasure with Honi is not based on his scepticism toward the story. The theological implications of Honi's behavior raise his ire. Again, in the *Baraitha*, we are told that, after Honi's prayer for the end of the rain is answered, Simeon ben Shetah sends him the following message:

> Were you not Honi I would have you excommunicated! If[22] these years were like the years in the time of Elijah, when the keys of rain were in the hands of Elijah,[23] would not the Name of Heaven have been desecrated by you![24] But what am I to do with you when you luxuriate before the Divine and He does your will for you, like a child who luxuriates with his father and has him do his will: When he says to him, "Wash me with warm water", he washes him, "Rinse me with cold water", he rinses him, "Give me nuts, peaches, almonds and pomegranates", he gives him.[25] And concerning you the verse says, "Let thy father and thy mother be glad, And let her that bore thee rejoice".[26] (Ibid.)

Simeon is not immune to Honi's charm and the sage's words are a mixture of stern disapproval and sensitivity, even sympathy. The picture of a child taking advantage of his father's indulgent love implies that it is childish to suppose that this really is the way in which the divine order is worked out. For a sage of the Law, the true way is much longer and far more arduous than the childish (for Simeon) demand for immediacy that leads to martyrdom. That there is in Honi's way a certain obviation of the need for the way of the Law, we may see in the following story:

> There was a plague in Sepphoris. It did not enter the square in which R. Hanina [bar Hama, the first half of the third century] lived, and the Sepphorians were saying: "What is [with] this old man among us, that he sits soundly, he and his neighbors, while the city is going from bad to worse!" He entered [the community's gathering place] and said before them: "Zimri[27] was alone in his generation and yet twenty-four thousand of Israel fell;[28] and we, how many Zimris are there in our generation and you are making a commotion!" It happened that it was necessary to make a fast-day [because of drought] and yet no rain fell. R. Joshua [ben Levi] made a fast-day in the South and rain fell, and the Sepphorians were saying: "R. Joshua ben Levi brought the rain to the Southerners while R. Hanina held back the water from the Sepphorians!" It was necessary to make [a fast-day] a second time. [R. Hanina] sent for

> R. Joshua ben Levi saying, "Would my master take care to come out with
> us to the [prayer ritual of the] fast-day? They went out together to the
> fast-day. And no rain fell. [R. Hanina] entered and said before them: "It
> is not R. Joshua ben Levi who brings the rain to the Southerners nor is it
> R. Hanina who holds back the rain from the Sepphorians. Rather, the
> Southerners—their hearts are sensitive and they hear the words of the
> Law and give in; while the Sepphorians—their hearts are hard and they
> hear the words of the Law and do not give in. When he [R. Hanina]
> went in he gazed upward and saw that the air was clear. He said, "Even
> now it is so?" Whereupon it started to rain, and he vowed not to do so
> again, saying, "Am I to tell the creditor not to claim his debt? (PT
> *Ta'aniot* 3:4 [66c])[29]

How different is R. Hanina from Honi ha-Me'aggel. When the people were hard pressed by drought they turned to Honi to alleviate their
suffering by intervening with their Father, his Father. But when the people of Sepphoris come upon calamity, the very presence of R. Hanina in
their midst makes them uneasy. R. Hanina is undaunted by their attitude
and exhorts them to bear the yoke of punishment rather than shirk it.
Divine justice is not worked out in the immediacy of the individual.

> R. Ze'eira [said] in the name of R. Hanina [bar Hama]: What are the
> great [sages] of the generation to do when the community is judged only
> in consequence of its majority. For so we find that throughout the thirty-
> eight years that Israel were as if excommunicated He did not speak with
> Moses, as the verse says, "So it came to pass, when all the men of war
> were consumed and dead from among the people" (Deuteronomy 2:16).
> What is written after that? "that the Lord spoke unto me, saying".[17]
> (continuation of ibid.)

Deliverance occurs in the dimension of peoplehood and this takes a long,
long time. Even Moses our teacher, about whom it is said "with him do I
speak mouth to mouth, even manifestly, and not in dark speeches; and the
similitude of the Lord doth he behold" (Numbers 12:8), was denied the
Divine vision for thirty-eight years, until the Divine way was worked out
in the wanderings of Israel through the desert. No wonder the Sepphorians are made uneasy! They do not hesitate to blame the Rabbi for the
continuation of the drought. R. Hanina is moved to annoyance. He asks
R. Joshua ben Levi, reputed to have brought the rains to his native Judaea,
to join the fasters in the Galilee. When even the participation of the
famous guest from the South does not effect rain, R. Hanina announces to
the community that the way to deliverance is through the Law and not
histrionics.

The day of fasting and prayer is ended, the drought continues, and R. Hanina has tried his best to help the community through the difficulty of reality. Now he returns to his study, tired, drained, and alone. He stands by the window, enjoying the quiet, and looks out. There are no signs of let up in the shriveling weather, the sky remains barren. And then weariness finally gets the better of the rabbi, and he blurts out, "Even now it is so?" Immediately the rain comes down. And then the rabbi is ashamed of himself. He promises himself that he will not succumb again. "Am I to tell the creditor not to claim his debt?" To grasp for immediate salvation can only mean abandoning the way of the Law. One must plod through the cumbersomeness of day-to-day events, tedious as they are, for only along the axis of patient time can the divine be lived out. Unlike the heroic Honi, R. Hanina would not willingly seek out the way of martyrdom; his is the way of the Law.

R. Hanina's way is indeed the long and patient way. Though Rabbi Judah ha-Nasi directed on his deathbed that R. Hanina be appointed head of the academy, the latter refused the position because he considered R. Effes more worthy than himself. Only after the death of R. Effes did R. Hanina accept the position.[30] And R. Hanina saw his own longevity as homeomorphic with actions of his:

> R. Hanina said: I was graced with longevity either because of this [his acceptance of delay in his appointment], I don't know, or because when I used to go up from Tiberias to Sepphoris I would make the way longer by stopping in for a cordial visit with R. Simeon ben Halaphta in Ein-Te'enah, I don't know. (Ibid. 4:2 [68a])

For R. Hanina longevity is a blessing. Would it be so for Honi? Simeon ben Shetah and R. Hanina are together in their rejection of Honi's way.

Both the Palestinian and Babylonian *Talmudim* recount how Honi ha-Me'aggel slept for seventy years. Of course, this is a folk motif, but by making it a part of the Honi stories, tradition has given further expression to the make up of the personality of the rain maker. In the Palestinian Talmud's version, Honi is said to have slept through the destruction and rebuilding of the Temple, while in the Babylonian version the Exile is referred to only through the exegesis of verse, Honi himself living at a later period. The Palestinian Talmud explains the obvious chronological descrepancy (according to the tannaitic sources, Honi lived contemporaneously with Simeon ben Shetah, in the first century B.C.E.) by associating the legend with a Honi ha-Me'aggel who is supposed to have been the grandfather of the later Honi. If we listen carefully to the telling of both stories about a Honi Ha-Me'aggel, one associated with a grandfather and the other with a grandson, we may discern a diachronic series of events concerning an organic personality, that of Honi the rain maker and the martyr. Let us listen first to the Palestinian Talmud's recounting, for that is the story of the grandfather.

> R. Yudan Giria[31] said: This Honi Ha-Me'aggel is the son of the son of Honi Ha-Me'aggel who lived about the time of the destruction of the Temple. He went out with the workers at the mountain. While he was there it started to rain. He entered a cave and while sitting there he fell into a deep sleep and slumbered for seventy years, while the Temple was destroyed and built again. At the end of seventy years he awoke from his sleep. He emerged from the cave and saw a a changed world: Instead of what was once vineyards, now olives were cultivated, instead of what was once olives, now corn was sown. He sought out the neighbors and said to them, "What is the news in the world?" They said to him, "And you don't know what the news in the world is?" He said to them, "No". They said to him, "Who are you?" He said to them, "Honi Ha-Me'aggel". They said to him, "We've heard that when he used to enter the Temple court it would be lit up!" He entered [the Temple court] and it lit up, and he proclaimed, in reference to himself, the verse, "When the Lord brought back those that returned to Zion, We were like unto them that dream" (Psalms 126:1). (PT *Ta'aniot* 3:10 [66d])

Honi sleeps through the terrible catastrophe of destruction and exile, and is equally oblivious to the jubilation of rebuilding. When he does finally wake up from his peaceful sleep, he stretches his limbs and steps out of the cave into the blinding sunlight. He sees that the world has changed its face. Where there were vineyards there are olive trees, where there were olive trees cornfields stretched out instead, indicating not only a change in the type of crops cultivated but a change in the places cultivated as well.[32] Honi is only vaguely confused; he asks the people, "What's new?" They in turn are shocked and incredulous that one could be so ignorant of the auspicious events of recent history. When Honi assents laconically that he is indeed ignorant, they inquire wonderingly as to his identity. When he tells them that he is the famous Honi Ha-Me'aggel, his listeners nostalgically recall legends of a generation that is no more. For Honi, the past and the present are the same, or rather, there is only the present for him and it is unchanged. He enters the Temple and is impressed only by the fact that it does indeed light up, as always. It is as if nothing has happened during those long seventy years.

Honi has lived through one of the most eventful and momentous periods of Jewish history, but he is unmoved. It is as if for him neither destruction nor return has taken place. He is oblivious of the time–history axis.

For Honi the rain maker, as we have seen, deliverance does not take time; it may be fully realized in the immediacy of the now, as it is in an act of martyrdom. The story thus is a caricature of Honi. He expects deliverance to be immediate; he does not learn the lesson of history. When return and rebuilding finally take place, he is blind to the tortuous way of history and sees only the immediacy of divine intervention. For this tradition, which identifies the legendary sleeper with Honi Ha-Me'aggel and the period of slumber as the years of Exile, redemption through history is so real that only unconsciousness could dim the fact. It is very unhistorical to attribute this story to Honi, who lived at the time of Simeon ben Shetah, but what better way to caricature his personality than to have him sleep through the destruction and rebuilding of the Temple! And Honi, convinced of his way, is certain that Scripture itself sanctions his view of deliverance. For him the verse "When the Lord brought back those that returned to Zion, we were like unto them that dream" can only mean here that deliverance does not take place along the axis of time–history.

With this, we are ready to listen to the Babylonian Talmud's version of the same story, remembering the diachronic nature of the two versions. The one we have already heard tells of the grandfather, the following one of the grandson. But both are Honi Ha-Me'aggel!

R. Johanan said: All his days that righteous man [Honi Ha-Me'aggel, as spoken of in the Mishnah in the time of Simeon ben Shetah] was unhappy with this verse, "When the Lord brought back those that returned to Zion, We were like unto them that dream" (Psalms 126:1), saying: "Is there such a person who slumbers in a dream for seventy years!" One day he was going along the way. He saw a certain man who was planting a carob tree. He [Honi] said to him, "How many years until this gives fruit?" He said to him, "Seventy years". He said to him, "Are you sure that you'll live another seventy years?" He said to him, "I found this world full of carob trees: Just as my fathers planted for me, so I, too, plant for my children." He [Honi] sat down and while he was eating he was overcome with sleep and he slumbered. He became enclosed in a grotto, was hidden from the eye, and slumbered for seventy years. When he awoke he saw a certain man who was picking from it [the fruit of the carob]. He said to him, "Are you the one who planted it?" He said to him, "I am his grandson". He said, "That means that I have slept seventy years!" He saw that his donkey had mothered several generations. He went to his home. He said to them, "Is the son of Honi Ha-Me'aggel alive?" They said to him, "His son is no more but his son's son is here." He said to them, "I am Honi Ha-Me'aggel." They did not believe him. He went to the House of Learning. He heard the Rabbis saying, "The words of tradition are as luminous as in the days of Honi Ha-Me'aggel; for when he would enter the House of Learning, any difficulty which the

Rabbis had, he would resolve." He said to them, "I am he!" They did not believe him and did not honor him as much as was his due. He broke down, prayed for mercy and died.[33] (BT *Ta'anit* 23a)

R. Johanan, the famed third century Palestinian amora, tells us, according to the Babylonian Talmud, that the verse, "We were like unto them that dream" caused Honi Ha-Me'aggel profound uneasiness. Is it possible, asked Honi, that one should sleep and dream for seventy years?

Because the Palestinian version of our story "precedes" this one, we understand why the verse made Honi uncomfortable, but this insight of ours will be strengthened with further listening. In the Palestinian version, Honi understands the verse by applying it to his own seventy years' sleep; that is, to his own acceptance of the existence of the second Temple and the deliverance implicit in it as an immediate given rather than as something to be awaited patiently. He dreams through Exile and Return, unconscious of the agonizingly long process of history, knowing only the now of achieved salvation.

But, in the Babylonian version Honi knows only his own isolated personal biography, a biography that is naively incompatible with events of the order of history. He has not "slept" through the destruction of the first Temple—he would certainly not be capable of living through them. He cannot even imagine one suffering patiently through seventy years of exile, certainly not dreaming through them. When he reads the verse just quoted, he imagines, rightly so, the day-to-day suffering of Israel, the eyes of the people dreamily fixed on a future redemption, a redemption that for decades was very far away indeed. They were "like unto them that dream" in the sense, Honi must realize, that they shuffled unhappily through the day-to-day present, their gazes fixed on a future beyond the now. They truly dreamed because the vision of redemption often must have been ever so far away from the present reality.

> Immutable, bring forth thy strength of hand this day, for how can Thou
> ignore?
> Broken, in the pit of Exile, Thy salvation dreaming—a slave of his
> redemption dreaming
> He begs the end yet no reply is heard, he is as blind, he asketh dumb;
> A thousand years he waits, perhaps the foeman's sins You'll see—and yet,
> not yet.
> Lord return, Thine altar to Your People give, and Jacob, whole, returneth.
> (Judah ben Solomon Al-Harizi, *Tahkemoni*, 50)

"Is there such a person who slumbers in a dream for seventy years," asks Honi in wonderment. Is it possible to sustain oneself with a faraway

dream for seventy years? Can one live through Exile without an immediately achievable salvation, with only the dream of redemption through
political change, an arduous Return, a long resettling and rebuilding?
Such a notion made Honi the rain maker extremely uncomfortable, says
R. Johanan, because Honi was not made of that stuff. And so, Honi had
to be taught a lesson. Or, following R. Yudan Giria in the Palestinian
Talmud, the grandson had to learn of the unreality of the grandfather's
way, a way that (thus R. Johanan in the Babylonian Talmud's version)
Honi does not even contemplate because he has never confronted history;
he only goggles at the image painted in the verse.

So one day, while Honi is wandering along the road, he sees a man
planting a carob tree. This causes Honi some wonder, and he stops to talk
to the busy farmer. "How many years does it take this tree to bear fruit?"
he asks, too polite to say outright what is bothering him. "It takes seventy
years," answers the farmer laconically. Honi can no longer contain his
wonder. "Are you so sure that you will live that long?" he asks. The dusty
farmer looks up at the wayfarer for a moment and then explains patiently
to him that we are born into a world laboriously prepared for us by others
and we join that continuous toil for the sake of our children and our
children's children.

> Thus saith the Lord of Hosts, the God of Israel, unto all the cap-
> tivity, whom I have caused to be carried away captive from Jerusalem
> unto Babylon:
> Build ye houses, and dwell in them, and plant gardens, and eat the
> fruit of them; take ye wives for your sons, and give your daughters to
> husbands, that they may bear sons and daughters; and multiply ye there,
> and be not diminished . . .
> For thus saith the Lord of Hosts, the God of Israel: Let not your
> prophets that are in the midst of you, and your diviners, beguile you,
> neither hearken ye to your dreams which ye cause to be dreamed. For
> they prophesy falsely unto you in My name; I have not sent them, saith
> the Lord.
> For thus saith the Lord: After seventy years are accomplished for
> Babylon, I will remember you, and perform My good word toward you,
> in causing you to return to this place. For I know the thoughts that I
> think toward you, saith the Lord, thoughts of peace, and not of evil, to
> give you a future and a hope . . . .
> The captivity is long; build ye houses, and dwell in them; and plant
> gardens, and eat the fruit of them. (Jeremiah 29:4–28)

Honi shrugs his shoulders and sits down in the open field to eat his
modest meal. "To labor over a tree whose fruit will be eaten in another

seventy years!" he mumbles to himself as he carefully chews the dry bread. The field is his bed and he falls asleep easily. He sinks into a deep, deep sleep; he is now being taken on a very different journey. He neither sees nor is seen for seventy years.

Honi awakens to a mildly changed world. He notes this and deduces that he has slept for seventy years. He returns to his home and asks if his son is still alive, all the while trying to remain calm. When he is told that his son is dead and his grandson is head of the house he blurts out: "I am Honi Ha-Me'aggel!" He is mocked and hurries away to the House of Learning. He stands hesitatingly at the entrance and he hears the scholars admiringly comparing present times to the days of the famous Honi Ha-Me'aggel, who could illumine any problem (here the light of knowledge replaces the Palestinian Talmud's "light" in the Temple court). In the House of Learning, he feels at home again, comfortable with the familiar. He strides into the midst of the crowded room and says excitedly, "I am he!" But he does not get the expected reaction. They look at the ancient man as at an eccentric stranger. They treat him with studied respect, but he senses the affectedness of their behavior. He breaks down and can accept only death.

For Honi the rainmaker deliverance is always imminent. His only way to understanding, therefore, lies in his being removed from the present of family and friends and thrown seventy years beyond it. Suddenly, he, too, becomes a dreamer, not of a future but of a past. In this cruel state of dispossession, he discovers that deliverance is no longer imminent; it lies far removed along the axis of time. For Honi, this situation is fatal, because he is incapable of the vision of future. He can only dream of the past, and the past constantly recedes from his grasp. Honi believes in a euphoric present and he cannot cope with the realization that he is now in need of a redemption that can only take time. He is unable to go the patient way of rediscovering love and reputation. He is not made of the stuff that the returners to Zion are.

> When the Lord brought back those that returned to Zion,
> We were like unto them that dream.
> Then was our mouth filled with laughter,
> And our tongue with singing;
> Then said they among the nations:
> "The Lord hath done great things with these."
> The Lord hath done great things with us;
> We are rejoiced.
>
> Turn our captivity, O Lord,
> As the streams in the dry land.

They that sow in tears
Shall reap in joy.
Though he goeth on his way weeping that beareth the measure of seed,
He shall come home with joy, bearing his sheaves. (Psalms 126)

We have in this psalm, whose initial verse opens the Babylonian Talmud's version of the story of Honi and closes that of the Palestinian Talmud, the source of the peculiar content of the former's version. The dreamers of redemption are like "those who sow in tears." They sow their fields at the very end of the long hot summer of the Land of Israel. The ground is parched, the wells and rivulets are dry, the lush yellow and green of spring are long since shriveled. Thirst closes in, hunger is palpable, pestilence threatens, and death lies waiting in the lengthening shadows. They go on their way, throwing this way and that the dry seed, weeping because they are frightened by the long wait till the rains of blessing come and the land comes to life again and bears fruit for man once more. How many of the sowers' children will breathe the sweet damp freshness of the coming spring? But they sow nonetheless, not stopping to think, dreaming of a better future. And it is only those who weep yet sow that reap with joy. Those who weep not are not prepared for the long way; they will not survive the fall and winter. And those that sow not are the ones resigned to death. Finally, the rains and rebirth come like "the streams in the dry land" and man is saved. "Whoever mourns for Jerusalem shall worthily partake in its joy; and who does not mourn for Jerusalem shall not partake in its joy" (BT *Bavli Ta'anit* 30b).[34] Man must know that he needs to be redeemed. But he must also know that redemption takes ever so long. He who is not "like unto them that dream" can never laugh the laughter of redemption, no matter how much he toils, because he is never on the way. And, he who does not mourn the Exile, who does not know the need for redemption, may find himself resigned to death.

The planter of the carob tree in the story of Honi is a dreamer of redemption, lackluster though he appears to Honi and even to us. His dream is realized, albeit after seventy years, though the beneficiaries of his dream must themselves continue to plant for the future. Honi, who neither weeps in the present nor sows for the future, mocks the farmer. When the age dreamed about finally comes, Honi cannot rejoice; on the contrary, he is dispossessed. So, Honi is finally resigned to death.

Thus, the Palestinian and the Babylonian *Talmudim* together are telling one story about one man. It is a story of euphoria in the present, of oblivion to Exile, of poverty of vision, of dispossession from history. It is the story of a person for whom martyrdom is unavoidable. In the Babylonian Talmud's version, Honi is denied the heroism of his death. He dies out of despair in weakness, not courageously in resolution. In truth, rabbinic sources do not record Josephus' story of the martyrdom of Honi Ha-Me'aggel, though Honi was a righteous man. We may correctly read in all this a rabbinic criticism of Honi's one-sided tendency toward martyrdom, a tendency unrelieved by the ability to draw back into the day to dayness of the Law. Martyrdom is *Akedah*, it is *kiddush ha-Shem*, Sanctification of the Name, only if the hand of death is held back with the same devotion with which it plunges. Honi's story, as the Rabbis tell it, is not so much tragic as pathetic.

Honi Ha-Me'aggel, we are told, had a grandson by the name of Abba Hilkiah and he, too, was a rain maker! This gives us a further opportunity to explore a personality as painted and connected by tradition to that of Honi.[35]

> Abba Hilkiah was the son of Honi Ha-Me'aggel's son. Once the world was in need of rain.[36] The Rabbis sent to him two Rabbis [asking him] to beg mercy so that the rain should come. They went to his house but did not find him. They went into the fields and found him as he was hoeing. They greeted him but he did not react warmly. Towards evening [setting out for home] as he took wood, he carried the wood and the hoe on one shoulder, moving his cloak over to the other shoulder. The whole way he did not wear his shoes; when he came upon water he put his shoes on. When he came upon brambles he hitched up his garment. When he arrived at the town his wife came out to meet him, all dressed up. When he arrived home his wife entered first and afterwards he entered and afterwards the Rabbis entered. He sat down and broke bread and did not invite the Rabbis to join him. He divided bread among his children, giving the older one one piece and the younger one two pieces. He said to his wife: "I'm certain that the Rabbis have come because of the rain. Let us go up to the roof and beg for mercy, perhaps the Holy One Blessed is He will be appeased and rain will come. And we will not cause anyone to feel beholden to us." They went up to the roof. He stood in one corner and she in another; the clouds began coming from the direction of his wife's corner. When he came down he said to them: "Why have the Rabbis come?" They said to him: "The Rabbis have sent us to you, sir, that you should beg for rain." He said to them: "Blessed is the Holiness that He did not put you in need of Abba Hilkiah!" They said to him: "We know that the rain came because of you, sir, but please, sir, tell us about the following things which we have found strange. Why is it that when we greeted you, sir, you, sir, did not react warmly?" He said to them: "I was a day-laborer and I meant not to interrupt [my work]." "And why did you, sir, carry wood on one shoulder, moving the cloak over to the other shoulder?" He said to them: "It was a borrowed cloak: I borrowed it for this purpose [to wear] but not for that [to cushion the

wood]." "Why did you, sir, not wear your shoes the whole way and when you came, sir, upon water you put your shoes on?" He said to them: "During the whole way I was able to see [where I stepped], in the water I was not able to see." "Why did you, sir, when you came upon bramble, hitch up your garment?" He said to them: "This [the skin] heals while this [the cloth] does not heal." "Why is it that when you, sir, arrived at the town your wife, sir, came out all dressed up?" He said to them: "In order that I should not gaze upon another woman." "Why did she enter [the house] first and afterwards you, sir, entered behind her and afterwards we entered?" He said to them: "Because I was not acquainted with you." "Why is it that when you, sir, broke bread you did not invite us to join you?" "Because there is not much bread and I meant not to make the Rabbis beholden to me for nothing [as the invitation would have been insincere, formal and hopeful of refusal]." "Why did you, sir, give the older child one piece of bread and the younger one two?" He said to them: "This one stays home while this one sits in school." "And why did the clouds begin coming from the direction of the corner in which your wife, sir, stood?"[37] "Because the woman is usually at home and gives the poor bread which is readily enjoyable. But I give [them] money which is not readily enjoyable. Or perhaps also [because] concerning some delinquents who were in our neighborhood, I begged mercy that they should die while she begged mercy that they should repent."[38] (BT *Ta'anit* 23a–b)[39]

This story underlines two important components of the biography of Abba Hilkiah the rain maker: poverty and an earthy immediacy of attitude. Let us examine each.

Abba Hilkiah is not merely poor, he is hungry. When he divides the few pieces of bread among his children he must carefully count out each child's portion, compassionately weighing hunger and other needs. He walks through the dried brush of the fields without flinching, though the thorns tear at his legs. No matter; he is used to that, and he must get home before dark to feed his family. Some rags to protect his flesh are an unaffordable luxury, and the skin will heal of its own. We picture a lean and burnt man striding over the coarse ground, pondering with furrowed brow how he and his family will meet the demands of living. When the Rabbis come to see him, they are apparently surprised not to find him at home yet. But, Hilkiah lacks even the luxury of a spare moment. We must imagine him completely involved in his struggle to live, never certain how far into the future he may dare to look, if even to the evening of the morrow.

A religious soul, when confronted by such extreme poverty, may be tempted to escape. When the here and now becomes oppressive, the imaginative soul stretches its ample wings and light-headedly floats upward toward the light. When the experience of life becomes suffocating and dark, man may sense that being in the world is an imprisonment of his real self. He begins to "know" that he is foreign to this world, an unwilling guest. Reality is then the hidden, the beyond. Salvation then lies in the renuncation of appearances and even of this-worldliness in order to break the bonds of imprisonment. Then, yearning for the attainable replaces hunger for temporary satisfaction, and man knows a goal the way to which is not ended by death nor impeded by poverty. The way to mystic tempta-tion begins, sometimes, in the confines of an unsatisfied present.

We should not be surprised were we to discover that Abba Hilkiah is a mystical ascetic. But, he is the son of Honi Ha-Me'aggel's son, and that is not his way. There is nothing ascetically otherworldly about Abba Hilkiah's way of life, aside from the deprivations forced upon him by his lack of means. On the contrary, the earthy relationship between him and his wife, the way in which he cares for his clothing and watches where he steps, show a prudence drawn from respect for experience and apprecia-tion for reality. Certainly the inclusion of such details in a story about Abba Hilkiah creates an atmosphere of this-worldliness. Nor is there any sense of hiddenness in the story; appearance and reality are and remain one. At first sight, the hero's behavior seems strange, but in his explana-tions to the rabbis it turns out to be perfectly reasonable, based on a combination of folk wisdom and devotion to ideals that are the common property of the Jewish people, however idiosyncratic and even extreme his manner of devotion may be.

This brings us to another salient characteristic of Abba Hilkiah. Pov-erty has struck home to the heart of his being, but rather than reject being in the world he embraces it. He fights for life, and every moment of time is tapped for its life-giving potential. Hilkiah and his family live from hand to mouth. The father has slipped into that limbo of the present where even the near past cannot assure existence now and the future is too distant to be caressed. His intense engrossment in his labors in the field is a result of a religious soul embracing the fact of living in poverty. He sees his salva-tion in toil, and thus his ethic finds its dimension for expression in toil as well, in unyielding devotion to the momentariness of ploughing and tend-ing the harsh earth.

"'Lord, who shall sojourn in Thy tabernacle? Who shall dwell upon They holy mountain? He that walketh uprightly, and a laborer of righ-teousness, . . .' (Psalms 15:1, 2) 'A laborer of[40] righteousness,' like Abba Hilkiahu" (BT *Makkot* 24a). He has no leave even to greet the rabbis warmly because his labor of the moment is his survival and thus his sphere for ethical heroism. "I meant not to interrupt"; he dare not miss a minute of work. Devotion to toil goes together, in his ethic, with devotion to employer. And Abba Hilkiah is very much aware of the fact that poverty draws man into a breathless immediacy of living, an impatient prayer for sustenance in each new moment; he appreciates the sweetness of each morsel of bread that his self-sacrificing wife hands to the poor at her door and knows that hers is the loving charity (*hesed*). The sustenance the woman gives is "readily enjoyable," immediate and warm; therefore her prayer for rain is answered first. (In the next chapter we shall see the significance of repentance, for which Hilkiah's wife prays on behalf of the delinquents in their neighborhood.) How well Abba Hilkiah knows the power of immediacy! To eat today is the vision of his toil; to be saved now is the essence of his prayers; hence the form of his ethic and his charity.

> When they [the congregation] stand up in prayer [on a fast day called because of sustained drought or other calamities], they send down before the Ark [in order to lead in prayer] an old man who is conversant [with the prayers] and who has children and whose house is empty in order that his heart should be consummate in prayer. (M *Taʾanit* 2:2)

> The Rabbis repeated: When they stand up in prayer, even though there be present an old and wise man, they do not send down before the Ark save one who is conversant. Rabbi Judah says: One who is burdened [with children or the like] and has not [the wherewithal], and who has much toil in the field and his house is empty . . . (BT *Taʾanit* 16a)

By these criteria, Abba Hilkiah is indeed suited to pray for rain, for there is a genuine immediacy to his needs and impatience in his prayers. But, he is not merely one who prays for rain, he is a rain maker! There is an earthiness to his immediacy that marks him. When he comes home he sits down to eat with hardly a word to his guests, though he knows that he has no other hospitality to offer them. And his relationship with his wife has the honest earthiness of those who know their own erotic nature without any sense of shame. For Abba Hilkiah, not only is salvation to begin in the present, but the immediate moment is capable of containing all salvation without thoughts of past or future. He accepts the here and now, indeed embraces it, with an impressive earnestness. We can imagine him eating his bread with the same heartiness that he does everything else. We also could imagine him being tempted to the total embracing of the immediate in an act of martyrdom, as his grandfather did, though there is no hint of that in Abba Hilkiah's story.

Although we can only speculate on the potentially heroic nature of

Abba Hilkiah from the immediacy of his earthy living in poverty, the Palestinian Talmud tells other stories that clearly connect poverty and heroism. Let us examine two of them.

> The Rabbis had a vision, saying: "Should so and so the donkey driver pray, the rain will fall." The Rabbis sent and brought him. They said to him, "What is your work?" He said to them, "I am a donkey driver." They said to him, "And what good have you done?" He said to them, "Once I rented out my donkey to some woman, and she was crying on the way. And I said to her, 'What's the matter with you?' She said to me, 'My husband is imprisoned and I must look around to see what I can do.' And I turned away and I sold my donkey and gave her what it fetched, saying, 'Here you are! Redeem your husband but don't sin.' " They said to him, "You are worthy of praying and being answered."
>
> R. Abbahu [Caesarea, around the beginning of the fourth century] had a vision, saying: "Should Pentakakah [five sins] pray, the rain will come." R. Abbahu sent and brought him. He asked him, "What is your business?" He answered, "Every day I procure for prostitutes, I fix up their bordello, prepare their clothing, cavort and dance before them and I beat the drum for them." He said to him, "And what good have you done?" He said to him, "Once when I was fixing up the bordello some woman came and stood behind a pillar, crying. And I said to her, 'What's the matter with you?' And she said to me, 'My husband is imprisoned and I must look around to see what I can do.' And I turned away and I sold my bed and bedclothes and gave her what it fetched, saying, 'Here you are! Redeem your husband but don't sin.'" He [R. Abbahu] said to him, "You are worthy of praying and being answered." (PT *Ta'aniot* 1:4 [64b])

In the first story, the donkey driver sells his donkey and gives the money he receives for it to the weeping woman. There can be little doubt that, considering the already difficult economic plight of a donkey driver, this act of generosity is heroic and impoverishing. In the second story, Pentakakah sells his bedding in order to help the woman, no doubt indicating that he is already poor and will be reduced to sleeping on the ground. We get an ironic picture of Pentakakah. Not only does he survive by pandering, he is part of the prostitutes' coterie. But when, by chance, he meets the unhappy woman hesitating in the strange (for her) quarter of the city, he forgets himself in his compassion and on the spur of the moment gives her his only permanent belongings. With a smile on his lips, not thinking about where he will sleep from this night on, he brusquely sends her back to her family life. The retreating woman would be very shocked were she to know her benefactor a little better. Pentakakah is a martyrial figure in the sense that his heroically costly action cuts him off from his past and future. Both the donkey driver and Pentakakah are candidates for bringing the rain because they are martyrial and because they remain stranded in the hungry present of destitution. Their heroism lies in the fearlessness with which they jump into the total insecurity that is the lot of the poor. Their prayer will be impatiently demanding.

It is no accident that the rabbis learn about the auspiciousness of the two men through visions. Pentakakah, at least, is not exactly the type to move in rabbinic circles. In the case of Pentakakah, not only do we have a martyrial figure but we may also clearly sense the antinomian aspect of martyrdom. Martyrdom is, as we have seen, a liberation from the Law, and for Pentakakh deliverance lies in one-time heroism, not in the way of the Law. But, when people are shriveling up from thirst, they, even the Rabbis, do not think much about past and future, and they are capable of singling out their martyrial heroes. It is then that the Rabbis can see a Pentakakah in their dreams.

Chapter Five

R. Hanina ben Dosa

By tradition, R. Hanina ben Dosa is a person in whom several of the characteristics we have discussed are configurated. He lived in Arav in the lower Galilee during the first century of the Christian era, and his martyrial tendency is evident from his stance in prayer.

> It was said about R. Hanina ben Dosa that he was standing and praying and a *havarbar* [a poisonous mottled lizard][1] came and bit him, and he did not interrupt his praying. And that same *havarbar* was later found lying dead at the entrance to its burrow. It was said: "Woe is the man bitten by a *havarbar* and woe is the *havarbar* who bit Ben Dosa."[2] (PT *Berakhot* 5:1 [9a])[3]

This story is brought in order to illuminate the following Mishnah:

> One does not stand to pray save from a sense of seriousness. The early *hasidim* would linger for an hour and then pray[4] so that they could concentrate their hearts on the Holiness.[5] Though the king greet him he will not answer him. And though a snake be wound about his ankle he will not interrupt. (M *Berakhot* 5:1)

R. Hanina interpreted this to mean that one's concentration in the *Amidah* prayer must be so intense that one becomes oblivious even to the need for preserving one's life.[6] Simeon ben Azzai demands a similar intensity of devotion in love for God: "['And thou shalt love the Lord thy God with all thy heart, and with all thy soul, and with all thy might.'] (Deuteronomy 6:5). Simeon ben Azzai [beginning of the second century] says: '. . . with all thy soul', love Him to the utter exhaustion ['wringing out'] of your soul.'" (*Sifre* to Deuteronomy, 32 [p. 55]). Another exegete interprets the same verse as referring to actual martyrdom, "'and with all thy soul', even though He take your soul,[8] and so Scripture says, 'Nay, but for Thy sake are we killed all the day; We are accounted as sheep for the slaughter' (Psalms 44:23)" (ibid.).[9] Ben Azzai calls upon man to draw the love of God up through his very being with such intensity as to "wring out" the livingness of his soul.[10] The notion that prayer deserves martyrial devotion also is attributed to a "certain *Hasid*":

> The Rabbis repeated: It happened that a certain *Hasid* was praying on the road. An overlord came along and greeted him, and he did not acknowledge the greeting. He [the overlord] waited for him to finish his prayer. When he had finished his prayer he [the overlord] said to him, "Fool! And is it not written in your Law, 'Only take heed to thyself, and keep thy soul diligently' (Deuteronomy 4:9), and [is it not] written, 'Take ye therefore good heed unto yourselves' (ibid., 15)? When I greeted you why did you not acknowledge my greeting? If I had cut your head off with a sword who would have brought me to task for your spilt blood?" (BT *Berakhot* 32b)

The Palestinian Talmud records R. Hanina as saying that his devotion to prayer made him insensitive to the bite of the poisonous reptile: "His students said to him [R. Hanina ben Dosa], 'Rabbi, did you not feel [the bite of the *havarbar*]!' He said to them, 'I swear that due to my devotion in praying I did not feel it'[11]" (PT *Berakhot* 5:1 [9a]). But the Babylonian Talmud has a tradition in which R. Hanina's behavior sounds theatrically deliberate:

> The Rabbis repeated: It happened that there was an *'arod* [a poisonous lizard] in a certain place and it would harm people. They came and told R. Hanina ben Dosa. He said to them, "Show me its burrow." They showed him its burrow. He put his heel on the opening, it came out and bit him, and that same *'arod* died. He took it on his shoulder and brought it to the House of Learning. He said to them, "See, my sons, it is not the *'arod* that kills, rather it is sin that kills." It was then that it was said: "Woe is the man who was accosted by an *'arod*, and woe is the *'arod* that was accosted by R. Hanina ben Dosa." (BT *Berakhot* 33a)

We may conclude that for tradition R. Hanina's devotion in prayer was intense to the point of "wringing out" life itself; that the story of his encounter with the poisonous lizard is a description of a prayer stance; that his "insensitivity" to the lizard results from a conscious devotion even unto death, so that his behavior was a fearless defiance of danger; in short,

that R. Hanina ben Dosa's behavior was martyrial.[12] And the connection
between prayer and martyrdom points again to an impulse toward martyrdom welling up, like prayer, from the depths of the religious soul.

Tradition stresses the poverty of R. Hanina ben Dosa:

> His wife said to him [R. Hanina ben Dosa], "Till when will we continue
> to suffer so much?" He said to her, "What should we do?" She said to
> him, "Beg for mercy that you should be given something." He begged
> for mercy. Something like a hand came out and he was given a leg of a
> golden table. His wife heard in a dream: "In the future the righteous will
> eat on a golden table having three legs while you will eat on a table
> having two legs." She said to him, "Does it please you that everybody
> will be eating on a complete table and we on an incomplete table?" He
> said to her, "And what should we do?" She said to him, "Beg for mercy
> that it should be taken from you." He begged for mercy and it was taken.
> It was repeated: The latter miracle was greater than the former. For we
> are taught that things are given [miraculously] but are not taken [thus].[13]
> (BT *Ta'anit* 25a)

Thus R. Hanina's poverty is seen as finally willed by him. "Rav Judah said
in the name of Rav: Each and every day an Echo goes forth saying, 'The
entire world is nourished for the sake of Hanina my son, and Hanina my
son is satisfied with a kab of carobs from one Friday to the next'" (Ibid.
24b). In the eyes of the Master of the World, all of existence is sutained
because R. Hanina ben Dosa is part of it. But R. Hanina himself does not
see beyond the need for a basketful of carobs in order to get through the
week. There is pain enough for him in that daily personal struggle.

R. Hanina also is a rain maker and even a rain stopper. Here again we
sense the difference between the world seen through the intimacy of a
man's self and the world as a cosmos.

> R. Hanina ben Dosa was walking along the way. The rain came. He said
> before Him, "Master of the World, the whole world is pleased and
> Hanina is suffering." The rain stopped. When he arrived home he said
> before Him, "Master of the World, the whole world is suffering and
> Hanina is pleased." The rain came. (Ibid.)

R. Hanina walks alone along the road on a dark wintry day. The rain starts
to pour heavily and the damp penetrates his bones. He thinks about those
who can afford to enjoy the winter months, knowing that the stormy
weather will fertilize their fields and yield the richness of spring. He
wonders why must it be the lot of some to shiver in the cold without the
hope of a happier summer. Is it fair that many are happy while the lonely

poor man ineffectually gathers his thin coat around his shoulders, the splattering rain making him inseparable from the muddy landscape? Master of the Universe, the whole world is at ease while Hanina suffers! Reality is too much to bear, and the rain ceases. He hurries home in the ensuing quiet. When he enters the coziness of his humble home he smiles. He is happy with his lot. How could he have prayed for the rain to stop? Is it right that Hanina should be happy while others are upset that the rain has stopped? R. Hanina, in the warmth of his hearth, has already forgotten the hardships of the long day out in the winter wind, just as in the storm he did not see beyond the suffering of the lonely poor. The harsh reality outside may resume its course, the rain begins to splash against the windows as the night gathers.

R. Hanina is not a rain maker in the sense that Honi Ha-Me'aggel was. Honi prayed for rain because the land of Israel had withered and its people thirsted. But, as Honi lacked the historical dimension, so R. Hanina does not sense the public dimension with the same intensity that he does the private. Or, put differently, the pain of the lonely self in the present preoccupies him, though not in the selfish sense, and this marks his miracle-working biography. It is not surprising that the sages of the Law were not altogether happy about his ability to see only the immediacy of the self.

> Rav Joseph said: What did the high priest's prayer help where R. Hanina ben Dosa was concerned. For we repeat: And he [the high priest] prays a short prayer [during an interlude in the Temple ritual on the Day of Atonement] in the outer chamber [of the Temple] (M *Yoma* 5:1). What did he pray? Ravin bar Rav Ada and Rava bar Rav Ada both said in the name of Rav Judah: May it be desirable before You Lord our God that this year should be rainy and warm . . . and with abundant dew; and may the prayer of the wayfarers [to stay the rain] be unacceptable before You. (Ibid.)

R. Hanina ben Dosa's preoccupation is with the personal, and therefore, he was famous mainly for healing and the like. The story of his rain making shows that he was capable of seeing even the patently public in the most personal of ways.

> It happened that R. Hanina ben Dosa went to learn Torah with R. Johanan ben Zakkai, and the son of R. Johanan ben Zakkai fell sick. He said to him, "Hanina my son, beg for him mercy and he will live." He put his head between his knees and begged for mercy for him and he lived. R. Johanan ben Zakkai said, "If Ben Zakkai would have pushed his head between his knees[14] for an entire day no attention would have been paid

to him." His wife said to him, "But is Hanina greater than you?" He said to her, "No, but he is like a servant before the king while I am like a minister before the king." (BT *Berakhot* 34b)

R. Hanina was not a sage and it was difficult for the wife of so illustrious a leader as R. Johanan ben Zakkai to appreciate the greatness of the compassionate pauper. But, when R. Johanan looked at his fevered son, he turned to the empathy of the miracle worker. R. Hanina felt the pain of the sufferer as if it were his own and begged, crumpled up on the floor, for mercy. And the great sage of the Law sensed his own impotence.

> He [R. Hanina ben Dosa] had a certain neighbor who was building a home but the beams did not reach. She came before him saying, "I've built my home but my beams don't reach!" He said to her, "What is your name?" She said to him, "Ikhu." He said, "*Ikhu* [meaning: would that] your beams will reach." (BT *Ta'anit* 25a)

He can pray for the woman only when he knows something personal about her, when she ceases to be anonymous. And then, charmed by her name, he turns it into a sigh for help.

R. Hanina ben Dosa was not a sage; *halakhot* are not quoted in his name. He is remembered for intimating that the significance of fearing sin and the importance of behavior take precedence over that of learning.

> R. Hanina ben Dosa says: He whose fear of sin precedes his learning, his learning will endure. And he whose learning precedes his fear of sin, his learning will not endure. He was wont to say: He whose deeds are more than his learning, his learning will endure. And he whose learning is more than his deeds, his learning will not endure. (M *Avot* 3:9)

He is careful not to denigrate learning; but learning is overshadowed by the possibility that, though one has it now, it may not endure. However, fear of sin and good deeds, the dual aspects of a piety that R. Hanina intimates is separable from learning, are not threatened by ephemerality. Their essence is to be wholly present and hence authentic. In R. Hanina's view the heart and hands are the reality before God, because they are the daily, brittle, human struggle, while learning is an outstretching—if the arm weaken, should man be lost?

The religiosity of R. Hanina ben Dosa is epitomized in the following enigmatic traditions.

> The Rabbis repeated: It happened that the daughter of Nehunya the ditch-digger (M *Shekalim* 5:1) fell into a big pit. They came and

informed R. Hanina ben Dosa. At the first hour he said to them, "[She] is well". At the second [hour] he said to them, "[She] is well." At the third [hour] he said to them, "She has come up." He said to her, "My daughter, who brought you up?" She said to him,[15] "A ram came by me and an old man was leading him." They said to him [R. Hanina ben Dosa], "Are you a prophet?" He said to them, "I am no prophet, neither am I a prophet's son,[16] but I said to myself, '[Is it possible that] the offspring of that righteous man should come to harm in the very thing for which he shows so much concern?'" R. Aha[17] said: Nevertheless his son[18] died of thirst, as Scripture says: "Our God cometh, and doth not keep silence; A fire devoureth before Him, And round about Him it stormeth mightily" (Psalms 50:3): This teaches that the Holy One Blessed is He is exacting with those around Him even to the breadth of a hair.[19] R. Nehunya[20] said: [Rather] from this verse: "A God dreaded in the great council of the holy ones, And feared of all them that are round about Him (Ibid. 89:8)." R. Hanina said: Whoever says that the Holy One Blessed is He easily overlooks [man's actions], let his life be thus overlooked,[21] as Scripture says: "The Rock, His work is perfect; For all His ways are justice; A God of faithfulness and without iniquity, Just and right is He" (Deuteronomy 32:4). (BT *Bava Kama* 50a)[22]

In order to know what it is that tradition hears in this story, we shall have to reconstruct the image that, philologically speaking, is beyond this text. We will accomplish this by the analysis of several associated texts, which will enrich our listening and make it attuned to tradition.

"Nehunya the ditch-digger" [enumerated in M *Shekalim* 5:1, as one of the Temple functionaries, is so called] because he was digging ditches and caves [in order to supply pilgrims with water]. . . . R. Aha[23] said: And his son died of thirst. R. Hanina said: One who says that the Merciful One easily overlooks [man's actions], let his bowels be thus overlooked: But rather He is long suffering and collects His own. R. Aha said: It is written in Scripture: "Our God cometh, and doth not keep silence; A fire devoureth before Him, And round about Him it stormeth mightily" (Psalms 50:3): He is exacting with them [who are "about Him"] even to the breadth of a hair.[19] R. Yose[24] said: Not for this reason but rather because of what is written in Scripture: "A God dreaded in the great council of the holy ones, And feared of all them that are round about Him" (ibid. 89:8): His fear is greater upon those near Him than upon those who are far away. R. Haggai [said] in the name of R. Samuel bar Nahman: It happened that there was a certain *Hasid* who used to dig wells, ditches and caves for [the benefit of thirsty] passersby. Once, his daughter was on her way to be married when the river she was crossing swept her away. And everybody came in to his home, trying to console him, but he would not be consoled. R. Phinehas ben Jair [the second half of the second century, around Lydda] came in to his home; he tried to console him, but he would not be consoled. He said to them, "This is your *Hasid!*" They said to him, "Rabbi, this is what he was wont to do . . . and this is what happened. . . ." He said, "Is it possible that he glorified his Maker through water and He should break him through water?" Immediately a murmuring broke out in the town: "The daughter of that man has come!" Some say that she got caught up in a branch [and was thus saved] and some say that an angel in the image of R. Phinehas ben Jair came down and saved her. (PT *Shekalim* 5:2 [48d])[25]

The Babylonian version is not merely a combination of two stories which appear separately in the Palestinian Talmud. Rather, the two *Talmudim* together inform us of a story that, as I have said, in order to hear we must know the rich imagery with which tradition is suffused.

The "*Hasid*," the righteous man, in the Palestinian version laboriously digs wells for thirsty wayfarers. Either he does this without recompense or very devotedly, and in this lies his righteousness. Now his daughter, on her way to her wedding, is swept into a torrential river. Her father refuses to be consoled. When R. Phinehas ben Jair sees the man's behavior, he scoffs at the man's reputation for being righteous. The man's way is not the way of the rabbis!

> When it rains and upon hearing good tidings one says: "Blessed is He Who is good and beneficent." And upon hearing bad tidings one says: "Blessed is the Judge of truth."
> Man must bless [God] in the event of bad just as he blesses [Him] in the event of good. (M *Berakhot* 9:2, 5)

But, when R. Phinehas hears the man's personal tragedy, he is moved. He joins him in his demand to heaven. The divine order is to be complete in the here and now!

Imagine the people gathering sadly in the house of the man who has lost his daughter, in the house where the happy preparations for marriage have been replaced by a dumbfounded weeping. Each one walks hesitantly to the father and speaks with him briefly. "She was a wonderful young lady; Your loss is our loss; God Himself shall console you; we all cast our eyes to a happier future, in this world and in the next. Even the mourning for Zion and Jerusalem shall come to an end." The father is unmoved and glances impatiently around the room. "God *shall* console? And what about now?" murmurs the father to himself. When R. Phinehas ben Jair enters the room, he, too, offers perfunctory condolences. But when the story of this man, whose hands are grimy with thankless toil for others, penetrates the Rabbi's consciousness, he is moved. The confrontation with this

pathetic man, no longer anonymous but uniquely sad, causes R. Phinehas's real feelings to well angrily up inside him. "This is the divine way?"
he asks, he demands. "Do You smite him whose labor was the worry lest
others thirst for water, with water itself? Is the world of here and now that
insensitive to the struggles of man?" The tension in the room is far too
much to bear, and reality itself gives way. The whispers go from the
oppressively stuffy room out into the meandering streets—the girl lives!

It is no accident that it is R. Phinehas ben Jair who joins the father's
cry to heaven, forgetting his own initial displeasure with the mourner's
attitude.

> He [R. Judah ha-Nasi, "Rabbi"] said to him [R. Phinehas ben Jair],
> "Would you like to dine with me?" He said to him, "Yes". Rabbi's face lit
> up. . . . When he [R. Phinehas] arrived, it happened that he came in by
> the entrance where some white mules were standing. He said, "The angel
> of death [referring to the white mules because of their supposed antago-
> nism][26] is in this man's house and shall I dine with him?" Rabbi over-
> heard, came out towards him and said to him, "I'll sell them." He said to
> him, "Thou shalt not . . . put a stumbling block before the blind [Levi-
> ticus 19:14; the buyer would be blind to the seriousness of his step]."
> "I'll abandon them." "You're spreading the harm." "I'll hamstring them."
> "That is [causing] pain to living creatures." "I'll kill them." "There is [the
> prohibition of] 'Thou shalt not destroy (Deuteronomy 20:19).'" He
> pressed him greatly: A mountain rose up between them . . . (BT *Hullin*
> 7b)

In R. Phinehas's view even the great R. Judah ha-Nasi has his road to
deliverance blocked—or, rather, the way of the Law is not always the way
to deliverance. For the ditch digger who has lost his daughter, the way of
the Law also is closed; it is too long. And R. Phinehas ben Jair joins him in
the vision of a different way, a way of immediacy. It should be noted that
there are significant parallels between R. Phinehas ben Jair (second century C.E.) and R. Hanina ben Dosa (first century C.E.) besides their connection through the story of this tragic digger of ditches.

So the Palestinian story of the *hasid* is about the demand for immediate deliverance despite promises of consolation and redemption. The
attempt at a rationalistic "explanation" in the Palestinian Talmud—"Some
say that she got caught up in a branch"—merely highlights this basic
tendency, as its incongruousness with the rest of the story strengthens our
initial awareness that the attitude of the father, and of R. Phinehas ben Jair
as well, is not congruous with mainstream rabbinic thinking. Let us turn
now to an examination of what we are told about Nehunya "the ditch
digger" in the Palestinian Talmud.

R. Aha tells us that Nehunya's son "died of thirst". This immediately raises our curiosity as to why tradition specifically remembers this point. For this, we are offered two different explanations.[27] "R. Aha said: It is written in Scripture: 'Our God cometh, and doth not keep silence; A fire devoureth before Him and round about Him it stormeth mightily': He is exacting with them [who are 'about Him'] even to the breadth of a hair." If we read this verse in its entire context we get a very good sense of R. Aha's point.

A Psalm of Asaph

God, God, the Lord, hath spoken, and called the earth
From the rising of the sun unto the going down thereof
Out of Zion, the perfection of beauty,
God hath shined forth.
Our God cometh, and doth not keep silence;
A fire devoureth before Him,
And round about Him it stormeth mightily
He calleth to the heavens above,
And to the earth, that He may judge His people:
5 "Gather My saints together unto Me;
Those that have made a covenant with Me by sacrifice."
And the heavens declare His righteousness;
For God, He is judge.   Selah
"Hear, O My people and I will speak;
O Israel, and I will testify against thee:
God, thy God, am I.
I will not reprove thee for thy sacrifices;
And thy burnt-offerings are continually before Me.
I will take no bullock out of thy house,
Nor he-goats out of thy folds.
10 For every beast of the forest is Mine,
And the cattle upon a thousand hills.
I know all the fowls of the mountains;
And the wild beasts of the field are Mine.
If I were hungry, I would not tell thee;
For the world is Mine, and the fullness thereof.
Do I eat the flesh of bulls,
Or drink the blood of goats?
Offer unto God the sacrifice of thanksgiving;
And pay thy vows unto the Most High;
15 And call upon Me in the day of trouble;
I will deliver thee, and thou shalt honor me."

But unto the wicked God saith:
"What hast thou to do to declare My statutes,

And that thou hast taken My covenant in thy mouth?
Seeing thou hatest instruction,
And castest My words behind thee.
When thou sawest a thief, thou hadst company with him
And with adulterers was thy portion.
Thou hast let loose thy mouth for evil,
And thy tongue frameth deceit.
20 Thou sittest and speakest against thy brother;
Thou slanderest thine own mother's son.
These things hast thou done, and should I have kept silence?
Thou hadst thought that I was altogether such a one as thyself;
But I will reprove thee, and set the cause before thine eyes.

Now consider this, ye that forget God,
Lest I tear in pieces, and there be none to deliver.
Whoso offereth the sacrifice of thanksgiving honoreth Me;
And to him that ordereth his way aright
Will I show the salvation of God." (Psalms 50)

God, the Lord of all the earth, appears here in awesome aspect. The "perfection of beauty" out of which he "shines" is an unearthly beauty, almost cold. His presence here is preceded by a devouring fire and it surrounds him stormily so that no man dare draw near. He appears here as the Supreme Judge. His decision is clear-cut. He addresses the righteous and the wicked separately. To his "saints" he is mangnanimous and understanding. He "that ordereth his way aright" may dare bring a sacrifice of thanksgiving. Not in order to give the Almighty anything—he does not need man's sacrifices, there is nothing that man can actually give to God. All that man can do is to know how much he gets from the divine bountifulness and to be thankful for it. In being thankful, man makes himself a part of creation, open and receptive to all the good the merciful Creator has abundantly scattered. Man also thus recognizes the awesomeness of being and so of God. God is the infinite source of good, and man is great in his ability to enjoy that good as well as small in his dependence on God. In finding his place in the cosmos, man forms a covenant with God, a covenant of being in the goodness of the world, with a sense of God's awesome greatness and his own concomitant smallness. With this self-knowledge, man must realize that the way to "salvation" is through harmony with the creation, a harmony actualized in the acting-out of the divine Law, which is the cosmic law. A thanksgiving sacrifice by the righteous thus is pleasing because it means an admission of the truth and an understanding of its implication, the auspiciousness of the Law. The evil ones, who do not follow the divine Law, are dispossessed from creation itself, from being; their lot is chaos, a "tearing in pieces," destruction.

The idea expressed by R. Hanina (*not* the son of Dosa) is in the same vein. To say that God is indifferent to the transgression of the Law by man is tantamount to saying that he is indifferent to the breakdown of the laws of nature. Let anyone who entertains the notion of the laxness of the Creator suffer in his bowels the laxness of nature.

R. Aha and R. Hanina explain the death of the righteous Nehunya's son by the exactness of divine justice. God is long-suffering, says R. Hanina, but finally there you have it: divine retribution. "God sees the truth but waits" and finally exacts what is right. R. Aha adds that the righteous, even more than others, are subject to divine justice. Precisely because they are covenantally a part of the cosmos in self-knowledge, in knowledge of the world and in living, as we have seen, they are the most intimate partners to the working-out of divine order.

R. Yose objects to this explanation. "R. Yose said: Not for this reason but rather because of what is written in Scripture: 'A God dreaded in the great council of the holy ones, And feared of all them that are round about Him': His fear is greater upon those near Him than upon those who are far away."

Here, too, the sage's idea becomes clear if we read the Psalm he refers us to.

Maskil of Ethan the Ezrahite

I will sing of the mercies of the Lord for ever;
To all generations will I make known Thy faithfulness with my mouth.
For I have said: "For ever is mercy built;
In the very heavens Thou dost establish Thy faithfulness.
I have made a covenant with My chosen,
I have sworn unto David my servant:
5   For ever will I establish thy seed,
And build up thy throne to all generations.   Selah

So shall the heavens praise Thy wonders, O Lord,
Thy faithfulness also in the assembly of the holy ones.
For who in the skies can be compared unto the Lord,
Who among the sons of might can be likened unto the Lord,
A God dreaded in the great council of the holy ones,
And feared of all them that are round about Him?
O Lord God of hosts,
Who is a mighty one, like unto Thee, O Lord?
And Thy faithfulness is round about Thee.

10   Thou rulest the proud swelling of the seas
     When the waves thereof arise, Thou stillest them.
     Thou didst crush Rahab, as one that is slain;
     Thou didst scatter Thine enemies with the arm of Thy strength.
     Thine are the heavens, Thine also the earth;
     The world and the fulness thereof, Thou hast founded them.
     The north and the south, Thou hast created them;
     Tabor and Hermon rejoice in Thy name.
     Thine is an arm with might;
     Strong is Thy hand, and exalted is Thy right hand.
15   Righteousness and justice are the foundation of Thy throne;
     Mercy and truth go before Thee.
     Happy is the people that know the joyful shout;
     They walk, O Lord, in the light of Thy countenance.
     In Thy name do they rejoice all the day;
     And through Thy righteousness are they exalted.
     For Thou art the glory of their strength;
     And in Thy favor our horn is exalted.
     For of the Lord is our shield;
     And of the Holy one of Israel is our king.

20   Then Thou spokest in vision to Thy godly ones,
     And saidst: 'I have laid help upon one that is a hero[28]
     I have exalted one chosen out of the people.
     I have found David My servant;
     With My holy oil have I anointed him;
     With whom My hand shall be established;
     Mine arm also shall strengthen him.
     The enemy shall not exact from him;
     Nor the son of wickedness afflict him.
     And I will beat to pieces his adversaries before him,
     And smite them that hate him.
25   But My faithfulness and My mercy shall be with him;
     and through My name shall his horn be exalted.
     I will set his hand also on the sea,
     And his right hand on the rivers.
     He shall call unto Me: Thou art my Father,
     My God, and the rock of my salvation.
     I also will appoint him first-born,
     The highest of the kings of the earth.
     For ever will I keep for him My mercy,
     And my covenant shall stand fast with him.
30   His seed also will I make to endure for ever,
     And his throne as the days of heaven.
     If his children forsake My law,
     And walk not in Mine ordinances;

If they profane My statutes,
and keep not My commandments;
Then will I visit their transgression with the rod,
And their iniquity with strokes.
But My mercy will I not break off from him,
Nor will I be false to My faithfulness.

35 My covenant will I not profane,
Nor alter that which is gone out of My lips.
Once have I sworn by My holiness:
Surely I will not be false unto David;
His seed shall endure for ever,
And his throne as the sun before Me.
It shall be established for ever as the moon;
And be steadfast as the witness in the sky."   Selah
But Thou hast cast off and rejected,
Thou hast been wroth with Thine anointed . . .

How long, O Lord, wilt Thou hide Thyself for ever?
How long shall Thy wrath burn like fire?
O remember how short my time is;
For what vanity hast Thou created all the children of men!
What man is he that liveth and shall not see death,
That shall deliver his soul from the power of the grave?   Selah
50 Where are Thy former mercies, O Lord,
Which Thou didst swear unto David in Thy faithfulness?
Remember, Lord, the taunt of Thy servants;
How do I bear in my bosom [the taunt of] so many peoples;
Wherewith Thine enemies have taunted, O Lord,
Wherewith they have taunted the footsteps of Thine anointed.

Blessed be the Lord for evermore.
Amen, and Amen. (Psalms 89:1–39, 47–53)

I have quoted verses from Psalms at length because the homilies we are discussing can be seen as developing naturally out of these verses, which shows how deeply rooted, historically speaking, is the consciousness underlying these homilies.

The central theme of Psalm 89 is a prayer for the deliverance of the Davidic dynasty, shortcomings and sins notwithstanding. The notion of the immutability, or the promised immutability, of that hegemony has here a naive lack of historicity. Put differently, it is difficult to see the biblical God of history as maintaining the chosenness of each and every Davidic king despite his historical uniqueness. Promise of a millenium in which the deservedly anointed scion rules, yes; that is a historic notion because it is a prophetic vision of a development, albeit a guided development, along the historical axis. But here we are not speaking of a "Messiah." Rather the poet is asking that any Davidic king of the present moment benefit from the glory that befits a true David. In order for that to make sense, we have to see the "covenant" made with David as looming in the present, and history as fading into the background. This is not a notion of "timelessness." We do not sense that the poet is speaking *beyond* time, referring to an idea or a symbol. On the contrary, he has in mind specific historical calamities that are befalling the king or kings and, no doubt, specific sins that tarnish the image of real men. Rather, the Davidic kings are viewed as having an amaranthine quality. It is as if one could overlook the historically real decadence of the dynasty and bathe in the sun of Davidic rule, as if nothing has changed since the days of the legendary David.

It is not surprising that early in the psalm a particular aspect of God is brought out, that of Creator. But the picture of creation has little in common with that of Genesis. Here the poet deliberately chooses language with mythical memories, distant as they are. It is reminiscent of the book of Job:

The shades tremble
Beneath the waters and the inhabitants thereof.
The nether-world is naked before Him,
And Destruction hath no covering.
He stretcheth out the north over empty space,
And hangeth the earth over nothing.
He bindeth up the waters in His thick clouds;
And the cloud is not rent under them.
He closeth in the face of His throne,
And spreadeth His cloud upon it.
He hath described a boundary upon the face of the waters,
Unto the confines of light and darkness.
The pillars of heaven tremble
And are astonished at His rebuke.
He stirreth up the sea with His power,
And by His understanding He smiteth through Rahab.
By His breath the heavens are serene;
His hand hath pierced the slant serpent.
Lo, these are but the outskirts of His ways;
And how small a whisper is heard of Him!
But the thunder of His mighty deeds who can understand? (Job 26:5–14)

Despite the "demythologization" of the overpowering of the forces of chaos, both this passage and Psalm 89 convey a strong sense of the immediacy of the creative power of God. True, the "smiting of Rahab" is firmly established and one need never fear the reassertion of the primeval chaos over the created order. But, God is still *now* the God of such staggering power that the very "pillars of heaven tremble . . . at His rebuke."

This is not merely the creation of an imperfect world that is just a beginning. The victory over chaos is total because God is almighty. As far as the suppression of chaos is concerned, we are speaking of completeness, of perfection. The just quoted speech by Job is an answer to the following speech by Bildad the Shuhite:

> How then can man be just with God?
> Or how can he be clean that is born of a woman?
> Behold, even the moon hath no brightness,
> And the stars are not pure in His sight;
> How much less man, that is a worm!
> And the son of man, that is a Maggot! (Ibid. 25:4–6)

If the act of creation is a perfect stilling of chaos, then surely the creation, the world, and man must partake of a nobler quality than the Shuhite admits.

The psalmist deliberately conjures up the image of God the crusher of Rahab because this is the aspect of God that the psalmist wishes to invoke in connection with the choosing of David. For the God of history, election and covenant take a long time, the time of history, to be worked out. But God as creator, the vanquisher of chaos, has the almighty power to achieve completeness in the present, without treading the weary way of time. (How like God is the martyr!) It is God as creator who can infuse the choosing of David with such numinosity that even the reality of time and history can be ignored. If we can escape history, then nostalgia can hide a great deal of evil and make us at peace with the world now.

The word *faithfulness* appears seven times in our psalm and other derivatives of its root, אמן, four times. The Hebrew word for faithfulness, אמונה, means devoted constancy, undying loyalty and truthful and righteous perseverance. Parallel to, or together with, faithfulness comes, in this psalm, the word חסד, translated as "mercy." In context, it should be rendered rather as "grace." It is the divine bountifulness promised to David and his dynasty as an irrevocable gift, or so the psalmist wants to see it. The "faithfulness of divine grace" means that indeed the grace conferred on the house of David will be continuous and perpetual—this is the psalmist's entreaty.

> Where are Thy former mercies [grace], O Lord,
> Which Thou didst swear unto David in Thy faithfulness? (Ibid. 50)

The psalmist would not be satisfied with a vision of future redemption for the house of David. He does not even allude to that. He wants that the deliverance of grace should be uninterrupted, or more correctly, that it should be eminently evident in the constant present. Not only does he deny the efficacy of history, he wishes to escape the flux of time as well. Faithfulness and time caress at the expense of one another. In time as change, the present is a fluctuating montage; if that is "real" then the faithful is imaginary, and if the faithful is "real" then the flux is not. One escapes that antinomy either by transcending time into History (can that be called *faithfulness*?) or by concentrating passionately on the present. The poet has chosen the latter—for only that is true faithfulness—and will not allow any lapse of the divine grace in the present. His way is an exodus from the flux of time, from the changing character and behavior of the Davidic kings. He wants to embrace the nowness of time and ignore its faithlessness. In the faithfulness of the divine, there can be no lapse of grace in the dimension of the now, prays the desperate psalmist.

But the dream of escape from time as change is barred, so it seems. In the way of the Law, each nuance of change, each rattling of time, is fraught with meaning. The arithmetic of sin piles up more surely than the creakings of any clock. The transgression against God's Laws makes the passage of vigor sadder. The knowledge of the Law makes self-knowledge necessary and painful. Could one who knows how long and arduous is the way of the Law expect the constancy of divine grace? The answer, simply, is no; that is why the psalmist stresses the faithfulness of grace at the expense of Law:

> If his children [David's] forsake My law,
> And walk not in Mine ordinances;
> If they profane My statutes,
> and keep not My commandments;
> Then will I visit their transgression with the rod,
> And their iniquity with strokes.
> But My mercy [grace] will I not break off from him,
> Nor will I be false to My faithfulness. (Ibid. 31–34)

Their sins are to be punished. The psalmist says so, in one verse out of fifty-three. Perhaps their punishment is like a beating administered by a father to his children. But such punishment clearly is not to be a lapse in the Divine grace. The awesomeness of the Law is to fade back before God's faithfulness. The Law is not to be allowed to include the present in working out a meandering way. God's faithfulness is not to relinquish the present to the axis of flux, not even to an ordered flux.

For the poet, such faithfulness, rather than the Law, is the dimension in which a relationship of happiness between God and Israel is to take place. "Righteousness and justice are the foundation of Thy throne;" but, "Mercy [grace] and truth go before Thee" (15). Contrast that to "A fire devoureth before Him, And round about Him it stormeth mightily" in the psalm quoted previously (50:30). A God before whom is fear is unapproachable. A God before whom is grace is a God with whom

> Happy is the people that know the joyful shout;
> They walk, O Lord, in the light of Thy countenance.
> In Thy name do they rejoice all the day;
> And through Thy righteousness are they exalted. (Ibid. 16–17)

But the poet's real intention is more personal. He is focusing on the divine relationship with an individual. It is true that that individual is the king of Israel (or of Judah). Nevertheless, the poet speaks of his relationship with God in personal terms. God "finds" His servant David, and he anoints *this* person to be king. The faithfulness of divine grace is now with an individual not just a People. Here is an intimate relationship, one between a father and a son. In the middle verse of the psalm, or the first of the two middle ones, if we do not count the title verse of the psalm, we read:

> He shall call unto Me: Thou art my Father,
> My God, and the rock of my salvation. (Ibid. 27)

The prophet Jeremiah, too, calls God father in this sense: "Didst thou [Israel] not just now cry unto Me 'My father, Thou art the friend of my youth'" (Jeremiah 3:4). And in the psalm, the following verse, God reciprocates:

> I also will appoint him first-born,
> The highest of the kings of the earth. (Ibid. 28)

Indeed the poet almost ends the psalm with this personal note.

> Remember, Lord, the taunt of Thy servants;
> How I do bear in my bosom [the taunt of] so many peoples;
> Wherewith Thine enemies have taunted, O Lord,
> Wherewith they have taunted the footsteps of Thine anointed. (Ibid. 51–52)

The poet dwells, finally, on the inner suffering of the servant who is to have grace. Through this personalism, in the final verse, he arrives at a statement of his own faithfulness to God:

Blessed be the Lord for evermore.
Amen, and Amen. (Ibid. 53)

R. Yose takes the melody of this psalm and connects it, through verse 8 ("A God dreaded in the great council of the holy ones, And feared of all them that are round about Him"), with the context of righteousness and death. By doing so he first of all replaces the Davidic scion with the *zaddik*, the righteous man, or at least equates the two in some sense. Ironically, the psalmist has unwittingly prepared the way for this use of his words by removing the personality of David from the historic context. Nevertheless, the homilist's move tends to complicate the relationship among grace, sin, and deliverance and to render it more ominous in the homily, as we shall see. That this is really what the homilist is doing will become manifest when we begin to understand what connection R. Yose sees between this text and the occasion of death in the circle of the *zaddik*. As for R. Hanina and R. Aha, discussed earlier, their homiletical juxtaposition is clear. The son of Nehunya the ditch digger dies because of Divine retribution for sin, an extreme retribution because of the father's unusual righteousness. We have not the slightest idea what that sin was, but the homiletical structure is transparent. However, R. Yose stresses that he is giving a *different* "explanation" and from the psalm he refers to we see that he definitely is not creating a context of divine retribution in the earlier sense. Psalm 89 contains no hint of a connection between sin and death other than words such as *dreaded* and *feared* in verse 8, which R. Yose quotes directly. What, then, is the connection between the notion of God as the God of creation, the removal from history and time as change, grace and deliverance, a dreadedness of God that is not the threat of retribution and the story of Nehunya the ditch digger and his son? We do not yet make out the homiletical structure involved in R. Yose's words.

Thus, we can say that the expression of tradition—and so far we are referring to it as it appears in the Palestinian Talmud—is fragmentary. We sense that the structures and images involved are richer than the literary expressions of tradition surviving here. Our own exegesis, therefore, is an attempt at reconstructing a reality, a reality of tradition, beyond the text that survives in the Palestinian Talmud and, as we shall see, beyond the Babylonian text as well. Armed with our sense of intimation and incompleteness, let us return to the text from the Babylonian Talmud. I quote it again.

The Rabbis repeated: It happened that the daughter of Nehunya the ditch-digger (M *Shekalim* 5:1) fell into a big pit. They came and informed R. Hanina ben Dosa. At the first hour he said to them, "[She] is well". At the second [hour] he said to them, "[She] is well." At the third [hour] he said to them, "She has come up." He said to her, "My daughter, who brought you up?" She said to him, "A ram came by me and an old man was leading him." They said to him [R. Hanina ben Dosa], "Are you a prophet?" He said to them, "I am no prophet, neither am I a prophet's son, but I said to myself, '[Is it possible that] the offspring of that righteous man should come to harm in the very thing for which he shows so much concern?'" R. Aha said: Nevertheless his son died of thirst, as Scripture says: "Our God cometh, and doth not keep silence; A fire devoureth before Him, And round about Him it stormeth mightily" (Psalms 50:3): This teaches that the Holy One Blessed is He is exacting with those around Him even to the breadth of a hair. R. Nehunya said: [Rather] from this verse: "A God dreaded in the great council of the holy ones, And feared of all them that are round about Him (Ibid. 89:8)." R. Hanina said: Whoever says that the Holy One Blessed is He easily overlooks [man's actions], let his life be thus overlooked, as Scripture says: "The Rock, His work is perfect; For all His ways are justice; A God of faithfulness and without iniquity, Just and right is He" (Deuteronomy 32:4). (BT *Bava Kama* 50a)

In this version, the man referred to as "a certain *Hasid*" in the Palestinian Talmud is identified as Nehunya the ditch digger. Let us first analyze the story of the ditch digger's daughter as it is enriched through listening to the versions of the Babylonian and Palestinian *Talmudin* together. Since it is clear that both are versions of the same story, we are justified in bringing them together even before considering the historical and other problems.

Remember that the Palestinian version is about a man who refuses to, or cannot, accept condolence for the death of his daughter. His life is marked by his own sensitivity for the simple and immediate need of thirsty wayfarers for water. Precisely because of this, perhaps extreme, sensitivity, the words of condolence said to him sound meaningless. The essence of condolence is the reality of time and the temporality of that which is lost. The former is to heal the pain of the latter. One is to accept loss in the passage of time, to forget, and to concentrate on and find comfort in that which remains after the loss, that which is becoming, that which will be in the future for the individual and for all of Israel. The refusal of the *hasid* to be consoled is a refusal to go along the painful road of time and to accept the working out of things along its way. Time holds out no hope for the man who cannot bear that people thirst and suffer; his is a demand for deliverance now.

In the Babylonian Talmud, this deprecation of the way through patient time is acted out dramatically. In the "first hour," R. Hanina ben Dosa calmly tells those anxiously awaiting news of the girl that she is well now but says nothing about what will be. Imagine their consternation! The girl's very life is threatened, her relatives and friends are frantic, and the man they have turned to tells them that she is well! In the "second hour," he repeats the same thing while those around him are besides themselves with mounting panic. And then, in the third hour, he throws off his mask. His "patient waiting" was merely a mocking imitation of the hope that things "work out" through time. His calmness was a knowledge, a disdain for the normal course of events. Now "two hours" have passed, time has been "given its chance" and, as expected, has failed, there is still no news of the girl. R. Hanina ben Dosa has waited patiently for two hours and now he flaunts the failure of patience, the impotence of time: no deliverance grows through it, no development of events has saved the girl. Her very life is in the gravest danger and only an actualization of deliverance in the immediate present, without recourse to any futher waiting, will do. This is the miracle worker's demand and conviction. And now that what he knew already is clearly manifest—that time brings no help—he impatiently waves his hand, and time and pain and suffering surrender to the present. It is not possible but that the girl has risen from the depths of the pit, she is saved now, miraculously. What a mockery of the notion that one must be patient and struggle through the meanderings of life! As soon as one realizes that it is an unbearable thought that the ditch digger's daughter should die in a pit, then one realizes, if one has the strength to conquer the present, that deliverance must be immediate. And so it is. The impossible, the unplanned, the unexpected wrenches the girl out of a reasonable course of events, and she is saved not because an alternatively reasonable course of events has replaced the first but because the sudden has replaced it. R. Hanina ben Dosa could no more accept condolence than could the *hasid* of the Palestinian Talmud; nor would that *hasid* be any more surprised than R. Hanina ben Dosa at the latest example of the fallacy of patience with the course of events through unperturbed time.

Those gathered around R. Hanina ben Dosa ask him if he is a prophet. They have misinterpreted his conduct. They have assumed that when in the "first hour" he told them that Nehunya's daughter was well, he already knew that the girl would be saved in the "third hour." Unlike Amos (7:14), who meant that he was not a "professional" prophet but rather that his prophecy came to him uncalled, spontaneously, perhaps even against his will, R. Hanina ben Dosa means that he himself is indeed no prophet. He did not know, two hours before it happened, how the drama would be worked out. On the contrary, the thought of things "working out" through time is foreign to him; therefore, he cannot be a prophet, far less a prophet of history like Amos! When R. Hanina ben

Dosa first told his listeners that the girl was well, it was a faith in the present, a faith without a thought of when or how she would get out. In the third hour, when he can wait no longer, when he is overcome with the terrible need for immediate deliverance, when he can no longer play the part of those who have faith in history, not even the history of a few short hours, he still does not have a vision of how it is to happen. He is overcome with the conviction that something *must* happen and happen *now*. His is not the prophetic conviction that something *will* happen. In the beginning, he knows that the girl is well *now*—it cannot be otherwise—though he does not yet think of rescue; he leaves that mockingly to time. In the "third hour," his bated breath overcomes the events, and time and history disintegrate before the impatient miracle worker. In the Palestinian Talmud, there is one tradition according to which the girl is saved from the overpowering flow of water by being caught in an overhanging branch. This is *not* an attempt at a "rationalization" of the story. Rather, it is a recognition that the remarkable element in the story is the seizing of deliverance in the immediate present. R. Hanina ben Dosa's conviction— "[Is it possible that] the offspring of that righteous man should come to harm in the very thing for which he shows so much concern?" (BT)—is not the attitude of a sorcerer or shaman who brings order to chaos, who overpowers the forces of darkness, who has powers unattainable by others. His, rather, is a knowledge of a different reality: not a reality to which one must ascend by shunning the here and now, but the reality in which one finds oneself when embracing the here and now. And, it is not a reality hidden in the secret of inwardness but one that is manifest—if one is heroic enough to look. We must not forget that R. Hanina ben Dosa belongs to a tradition intimately connected with martyrdom, and to the martyr belongs the immediate.

Thus far, we have seen how the image known to tradition becomes more visible to us as we hear the same story retold. The live meaning in tradition comes out more when we pay attention to the way in which material found in both *Talmudim* configurates peculiarly in the Babylonian.

In the Babylonian Talmud, the "certain *Hasid*" is none other than Nehunya the ditch digger. Following the view of R. Hanina (*not* ben Dosa) and R. Aha[29] that the reason for the death of Nehunya's son is divine retribution for sin, the identification of the *hasid* and Nehunya would seem to be merely coincidental, a result of the similarity in their stories as handed down by tradition. However, if we follow the view of R. Yose[30] that the son's death is not connected to this notion of sin but has rather to do with the constellation of ideas in Psalm 89, then the identi-

fication of the *hasid* who dug water ditches for wayfarers and whose
daughter was nearly lost in an accident, with Nehunya the ditch digger
whose son died of thirst—becomes meaningful indeed.

If the death of Nehunya the ditch digger's son is not retribution for
sin then it takes on (if we insist on a meaning, as R. Yose does) a meaning
centering around the *nature* of his death. The son dies of thirst, according
to all our sources. If we remember that his father devoted much effort to
the alleviation of the thirst of wayfarers by preparing water for them along
the roads, then we see the point: Nehunya's labors have been completely
and totally selfless! If his own son died of thirst, then Nehunya has not had
even the most rudimentary benefit from his efforts. He labors his whole
life lest some unknown and thankless traveler suffer from thirst, and he has
not eased in the slightest the suffering of one who is closest and most
beloved. Is this not an *Akedah*? By this tragic and unwitting sacrifice he has
lost what is most dear to him and at the same time has made his life work a
perfection of self-sacrifice for others only. The symbolism of the death by
thirst of the son of the water-ditch digger thus is clear: it is sacrificial like
the Binding of Isaac in that the tragedy of total loss in one moment
epitomizes the sweating labor of years.

Now, we finally recognize in Nehunya the ditch digger the "certain
Hasid." Whether it is the attitude of the *Hasid* himself or it is R. Hanina
ben Dosa who senses in the father's work a certain truth, it is the same.
The ditch digger cannot bear the thought of the slow steps of deliverance.
The picture of some traveler looking for water, searching, waiting, slowly
drying up, and dying; of the divine way being worked out without that
dusty traveler, in children, in a People, in the future, is too painful for his
compassionate imagination. He will dig wells so that each wayfarer will
have his sweet needs as close as possible to the request for them. He
cannot imagine for a moment that the divine mercy is any different. Is God
less loving and caring than the lowly ditch digger? And, when he hears
that his daughter is lost, do we expect him to be consoled? Do we expect
his pain to be softened by knowing that in time the wounds will heal?
Would he have told a thirsty man that in time things will somehow work
out? Is R. Hanina ben Dosa not right in mocking the thought that the life
of this man's daughter must await a working out through the course of
events? But this is not all. The *hasid*'s demand for deliverance in the
present, so powerful that it overcomes the smallest and hardest of history's
facts, marks his story with terrible tragedy. Finally, he has the perfection of
the immediate moment; but this leaves no room for slowness, for working
out, for the play of grays. If the present moment is to be so laden with
meaning, then it can contain only a drama of life and death. His daughter

is saved in the seizing of the present. And he unwillingly loses his son in a sacrificial moment so laden with meaning that it epitomizes the father's life. A complete drama of life and death must be compressed into a moment for the man who demands immediacy. For his daughter the drama ends in life; for his son it ends in *Akedah*.

Now the connection between Psalm 89 and Nehunya the ditch digger, who is the "certain *Hasid*," finally may be seen. According to R. Yose the psalm is about the *zaddik*, the righteous man, who is compared to the Davidic scion. Or, rather, we will use the word *hasid* to note the uniqueness of his righteousness, as we shall see. God the Creator, who crushes Rahab and vanquishes chaos, is almighty in the completeness of momentary action. He does not need the creeping of history nor the patience of time for his way. He finds a partner for covenant in the *hasid* because the latter is capable of receiving the awesome and complete love of the Creator. The *hasid* can forget history and continue in the lonesomeness of the present, despite the horrible truth of history. Or, he is capable of forgiving history and continues living despite it, without being gripped to oppression by it. He does not need the grand vision of the "end of the days": in his simplicity and heroism he may find deliverance in the present. He is capable and deserving of the faithfulness of God. Through change, old age, disillusionment, and disappointment, he does not see the waning of man, he does not see the nakedness and weakness of man. He loves men in all their frailty and believes in their godliness and beauty always. He struggles to live through the present moment and is happy with life now. Now he lives, now he enjoys what little is still left him. He forgets the passion of yesterday and tomorrow is still a dream for him. He is like R. Hanina ben Dosa for whom the world exists but who is oblivious of the fact and is content in his hut with his basket of carobs. For him there is indeed divine faithfulness, for not a moment goes by without an overwhelming sense of divine closeness and love. His own way is one of love and concentration on things as they are in the apparentness of the present, not in the sophistication of long duration, pattern, structure, and Law. He is a chosen one and full of divine grace. Was ever a David more chosen, more unique, more brilliantly outstanding in the dullness of the present? It is the Creator who loves this man and sees his greatness, for it is the Creator who can caress the present in totality. What would men who measure by the grandness of history see in this humble *hasid*? For men with prophetic vision, the present is dull and gray indeed. For the *hasid*, the present is a world.

R. Yose has singled out one particular verse in Psalm 89 as a handle for the psalm:

> A God dreaded in the great council of the holy ones,
> And feared of all them that are round about him. (8)

And remember that he connects this with the death by thirst of the son whose father dug cool wells for dusty wayfarers. God is truly dreadful for this Nehunya, or rather the being in the world through which the *hasid* turns to God is fraught with dread. Nehunya compresses his life into the immediate care for thirsty travelers because in the intimacy of such closeness he does not feel homeless. He knows their needs. Perhaps, this gives him a feeling that in some way he knows them. Perhaps, they are not anonymous to him because he knows they have the same cry for immediate needs that he has. This is a tiny world that he knows and is able to bring some happiness to. On his way home at dusk, he must think about someone wetting his cracked lips with his sweet water. Or caressing its coolness with naked wrists. The world beyond that vision is frightening. Far from his wells, people suffer and are lost, strangers in a mute world. In that world, he himself is unknown, impotent, and homeless. He returns home always to the warm and immediate cares, to his own present and that of others with needs like his own, because he knows the frightening indifference and awesome and cruel immensity of the world beyond the reachable present. Therefore, he is ready to embrace the close present whatever the cost. He is driven to a completeness of living in the present, he needs a living that will encompass all that is pent up inside him in the immediacy of the moment. He might seek the heroic because there one may do ever so much, frighteningly much, in the comforting and known closeness of the most intimate of worlds. In heroism, the action of the hero makes sense, in martyrdom all of meaning radiates out from the 'I' of the martyr, mocking the foolish and the absurd, and in relinquishing all in *Akedah* man makes the final covenant with the present. He is at peace with the knowledge that labor is thankless, that the future is an illusion. Nehunya's loss of his son to the encroaching death he has laboriously fought against stamps his life with the meaning he has been searching for: selflessness, a certain knowledge of the immediate needs of men without any thought about a lingering tale of give and take, of barter, of ambition and status, of growth and power. His dread of the world of history and grandness has brought him into a world of heroic immediacy where the sacrificial, the *Akedah*, is a meaningful finality. God calls upon the *hasid* to sacrifice his son because he knows the father, he beckons him into the ultimately heroic and complete.

Implicit, then, in the fragment of tradition attributed to R. Yose is a powerful intimation of the images that lie behind all the bits and pieces we have discussed. Again, it is only through a developed sensitivity to the resonance of all the fragments that we can actually glimpse the perception of reality that is the substratum of tradition.

Perhaps the most enigmatic point, at first glance at least, has been the "ram . . . and an old man was leading him" who, according to the Babylonian Talmud, saved Nehunya's daughter. This scene now presents a dazzling invitation to interpretation, an interpretation already given, at least partially, by Rashi, the medieval scholar whose commentary on the Babylonian Talmud represents an accrual of ancient Ashkenazic traditions.[31] Rashi writes that the ram is the ram of Isaac and the old man leading it is Abraham. Whether this interpretation is an old traditional one or Rashi's own insight, I do not know, although I suspect it is the former. In any case, this interpretation makes the scene strikingly epitomize what seems to be fragmentarily adumbrated in our texts. Through it the texts belonging to a wholeness beyond them is more manifest. Nehunya's daughter is saved in the story of the Binding of Isaac. But it is not Isaac himself who appears here, it is his ram. As we saw previously, the ram represents the fullness of the dialectic of *Akedah* because it is slaughtered; it represents not only the redemption of Isaac but also death. It is through the uncompromising embrace of the present as represented in the sacrificial death of Nehunya's son that deliverance is immediate for the daughter. The symbolism of Abraham and the ram means here the *Akedah*'s sacrificial aspect, its embracing of the present, which results in the saving of the daughter and the death of the son, and not its aspect of the covenant of history, in which redemption takes the long and arduous way.

In a society where tradition is taken seriously, the entire sense of reality may be determined by tradition. The way one eats, let alone what one eats, the way one dresses, talks, and acts become stylized because they thereby contain the messages of tradition. Moreover, the meaning of man, woman, time, and space—in short all the elements making up the kaleidoscope of living, as well as the structure that connects these images—become an incarnation of tradition. But, if tradition is an attitude towards living itself, then it is naive to suppose that the literary expressions of such a tradition are anything but fragmentary. At best, they are still-life photographs. We all know how far even an endless series of photographs, taken from an endless number of angles and with endless variations in the lighting, fall short of the reality of living. This is no less true of literary sources. And, if we are speaking of an *attitude* toward living, then we are speaking of man's very spirituality and our search is ever more complex and its object ever more elusive and meta-artifactual. Therefore, when interpreting our sources, we are justified in pursuing much more than their philological connotations.

Following this, the connection between the story of Nehunya the ditch digger and the personality of R. Hanina ben Dosa is no less important than any of the other aspects alluded to. That the Babylonian Talmud allows R. Hanina ben Dosa's share in the story to swallow up part of Nehunya's share shows how deeply one part of tradition felt it knew the miracle worker. It therefore felt that by attributing to him the actions or sayings of Nehunya, it would convey a more transparent message. This transferral is legitimate on the assumption that the two personalities are similar. Therefore, I have stressed that similarity. The choice of R. Hanina ben Dosa as the giver of meaning in the Babylonian version certainly does not derive merely from the chronological nexus with Nehunya the ditch digger. The attribution of a partially similiar role to R. Phinehas ben Jair in the Palestinian version also results from a conviction of insight into his personality, and I have already mentioned the existence of important parallels between what is remembered about him and about R. Hanina ben Dosa. The Palestinian version does not include the identification of the "certain *Hasid*" as Nehunya the ditch digger, and therefore, there is no chronological consideration there. This does not prove that one version is either more pristine than the other or more historical. In any case, behind both versions images move that are richer than any surviving material concerning either R. Hanina ben Dosa or R. Phinehas ben Jair.

To sum up, I have tried to show how R. Hanina ben Dosa is connected with the phenomenon of martyrdom and how that recognition sheds light on the meaning of martyrdom and, consequently, on the nexus of *Akedah*—martyrdom that we have discussed. In martyrdom, man stands before God as Creator (the crusher of Rahab and the vanquisher of chaos) and not as the God of history. Martyrdom is itself, for the martyr, an act of creation in the sense that it is complete and perfect and enduring, like the victory of God over the forces of chaos; and it is accomplished in the immediacy of the present, not as an ongoing processes. In the stance of martyrdom, the individual is the center and the moment is supreme. The nexus of miracle worker and martyr is not uncommon, and when it occurs, it is essential and not accidental. For both, deliverance is immediate and not through long, patient ways of redemptive history and Law. I have identified this martyrial syndrome as the sacrificial aspect of *Akedah*.

After his death, the great miracle worker, who was distinguished by self-sacrifice and not by learning, was mourned by rabbinic tradition in the following words, "With the death of R. Hanina ben Dosa men of deed disappeared"[32] (M *Sotah* 9:15). His predilection for martyrdom and the confinement of his vision to the immediate and the personal perhaps were not condoned by the rabbis, but they nevertheless mourned the loss of men who could conquer the present with their heroism.

Chapter Six

Nahum ish Gamzo and R. Hananiah ben Teradyon

N ahum ish Gamzo, who lived at the end of the first century and the beginning of the second, apparently in Gimzo, in central Palestine, affords us an opportunity of tracing some of our motifs through an interplay with more mainstream rabbinic views.

It was said about Nahum ish Gamzo that he was blind in both eyes, that he had lost his hands and feet, and that his whole body was covered with boils, and that he was lying in a shaky house and the legs of his bed were standing in cups of water so that ants should not crawl up on him.[1] Once, his bed was placed in a shaky house. His students wanted to take his bed out and afterwards to take out the furnishings. He said to them, "My sons, take the furnishings out and afterwards take out my bed, for you can be assured that as long as I am in the house it won't collapse." They took out the furnishings and then took out his bed, and the house collapsed. His students said to him, "Rabbi, since, then, you are a completely righteous person, why did this happen to you?" He said to them, "My sons, I brought it upon myself: Once, I was going on the way to my father-in-law's house and I had with me three loaded donkeys; one with food and one with drink and one with various delicacies. A poor man came along and stood in my way and said to me, 'Rabbi, feed me.' I had not yet finished unloading the donkey when he breathed his last breath and died. I went and fell on his face and said, 'My eyes, which would not spare your eyes, should be blinded; my hands, which would not spare your hands, should be hacked off; my legs which would not spare your legs should be severed'; nor was I calmed until I said, 'Let my whole body be covered with boils'." They[2] said to him, "Alas for us that we see you so!" He said to them "Alas for me if you saw me not so." (BT *Ta'anit* 21a)[3]

Nahum's students see a righteous, suffering man. But more indelibly imprinted on Nahum's vision is the scene where he becomes what he is. He is pushing ahead on the road to his father-in-law's home, laden down with worldly refreshment, anxious to proceed, when a poor man stands in his way obstructing his progress. The poor man is hungry and asks, almost curtly, that Nahum feed him. Nahum is forced to make a stop here; he asks the man to wait while he unloads the donkeys and thus prepares for camp. All this is a rich man's rigmarole, in the eyes of the pauper. By the time Nahum is finished with his preparations the poor man has collapsed with weakness and is beyond saving. The terrible shock is a revelation for Nahum. Suddenly he hates his way of living. He wants desperately to be a different Nahum, immediately. He wants the road of the past, which he walked mindlessly, to disappear; and all thoughts of continuing, laden with goods, to his father-in-law's home are trivial now, nonsensical. The very future becomes vague for him; all that matters is his passionate need for immediate and complete atonement. He has become like the poor man desperately seeking—not bread but salvation—in the moment. Only when the enterprising Nahum is destroyed, leaving a helpless and repulsive Nahum, is he at peace with himself. Dying has been his salvation. He has acted out a martyrdom and he reiterates his readiness for that martyrdom constantly anew. Rather than the the pitiful old man his students saw, Nahum is a heroic embracer of his own dread fate, giving it an immanent meaning rather than mourning it as a fall from a better past.

The Talmud continues immediately the story of Nahum as follows:

And why was he called Nahum ish Gamzo?[4] Because at everything that befell him he said, "This, too, is for the good." Once the Jews wanted to send a gift to Caesar's court. They said, "Who should go? Nahum ish Gamzo should go because he is accustomed to miracles." They sent with him a bag full of precious stones and pearls. He set out and stayed over at a certain dwelling. At night the neighbors got up and took his bag and refilled it with earth. The next day, when he saw that, he said, "This, too, is for the good."[5] When he arrived there, his bag was opened and found to be full of earth. The king wanted to kill them all, saying "The Jews are making fun of me!" He [Nahum] said, "This, too, is for the good."[6] Elijah came. He appeared to them as one of them [the Romans]. He said to them, "Perhaps this earth is from the earth of their father Abraham; for when he would throw earth [at his enemies] it became swords while the chaff in it became arrows."[7] . . . There was a certain city which they could not conquer: They tried some of it [the earth] and conquered it. They took him [Nahum] into the treasure-house and filled his bag with precious stones and pearls, and they sent him off with great honor. On his way he stopped at the same dwelling. They said to him, "What did you bring with you that they should have done you so much honor?" He said to them, "What I took with me from here I brought there." They tore down their dwelling and brought [earth from] it to the king's court. They said to him, "That earth which he [Nahum] brought here is from ours!" They tried it out and nothing happened, and they killed those neighbors. (Ibid. and BT *Sanhedrin* 108b)

Nahum is famous for the manner in which he has embraced his calamitous physical breakdown. It seems clear, then, that the epithet *this too, (gam zo)*, short for This, too, is for the good, is homiletically attached to his name because of the way he embraced each successive disablement. However, in the parallel in Tractate *Sanhedrin*, the homily on Nahum's name is brought without any previous mention of the story about his being crippled. In both sources, the homily is further quoted in connection with Nahum's adventure with the box of jewels. But, there, it is incongruous and must represent an alteration of the original tradition. The fact that the jewels are stolen and replaced with earth is not "good"; it turns out not to be a disaster because of Elijah's miraculous intervention. We are given no reason to suppose that had Nahum continued to the Roman ruler with the original jewels his bribe would have been unsuccessful. And it is unlikely that the faith Nahum expresses upon seeing the earth is a faith that, in addition to the success of his important mission, he also will return enriched. When, upon seeing the earth-filled box, the Roman angrily threatens the Jews with death, again there is nothing identifiable here as "good"; rather it spells certain disaster, which Elijah miraculously overcomes so as to ensure the initially expected success of the mission. Interpreting "this, too, is for good" to mean that even apparently evil phenomena are not bad because they will be corrected by miracles reduces it to triviality. The reliance on the miraculous implies that evil is seen not as good but as true evil, which is to be changed or overcome, however imminent the miracle may be. In any case, our initial interpretation of the homiletical epithet seems more cogent.

That Nahum's real distinction is his martyr's embracing of calamity and that the homiletical epithet has been reinterpreted is thrown into relief by contrast with the views of the famous R. Akiva, who died at the hands of the Romans toward the end of the Bar Kokhba uprising. R. Akiva comes down to us in tradition too rich to epitomize in a work of this size, and we shall merely touch on one point of contact where he differs with Nahum ish Gamzo.

> R. Akiva went to visit him [Nahum, after the latter had been struck down]. He said to him, "Woe that I see you in such a state!" He [Nahum] said to him, "Woe that I do not see you in such a state." He said to him, "Why are you cursing me?" He said to him, "And why do you scorn suffering?" (PT *Pe'ah* 8:9 [21b]; *Shekalim* 5:6 [49b])

What R. Akiva perceives as a curse, Nahum embraces positively and even wishes on the former.

> Rav Huna said in the name of Rav[8] who ascribed it to R. Meir [second century], and so someone repeated it in the name of R. Akiva:[9] Man should always be accustomed to saying, "Whatever the Merciful One does He does for the good." Like this [story] concerning R. Akiva, who was going along the way. He came to a certain town and tried to find lodgings but was unsuccessful. He said, "Whatever the Merciful One does is for the good." He went to spend the night in a field. And he had with him a rooster, a donkey and a candle. A sudden wind blew out the candle; a cat came and ate the rooster; a lion came and ate the donkey. He said, "Whatever the Merciful One does is for the good." During that very same night an armed band came and took over the town. He said to them [his companions], "Didn't I say to you, 'Whatever the Holy One Blessed is He does, all is for the good'."[10] (BT *Berakhot* 60b)

This story of how R. Akiva lived out the faith that "Whatever the Holy One Blessed is He does, all is for the good" is a reinterpretation of the saying that epitomized his teacher Nahum, "This, too, is for the good." That R. Akiva is denied lodging in the town is neither good of itself nor is it miraculously changed into anything other than it manifestly is. The losses of his rooster (his "clock," Rashi), his donkey (his "hands and legs"), and his candle (his "eyes") are neither celebrated as suffering nor do they turn out to be a ruse for his enrichment. The loss of these three items is a chain of events that follows, in orderly fashion, from the inhospitality he originally meets with. Camping out in the open field, his candle is snuffed out by the wind; with no fire to scare away the wild animals, his own animals are vulnerable to predators; and once the nervous and noisy rooster is gone the approach of the patient lion is unnoticed. This chain of events continues in such a way so that precisely because the events are really what they seem to be R. Akiva is saved. The darkness hides him from others as well; the loss of the rooster brings quiet and he sleeps through the dangerous events, and even when he does finally wake up he must move out on foot, slowly. He is saved because he is kept from the danger by both space and time, as well as hidden in the natural camouflage of the night. "All is for the good" because things work out through the orderly labyrinth of time. Evil prevails when one has only the immediate view of events. In the unraveling of things through history, so R. Akiva is convinced, good finally becomes the direction of reality. This is very different from Nahum's attitude toward life. For him salvation is immediately available, time takes too long. "He is accustomed to miracles" and does not need history. He has the strength of self to accept the present no matter how terrible it is; indeed, he is able to prevail over it without escaping to the metaphysical, to patterns, or to future. For him even the most terrible can be "this, too, is for the good" in all its naked reality; for R. Akiva the present, when unbearable, is acceptable only as part of history—albeit even a very limited history. R. Akiva reinterprets "This, too, is for the good" to mean that "this, too, is part of a process whose end is good." R. Akiva was a student of Nahum ish Gamzo in his sensitivity to the pain of evil and in the need for salvation (Nahum)/redemption (R. Akiva). But, in his working out of these sensibilities, R. Akiva is closer to mainstream rabbinic thinking. The telling of Nahum's own story has been influenced by his student's story, and this is the reason for the alteration of the original meaning of the homiletical epithet "this, too, is for the good" and the incongruous connection of that phrase with the episode about Nahum and the filled box of jewels.

The difference between the attitudes of Nahum ish Gamzo and R. Akiva comes out in the fact that R. Akiva supported Bar Kokhba as the Messiah.[11] There is a gulf between one for whom Elijah interferes, turning clods of earth into magic missiles (for the sake of the Romans!) and a threatening Roman into a patron, and one for whom the messianic redemption is to come about through liberation by military struggle from Roman rule. R. Akiva was tortured to death because of his refusal to suffer the Roman yoke,[12] but he is not a martyr in the sense we have discussed, at least not in his support of Bar Kokhba. We have seen that martyrdom may partake of the sacrificial aspect of the Binding of Isaac as a heroic embracing of the present and an escape from history. R. Akiva's vision of redemption through military struggle is not an escape from history, though it may be a misinterpretation of it, and therefore, does not partake of the *Akedah* aspect of martyrdom. R. Akiva's biography is extremely complex, even in its fragmentary form, as remembered in rabbinic literature, and it is possible, perhaps even probable, that he experienced his terrible death as a martyrdom in the sense that we have discussed. Perhaps, his life partook of that dialectic of Law and martyrdom discussed. But his support of Bar Kokhba was not the act of a martyr in that sense, even if it entailed the danger of death. This point will become clearer in the following discussion of R. Hananiah (or Hanina) ben Teradyon (second century) and R. Eleazar ben Parta; we shall return to R. Akiva himself later.

> The Rabbis repeated: When R. Eleazar ben Parta and R. Hanina ben Teradyon were arrested [by the Romans]. . . . They brought forth R. Eleazar ben Parta and said, "Why did you teach and why did you steal?" He said to them, "If a swordsman, then not a scholar, and if a scholar, then not a swordsman. . . ." "Why, then, are you called 'Rabbi' [master]?" "I am a master of weavers." They brought him two balls of thread and said to him, "Which is for the warp and which is for the woof?" A miracle took place for him: A queen bee came and settled on the warp while a drone came and settled on the woof. He said to them, "This is for the warp and this is for the woof." They said to him, "And why didn't you come to our house of worship?" He said to them, "I've grown old and I'm afraid you'll trample over me." They said, "And how many old men have been trampled so far?" A miracle took place: On that very day an old man was trampled. "And why did you set your slave free?" He said to them, "That never happened." One of those present stood up in order to bear witness against him. Elijah came, appearing to that man like one of the important people of the government. He [Elijah] said to him [the would-be antagonist], "Since all along the miraculous has occurred for his sake, now, too, a miracle will take place and you are just showing your meanness!" But he [the antagonist] paid him no attention. He stood up to speak to them [to bear witness against the Rabbi]. Now there was a letter written by important people in the government [waiting] to be sent to Caesar's court: And they sent it off with that man [the antagonist]. Elijah came and propelled him a distance of fifteen hundred miles [so that] he went but did not come. (BT *Avodah Zarah* 17b)

During the time of the Hadrianic persecutions, R. Eleazar ben Parta was arrested by the Roman authorities, apparently for revolutionary activity. Even the attendant miracles and the activity of Elijah cannot hide the fact that R. Eleazar is saved by his resourcefulness. He does not recognize the validity of the Roman rule, and all means are fair for escaping their talons. The addition of the miraculous to the story is intended to show approval of the Rabbi's behavior and not at all to belittle the weight of his own efforts. In fact, this addition emphasizes his daring determination to shirk the foreign oppressor. Even were R. Eleazar ben Parta to be executed finally, he would not be a martyr in the sense of *Akedah*. His intention is to struggle, not to sacrifice; he is aided, perhaps, by an optimistic conviction that things will work out in the end, and by a brave sense of humor.

R. Eleazar ben Parta said three things before the Sages and they upheld his words: Concerning a person in a town under a siege and a person on a ship foundering at sea and a person being taken out to be condemned; that they are assumed to be still alive. But [the wife of] a person in a town that was taken through siege, or on a ship that was lost at sea, or a person being taken out to be executed, is not given the legal benefit of the doubt: A woman of non-priestly lineage married to a priest, and a woman of priestly lineage married to a man of non-priestly lineage, do not eat *terumah* [which is reserved for priests and their immediate families]. (M *Gittin* 3:4)

This Mishnah gives a rabbinic view of an age when, for Judea, Roman law and order was worse than anarchy. Even in such times, the Rabbis retained their faith that the course of events might bring relief. R. Eleazar ben Parta holds this view, and his opinion—that even when death looms imminent before a man, his chances of survival still must be considered—is part of mainstream rabbinic thinking of that period. In later times, when the faith of a generation who dared war with the Roman Empire was incomprehensible, the Mishnah had to be partially reinterpreted: "Rav Joseph said: The Mishnah [which says "one being taken out to be executed" is assumed, in some sense, to be still alive] is referring to the instance of a Jewish court; but in the instance of a non-Jewish court,[13] once he has been condemned to death they surely kill him"[14] (BT *Gittin* 28b). Unless one alternative could be considered: "Abbaye said to him [Rav Joseph]: [In the instance of] a non-Jewish court[13] as well since they accept bribes" (ibid.).

The possibility of bribery always exists, and on that basis one could even give the Mishnah the opposite interpretation: "Others quote Rav Joseph as having said: The [same] Mishnah is referring to the instance of a non-Jewish court;[13] but in the instance of a Jewish court once a death sentence has been passed on him they kill him" (ibid. 29a).

R. Hananiah ben Teradyon is very different from R. Eleazar ben Parta:

They brought forth R. Hanina ben Teradyon. They said to him, "Why do you study the Torah?" He said to them, "As the Lord my God commanded me."[15] They condemned him at once to be burnt, and his wife to be killed, and his daughter to be put in a brothel. He [was condemned] to be burnt because he was wont to pronounce the name [tetragrammaton] according to its actual spelling. And how did he do so, when we repeat:

And the following have no share for the Coming World: Whoever says that [the belief in] the resurrection of the dead is not based on the Pentateuch[16] or that there is no such thing as a revealed Law, and an *apikoros*.[17] R. Akiva says: So, too, one who reads alien writings.[18] And one who whispers over a sore, saying, "I will put none of the diseases upon thee, which I have put upon the Egyptians; for I am the Lord that healeth thee" (Exodus 15:26).[19] Abba Saul says: So, too, one who pronounces the name [tetragrammaton] according to its actual spelling.[20] (M *Sanhedrin* 10:1)[21]

He did so for the purpose of learning [that pronounciation in theory but not for practice]. . . . Why, then, was he punished? Because he was pronouncing the name in public. And his wife [was condemned] to be killed because she did not restrain him. . . . And his daughter [was condemned] to be put in a brothel because of what R. Johanan [Palestine, third century] said: Once, his daughter was walking in front of some important Romans. They said: "How lovely is this young woman's manner of walking!" At that she began to walk deliberately. . . . While the three of them [the sage with his wife and daughter] were going out (to be executed) they justified the [divine] nemeses. He said, "'The Rock, His work is perfect. . . .'" (Deuteronomy 32:4). And his wife said, "'A God of faithfulness and without iniquity' " (ibid.). His daughter said, "'[The Lord is] great in counsel, and mighty in work; whose eyes are open upon all the ways of the sons of men. . . .'" (Jeremiah 32:19). Rabbi [Judah ha-Nasi, around the turn of the third century] said: How great these righteous people were, that they happened upon three verses whose subject is the justification of [divine] nemeses, at the very time when they themselves were justifying the divine judgment! (BT *Avodah Zarah*, ibid.)

In contrast to R. Eleazar ben Parta, the martyrial consciousness of R. Hananiah ben Teradyon stands out conspicuously. He is ready for his death even before it is pronounced on him, and his thinking is concentrated on the meaning of his martyrdom rather than on ways of avoiding it. The Roman regime, its laws and cruelty, its bureaucrats and executors who might be open to argumentation or bribery, who might even be vulnerable, are of little interest to him compared with the intense meaningfulness of his own willed steps. For him, the drama of man standing momentarily before God is far grander than all the grandeur of the Roman hordes, and he holds his breath before the smallest of his movements. He colors the moment of his death with the verse, "The Rock, His work is perfect; For all His ways are justice."

For the martyr, the ways of God are indeed perfect, since the martyr himself achieves perfection in his dying. And this is a perfection achieved in a moment of immanence, not required to be worked out through peoplehood and history. Thus "*all* His ways are justice," each and every one complete in itself, in the eyes of the martyr. R. Hananiah's wife quotes the verse,

> A God of faithfulness and without iniquity,
> Just and right is He.

We have already seen the connection between the notion of God's "faithfulnesss" and the martyrial consciousness. There is no "iniquity" in his ways, for he is faithful. No man and no moment is too small or fragmentary—on the contrary, he knows their grandness—to contain fully the divine grace. He is faithful to each and every moment, embracing with a passion only the martyr can know. There is no point of being that is abandoned by God; there is no "iniquity."[22]

> "The Rock", [meaning] the draftsman,[23] [in the sense] that He planned out [and created] the world first, and [only] then created man in it, as the verse says: "Then the Lord God formed man of the dust of the ground" (Genesis 2:7). "His work is perfect", His working is complete in every one who comes into the world:[24] And one must not entertain the possibility of even the slightest fault in His actions: And there is not one of them [His beings] who could look and say, "If I had three eyes or if I had three hands or if I had three legs or if I would walk on my head or if my face was turned backwards how lovely it would be for me"; the verse teaches us, saying, "For all His ways are justice", He sits in judgment with each and every one and gives him his due. "A God of faithfulness", [meaning] that He had faith in the world and created it. "And without iniquity", [meaning] that men were not created to be evil but rather [to be] righteous, and so the verse says: "Behold, this only have I found, that God made man upright; but they have sought out many inventions" (Ecclesiastes 7:29). "Just and right is He", He deals rightly with every one who comes into the world. (*Sifre* to Deuteronomy 32:4 [p. 344])

If we read this Midrash with the knowledge that its verse is quoted in connection with martyrdom, we gain insight into its meaning. The homilist interprets the verse as referring to God in his aspect as Creator, despite the fact that this is manifest neither in the verse itself nor in its context. The verse would seem to be referring to God as Judge, "For all His ways are justice," and so, too, the following verse:

> Is corruption His? No; His children's is the blemish;
> A generation crooked and perverse.

And, the context of the song of *Ha'azinu* indeed is the notion of the God of history judging His People in the historical dimension:

Remember the days of old,
Consider the years of many generations;
Ask thy father, and he will declare unto thee,
Thine elders, and they will tell thee. (7)
But Jeshurun waxed fat, and kicked . . . (15)

They sacrificed unto demons, nogods,
Gods that they knew not,
New gods that came up of late,
Which your fathers dreaded not.
Of the Rock that begot thee thou wast unmindful,
And didst forget God that bore thee. (17–18)

And He said: I will hide My face from them,
I will see what their end shall be;
For they are a very forward generation
Children in whom is no faithfulness. (20)

Venegeance is Mine, and recompense,
Against the time when their foot shall slip;
For the day of their calamity is at hand,
And the things that are to come upon them shall make haste. (35)

The fact that the homilist chooses to stress a different aspect of God, therefore, is of special interest. For him, God is "perfect" and "faithful," not in the patience of peoplehood and history but in his role as the Creator who forms and embraces each individual. Even when it comes to man's physical form and its symmetry, which easily could be viewed as relevant to humanity as a whole rather than to the individual, even on that score the individual's pain is heard. The Lord "sits with each and every one" even concerning the clumsiness of his limbs. And the world is created to be intrinsically without evil; evil derives from the way men work things out and not from the essential nature of men and the world. In other words, evil is not neutralized by the way things work out; on the contrary, the working out of things is the dimension in which evil enters. Moreover, the world is suppposed to be good not because humanity, or the soul of man, is essentially good but because each man in his fragile frame is initially good. "God had faith in the world and created it!" But how could man have so much faith in the world?

We ask, How could man have such faith in the world? The answer lies in connecting this homiletical tradition with the martyrial consciousness, with R. Hananiah ben Teradyon. If the martyr posseses a grand vision of man and the tragedy of man's death, then his own martyrdom is a power and a perfection. The martyr's strength of character, which enables him lovingly to hold his own life in his hands, is a power to negate all or to sustain all. The martyr is godlike because he determines a dreadful fate of life or death. When he determines his own death with superhuman strength, his dying is a perfection. In it good prevails over evil, the righteous man is powerful and the evil are impotent. The martyr's very being thus becomes a perfection, his sins pale into insignificance, his yearnings to become, to arrive, to achieve are realized triumphantly, albeit tragically. No matter how deformed or maimed man and the world may be, if he values his life and has the strength to give it up, then he is heroic and may know perfection. The martyr knows God as the Creator of perfection and is partner to him. It is the martyr who can have faith in the world of the present.

Thus, R. Hananiah ben Teradyon and the anonymous homilst quoted in the *Sifre* are closer to each other in their interpretation of the verse from the Deuteronomic song than either of them is to the apparent meaning of the verse itself. R. Hananiah's interpretation we deduce from his martyrial biography, from the homilist we have the actual interpretation of Scripture, though without knowledge of the man behind it we cannot be sure of its meaning. Nevertheless, the two do seem to meet and through them we get some further intimation of the martyrial consciousness subsisting, however marginally, in the rabbinic milieu.

R. Hananiah ben Teradyon's daughter quotes the verse: "Great in counsel, and mighty in work; whose eyes are open upon all the ways of the sons of men, to give every one according to his ways, and according to the fruit of his doings" (Jeremiah 32:19). Here, too, the biographical connection changes the meaning of Scripture, though more subtly. R. Hananiah's daughter is not a complete martyr, terrible as her fate is, and tradition tells us that she finally is redeemed by her brother-in-law R. Meir (BT *Avodah Zarah* ibid.). Her punishment appears to be a grotesque exaggeration of what tradition sees as a natural, but nevertheless improper, feminine weakness. Even R. Meir, when he comes to redeem her from forced prostitution, doubts her innocence, and so, too, it seems, does his wife (the famous Bruriah) who is the victim's sister.[25] Whereas the quoted verse refers, in context, to divine justice in the dimension of world, history, and peoplehood, the martyr's daughter is experiencing the extreme meaningfulness of apparently small moments in life, on the occasion of a punishment that in itself is very unjust indeed. But, to one for whom the moment is all-important, justice looks very different; and events weigh a great deal more on the impatient scale of immediacy than they do when subsumed in more transcendent structures. R. Hananiah ben Teradyon's daughter is the daughter of a martyr, and her perception of the meaningfulness of her fate is true to this.

The fact that Rabbi Judah ha-Nasi marvels at the Scripture quoted by the tragic family, apparently does not derive merely from his impression with their astuteness. His words intimate, I think, a certain disapproval of the martyrial tendency.

As the Talmud tells the story, R. Hananiah's death is seen as a punishment for "pronouncing the name (tetragrammaton) according to its actual spelling." Most probably, he was known for using the divine name for healing and the like.[26] This would fit in with what we have found to be the relationship of the martyrial consciousness to miracle working. Such a practice obviously is viewed by the Rabbis with great disapproval, and this telling of the story expresses a mainstream rabbinic view, an outsider's view, of the martyr's death.[27] The later Saboraic material,[28] "He did so for the purpose of learning," attempts to soften the censure of the great martyr of whose image we get an impressive glimpse through tradition despite differences of world view, as we shall see.

The Talmud continues:

> The Rabbis repeated: When R. Yose ben Kisma became ill R. Hanina ben Teradyon went to visit him. He said to him, "Hanina my brother, do you not know that this nation [the Romans] has been invested by Heaven; for[29] they have destroyed His house and murdered His pious ones and done away with His best: And yet they [the Romans] survive! And I have heard that you sit and study Torah, bringing together groups of people in public, holding the Scroll of Law to your bosom!" He said to him, "Heaven will be compassionate." He said to him, "I say reasonable things to you and you answer me 'Heaven will be compassionate'! I wonder if you and the Scroll of the Law won't be burnt in fire." He said to him, "Rabbi, what about me in the coming world?" He said to him, "Did any deed happen your way?" He said to him, "Money that I had put aside for Purim got mixed up with money that was intended for the poor and I divided all of it among the poor [without taking back what belonged to him]." He said to him, "If so, may my share partake of yours and may my fate partake of your fate." It was said: A short time later R. Yose ben Kisma died and all the important Romans went to his burial and eulogized him impressively. And upon their return they found R. Hanina ben Teradyon sitting and learning Torah, bringing together groups of people in public, holding the Scroll of the Law to his bosom . . . (BT ibid. 18a)

R. Yose ben Kisma sees the Roman rule as a divinely sanctioned order, for the present. History is an unalterable reality even if it seems to be antithetical to the divine will. The contrast between him and R. Hananiah ben Teradyon is expressed very succinctly in the short dialogue between them. R. Hananiah says: "Heaven will be compassionate." All of Roman might is ethereal compared to the significance of divine mercy for the individual. R. Yose is surprised by this answer—what has one thing to do with the other! The Romans are the reality of polity now and to ignore the implications of that fact is to ignore the real world. R. Hananiah asks the angered Rabbi whether their difference of vision is so great that R. Yose does not consider him worthy of life after death. R. Yose, on the verge of saying no, asks: "Perhaps, nevertheless, you have done some saving deed?" When R. Hananiah answers that he has been meticulously careful with charity R. Yose is relieved. The polity indeed is ruled by the "evil nation" but the sphere of interpersonal relations is free for the subsistence of the Law. For R. Yose ben Kisma redemption takes place through the Law and not, it would seem, through history. More precisely, insofar as man is an active partner in the process of redemption he does so in the realm of the Law and not in the realm of history.[30] Although R. Yose disagrees with R. Hananiah ben Teradyon, he is not necessarily representative of mainstream rabbinic thinking of that period. Certainly, he does not represent R. Akiva, who supported the Bar Kokhba revolt against the Romans. Perhaps, in a later and wisened period, his view would be more pervasive.

> they found R. Hananiah ben Teradyon sitting and learning Torah, bringing together groups of people in public, holding the Scroll of the Law to his bosom. They took him and wrapped him in the Scroll of the Law and piled up wood around him which they then kindled. And they brought woolen sponges and soaked them in water and placed them on his heart in order that he should not die quickly. His daughter said to him, "Father, am I to see you like this!" He said to her, "If I was burning alone it would be hard for me; now that I am burning and the Scroll of the Law is together with me, He who avenges the dishonoring of the Scroll of the Law He will avenge my dishonoring." His students said to him, "Rabbi, what is it that you see?" He said to them, "[I see] the parchments burning and the letters taking flight." They said to him, "You, too, open your mouth and let the flame enter you." He said to them, "It is better that He who gave her [the soul] should take her, and I shall not harm myself." The executioner[31] said to him, "Rabbi, if I increase the flame and take the woolen sponges away from your heart, will you bring me to the life of the coming world?" He said to him, "Yes". "Swear to me." He swore to him. He immediately increased the flame and took the woolen sponges away from his heart. He died quickly. He [the executioner] too leaped into the blaze. An Echo went forth saying, "R. Hanina ben Teradyon and the executioner are elected for the life of the coming world." Rabbi [Judah ha-Nasi] wept, saying, "There is one who makes his world in a moment while another makes his world in years." (Ibid.)

R. Hananiah ben Teradyon here has three different conversations: with his daughter, with his students, and with the executioner. From his answer to his daughter, we learn that being burnt with the Scroll of the

Law is deeply symbolical for him. In his answer to his students, we are told of his vision of the burning of the scroll but are moved by his apparent disassociation of that event from his own martyrdom. The martyrdom of the executioner seems to be only accidentally connected with that of R. Hananiah. The conversation between the two martyrs seems to cast a shadow of insincerity upon the Rabbi, who promises salvation to the non-Jew, and the discrepancy concerning the rabbi's approval of the hurrying of his own death is confusing. In order to view what is behind this fragmentary expression of tradition we must, again, turn to its parallel:

> When R. Haninah ben Teradyon was arrested, he was condemned to be burnt together with his Scroll. . . . A certain philosopher stood up to his overlord, saying, "My lord, do not let the fact that you have burnt the Torah go to your head, for whence she has emerged she has returned to her Father's house." He said to him, "Tomorrow you will suffer the same fate as they [the sage with his wife and daughter]." He said to him, "You have borne me good news: That tomorrow my share will be with them for the coming world." (*Sifre* to Deuteronomy 32:4 [307, p. 346])

The notion of the Torah "returning to her Father's house" is part of an imagery in which God is viewed as the father of Israel as well as her lover-bridegroom.

> "Go forth, O ye daughters of Zion, And gaze upon king Solomon, Even upon the crown wherewith his mother hath crowned him in the day of his espousals,[32] And in the day of the gladness of his heart" (Song of Songs 3:11). "The day of his espousals" is the giving of the Torah. "And in the day of the gladness of his heart" is the building of the Temple. (M *Ta'anit* 4:8)[33]

King Solomon is interpreted to mean God, "'upon King Solomon', the King to Whom peace belongs'[34]" (*Sifra* to Leviticus 9 [no. 15, p. 192]). And Israel is His "mother," "'his mother' can only mean Israel" (ibid.).[35] God is, first of all, Israel's father:

> R. Johanan said: R. Simeon ben Yohai asked R. Eleazar ben R. Yose, saying: Did you, perhaps, hear from your father what is the meaning of, ". . . upon the crown wherewith his mother hath crowned him . . ." He said to him, "Yes." He said to him, "What, then?" He said to him, "Like a king who had an only daughter and he loved her too much: And he would call her, 'my daughter'. And his love for her did not wane and he started to call her, 'my sister'. And his love for her did not wane and he started to call her, 'my mother'. In the same way, the Holy One Blessed is

He loved Israel too much. And He called them, 'My daughter' just as the verse says, 'Hearken, O daughter, and consider' (Psalm 45:11).[36] And His love for them did not wane and He started to call them, 'My sister', as the verse says, 'Open to Me, My sister, My love' (Song of Songs 5:2). And His love for them did not wane and He started to call them, 'My mother', as the verse says, 'Attend unto Me, O My people, And give ear unto Me, O My mother[37]' (Isaiah 51:4)." R. Simeon ben Yohai stood up and kissed him on the head and said, "Had I come for no other reason than to hear from you this interpretation it would have been worthwhile!" (*Song of Songs Rabbah* to 3:11)

The Song of Songs, in this reading, speaks of the relationship of God and Israel as an erotic, that is, mystical, relationship—a relationship emanating from a yearning grounded in the very being of the two partners. In this relationship, God views Israel the bride first as his daughter. This means that he, as it were, totally possesses her because he gives her life and meaning. In the maturing of the beloved and of love itself, passionate possession gives way to a practiced and accepted intimacy and oneness— Israel is then his "sister." Finally, in his "too great" love for Israel, the bride becomes a well of life and feeling, the People are the Mother, and God, as it were, is born out of the womb of the being in the world of Israel—as if without knowing them one cannot know him! What historian could describe more knowingly a love story between a People and God! Can only the martyr return to the pristine passion of possession?

In the marriage of God and Israel, the toiling in the Law (Torah study) and prayer (crystalized in the temple ritual) are a cohabitation (M *Ta'anit*, ibid.). Rabbinic tradition attempts here, perhaps too facilely, to combine the mystic way with that of the Law, as if the former may smoothly emanate from the latter. For the martyrial consciousness, even if it belongs to a sage of the Law, the way of salvation is immediate, personal, perhaps even impetuous; and he therefore is closer to understanding the erotic imagery of the Song of Songs.

In both versions, that of the *Sifre* and that of the Talmud, the burning of the Scroll of the Law is infused with metaphysical meaning. The two versions are based on the same unusual perception of the event, a perception by a martyial consciousness. In the *Sifre*, the Torah "returns to her Father's house." As in the Talmud, where the martyr R. Hananiah ben Teradyon sees the "parchments burning and the letters taking flight," the Torah survives the burning of its incarnation. But from the *Sifre*, we learn that the assurance of the Torah's survival is given because the Torah does pass through a cosmic crisis; the existence not merely of the individual Scroll but of the Law itself has been threatened. In the Talmudic version, the letters "take flight," an image used elsewhere to describe the Breaking of the Tablets by Moses at Sinai:

> It was repeated in the name of R. Nehemiah: The writing itself took flight [when Moses broke the Tablets]. R. Ezra said in the name of R. Judah bar R. Simeon: The Tablets weighed forty *se'ah* and the writing held them up. When the writing took flight they weighed down on Moses's hands and fell and broke. (PT *Ta'aniot* 4:8 [68c])[38]

When the Tablets of the Law lost all content, Moses could bear them no longer. The breaking of the first Tablets thus is viewed as a negation of the Receiving of the Law. In R. Nehemiah's imagery, too, the Breaking of the Tablets means a withdrawal of the Divine communication from Israel, though he does not deny the initiative of Moses in the event. We must conclude that in the vision of the burning of the Scroll of the Law and the "letters taking flight," the martyr sees the destruction of an individual scroll as so horrendous that he sees the very word of God as the possession of all Israel going up in flames. After R. Meir ben Baruch of Rothenburg witnessed the public burning of the Talmud in France in 1242 the learned martyr[39] wrote:

Inquire, one burned in flames, of the well-being of your mourners, who yearn
  to live in the court of your dwelling,
Who stretch out in pain on the very earth, who are bewildered at the burning
  of your parchments,
They wander in darkness, no glow to be seen, who hope for the light of day
  which will shine upon them and upon thee;

My rock in flame and fire, was it for this He gave thee, that in the end a fire
  should blaze around thee?
Sinai! Was it for this that He chose you, decrying the greater, to shine on your
  crest,
To herald the faith, that she should wane in dishonor?
Let me tell thee a parable:
Like a king who wept at his son's festivity, for he knew he would die, so are
  you in your words!
Hide in a cloak, Mount Sinai, clothe you in sackcloth, don the garment of
  widowhood, change you your garb.
I will shed my tears, till they become a stream and reach to the graves of your
  princes,
Moses, and Aaron on Mount Hor, and I will ask if there be a new Torah
  wherefore they have burnt your scrolls?

Let my eyes empty out all the wells of my tears, for all who still clutch at the
  hem of your cloak,
Let them sear on my cheeks, my compassion overwhelms me, at the wandering
  of your Husband.
He has taken His bag of silver with Him, He is gone a long journey, and with
  Him have not your soothing shadows fled?
And I have remained bereaved and alone without them, like a mast on the peak
  of your towers. (From the *Kinot* of the Ninth of Av according to the
  Ashkenazi custom)

This elegy is chanted to this day on the fast of the Ninth of Av (com-
memorating the destruction of the Temple).

It is in the martyrial consciousness that a local event takes on cosmic
proportions, because for the martyr all of existence turns on the immediacy of the here-and-now moment. For the martyr, the immediate
moment may suffer no compromise. Either he acts properly now or all is
lost; he therefore does not hesitate to relinquish now the completeness of
his living, sacrificing all, his world as he lives it now, in order to save all.
To the martyr, the fate of all too much pivots on the point of his immediate behavior; how else can we understand his readiness to sacrifice what
for many is all of being? We have here no mere egoistic stance but a
sensitivity to the intenseness of all being, a sensitivity that defines the
nature of all tragedy not merely of his own. Thus, R. Hananiah ben
Teradyon views the burning of the Scroll of the Law in the immediacy of
the here-and-now moment as a vortex around which all else pales; and
thus that local event becomes an event of cosmic import.

In the *Sifre*, the Torah returns "whence she has emerged . . . to her
father's house." A similar image is used by the Bavli in the account of the
destruction of the Temple:

> The Rabbis repeated: When the first Temple was destroyed young priests
> gathered around in groups, holding the keys to the sanctuary in their
> hands. And they went up on the roof of the sanctuary and said before
> Him, "Master of the World, since we were not worthy to be devoted
> trustees let the keys be held by You." And they threw them upwards. And
> something like the palm of a hand came out and received them from
> them. And they [the young priests] jumped and fell into the blaze. (BT
> *Ta'anit* 29a)

Youth possesses most completely because it is potential and hope. And the
priestly youth, the pride and the future of priestly yearnings, discern most
deeply the turning point that is the destruction of the Temple. They have

possessed most, they still dreamed of the future, therefore they know the tragedy most. For them the present suddenly has become everything and despair and nothingness all of reality. Naught remains but the all-embracing, all-meaning act of martyrdom. The tragedy of destruction was so great for them that history itself ended, there could not be anything else, no continuation, no afterglow, no redemption.

In the *Sifre*, the burning of the Scroll is an event of dispossession. The Torah "returns to her Father's house" as if in widowhood; the tragedy of the Torah is congruent with that of the martyr and thus with that of Israel. But the return to the father's house also is a return to a pristine state. Love may be again, there may ensue new relationships, there is a return to beginnings, to freshness, to openness, to dreams and possession, indeed to the father. The philosopher admonishes his overlord not to let his seeming power go to his head because, although the tragedy for Israel is real, it is at the same time a new beginning, an arrival. Unlike the talmudic version, where we might misunderstand the martyr's vision as a vision only of cosmic crises and survival, from the *Sifre* we understand that the event is not merely something to be survived; it has a positive meaning as well: In the talmudic version, we thus should view the "burning of the parchments and the flight of the letters" as an event of purification. Remember! The martyr's vision is determined by his understanding of his own death as a positive event; he does not view himself as surviving *despite* his martyrdom but rather he has real being *because* of his martyrdom.

This, then, is the key to grasping the image behind both versions. R. Hananiah ben Teradyon sees the burning of the Scroll of the Law in such a way because he is a martyr; and in turn, his vision says how the martyr views his martyrdom. For the martyr, his death is a death of Isaac, a destruction of all Israel. It is a cosmically shattering event. But, precisely because of its horrendousness, his death is a moment of real and complete being. In its tragedy lies its positive meaning, in the limbo of complete abandonment to the moment lies power and heroism. One may characterize the martyrial consciousness by saying that it is an infinitely developed sensitivity to the intenseness of the I-world in the immediacy of the present.

Now we understand the consoling quality that the burning of the Scroll of the Law has for R. Hananiah ben Teradyon according to the talmudic version. The martyr's vision assures him of the reality of his own death as a martyrdom. Both holocausts are cosmic events, and "If I was burning alone it would be hard for me; now that I am burning and the Scroll of the Law is together with me, He Who avenges the dishonoring of the Scroll of the Law will avenge my dishonoring." It is not surprising that, immediately following this remark his students gape at him and ask,

"Rabbi, what is it that you see?" And upon hearing a description of his vision they urge him to embrace death, since death is certain: "You, too, open your mouth and let the flame enter you."

At this point, there enters into the talmudic version an element that turns out to be incongruous. While the executioner "makes his world" by hastening the sage's death, as well as his own, the sage himself is said to have refrained from so doing. This is evidence that the story about R. Hananiah ben Teradyon concerns views that were significant and controversial in the rabbinic circles. Our seemingly unified story actually is made up from separate influences, together giving expression to a real tension and ambivalence.

I think it is fair to say that Rabbi's tears express a profound discomfort with the martyrial consciousness: "Rabbi wept, saying, 'There is one who makes his world in a moment while another makes his world in years.'⁴⁰" Remember the following story about the sage whose name the Mishnah bears (*Mishnat Rabbi Yehuda ha-Nasi*):

> On the day Rabbi [Judah ha-Nasi] died the Rabbis decreed a fast and prayed. And they said, "Whoever will say [first] that Rabbi died, let him be struck with a sword." Rabbi's maidservant went up on the roof. She said, "The upper ones want Rabbi and the lower ones want Rabbi: May it be the Will that the lower ones overcome the upper ones." Upon seeing how many times he was forced to cleanse himself, each time removing and replacing his *tefillin*, and how he suffered, she said, "May it be the Will that the upper ones overcome the lower ones." But the Rabbis were praying incessantly. [So] she took a jug and hurled it from the roof. The praying was [momentarily] silenced; and Rabbi died. The Rabbis said to Bar Kappara, "Go and inspect." He went and learned that he had died. He rent his clothing but turned the tear to the other side [so that it should not be seen]. He began by saying, "The celestial ones and the upright ones grasped the holy ark; the celestial ones were victorious over the upright ones and the holy ark was abducted." They said to him, "He died?" He said to them, "It is you who have said it, but I have not said it."
>
> As Rabbi was dying he raised his ten fingers upwards and said, "Master of the World, it is manifestly clear before You that I have labored in the Torah with my ten fingers yet have not taken any personal benefit even with my little finger. May it be desirable before You that there be peace in my resting." An Echo went forth saying, "He entereth into peace, They rest in their beds, [Each one that walketh in his uprightness]" (Isaiah 57:2) (BT *Ketubbot* 104a)

Rabbi Judah ha-Nasi, referred to by his students as Our Holy Teacher, was a pharisee's pharisee. Under his leadership, the long process of completing and editing the Mishnah, a process spanning several generations, was finally brought to completion, at the beginning of the third century. The mishnaic literature is the classic literary statement of the notion of the authority of the Law. And Rabbi Judah played an equally important role in the dissemination of the Mishnah throughout Israel and the Diaspora by virtue of his charismatic personality and political power, as well as through the untiring efforts of his devoted pupils. His primary interest was in the question How does a *talmid hakham*, a rabbinic Jew, act out his essential being? For him religiosity meant a particular mode of being in the world throughout a lifetime and not a breakthrough experience or a rite of passage.

> It was repeated: When Rabbi fell ill R. Hiyya came to see him and found him crying. He said to him, "Rabbi, why are you crying, has it not been repeated: If one died in the midst of smiling it is a comely sign for him, in the midst of crying it is an uncomely sign for him. . . ." He said to him, "I am crying because [I am parting with] Torah and *mitzvot*." (Ibid. 103b)

Rabbi's final prayer is not for death as a passage to a long preferred existence, it is the prayer of an exhausted man finally giving in to impotence. We have this same motif in the prayers of the maidservant. When she senses the shadow of death across her master's bed she cries out the cry of the living for life. But, in her sensitivity as a woman, she feels the sage's suffering, not only the agonizing pain of a man dying in the grip of intestinal disorder but also—no, more so—the anguish of a man who cannot accept the dehumanization brought on by his deteriorating condition. And so she prays that death be surrendered to, that Rabbi's being in the world be relinquished for a different-worldliness. It is important to sense that although we undoubtedly are dealing with a milieu in which belief in life after death is unquestioned—and indeed the very language of the story bears this out—nevertheless, the tragedy of death is unmitigated. The maidservant's second prayer thus is a surrender to death, a relinquishing. Her forceful stopping of the rabbis' prayer is an act of frustration and despair. So, too, when Rabbi raises his failing hands, he sees hands that are worn out with a labor of love, drained by the strain of striving to be as one should be. In his illness that struggle to be has intensified. The vast energy that the man has put into acting out the Law is now pitted against that which will end his very being in the world, and he is not up to his final striving, his strength finally is vanquished. Rabbi's death is not the heroic death of the martyr who "makes his world in a moment," but the passive death of exhaustion.

This, then, is the struggle between the "celestial ones and the upright ones," in the words of Bar Kappara. He is quoted as using the words "celestial ones and upright ones" rather than the phrase attributed to the maidservant, "the upper ones and the lower ones." Bar Kappara's words are chosen differently. It is not a struggle between two modes of human existence, a lower one and a higher one. It rather is a struggle between the drive to be in the only sense meaningful to man as he knows himself—that is, to live—and a beingness that is knowable by the angels but separated from man by death. It is a struggle man wins by being man, by living, by being mortal, and that the angels can win only when man dies. To be alive contradicts the truth of death. We live as if we will never die, as if we could escape death by overlooking it. The prohibition, imposed by those who surround Rabbi during his death agonies, against speaking of the sage's death, would be a parody of the way we live, except that in desperation and despair there is no sense of humor.

Thus, as in Rabbi's prayer, death is man's defeat. Should we be surprised, then, to be told that Rabbi wept when he heard that death was a victory?

It is not surprising, therefore, to discover that the literary remains of the martyrdom of R. Hananiah ben Teradyon bear witness to different attitudes toward his stance. In the Babylonian Talmud, these attitudes are mingled together in a seemingly organic story. Such piecing together of literary fragments is not an uncommon phenomenon in the talmudic literature. Thus, the traditions concerning the improper behavior of R. Hananiah and his family (the later saboraic softening of some of this material not withstanding) represent a negative opinion of the martyrial posture, while the denial of death by the martyr himself is an adjustment of the original story because of a discomfort with its implications. In that version of the story where the martyrial consciousness is looked upon positively, the promise of salvation to the executioner does not ring false because it is in keeping with the martyr's view of the auspiciousness of heroic death. Note that, in the *Sifre*, the notion of the Torah "returning to her Father's house," the parallel to R. Hananiah ben Teradyon's vision of the ascending letters, is attributed to the "philosopher," a non-Jew! That is clear evidence that we have before us the fragmentary remains of more than one telling of the martyr's story.[41]

Chapter Seven

If I Am Here, All Are Here

We may effect a clearer vision of the martyrial consciousness, and perhaps even move toward a synthesis of all we have discussed on the matter till now, by looking at a different but, as we shall see, parallel biographical story. We shall examine some aspects of the remembered religiosity of the famous sage Hillel the Elder, who flourished around the time of the birth of Jesus.

> It was repeated: It was said about Hillel the Elder that when he rejoiced in the *Simḥat Bet ha-Sho'avah* [Temple festivity during *Sukkot*] he said thusly, "If I am here, all are here, and if I am not here, who is here?" He was wont to say thusly, "To the place I love, that is where my legs take me.[1] If You will come to my house, I will come to Your house, if You will not come to my house, I will not come to Your house. . . ."[2] It was he, too, who saw a skull floating on the water: He said to it, "Because you drowned another, you were drowned, and he who drowned you will drown."[3] (BT *Sukkah* 53a)

The Palestinian Talmud describes this scene differently, thereby allowing us a wider insight into the figure behind the brittle literary pieces:

> Hillel the Elder, when he saw us doing so [rejoicing in the *Simḥat Bet ha-Sho'avah*] hastily, would say, "If we are here, who is here? And does He need our praises? Is it not written, 'Thousand of thousands ministered unto him, and ten thousand times ten thousand stood before him' (Daniel 7:10)." When he saw us doing so properly he would say, "If we were not here, who would be here? For though there are before Him

many hymns of praise, the praises of Israel are dearer than all. Why? [Because it is written,] 'the sweet singer of Israel' (II Samuel 23:1) [and] 'enthroned upon the praises of Israel' (Psalms 22:4)." (PT *Sukkah* 5:4 [55b–c])

The Palestinian tradition recalls Hillel's view as being given over by a teacher to his students. There, the stress is on his encouragement of a more authentic religious devotion on the students' part. The Babylonian Talmud, on the other hand, describes Hillel not as he preaches but rather as he himself rejoices before God. With this in mind, the Palestinian Talmud's version can serve as a background for a more living understanding of the Babylonian's. The Palestinian version begins with a sense of man's smallness. If man does something hurriedly, then his inner depth, which is the uniqueness of his self, is blurred and is as naught. Man in a hurry is small indeed, it is as if no one were there, as if the Temple court were empty, the impatient students mere shadows. When man dares stand before God in haste, let alone to praise him, he is negated in the awesomeness of the Lord of Hosts. But, when a man does something with concentration, when he brings his "holiest depths" to bear on his actions, then he is being his inimitable and true self, then he may sense that he is unique, irreplaceable. Remember that Hillel tells this to his students as a group and therefore uses the plural pronoun. For the dimension of personal experience, we have the testimony of the Babylonian Talmud, to which we shall return in a moment. But, even in the Palestinian version, we sense the struggle in the sage's words between the perception of experience as 'we' and as 'I'.

"The praises of Israel are dearer than all. Why? [Because it is written,] 'the sweet singer of Israel' [and] 'enthroned upon the praises of Israel'."

> Now these are the last words of David:
> The saying of David the son of Jesse,
> And the saying of the man raised on high,
> The anointed of the God of Jacob,
> And the sweet singer of Israel:
> The spirit of the Lord spoke by me,
> And His word was upon my tongue. (II Samuel 23:1, 2)

The poet is the "sweet singer of Israel," but he speaks nonetheless as David, "the anointed of the God of Jacob," as the chosen individual to whom and by whom God speaks.

> My God, My God, why hast Thou forsaken me,
> And art far from my help at the words of my cry?

O my God, I call by day, but Thou answerest not;
And at night, and there is no surcease for me.
Yet Thou art holy,
O Thou that art enthroned upon the praises of Israel.
In Thee did our fathers trust;
They trusted, and Thou didst deliver them.
Unto Thee they cried, and escaped;
In Thee did they trust, and were not ashamed.
But I am a worm, and no man;
A reproach of men, and despised of the people. (Psalms 22:2–7)

Be not far from me; for trouble is near;
For there is none to help. (Ibid. v. 12)

My strength is dried up like a potsherd;
And my tongue cleaveth to my throat;
And Thou layest me in the dust of death. (Ibid. v. 16)

I will declare Thy name unto my brethren;
In the midst of the congregation will I praise Thee:
'Ye that fear the Lord, praise Him;
All ye the seed of Jacob, glorify Him;
And stand in awe of Him, all ye the seed of Israel.
For He hath not despised nor abhorred the lowliness of the poor;
Neither hath He hid His face from him;
But when he cried unto Him, He heard.'
From Thee cometh my praise in the great congregation;
I will pay my vows before them that fear Him. (Ibid. v. 23–26)

The poet knows the depth of suffering, the terrible need for deliverance, as a lonely I, as "a worm, and no man; A reproach of men, and despised of the people" (7). That recognition of need is so great that in it man finds the unbelievable strength to beseech God, the Almighty God of Israel. The need for deliverance is in the greatness of humility. But David, "the anointed of the God of Jacob" (II Samuel 23:1), becomes "the sweet singer of Israel" (Ibid.) "in the midst of the congregation" (Psalms 22:23). Only through a vision of the Almighty that comes with the ecstasy of participating in Peoplehood does man rise to the summit of poetry, daring to praise God. For praise stems not from the depths of need but from the grand vision of beauty and perfection.

From Thee cometh my praise in the great congregation;
I will pay my vows before them that fear Him. (Ibid. v. 26)

Man cannot praise God without knowing the need for deliverance, and this he knows in the lonely cry of "My God, my God, why hast Thou forsaken me" (ibid. v. 2). But the ability to praise God is an ecstatic one, it stems from man's drawing out beyond himself. It is the humble man with knowledge of his own need who rises above himself in the being that is ever greater than himself and becomes the religious poet:

> The preparations of the heart are man's,
> But the answer of the tongue[4] is from the Lord. (Proverbs 16:1)

Thus, the context of the verses quoted by Hillel reveal to us a sense of the self in dialectic with the People. The joyful praise of God is said by Israel; but it is grounded in the being of the self. This interpretation is borne out by the tradition preserved in the Babylonian Talmud, but we have not, as yet, listened carefully enough to the Palestinian version.

The Palestinian version centers around a point that is only implicit in the Babylonian. Hillel perceives the organic connection between the sense of joy and the sense of potency. Joy is incomplete when the praise of God is incomplete. Haste, in blurring the self, causes man a profound impotency, his joy is then not genuine, it is not harmony with the self but a forgetting of the self, a mere dancing to a tune heard from afar. Man may praise God only when he has a strength rooted in his depths. Without that, no ecstasy of belonging can raise him to any heights. Joy, in this sense, can never occur unless man is happy with himself; and in the *Simhat Bet ha-Sho'avah*, for Hillel, that happiness with oneself stems from the sense that one is potent in the ability to praise God. Thus, in stressing the importance of how his students are acting, Hillel is stressing the stance of the I before God in the joyousness of the Temple court. This notion is important for understanding the Babylonian version, which, in turn, shows us beyond doubt that for Hillel the experience of the self is central.

The scene depicted in the Babylonian Talmud, as I have said, does not show Hillel teaching but Hillel acting out his teachings. In the personal experience of joy before God, the content of the sage's teaching takes on a concrete reality that requires it to be described in different language than that which couches his teaching as such. Here, the self is not a theoretical grounding for the personal strength that must be available to one who would truly praise God. Here, the theological vision, so ripe as to burst into the flowering of an experience of the self, is overwhelmed by the vitality the self actually shows. As moderns we may comment that man's perception of the world as an I is a reigning of the self over the world. Man experiences being only in so much as he is a perceiving self. Thus, the world he knows is one in which his perception of it is a pivotal point. In the religious experience described, Hillel intuitively recognizes the central-ity of the self.

When Hillel says, "If I am here, all are here, and if I am not here, who is here?" he obviously does not mean that he is totally alone and complete as a man in the third person. Surely, for others, Hillel's presence in the Temple is neither a presence of all men nor does his absence deprive them of all men. Although it may be historically unconvincing to attribute to a first century sage a modern sensibility of the self, we must admit that Hillel at least distinguishes between a man's experience as himself and another's perception of that event. The man standing before God can say "If I am here, all are here"; this cannot be said of him by another.

Hillel experiences the overwhelming vitality of the self in a moment of joy. We have learned from the Palestinian version that that the sense of joy is organically connected with the sense of personal spiritual potency. In the language of a modern sensibility, we may say that in a moment of elation, stemming from a personal sense of achievement or power, the I-perception of the world (the fact that we perceive the world subjectively, as selves, that is) legitimates the conviction that the totality of humanity is included in the self's perception of being. If being is known as a subjective reality, as a perception of the I, then my own perception of the world, precisely because it is subjective, is a complete perception of being as well as the only perception of reality, for me, because others' perception can add nothing to the completeness of my subjective perception. If it could, it would do so only by being absorbed into my perception as an I. And, conversely, what I do not perceive is not, for my self, a perception by an I, it is not a subjective reality, it does not partake of being as I know it (leaving aside completely the question What is truth?). That perceived by others, inasmuch as it is transmittable to me, is by its very nature "objec-tive", that is, it is an object of which I can speak without including the word *I*. Unless, as we said, that "objective" knowledge is absorbed by my self in such a way that it becomes my own perception and, by definition, subjective, for me, it is not a true knowledge of reality. To get back again to Hillel: his experience of rejoicing before God is so rich that he knows that were others to join him it would change the quantitative reality of the experience but not its qualitative reality. And were he himself not to experience it, it would remain, for him, a hearsay experience, an experience of man in the third person, not an experience of reality as he knows it. Thus, Hillel's experience is microcosmic; it stands for the experience of all humanity.

The model of the psyche–world relationship that I have used here is a modern one and, of course, must be applied to Hillel with caution. Still, I think it is legitimate to picture his psychological experience by using a model that is familiar to us. This can help us at least to get some feeling for what is behind the unusual literary crystallizations that tradition has left us concerning Hillel. "He [Hillel the Elder] was wont to say: If I am not for me, who is for me?" No other can replace the being of self. On the other hand, "And when I am for myself, what am I?" (M *Avot* 1:14). One must know, too, that the being of the self is a being that encompasses the entire experienced world, especially other people. "Hillel [the Elder]5 says: . . . And do not judge your friend until you find yourself in his place" (ibid. 2:4). Remember the being of your friend as a total self as well!

Hillel does *not* speak of a solipsistic self nor does he even speak of the importance of an "inner world" as compared to an "outer world." Man's being remains always a living in the world. Hillel is speaking of man's standing before God, or confronting the world, as a self. This event is not a "subject–object" relationship where one "half" can be discussed without the other. As we saw earlier, man can feel that his rejoicing before God is complete and all encompassing because *God wants* man, "'For though there are before Him many hymns of praise [from the angels], the praises of Israel are dearer than all'" (PT ibid.). That is to say, man's stance is meaningful because it is before God, who turns toward man in love.

"He was wont to say thusly, 'To the place I love, that is where my legs take me'" (BT ibid.). Man's love is true in his expression of it. Hillel feels he is borne along toward the goal he himself loves, as if he were carried there without conscious volition. This is very interesting for our discussion for two reasons. First of all, it presents the awareness of self. The "real I" is the "I love," the self in the modern sense, and the legs are completely subservient to the impassioned determination of the self. Second, Hillel's insight recognizes that the true drives of the self are not experienced as "free choice." The self is the totally autonomous agent in the sage's movement to "the place," but the sage experiences that movement as something that overwhelms him. The experience of man as an I before God is one of love and of movement, both indicating the sense of self as always in a relationship with some other. And "that is where my legs take me" indicates that that relationship is always an action. "If You will come to my house, I will come to Your house, if You will not come to my house, I will not come to Your house." Man's "coming to God" is inseparable to "God's coming to man"; both are one event. Whereas the "coming to God" would be experienced as being carried along by one's legs, without a volitional motor decision, the "not coming to God" would be a conscious, and no doubt painful, decision. It would not be a true expression of self; that is to say, for Hillel the Elder, it would be inauthentic of the being as self.

For Hillel, being as self means living the "I love." Compare this with the material in the Babylonian Talmud immediately following that concerning Hillel:

> R. Johanan said: A person's legs, they are responsible for him; to the place where he is required, thither do they bring him. Two black men who were at Solomon's court, Elihoreph and Ahijah the sons of Shisha, were Solomon's scribes (I Kings 4:3). One day he [Solomon] saw the Angel of Death who was unhappy. He said to him, "Why are you unhappy?" He said to him, "Because these two black men who sit here are being required of me." He [Solomon] gave them over to demons and sent them off to the province of Luz [wherein the Angel of Death is, supposedly, not permitted to pass; BT *Sotah* 46b]. When they arrived in the province of Luz they died. The next day he [Solomon] saw the Angel of Death who was happy. He said to him, "Why are you happy?" He said to him, "To the place where they were required of me, thither did you send them." Whereupon Solomon pronounced: A person's legs, they are responsible for him; to the place where he is required, thither do they bring him. (BT *Sukkah* ibid.)

The parallel in form between R. Johanan's (Palestine, third century) words, "A person's legs . . . to the place where he is required, thither do they bring him," and Hillel's, "To the place I love, that is where my legs take me," is striking.[6] The difference is that Hillel is speaking about the determining quality of the "I love" while R. Johanan is speaking about a fate. "Man's legs, they are responsible for him" indicates a certain sense of dissociation between man's movement and his self, a certain sense of alienation with the self. And that sense of fate, "where he is required," to which R. Johanan alludes so softly from a knowledge of inescapability, is ironically and tragically developed in the story about King Solomon's scribes. The fate alluded to, says the story, is the most powerful and final fate of all, death. Thus, an image Hillel uses to convey the determining nature of self is used, in the later material, to suggest the ineluctable and frightening power of the Angel of Death!

"It was he [Hillel], too, who saw a skull floating on the water. He said to it, "Because you drowned another, you were drowned, and he who drowned you will drown.'" To Hillel, the stance of the self in the world is the essence of man's living for evil man as well. The murderer determines his living through a life of violence and his own action becomes his fate. Hillel sees this not as a prophecy but as an interpretation of the ghastly sight he comes across.

> The Rabbis repeated: It happened that Hillel the Elder[7] was coming on the way when he heard the sound of a scream in the city. He said, "I am assured that it is not in my house." And about him scripture says: "He

shall not be afraid of evil tidings; His heart is steadfast, trusting in the Lord" (Psalms 112:7). (BT *Berakhot* 60a)[8]

The sage, who is convinced of the truth of the self–world stance, who in rejoicing before God says, "If I am here, all are here," has the inner strength of vision to see a personal light in the world, to live even in hell (as we might call it) with the conviction that the warmth of his home is real and enduring whereas the swirling chaos without can be warded off. This strength, by which man in his faith overtakes the world, we have already seen in our discussion of the martyrial consciousness. Once again, Hillel and the martyr meet.

The preoccupation with the self–world stance carries with it the perception of the present, the here and now, as the real dimension of being:

> He [Hillel the Elder] was wont to say: If I am not for me, who is for me? And when I am for myself, what am I? And if not now, when? (M *Avot* 1:14)

> Hillel [the Elder][9] says. . . . And don't say, "When I find time I'll study"; lest you not find time. (Ibid., 2:4)

Religious man is to live with the sense that if there is not a present, that if his religiosity does not take place now, then all is lost. One is to learn Torah with the sense that other than in the present the nothingness of death closes in. The awareness of impending death must force us to accept the tyranny of being in the present. It is interesting to compare Shammai's statement: "Shammai [a colleague of Hillel the Elder] says: Make your [studying of] Torah your fixed [main] occupation" (ibid., 1:15). Since the word *Torah* is in the possessive, your Torah, we may assume that Shammai is referring to the studying of Torah, like Hillel (ibid., 2:4).[10] Both sages see man's being in the dimension of time as critical to the study of Torah. But, for Shammai, one must bring a certain order to the flux of time, by studying regularly as one's fixed and main occupation; while for Hillel, the realization of the unique reality that belongs to the present is important. Here, again, we note a parallel between Hillel and the martyr, who "makes his world in a moment"—now; and "If not now, when?"

> It was repeated: It was said about Shammai the Elder that throughout all his days he ate in honor of the Sabbath:[11] If he found nice meat he would say, "This is for the Sabbath." If he found a nicer one he would put the second one aside [for the Sabbath] and eat the first. But Hillel the Elder had a different characteristic: That all his actions were for the sake of Heaven, as the verse says, "Blessed be the Lord, day by day He beareth

our burden, Even the God who is our salvation" (Psalms 68:20). It was also repeated thusly: Bet Shammai say: [prepare] from Sunday for the Sabbath. And Bet Hillel say: "Blessed be the Lord day by day . . ." (BT *Bezah* 16a)

Shammai lived his life in a rhythm of the limbo of expectation and the satisfaction of arrival, as it were of the awaiting of salvation and its arrival. As if the fullness of the here and now was not to be had except on the Sabbath, as if the six days of the week were to be lived out somewhat surreptitiously, a mere expectant prelude to the seventh day. But for Hillel, the present is too dear to be merely an intermezzo, and the Lord is to be blessed day by day. And how could that which is only becoming, which still hides in the uncertainty of the future, bear down more heavily on religious man's attention than the earthy now? Similarly, how could the martyr bear any delay in the fullest realization of his being?

Can we find evidence of a martyrial tendency in the biography of Hillel the Elder?

The Rabbis repeated: A poor man, a rich man and an evil man come to Judgment. To the poor man it is said, "Why did you not busy yourself with the Torah?" If he answers, "I was poor and was taken up with my living", he is told, "Were you any poorer than Hillel?" It was told about Hillel the Elder that every day he would work enough to earn a *victoriatus*; half of it he would give to the caretaker of the house of learning and half of it was for the support of him and his family. Once it happened that he was not able to earn anything and the caretaker of the house of learning did not let him enter. He went up and sat on the edge of the skylight, leaning over in order to hear the words of the living God[12] from the mouths of Shemaiah and Avtalyon. It was told that that day was the eve of the Sabbath and in the deep of winter, and snow poured down on him from the sky. When the dawn rose, Shemaiah said to Avtalyon, "Avtalyon my brother, every day the house is illuminated yet today it is dark, is it perhaps, that the day is so cloudy?" They looked up and saw the silhouette of a man in the skylight. They went up and found four feet of snow piled up on top of him. They took him down and washed him and oiled his body and made him sit opposite the blazing fire. They said, "This one is worthy of having the Sabbath profaned for him [in order to save him]." (BT *Yoma* 35b)

It is possible that this tradition, attributing to Hillel, in his early period[13], behavior whereby he seems to be consciously endangering his very life, is evidence of a martyrial streak in the sage's biography. It also is possible, as I have more than hinted at, that the experience of joy before God meets the experience of martyrdom in a substratum of consciousness, the disproportion in their drama and greatness not sufficient to bifurcate them. That question remains for a study by itself.

Let us, in any case, remember the vision of the great martyr R. Hananiah ben Teradyon as the fire consumed him. He perceived the holocaust of the Scroll of the Law as he perceived his own. Its tragedy is the clear eye in the hurricane of chaos and absurdity, it is alone, it is unique, it is an epitome, it is all encompassing, it is cosmic. The martyr achieves a pinnacle of spiritual strength in his ability to concentrate all of his humanity in a single here-and-now moment of being. And he makes that tiny pinpoint of a moment in the vastness of time into an infinite one; and all history may tremble. Does not the martyr surely say, "If I am here, all are here, and if I am not here, who is here? And if not now, when?"

Chapter Eight

If Not Now, When? Repentance

We have seen that martyrdom as a Binding of Isaac is part of a scenario in which religious man is drawn into a dialectic of Law and martyrdom because he takes being in the world seriously and therefore is painfully sensitive to the existence of evil in the world. We shall now examine an experiential phenomenon that may serve as a focal point for viewing the directions of Law and martyrdom because of its central place in an experience of their dialectic. The phenomenon we have in mind is that designated by the Hebrew word *teshuva*, "return," which in a religious context is translated as "repentance."

> Wisdom was asked, "What shall be the sinner's punishment?" She answered, "Evil pursueth sinners" (Proverbs 13:21). Prophecy was asked,"What shall be the sinner's punishment?" She answered, "The soul that sinneth, it shall die" (Ezekiel 18:4). The Holy One Blessed is He was asked, "What shall be the sinner's punishment?" He answered, "Let him repent and thus be atoned." This is what is written, "Therefore doth He instruct sinners in the way" (Psalms 25:8): He instructs sinners in the way of repentance. (PT *Makkot* 2:7 [31d])

The nature of man as known by Wisdom points to a certain continuity and inevitability. Punishment in that view is an epitomization of the sinner's life. In sinning he spins a thread of fate into destruction. So, too, the prophet in his vision sees that road upon which the sinner is treading as a self-entrapment (the homilist has intentionally overlooked the context of Ezekiel's words). The man caught up in that way surely has surrendered to nothingness and death.

But the Holy One, blessed is he, knows man as he turns to God in yearning:

> Unto Thee, O Lord, do I lift up my soul.

> Show me Thy ways, O Lord;
> Teach me Thy paths.
> Guide me in Thy truth, and teach me;
> For Thou art the God of my salvation;
> For thee do I wait all the day.
> Remember, O Lord, Thy compassions and Thy mercies;
> For they have been from old.
> Remember not the sins of my youth, nor my transgressions;
> According to Thy mercy remember Thou me,
> For Thy goodness' sake, O Lord:
> Good and upright is the Lord:
> Therefore doth He instruct sinners in the way.

> For Thy name's sake, O Lord,
> Pardon mine iniquity, for it is great.

> See mine affliction and my travail:
> And forgive all my sins. (Psalms 25:1, 4–8, 11, 18)

Neither through wisdom nor through vision into the future can the way of repentance be known. As we shall see later, this statement does not arise merely in the whim of the homily. It rather echoes, albeit distantly, different attitudes toward the phenomenon of repentance. We shall have to ask and answer the question What is it about repentance that makes it knowable through God alone and not through Wisdom and Prophecy? If we gain insight in this question we shall be able to understand the different attitudes toward repentance as they find expression in our sources.

In Ezekiel we find an already developed and clear notion of repentance:

> And the word of the Lord came unto me, saying: "Son of man, when a land sinneth against Me by trespassing grievously, and I stretch out My hand upon it, and break the staff of the bread therefore, and send famine upon it, and cut off from it man and beast; though these three men, Noah, Daniel, and Job, were in it, they should deliver but their own souls by their righteousness, saith the Lord God. If I cause evil beasts to pass through the land, and they bereave it, and it be desolate, so that no man may pass through because of the beasts; though these three men were in it, as I live, saith the Lord God, they shall deliver neither sons nor

daughters: they only shall be delivered, but the land shall be desolate. Or if I bring a sword upon that land, and say: Let the sword go through the land, so that I cut off from it man and beast; though these three men were in it, as I live, saith the Lord God, they shall deliver neither sons nor daughters, but they only shall be delivered themselves. Or if I send a pestilence into that land, and pour out my fury upon it in blood, to cut off from it man and beast; though Noah, Daniel, and Job were in it, as I live, saith the Lord God, they shall deliver neither son nor daughter; they shall but deliver their own souls by their righteousness. (Ezekiel 14:12–20)

Ezekiel here views the biography of an individual as self-contained. A complete drama of action and deliverance may take place in the unity of a single man's life. Though God's will is acted out in history, in the retribution wrought on the land and its people through war and pestilence, and though no man amidst that death and chaos could possibly feel totally isolated and safe, nevertheless man's sense of the autonomy of his own personal being, of the intrinsic meaning of what happens around and within his personal sphere, is legitimate. For the sensitive soul, all happenings that caress or smite from even the distant outside drive home to an inner happiness or pain. That sense of the organismic nature of experience as centering around the self is true, says the prophet. As great as the shuddering of the righteous in the winds of chaos may be, his experience of deliverance will be as an individual. The prophet has focused on the world of man as an 'I' in the world of experience.

And the word of the Lord came unto me, saying: "What mean ye, that ye use this proverb in the Land of Israel, saying:

The fathers have eaten sour grapes,
And the children's teeth are set on edge?

As I live, saith the Lord God, ye shall not have occasion any more to use this proverb in Israel. Behold, all souls are Mine; as the soul of the father, so also the soul of the son is Mine; the soul that sinneth, it shall die." (Ibid. 18:1–4)

God knows the soul of each man—a complete knowledge in which the world which the soul is is known to Him. And so each and every man stands before God in the loneliness that is wholeness. Each man walks as an 'I' and bears his burden alone before God.

But if a man be just, and do that which is lawful and right, . . . hath walked in My statutes, and hath kept Mine ordinances, to deal truly; he is just, he shall surely live, saith the Lord God.

If he beget a son that is a robber, a shedder of blood, and that doeth to a brother any of these things, whereas he himself had not done any of these things, . . . shall he [the son] then live? He shall not live—he hath done all these abominations; . . . Now, lo, if he beget a son, that seeth all his father's sins, which he hath done, and considereth, and doeth not such like, . . . he shall not die for the iniquity of his father, he shall surely live. As for his father, . . . behold, he dieth for his iniquity. . . . The soul that sinneth, it shall die; the son shall not bear the iniquity of the father with him, neither shall the father bear the iniquity of the son with him; the righteousness of the righteous shall be upon him, and the wickedness of the wicked shall be upon him.

But if the wicked turn from all his sins that he hath committed, and keep all My statutes, and do that which is lawful and right, he shall surely live, he shall not die. None of his transgressions that he hath committed shall be remembered against him; for his righteousness that he hath done he shall live. Have I any pleasure at all that the wicked should die? saith the Lord God; and not rather that he should return from his ways and live?

But when the righteous turneth away from his righteousness, and committeth iniquity, and doeth according to all the abominations that the wicked man doeth, shall he live? None of his righteous deeds that he hath done shall be remembered; for his trespass that he trespassed, and for his sin that he hath sinned, for them shall he die.

When the righteous man turneth away from his righteousness, and committeth iniquity, he shall die therefor; for his iniquity that he hath done shall he die. Again, when the wicked man turneth away from his wickedness that he hath committed, and doeth that which is lawful and right, he shall save his soul alive. Because he considereth, and turneth away from all his transgressions that he hath committed, he shall surely live, he shall not die.

Therefore I will judge you, O house of Israel, every one according to his ways, saith the Lord God. Return ye, and turn yourselves from all your transgressions; so shall they not be a stumbling-block of iniquity unto you. Cast away from you all your transgressions, wherein ye have transgressed; and make you a new heart and a new spirit; for why will ye die, O house of Israel. For I have no pleasure in the death of him that dieth, saith the Lord God; wherefore turn yourselves, and live. (Ibid. 18:5, 9–11, 13, 14, 17, 18, 20–24, 26–28, 30–32)[1]

Not only does Ezekiel turn to the world of man as an individual, he focuses on what is most vivid in the experience of the self and thus most real—the present. In man's experience as an individual, the greater the distance of events from the self the vaguer they are and the more he must exert his power of ordering so as to bring those events into focus through some vector pointing to or from the self. So, too, with memory and anticipation. The further away they are, the more likely they are to be forgotten, unless he can succeed in drawing their meaning toward the present. Thus, memory, the one dimension in which the past still has being for man, is always surveyed from the vantage point of the present and looking outward. For experiencing man, the present is the vortex of being. If God is fascinated by man as he subjectively experiences the world, then God looks most fascinatedly on the present. Therefore, man must learn to live every moment with the absolute seriousness that his being before God demands. Here we are speaking neither of a cultic penitence for sin, nor of a forgiving judgment by God of the repentant man, nor even of a compassionate erasure of guilt. For Ezekiel here, repentance means man's being as essentially a being of the present, and thus both the righteous man and the evil man are judged by their present living and not by their past. Repentance thus says man's freedom in the sense that he is what he is now, not his memories nor his plans and promises. That is, of course, provided his actions in the present well up out of his sense of the absolute seriousness of the present, which makes the past fade away; this has nothing to do with that overflowing of a frivolity that prefers the immediate because it is at hand. This is acting in the present before God who judges man for life or death; it is not filling up time merely because it is there.

Although the stark centrality of the present in man's behavior before God may have been very luminous to the mighty visionary Ezekiel, it is not surprising that in Psalm 25, as we have seen, the psalmist can only imagine his own completeness of being in the present as God's merciful answer to his entreaties. Indeed, Ezekiel himself perceives the radical implication of the strength to live in the loneliness of the present: "Cast away from you all your transgressions, wherein ye have transgressed; and make you a new heart and a new spirit; for why will ye die, O house of Israel?" (Ibid.18:31). Man can escape the web of his own past only by boldly stepping into a new being, a being of the present.

> Included in the ways of repentance are that the repenter should . . . draw away greatly from that in which he sinned, and should change his name as if to say, "I am someone else—I am no longer the same man who did those deeds", and should change his actions—all of them—for the better and to follow the proper path . . . (Maimonides, *Yad, Teshuva* 2:4)[2]

This is no simple step, it is a task of "making a new heart and a new spirit." But the alternative to making oneself now, says Ezekiel, is death. It is no wonder that this gaping genius finally saw the salvation of Israel as a rising up of faded bones by the will of their God.

> And He said unto me: "Son of man, can these bones live?" And I answered: "O Lord God, Thou knowest."

> Therefore prophesy, and say unto them: Thus saith the Lord God: Behold, I will open your graves, and cause you to come up out of your graves, O My people; and I will bring you into the land of Israel.

> And I will put My spirit in you, and ye shall know that I the Lord have spoken, and performed it, saith the Lord." (Ibid. 37:3, 12, 14)

If we put these bold visions together: Man as an individual can escape death only by realizing the hope of his being in the lonely present; and this is to be done, finally, through God, who entreats Israel to repent and fills them with his spirit, lest Israel rely on its past and perish.

In the book of Jonah, we find a story that centers around the notion of repentance. Jonah is called by God to warn the people of the great Assyrian capital, Nineveh, that their sinfulness is overwhelming. He tries to deny this calling, and the fragment of Jonah's biography is the story of how he finally comes to fulfill his mission. Since the story ends with a justification of the acceptance by God of the city's repentance, by paying attention to the progress of Jonah's biography, we can learn something of the nature of repentance as seen by the book's author and, more important, as seen by those who solemnly read the book as the Day of Atonement wanes. We shall examine two questions: What is it that Jonah must live through before *he* can accept the repentance of the people of Nineveh? and What is true repentance?

Jonah reacts to God's calling by fleeing the divine word. One may say that he does so laconically. He does not say a word, he does not hesitate, we have not the slightest hint of an inner struggle or even of an attempt at justification of his behavior. This is not because the author lacks the literary sophistication to do so; when necessary, the few words Jonah utters are vivid and emotional (cf. Jonah 4:9). It is rather because the author wants to illustrate Jonah's total lack of readiness to consider the mission he is called upon to take. It is important for us to know this in order to appreciate the long journey the prophet takes from this simplistic beginning until the understanding incarnate in the final verse.

Jonah boards the boat bound for Tarshish, and the drama has begun, unfolding swiftly and surely. The little ship, no doubt clinging timidly to the shore line, is flung by God into a storm that threatens to break up the vessel into pieces. Indeed the mariners are frightened—they are not our story's hero—and they pray to their gods as well as make every desperate effort to save their lives. But not so Jonah. He goes down into the dark and damp hull of the lurching ship (a shirking soul descending into the imprisoning refuge that is this earth?), lies down, and has no trouble falling into the sleep of oblivion. The shipmaster, exuding responsibility, seeks him out and admonishes him to pray to God. But, to the prophet of God, prayer does not come as easily.

Then, the sailors, with the practicality of men of action, decide to cast lots in order to discover the cause of evil. Jonah is found out. His listeners are horrified to learn that he is fleeing God, who brings such a terrible storm upon them. Jonah tells them how they may escape God's wrath, which is not directed against them; he himself thinks to escape its pursuit by drowning. Upon seeing how the storm suddenly lets up after they cast the Hebrew into the sea, the sailors all become God fearing. But, the way is far from over for the man of God.

Jonah is not permitted the oblivion of death's sleep. He is swallowed by a great fish, in whose stinking belly he squirms for three whole days, having descended to the very bowels of the earth (mockingly drawn down in the vector of his own plunge). For three days and three nights, the prophet lies suffocating, sick unto his depths. And, finally, the transformation takes place. Finally, Jonah prays from the farthest depths to the God of Israel.

In the short book of Jonah, we have at this point a comparatively long, beautiful prayer. However we view the history of the book, it is clear that in the canonical book of Jonah this prayer is central, as it most certainly is in the reading of the book in the synagogue.

3 I called out of mine affliction
Unto the Lord, and He answered me;
Out of the belly of the netherworld cried I,
And Thou heardest my voice.
4 For Thou didst cast me into the depth,
In the heart of the seas,
And the flood was round about me;
All Thy waves and Thy billows
Passed over me.
5 And I said: "I am cast out
From before Thine eyes";
Yet I will look again
Toward Thy holy temple.
6 The waters compassed me about, even to the soul;
The deep was round about me;
The weeds were wrapped about my head.

> 7 I went down to the bottoms of the mountains;
>   The earth with her bars closed upon me for ever;
>   Yet hast Thou brought up my life from the pit,
>   O Lord my God.
> 8 When my soul fainted within me,
>   I remembered the Lord;
>   And my prayer came in unto Thee,
>   Into Thy holy temple.
> 9 They that regard lying vanities
>   Forsake their own mercy.
> 10 But I will sacrifice unto Thee
>   With the voice of thanksgiving;
>   That which I have vowed I will pay.
>   Salvation is of the Lord. (Jonah 2:3–10)

In verses 3 and 10, Jonah speaks as if his prayer is already answered. In the context of the book this means that Jonah realizes the omnipresence of God while he is still a hopeless captive in the fish's belly. His prayer is already answered in as much as, despite the cold and the stench, he can yet sense the lighting presence of God, whom he loves. In verses 4 and 5, the prophet speaks as one who has been cast into the furthest depth, overwhelmed by the floods of God's wrath, severed from being with God. But the prophet hastens on from this too terrible thought; he continues to "look again toward Thy holy temple." God, even in his anger, does not push man from his presence. In verses 6 and 7, the poet says that though his very life is smothered by the waters, though he descends to the world underneath the world, though the fertile earth of life closes its entrance to him forever, yet this, too, is no barrier between him and his God, who brings "up my life from the pit." God thus is omnipresent in a double sense. He is omnipresent in the world of man's psyche. No matter how desperate and dark man's psyche may be, it need not keep God out; His light penetrates even the most unfathomable of man's depths. And because of this God is omnipresent in the cosmic sense as well; he is God even of the Underworld. How deeply Jonah has learned that he cannot flee God or his word! In verse 8:a, we have the center of movement of the whole psalm. Jonah reveals to himself the essence of the divine being precisely in his almost fatal despair. When his soul "fainted within" him he remembers God. In his total despair, man finally is able, even in his blindness, to discern the closeness of God. From where else, in the cold of chaos, comes the strength to be? How utterly alone we sometimes must be in order to know that we are not alone. Jonah discovers the omnipresence of God in his own seemingly uncrossable distance from God. Thus, his prayer is answered. Verses 9 and 10 together with verse 3 are the formulistic frame of the psalm; they designate it as a psalm of thanksgiving. This means that Jonah has passed through the first stage of his long journey to Nineveh. He has gained knowledge and he is happy with that knowledge.

All this does not yet amount to a justification of Jonah's calling, and he has to be told again to go. This time God intimates a more specific message that is to be delivered, easing somewhat Jonah's burden. In any case, Jonah feels that he must separate his being from his will, and he reluctantly sets out for the bustling metropolis. He calls out, like one selling pretzels, "Yet forty days, and Nineveh shall be overthrown" (3:4). The prophet is flabbergasted by the fact that the people do indeed show contrition and repent. What the prophet can accomplish only by descending to hell presents no great difficulty for the people of Nineveh, their leaders included. To be sure, their behavior is downright ludicrous, when they make even their beasts fast and don sackcloth. But "God saw their works, that they turned from their evil way; and God repented of the evil, which He said He would do unto them; and He did it not" (3:10)—despite, or perhaps because of, their silliness, shallowness, and facileness.

If we have had any doubts till now about Jonah's attitude toward people's repentance, it is now made abundantly vivid.

> But it displeased Jonah exceedingly, and he was angry. And he prayed unto the Lord, and said: "I pray Thee, O Lord, was not this my saying, when I was yet in mine own country? Therefore I fled beforehand unto Tarshish; for I knew that Thou art a gracious God, and compassionate, longsuffering, and abundant in mercy, and repentest Thee of the evil. Therefore now, O Lord, take, I beseech Thee, my life from me; for it is better for me to die than to live." (4:1–3)

The same Jonah who cried out from hell to God now wishes death. He found the omnipresent God in his own deepest depths, but God apparently is not omnipresent enough to be with these facile pagans of Nineveh. How lovingly Jonah touches the memory of when he was in his own land and with his own people, where surely God could be said to be! And God answers him, almost sarcastically: "Art thou greatly angry?" (4:4) So Jonah, still fuming, leaves the noisy city to watch from the quiet of the desert. He makes himself a tiny hut to sprawl in, he is not at all intent on getting on with living.

> And the Lord God prepared a gourd, and made it to come up over Jonah, that it might be a shadow over his head, to deliver him from his evil. So Jonah was exceeding glad because of the gourd. But God prepared a worm when the morning rose the next day, and it smote the gourd, that it withered. (4:6–7)

Just as the sun is to rise and cast the "gourd's" soft and caressing shade over Jonah's body, the gourd succumbs to death and dust. "And it came to pass, when the sun arose, that God prepared a vehement east wind; and the sun beat upon the head of Jonah, that he fainted, and requested for himself that he might die, and said: 'It is better for me to die than to live'" (4:8). When the cool caress of the "gourd" is withdrawn, the same life that had seemed so dear to the man in the fish's belly becomes unbearable. The man who was called upon to go to the great city of Nineveh and bring God's message, who but last evening was "exceeding glad because of the" simple yet ever so real "gourd," is now, with the loss of the green bush, again left without any reason to live! "And God said to Jonah: 'Art thou greatly angry for the gourd?'" (4:9). This time, saying it with compassion rather than sarcasm.

> And he said: "I am greatly angry, even unto death." And the Lord said: "Thou hast had pity on the gourd, for which thou hast not labored, neither madest it grow, which came up in a night, and perished in a night; and should not I have pity on Nineveh, that great city, wherein are more than sixscore thousand persons that cannot discern between their right hand and their left hand, and also much cattle?" (4:9–11)

Was ever one of those one hundred and twenty thousand people who, like the beasts, know not to "discern between their right hand and their left hand," more humble than that "gourd" plant?

> For ye shall be as a terebinth whose leaf fadeth,
> And as a garden that hath no water. (Isaiah 1:30)

> And we are all become as one that is unclean,
> And all our righteousnesses are as a polluted garment;
> And we all do fade as a leaf,
> And our iniquities, like the wind, take us away. (Ibid. 64:5)

> Fret not thyself because of evildoers,
> Neither be thou envious against them that work unrighteousness.
> For they shall soon wither like the grass,
> And fade as the green herb. (Psalms 37:1–2)

> And he shall be like a tree planted by streams of water,
> That bringeth forth its fruit in its season,
> And whose leaf doth not wither;
> And in whatsoever he doeth he shall prosper. (Ibid. 1:3)

Jonah's "gourd" plant is a symbol of a man at his most humble, in his sinful and fleeting existence. Even so, his caress is a comfort and his grip a clutching on to life, a reason (for someone else) ever so rich and vivid to go on living. In him, too, God is omnipresent. Should God not seek every man's salvation and accept his repentance?

With this, the story of Jonah ends. His calling has been justified, though he has been called to a great deal more than to announce doom to an ancient heathen city. The message of his book is the efficacy of repentance as rooted in the very nature of man. Man is frail and not constantly capable of the continuous intensity of the proper way of living. God therefore allows man to be drawn into the immediacy of repentance, allowing him to forget his past and to grasp being in its present only. It is doubtful whether this knowledge, which Jonah gains so arduously, allows him to return to the sedentary life of land and hearth.

It is important to see that Jonah's story affirms the *potential* efficacy of repentance for all men in their utmost lowliness. Therefore, Jonah was wrong in fleeing the call to Nineveh. But this does not mean that true repentance is facile. Jonah was wrong in in his a priori denial of repentance for the Assyrian heathens, and his story tells how he finally came to complete his mission—up to the point that the sinners even changed their evil ways, for the time being at least. But the story says no more on this point than that the way to salvation through repentance is open to all, even the heathens of Nineveh. The book of Jonah really ends in the middle. Jonah still waits outside the city to "see what would become of the city" (4:5). The incident with the gourd is directed toward his anger not toward his desire to follow later events, and God speaks to him only of his anger. After this, Jonah neither answers God, signifying final consent, nor are we told of his return home. There is a definite sense that, as told, the story has no closure. The reason for this is that the Israelite who heard the story could well supply the end by himself, and with a wry smile. The ludicrous behavior of the Ninevites upon hearing Jonah's tinny announcement, the all-too-facile changing of their ways, is impossible to overlook, and it is very much in keeping with the ending of the story as Israel no doubt finished it. Nineveh, after all, was the capital of the Assyrian empire, which brought destruction and exile to the northern Israelite kingdom toward the end of the eight century B.C.E. and carried on campaigns in Judah during the rule of Sennacherib. The book of Jonah was written, in all probability, after the pillage and total destruction of Nineveh by the Medes and Babylonians in the summer of 612 B.C.E.. The prophet Zephaniah foresees the bitter end of the city in terms that leave no doubt as to its indictment:

And He will stretch out His hand against the north,
And destroy Assyria;
And will make Nineveh a desolation,
And dry like the wilderness.
And all the beasts of every kind
Shall lie down in the midst of her in herds;
Both the pelican and the bittern
Shall lodge in the capitals thereof;
Voices shall sing in the windows;
Desolation shall be in the posts;
For the cedar-work thereof shall be uncovered.
This is the joyous city
That dwelt without care,
That said in her heart:
"I am, and there is none else beside me";
How is she become a desolation,
A place for beasts to lie down in!
Every one that passeth by her
Shall hiss, and wag his hand. (Zephaniah 2:13–15)

And the prophet Nahum says on Nineveh:

The Lord is long-suffering, and great in power,
And will by no means clear the guilty; (Nahum 1:3)

Woe to the bloody city!
It is all full of lies and rapine;
The prey departeth not. (3:1)
And it shall come to pass, that all they that look, upon thee
Shall flee from thee,
And say: "Ninevah is laid waste;
Who will bemoan her?" (3:7)

All that hear the report of thee
Clap the hands over thee;
For upon whom hath not thy wickedness passed continually. (3:19)

What, then, are we to think of Nineveh's "repentance"? Surely, that city is chosen for Jonah's calling precisely because, in their evil, prideful aggression, they are the least likely candidates for repentance. Their grasping at the immediacy of repentance for a time is accepted by God for the time because he is everywhere open to the reach of man, even the blackest and lowest of men, even to man who is like the "gourd." That divine receptiveness is stated most sharply in the temporary pardon offered the Assyrian horde who, it turns out, are not truly repentant and richly deserve the divine wrath.

If so, what is true repentance for the author of the book of Jonah? The answer to this question is clearly implicit in the story. The truly repentant person in the book, of course, is the hero (not the antihero), Jonah himself. His long and painful journey to the eastern outskirts of Nineveh is an arduous adventure of learning and repentance. The same Jonah who at the outset flees God and then life without any second thoughts, finally comes to await events in Nineveh. His denial of the divine way, his anger, and his disgust with life change to a watchfulness rooted in compassion for even sinful men. Or perhaps, Jonah even learns to accept the greatness that is in the smallness of the present, in the meagre moments of life; he learns to see the people of Nineveh in their sudden fear before death, overlooking, for a time, the monstrousness of Assyrian greed and power. We do not know—and that is, I think, part of the greatness of the book's prophecy. We have been shown a very vivid picture of the prophet's way through repentance. But precisely because that repentance is so genuine, the author barely alludes to the outcome of that way, to the new living of Jonah. The outcome of Jonah's repentance is to be too rich and profound to understate in banal formulas of a "happy ending" or facile promises of righteousness in the future. How different is the end of this chapter in the life of Jonah from the happy ending of Nineveh's chapter! After all, this is a book that tells the story of a man of God; how much dare the writer assume that he is capable of constructing on the dry parchment? And so, the little book ends abruptly, in the very middle.

In summary, the justification of repentance, for Jonah, is in the omnipresence of the Almighty even in the remotest smallness or evilness of man, and in the legitimacy of the dimension of the present. Furthermore, the true path to repentance as trekked by Jonah is through the painful recognition of one's own smallness, leading to an appreciation of the godliness in man, which enables him to reach out, "from the pit," toward God, and to a compassion for every man in the immediacy of his fleeting present.[3]

These notions of the meaning and efficacy of repentance continue into rabbinic thinking.

> R. Simeon ben Yohai [second century] says: Even if one were completely righteous all his life yet rebelled in the end, he would lose what was beforehand,[4] as the verse says, "The righteousness of the righteous shall not deliver him in the day of his transgression" (Ezekiel 33:12). And even if one were completely evil all his life but repented in the end, he is no longer reminded of his evilness,[5] as the verse says, "and as for the

> wickedness of the wicked, he shall not stumble thereby in the day that he
> turneth from his wickedness" (ibid). (BT *Kiddushin* 40b)

The sage's need to stress the prophet's words is understandable in view of
their possible implications—which caused another rabbi to stress: "R.
Simeon ben Lakish [Palestine, third century] said: [Only] if he is shocked
by his earlier actions" (Ibid.).

On the verses in Leviticus 26,

> And they shall confess their iniquity, and the iniquity of their fathers, in
> their treachery which they committed against Me, and also that they have
> walked contrary unto Me. I also will walk contrary unto them, and bring
> them into the land of their enemies; if then perchance their uncircum-
> cised heart be humbled, and they then be paid the punishment of their
> iniquity;[6] then will I remember My covenant . . .

a homilist in the *Sifra* comments:

> "And they shall confess their iniquity, and the iniquity of their fathers",
> this means repentance. [God says:] "Immediately upon their confession
> for their sins I—immediately—return to having compassion for them."
> ". . . If then perchance their uncircumcised heart be humbled", this means
> repentance: "Immediately upon their subjugating[7] their hearts in repen-
> tance I—immediately—return to having compassion for them."[8] (*Sifra*
> to *Behukkotai* 26:40–41)

Forgiveness does not come because of a meekness of heart and a broken
spirit, a humbleness engrained through the long suffering described in the
previous biblical verses, nor does it come through an admission of man's
lowliness and ineluctable sinfulness. Rather, says the Rabbi, man faces up
to his guilt and admits it. In so doing, he takes responsibility for his past,
even the lack of a sustaining righteousness on his parents' part. And
through this admission of guilt comes the submission to the divine ways
and a sense of determining one's ways rightly from the present onward. In
this experience, there is a freeing of man—for "immediately," *now*, is
God's mercy fully partaken of. The story of sin and punishment is a long
one, about famine and pestilence and conquest and fear and dispossession
of the Land and Exile and deep humiliation and shame and, finally, hatred
of life and oneself. It is a biblical story of history. Who can deny the
terrible burden of its truth for us? But, in repentance, says the Rabbi, man
escapes history, or more powerfully, the God of history himself returns to
his mercy for man in the tinyness and greatness of the present. Israel need
not retrace the tortuous way through history in order again to be home in
their Land, the mercy of God is imminent in the strength of repentance.

"R. Berekhiah said: It is written, 'My doctrine shall drop as the rain' (Deuteronomy 32: 2): If they bend their necks in repentance then immediately the rains fall."9 (PT *Ta'aniot* 2:1 [65b]) If man can break his stubborn inertial grounding in the past, the "stiffnecked" being of the Bible,10 if he can admit his guilt and yet escape it by fully embracing the present with its awesome implications, then even tiresome nature yields to man's immediacy.

This conviction of the efficacy of repentance is even institutionalized in the order of fast days as described in an old Mishnah:

> What is the Order of the Fast-Days? . . . The eldest one among them preaches a sermon of admonition [such as]: Our brothers! It is not said about the people of Nineveh, "And God saw their sackcloth and their fasting" but rather, "And God saw their works, that they turned from their evil way; and God repented of the evil, which He said He would do unto them; and He did it not" (Jonah 3:10). And in Tradition it is said, "Yet even now, saith the Lord, Turn ye unto Me with all your heart, And with fasting, and with weeping, and with lamentation; And rend your heart, and not your garments, And turn unto the Lord Your God; For He is gracious and compassionate, Long-suffering, and abundant in mercy, And repenteth Him of the evil" (Joel 2:12–13). (M *Ta'anit* 2:1)11

By juxtaposing the verses from Jonah and Joel, the homilist lets the words of each prophet elicit an interpretation of the other's. Joel thus is understood as referring to the notions of repentance as turning away from sin and returning to the way of the Law, just as Jonah speaks of "their works, that they turned from their evil way." And Jonah, in turn, thus is understood as referring not merely to the outward behavior of the people of Nineveh but also to an inner wrenching—"and rend your heart, and not your garments," as Joel says.

The fasts described in this Mishnah are part of a long order of praying, fasting, and repenting following upon a deepening drought in the Land of Israel (or other calamities).12 But, such institutionalization notwithstanding, we must picture the terrible sense of urgent immediacy accompanying each fast and its order of praying and exhortations. With the passage of each fast day as the winter moves on without rain, indeed with the passage of each day, the farmer in Israel feels dusty death lurking in the wastelands closing in on him. His hunger increases as the hope of an early and rich crop recedes and pestilence threatens and finally strikes directly at man himself. Drought, in a country almost entirely dependent for its water supply on winter rains (even underground water supplies are influenced by the yearly rains) is a sense of very imminent suffering and death. So that even if the order of the fast days is prescribed, according to weather conditions, by old custom, nevertheless the praying, fasting, and repentance are shot through with an intense feeling of growing urgency and a demand for immediate mercy. One may spend the hours of light watching the sparsely clouded sky and entreatingly wait for the cruel blue sky to suddenly darken with the voluptuous wetness of life-giving rain clouds. In such conditions, even the most prearranged ritual has a real spontaneity, and those who gather together in fasting pray with a conviction that time has all but run out. A drama of life and death is played out in the very present. The old custom of fasting as described in the Mishnah, including as it does repentance as a central part of the ritual, thus is a clear expression of a positive rabbinic attitude toward repentance as a withdrawal into the present.

> We repeat there (M *Avot* 2:10): R. Eliezer [ben Hyrcanus, end of the first century and beginning of the second] says: Repent one day before your death. R. Eliezer's students asked him, "But does one know on which day he will die!" He said to them, "Then certainly he should repent today lest tomorrow he will die; and he will thus be repentant all his life. And so, too, Solomon in his wisdom said, 'Let thy garments be always white; And let thy head lack no oil' (Ecclesiastes 9:8)."[13] (BT *Shabbat* 153a)

This juxtaposition of R. Eliezer ben Hyrcanus' view with verses from Ecclesiastes has fascinating implications for the history of our theme, and in any case, a comparative analysis widens its understanding. Let us examine Ecclesiastes in its own dimensions. For this purpose we will compare the verse just quoted and its context (9:7–10) with a portion of the Epic of Gilgamesh (Old Babylonian version, Tablet x, iii, ANET, p. 90, column 1):[14]

Ecclesiastes	*Gilgamesh*
7 Go thy way, eat thy bread with joy And drink thy wine with a merry heart; For God hath already accepted thy works.	"Gilgamesh, whither rovest thou? The life thou pursuest thou shalt not find. When the gods created mankind, Death for mankind they set aside,
8 Let thy garments be always white; And let thy head lack no oil.	Life in their own hands retaining. Thou, Gilgamesh, let full be thy belly,
9 Enjoy life with the wife whom thou lovest all the days of the life of thy vanity, which He hath	Make thou merry by day and by night.

given thee under the sun, all the days of thy vanity; for that is thy portion in life and in thy labor wherein thou laborest under the sun.

10 Whatsoever thy hand attaineth to do by thy strength, that do; for there is no work, nor device, nor knowledge, nor wisdom, in the grave, whither thou goest.

Of each day make thou a feast of rejoicing,
Day and night dance thou and play!
Let thy garments be sparkling fresh,
Thy head be washed; bathe thou in water.
Pay heed to the little one that holds on to thy hand,
Let thy spouse delight in thy bosom,
for this is the task of [mankind]!"[15]

Gilgamesh, upon the death of his friend Enkidu, has set out to find immortality. He explains this to Siduri, the alewife (or cupbearer of the gods):

"He who with me underwent all hard[ships]—
Enkidu, whom I loved dearly,
Who with me underwent all hardships—
Has now gone to the fate of mankind!
Day and night I have wept over him.
I would not give him up for burial—
In case my friend should rise at my plaint—
Seven days and seven nights,
Until a worm fell out of his nose.
Since his passing I have not found life,
I have roamed like a hunter in the midst of the steppe.
O ale-wife, now that I have seen thy face,
Let me not see the death which I ever dread." (Ibid. ii, 1–13, p. 89, column
    2–p. 90, column 1)

He sets out, very much like Abraham, to find what is beyond the given, perhaps with a sense of the immediately given here and now closing in on him. But, unlike Abraham, who sets out to the Promised Land, a real land that flows with milk and honey and must be conquered and suffered for, Gilgamesh takes flight into a journey where Humbaba, a chaos monster, may be confronted and afflicted and where the heavenly Bull may be slain. His aim is a meeting with Utanapishtim the Faraway, who is faraway indeed, one must cross "the Waters of Death" to reach him. Utanapishtim is the only man to whom the gods have given the gift of immortality, and since the quest for him is a quest for that immortality, Gilgamesh must roam as faraway from the humdrum world as imagination will allow. To the initiated, that journey probably wound through ancient rituals connected with death and life after death, so that it was really a journey through this life; but it followed a road paved through a mythically constructed wayside and not the dry deserts trekked by Abraham. On this long way, Gilgamesh meets the alewife and she tells him what is really his final revelation—though he denies it until the weariness and fantasy of his journey exhaust him, and only then accepts the "truth."

The alewife tells the hero that, in his wanderings in search of immortality, he is really overlooking life itself. Not only is his quest in vain, but by seeking endless life so earnestly, he is losing that wonderful bit of life that the gods have really given to man. "The life thou pursuest thou shalt not find"—even that which already is given to you. The gods have given to man a life that is terminated by death, while they kept from him endless life. Therefore, man must passionately embrace what he really has. Man should make use of every moment of that life, he should caress its every voluptuousness and be happy with it "by day and by night." Each day is its own joy, each night its own ecstasy. Let man live the freshness and youth that is the becoming of each day, basking in the sensuousness of his bathed and anointed body. The little child that holds your hand does so with a sweaty urgency whose wisdom you should learn. Let your beloved enjoy the virile warmth of your enclosing arms because there you have life itself. For this is all of man! Life is a present, a here and now, and to overlook the present is to embrace death. Is there a more earnest embrace of life in Goethe's poetry than in the message of the story of Gilgamesh? I think that this epic contains some of the oldest seeds of a secular consciousness; it is surely a critique of some of the religiosity of its day.

Thus, the alewife's words are a legitimation of the dimension of the present and an intense recognition of its richness. Now we may reread Ecclesiastes.

Ecclesiastes, too, sets out from, among other starting points, the ineluctable ubiquity of death.

> All things come alike to all; there is one event to the righteous and to the wicked; to the good and to the clean and to the unclean; to him that sacrificeth and to him that sacrificeth not; as is the good, so is the sinner, and he that sweareth, as he that feareth an oath. This is an evil in all that is done under the sun, that there is one event unto all; yea also, the heart of the sons of men is full of evil, and madness is in their heart while they live, and after that they go to the dead. (9:2–3)

Living is all and everything, for death is an absolute end, a terminal. One must embrace life, but not out of love for it, rather out of the knowledge that that is all there is. "For to him that is joined to all the living there is hope; for a living dog is better than a dead lion. For the living know that they shall die; but the dead know not any thing, neither have they any more a reward; for the memory of them is forgotten" (9:4–5). Living man is conscious, he "knows," the lowly reality of consciousness as "a dog" is better than someone else's fading memory of "a lion." "As well their love, as their hatred and their envy, is long ago perished; neither have they any more a portion for ever in any thing that is under the sun" (9:6). Love and hatred are in the living of man, afterwards they are ludicrous. Should man then "eat his bread with joy and "drink his wine with a merry heart"? Yes, but with the overshadowing knowledge that the Almighty has already foreseen and accepted his works, such as they are, for what they are. Remember what man's consciousness is a consciousness of, what his knowledge is a knowledge of: "For the living know that they shall die"! To live is a greatness because one then knows that one shall die! Dress up and anoint yourself and enjoy life with a woman, whom, you have found, you love. Do so all your days till the bitter end, do so "all the days of the life of thy *vanity*, which He hath given thee under the sun, all the days of thy *vanity*: for that is thy portion in life."

The uniqueness of Ecclesiastes' thinking here undoubtedly comes through in the word used so often, *vanity*, the Hebrew word הבל. In order for its meaning to strike us, let us stop for a moment to note its meaning and connotation in biblical usage:

> When thou criest, let them that thou hast gathered deliver thee;
> But the wind shall carry them all away,
> A breath (הבל) shall bear them off; (Isaiah 57:13)

In the above, we probably have the word in its orginal meaning. "For Egypt helpeth in vain (הבל), and to no purpose;" (Ibid. 30:7). Connoting, here, nothingness.

> Unto Thee shall the nations come
> From the ends of the earth, and shall say:
> "Our fathers have inherited nought but lies,
> Vanity (הבל) and things wherein there is no profit." (Jeremiah 16:19)

Connoting nothingness, nonsense.

> Grace is deceitful, and beauty is vain (הבל);
> But a woman that feareth the Lord, she shall be praised. (Proverbs 31:30)

Connoting that beauty is "unreal." ". . . and they rejected His statutes, and His covenant . . . ; and they went after things of nought (הבל), and became nought (ויהבלו), and after the nations that were round about them" (II Kings 17:15; and see Jeremiah 2:5), connoting nonsense. In rabbinic literature, the word most commonly retains its apparently original meaning of breath, hot air or air, vapor. In Ecclesiastes itself, the word is used as:

> I have seen all the works that are done under the sun; and, behold, all is vanity (הבל) and a striving after wind. (1:14, and the same usage in 2:11, 17, 26; 4:4; 6:9)

> For there is a man whose labor is with wisdom, and with knowledge, and with skill; yet to a man that hath not labored therein shall he leave it for his portion. This also is vanity (הבל) and a great evil. (2:21)

> This also is vanity (הבל), yea it is a grievous business. (4:8)

> this is vanity (הבל), and it is an evil disease. (6:2)

> There is a vanity (הבל) which is done upon the earth: that there are righteous men, unto whom it happeneth according to the work of the wicked; again, there are wicked men, to whom it happeneth according to the work of the righteous—I said that this also is vanity (הבל). (8:14)

Throughout the word connotes purposelessness, meaninglessness, emptiness, nothingness, and mainly, nonsense. Furthermore, for Ecclesiastes the word has a definitely evil connotation. I have shown so many instances of the word's use, because Ecclesiastes' notion of the world as being הבל is extremely important for an understanding of rabbinic thinking, as we shall see.

Ecclesiastes, like Gilgamesh in his final wisdom, knows that living is all of being. He, too, therefore, embraces life with desperation. But while the alewife teaches the ancient hero to embrace life voluptuously, Ecclesiastes' awareness of the singularity of life is a melancholy one. Precisely because life is all there is, its meaninglessness is unbearable. "Whatsoever thy hand attaineth to do by thy strength, that do; for there is no word, nor device, nor knowledge, nor wisdom, in the grave whither thou goest" (9:10). There is an intense sense of tragedy in these words. All that counts—"work, device, knowledge and wisdom"—these most precious things are possible now; grab them now because they soon slip from your hands. One should sense, when one reads the verse, that as deep as is the silence of the grave, so vivid and important is life. How very harsh, then, is the fact that the world is הבל!

"I returned, and saw under the sun, that the race is not to the swift, nor the battle to the strong, neither yet bread to the wise, nor yet riches to men of understanding, nor yet favor to men of skill; but time and chance happeneth to them all" (9:11). How absurd that living eludes man who is nothing but a living being. How strange that swiftness, which is a running, does not win the race. How is it that strength, which is a doing, cannot win the battle? That wisdom, which is knowledge of the world, cannot grasp that world? That skill, which is a beauty of making, does not bring favor? How is it that time and chance, which are a flux and an undoing, are the way for all men?

Should man, then, wish death? No. Man is so caught up in living that death is beyond his willful caress. Death is so distant from living that the living can relate to it only in a shudder. "For man also knoweth not his time; as the fishes that are taken in an evil net, and as the birds that are caught in the snare, even so are the sons of man snared in an evil time, when it falleth suddenly upon them" (9:12). Death is not the final part of living; it is life's total negation.

What has all this to do with Rabbinic thinking? I think that the book of Ecclesiastes is included in the canon approved by the Rabbis for more impressive reasons than the few and scattered remarks which support, or seem to support, Rabbinic Judaism. I think that Ecclesiastes, that is to say the consciousness expressed in it, is actually a setting of the stage upon which Rabbinic thinking and acting take place. And I think that R. Eliezer ben Hyrcanus' remark on repentance, together with the homily on Ecclesiastes, may serve as an example of this fact. First let us examine, for a moment, the thesis in general.

Ecclesiastes makes three points, two explicitly and one implicitly. First, living is the essence of man's being as we know it. Whatever may be man's lot after death, from the point of view of the experience of living, death is a total negation.

> Who knoweth the spirit of man whether it goeth upward, and the spirit of the beast whether it goeth downward to the earth? Wherefore I perceived that there is nothing better, then that a man should rejoice in his works; for that is his portion; for who shall bring him to see what shall be after him? (3:21, 22)

And, "for a living dog is better than a dead lion" (9:4).[16]

Second, that dimension in which man has being, the world of time and space, tends to be absurd, even to the point, at times, of being downright evil.

Third, although Ecclesiastes does not explicitly say so, throughout one has the sense that the fact of man's living is not at all an act of will.

Man lives because that fact is given, he is forced to be. This is not so much because the Creator has made him, although this may underlie Ecclesiastes' mood, but rather because the very experience of being powerfully draws back from death.[17] Death is not an option.

Ecclesiastes, despite his few comments on the need to follow God's ways, leaves the reader with a profound sense of being in limbo. There is only this life in this world, but living is a deeply unsatisfying experience. Man should try very hard to "be happy" with his lot, says Ecclesiastes, but after reading the variegated wise teachings included in Ecclesiastes, one is most likely to feel like "one that hath been stunned, And is of sense forlorn," a wiser, yes, but sadder man thereafter. Man is intensely "stuck" with this world but he cannot really have it. The overwhelming mood of Ecclesiastes is a fateful unsatisfiable hunger for all that man has.

In such a mood is it at all surprising that man's greatest need should be to *correct* the chaos that darkens his world? This is what the sensibility of following the Law, as in rabbinic thinking, is all about, inasmuch as we are speaking of an attitude toward the world. Could there be a better introduction to rabbinic convictions than Ecclesiastes' mood? Living is all there is to man. But in the world as it is, with man as he is, that fact gives rise to terrible despair; and this provides the point of departure from Ecclesiastes' thinking. In rabbinic thinking, the uniqueness of living is taken so seriously that it *must* be filled out and enriched. Precisely because time and space is the dimension of being for man, man desperately needs the Law to make that dimension meaningful. The rabbinic mentality, unlike Ecclesiastes', is one of living not of the contemplation of living. The conviction that the world can and must be corrected is the sine qua non for the intenseness of being in the world that characterizes classical rabbinic thinking. In that thinking, moreover, belief in life after death is a corollary of the seriousness of being alive. The rabbinic way was one reaction to the unmitigated vision of this world. As we shall see, an alternative was available, the gnostic flight, the yearning for a being separated from living by eons.

Now, we shall follow Ecclesiastes' three points into rabbinic thinking.

> The Rabbis repeated: For two and a half years Bet Shammai and Bet Hillel contended, these saying: It were better for man had he not been created rather than being created. And these saying: It is better for man that he is created rather than not being created. Finally the consensus of the majority was: It were better for man had he not been created rather than being created; now that he is created let him probe[18] his actions. And some say it thusly:[19] Let him weigh[20] his actions. (BT *Eruvin* 13b)

The fact that the historicity of this controversy is suspect[21] increases the justification of a contemplative interpretation of the *Baraitha*. If one may say that "It were better for man had he not been created," then there is a recognition that no eschatology, public or private, can dim the vividness of living in this world. Thus, as in Ecclesiastes, we have here a sense of the experience of living as the focal point for our knowledge and understanding of man. The conclusion that "now that he is created let him probe . . . . weigh his actions" strengthens this feeling, since finally man is called upon to deepen his interest in his actions, to take them more seriously. We may say that for Bet Hillel "It is better for man that he is created" because they are convinced of the high degree of probability that man will make the best of his life. But for them, too, the controversy takes place in the uniqueness of a this-worldly dimension, and this is reflected in the final decision, which is probably a compromise. Living, the experiential essence of man, is heavy, but precisely because we view him in his being as a living man, it is incumbent on him to mend his ways, and Bet Hillel would say, it is quite probable that he will finally do so.

> Akavyah ben Mahalalel [first century c.e.) says:[22] Look at three things so that you will not come to sin: Know from where you have come; and to where you are going; and before Whom you are destined to give an accounting. From where have you come? From a stinking drop. And to where are you heading? To a place of dust and worms. And before Whom are you destined to give an accounting? Before the King of the kings of kings, the Holy One Blessed is He. (M *Avot* 3:1)

The point of Akavyah's "Know from where you have come and to where you are going," is not *that* man comes and goes on the road of life but rather *from where* he comes and *to where* he goes. Similarly, the point of "Know before Whom you are destined to give an accounting" is not *that* man must give an accounting but *to whom* he must give it. These are the three things upon which man should gaze: a stinking drop, dust and worms, and the King of the kings of kings. What Akavyah enjoins us to "Know"! is not an order of being that is beyond experience. Man's birth and his decomposition in the grave are common knowledge. Man knows accountability only too well from his experience, even if it is an unfair one. But the accountability one practices in life toward the powers of polity is a misplaced one, for man is finally accountable only to God. In this aphorism, too, man's essence is perceived in terms of the experience of living: becoming, dying, and accountability analogous to that one knows toward the power of polity. The societal power structure is to be replaced in its own dimension by a divine order sensed on its analogy.

Contrast this to the following Valentinian saying from the writings of Theodotus, the Gnostic (as copied by Clement of Alexandria [born c. 150 c.e.] 78:2):[23] "What liberates is the knowledge of who we were, what we became; where we were, whereinto we have been thrown; whereto we speed, wherefrom we are redeemed; what birth is, and what rebirth." "We were" a divine spark, and "we became" men; "we were" in a world beyond the Seven Heavens, in the being of the God of good, and "we have been thrown" into the dungeons of this world and of our humanity; "we are hurrying" to recross that unimaginable distance separating us from the good God; "we are redeemed" from the prison of this-worldliness; "birth" means a plunging into the grips of satanic forces; and "rebirth" means dying to this world and emerging to be in a dimension where neither hunger, frustration, nor death are imaginable. In Gnosticism, this knowledge itself liberates man from the claustrophobic here and now, because man knows about the spiritual world beyond in his capacity as one fallen from that world.

In both instances, the rabbinic and the gnostic, knowledge is redeeming, and in both man's source and destination are central. But whereas the gnostic knowledge frees man from this world, Akavyah's wisdom places man even more firmly in this world. If man really recognizes his nature, says Akavyah, then he will realize that his only hope—and as a religious soul his hope is a passionate yearning—lies in confronting what is for the sage the frailty of that nature. In other words, while both have a definite sense of man's uncomfortableness in this world, the rabbinic view knows that man's real nature nevertheless is flesh and blood, while the gnostic knows that man is a stranger to this world. Furthermore, the gnostic believer is truly liberated from this world by virtue of his knowledge. He is part of an order that is beyond this world and cannot be dimmed by the darkness of living. He travels on a circle of perfection that is only tangential to the here and now. This is an actual experience for him because he can "explain" his way of living, it "makes sense" according to that other order. The pain around him neither disturbs nor threatens him, because come what may, his sanity unfolds on a very different plane. His "real" world is always an ordered one. But, what is the student of Akavyah ben Mahalalel to say? He remains a being of the earth, he is truly born of humble parents and he truly dies. Whatever evil and suffering he encounters is only too real. And caught up in that, he must, nevertheless, explain his ways to God. Here is much more than an echo of Ecclesiastes' perception of man as a living and dying being.

The world that is so ineluctably the dimension of man's being is a world permeated with evil, even aside from the fact that man must die. The "stinking drop" that Akavyah speaks of signifies man's lowly nature, which is a source of evil in the world, as the rotting of man's body testifies to the baseness of his make up. This is very much in keeping with rabbinic thinking, where man himself is a source of evil in the world, the "evil inclination" being a part of man's essence as a human being.[24] But, as Akavyah points out, this does not free man from responsibility for his actions before God. No matter how deeply ingrained evil may be in man, he nevertheless is capable of good, as we shall stress later on, and this while remaining a creature of the earth. We must try to feel the religious sense of the evil in the world in order to follow the continuity of Ecclesiastes' mood into the rabbinic consciousness. Again, in order to feel the intenseness of these perceptions, let us pursue a gnostic description of them.

> He [the "chief archon"] made a plan with his authorities, which are his powers, and they committed together adultery with Sophia, and bitter fate was begotten through them, which is the last of the terrible bonds. . . . For from that fate came forth every sin and injustice and blasphemy and the chain of forgetfulness and ignorance and every difficult command and serious sins and great fear. And thus the whole creation was made blind, in order that they may not know God who is above all of them. And because of the chain of forgetfulness their sins were hidden. For they are bound with measures and times and moments, since it [fate] is lord over everything. (The Apocryphon of John II, 1 [28:11–15, 21–33])[25]

Here we have a very general description of the gnostic perception of the evil of this world. If we have listened with the proper sensitivity, perhaps we can understand the intensity with which the rabbis viewed the way of the Law as the redemption from evil. For the Gnostic mind, redemption is quite different:

> I went—I am the light which exists in the light, I am the remembrance of the Pronoia—that I might enter into the middle of darkness and the inside of Hades. . . . And I entered into the middle of their prison which is the prison of the body. And I said, "He who hears, let him get up from the deep sleep". And he wept and shed tears. Bitter tears he wiped from himself and he said, "Who is it that calls my name, and from where has this hope come to me, while I am in the chains of the prison?" And I said, "I am the Pronoia of the pure light; I am the thinking of the virginal Spirit, he who raised you up to the honored place. Arise and remember that it is you who hearkened, and follow your root, which is I, the merciful one, and guard yourself against the angels of poverty and the demons of chaos and all those who ensnare you, and beware of the deep sleep and the enclosure of the inside of Hades." (Ibid. [30:32–31:22])[26]

The gnostic can be redeemed from the terrible bonds of this world, as he perceives it, only through flight to the light that is beyond being as we experience it. "And I raised him up and sealed him in the light of the water with five seals, in order that death might not have power over him from this time on" (Ibid. [31:22–25]).

But, for the rabbis, man counters evil by recognizing it yet deepening his being in the world and following the Law. In order to appreciate Akavyah's language in this atmosphere, read the following:

> After the day of rest, Sophia sent Zoe, her daughter, who is called "Eve [of Life]", as an instructor to raise up Adam, in whom there was no soul, so that those whom he would beget might become vessels of the light. [When] Eve saw her co-likeness cast down, she pitied him, and she said, "Adam, live! Rise up on the earth!" Immediately her word became a deed. For when Adam rose up, immediately he opened his eyes. (On the Origin of the World II, 5 [115:31–116:5])[27]

But "Eve [of Life]" is soon replaced by the "carnal woman":

> Then the authorities were informed that their molded body was alive, and had arisen. They were very much disturbed. They sent seven arch-angels to see what had happened. They came to Adam. When they saw Eve speaking with him, they said to one another, "What is this [female] light-being? . . . Now come, let us seize her and let us cast our seed on her, so that when she is polluted she will not be able to ascend to her light, but those whom she will beget will serve us.
>
> Then [the Life]—Eve, since she existed as a power, laughed at their [false] intention. She darkened their eyes and left her likeness there stealthily beside Adam. . . . [And] when they saw the likeness of that [woman] with him, they were troubled, thinking that this was the true Eve. And they acted recklessly, and came to her and seized her and cast their seed upon her. They did it with a lot of tricks, not only defiling her naturally but abominably . . . And they were deceived, not knowing that they had defiled their own body. It was the likeness which the authorities and their angels defiled in every form.
>
> She conceived Abel first from the prime ruler; and she bore the rest of the sons from the seven authorities and their angels. Now all this came to pass according to the foresight of the First Father, so that the first mother might beget within herself every mixed seed which is joined together with the Fate of the world and its schemata and [Fate's] justice. (Ibid. [116:8–117:24])[28]

In the gnostic order of things, as it comes out in these works, there are different types of men depending on their ancestry, the descendants of

Cain, or Seth, being superior to those of Abel. The source of evil, and thus of evil men, is the sinfulness of sexuality: "Now up to the present day sexual intercourse continued due to the chief archon. And he planted sexual desire in her who belongs to Adam. And he produced through intercourse the copies of the bodies, and he inspired them with his opposing spirit" (The Apocryphon of John II, 1 [24:26–31]).[29]
Or, put more abstractly:

[The man followed] the earth,
The woman followed [the man],
And marriage followed the woman,
And reproduction followed marriage,
And death followed reproduction. (On the Origin of the World II, 5 [109:22–25])[30]

Thus, we have in Gnosticism one of the mightiest myths of the evil of the world. Generally speaking, it shares with Ecclesiastes a bleak perception. Of course, there is a gulf between the two in that Ecclesiastes sees the hypostasis of evil in society and flux, whereas for the gnostics it is much more in the intimate spheres of sexuality and the make up of the human psyche. In this sense, Akavyah ben Mahalalel's imagery lies in between the perception of Ecclesiastes and the Gnostic one. He sees the importance of properly placed accountability, authority and Law being positive for him if they are a subservience to God; and in this there is no agreement between him and the gnostics. But, he also perceives evil as stemming not merely from the unordered (or venally ordered) structure of society or from inadherence to the Law. In man's base nature lies the tendency toward evil, and it is that awareness that makes accountability to God redeeming. The baseness of man has to do with his sexuality and his mortality. But, for the sage, it is not the fact of man's sexuality that gives rise to evil, just as it is not merely the fact that he dies that does so. Rather, man's sexual nature implies his frailty: he is born through the whim of physical passion and develops out of the most unimpressive of "drops." Thus, man has a very long way to go to be worthy of standing before God, and he never really attains that worthiness because his biography is cut short by death and, finally, he rots in the grave, all his plans, dreams, and constructions turn out to be truly humble indeed. For the gnostic, man's sexual drive is evil, whereas for Akavyah man's dependence on the physical, the earthy, points out his frailty.

This also explains the very different conclusions the two reach. The Gnostic must escape his humanity, a need echoed in Paul's cry, "O wretched man that I am! who shall deliver me from the body of this death?" (Romans 7:24). Whereas the rabbi must face up to his frailty and live with it and through it the way of God. "'And thou shalt love the Lord thy God with all thy heart, and with all thy soul, and with all thy might' (Deuteronomy 6:5). 'With all thy heart': With both your inclinations, with the good inclination and with the bad inclination" (M *Berakhot* 9:5)[31]

In summing up, we must remember the sensitivity of Ecclesiastes, the gnostics, and the rabbis to the existence of evil in the world. For Ecclesiastes, the hypostasis of evil is society and flux; for Gnosticism (or at least for one type of Gnosticism, represented by the passages discussed) it is man's humanity, particularly his sexuality; for the rabbis, as Akavyah's early and sharp saying exemplifies, it is man's frailty that portends evil. The perceptions of all three share an intensity that is most dramatically obvious in the Gnostic yearning for flight. In the rabbinic view, it leads to the conviction that man must ultimately give an accounting of himself before God, because in proportion to the tragedy of death is the belief that life continues strong. This is the seeming paradox of rabbinic thinking. The story of living is ultimately a tragedy in its climax and, all too often, in its plot as well. But no less intense is the belief that somehow man brings a redemption to his world, though the story seems to remain the same. But, then, this is not a paradox. Rather, it is precisely the profoundest sense of tragedy that brings the conviction of redemption, because otherwise sanity would not be of this world. Rather than theodicy, rabbinic consciousness has gone the way of a story, a story in which the most terrible tragedy "really" takes place and yet man is redeemed in the end. Since redemption takes place, in the rabbinic consciousness, through the way of the Law, one may sense the seriousness of the Law for the rabbis if one can grasp the mighty temptation of the gnostic flight. For the rabbis, the alternative to that flight is the way of the Law.

The rabbinic perception of man's personal accountability before God introduces an attitude toward death, and thus life, that is absent in both Ecclesiastes' and the gnostic's view.

> R. Eleazar ha-Kappar [third century] . . . He used to say: Those born will surely die; and the dead will surely rise; and the risen will surely be judged. To know, to let know, and to be known: That He is the Lord; He is the Maker; He is the Creator;[32] He is the One Who understands; He is the Judge; He witnesses; He is litigant; And He will surely judge. Blessed is He, for with Him there is no inequity and no forgetfulness and no partiality, and there can be no bribery for all is His. And know that everything is taken into account. And let not your inclination convince you that the netherworld will be a refuge for you: For ineluctably are you made, and ineluctably are you born, and ineluctably do you live, and inevitably do you die, and inevitably are you destined to give an accounting before the King of the kings of kings, the Holy One Blessed is He. (M *Avot* 4:22)

Here the perception of evil in the world is heightened. The absurdity of living in the world is emphasized by the sharp recognition that "Those born will surely die." Man at his very birth is a dying creature—what sense, then is the whole effort of living? This is indeed the mood of Ecclesiastes! But more than that, the consciousness expressed here is infused with the sense of God's omniscience and omnipotence and incorruptibility. Together with man's perception of the absurdity of the world and his own smallness and the transience of his living comes the conception of the existence of Perfection. And with that conception of an almighty God, man's vision of the imperfection of himself and the world becomes ever greater, but not as a confusion and a despair, rather as a knowledge of the truth. Man is not part of a chaotic and meaningless world where he can be only blind and confused. He is not in a prison that destroys his vision. Man indeed is imperfect, as is the world, but he possesses *knowledge*. Not a Gnostic knowledge of another, distant world but a clear, incisive knowledge of the real and only world—the same world in which he will finally find his life after death. The Rabbi's knowledge, like Ecclesiastes', is a highly critical analysis of living that enables him to go on living in that same world. But, stronger than Ecclesiastes' is the Rabbi's sense of the imperfection of the world before God, though this, too, is undoubtedly deep in the substratum of Ecclesiastes' thinking, coming to the surface in various, scattered verses. And, certainly more than Ecclesiastes, the rabbi stresses the potentially redeeming nature of that knowledge, because it can enable man to correct his living in the world. Here we are harking back through Jonah and Ezekiel.

In rabbinic thinking, the realization that "ineluctably do you live" is central. Man has no choice as to the dimension in which he works things out. There is no room for a gnostic flight, nor is there time for philosophical consternation as in Ecclesiastes. There should not be despair, because living, as terrible as it is, is all there is and the only alternative is nothingness; one must face that by virtue of being a man. Man must live fully in the world because "ineluctably do you live."

The rabbi shares with Ecclesiastes the sense of the onlyness of living, neither recognizes any alternative. The two also share the sense of the transience of life and the tragedy of death—"inevitably do you die." No matter how unwilling life is, death is always unwelcome. Even the suicide has not a desire not to be. Rather, in the final flight from life, death, remains a terrible tragedy. A suicide has chosen the vivid tragedy of death not the nothingness of oblivion—that can be had far less dramatically in alcohol and drugs. But, in the rabbinic consciousness, there is a new element; that is, *impatience*.

In the rabbinic theology, man must give an accounting of his ways before God: "inevitably are you destined to give an accounting before the

King of the king of kings, the Holy One blessed is He." This makes the prospect of death almost a desperation. Man has so much to do to perfect himself as a man. Can he accomplish that before death interrupts?

> It was repeated: When Rabbi [Judah ha-Nasi] fell ill, R. Hiyya came to see him and found him crying. He said to him, "Rabbi, why are you crying . . .?" He said to him, "I, I am crying because [I am parting with] Torah and good deeds." (BT *Ketubbot* 103b)
> As Rabbi [Judah ha-Nasi] was dying he raised his ten fingers upwards and said, "Master of the World, it is manifestly clear before You that I have labored in the Torah with my ten fingers yet have not taken any personal benefit even with my little finger . . ." (Ibid. 104a)

Although Ecclesiastes, with all his sense of the tragedy of death, will be expected to greet it with a certain philosophical equanimity, the rabbi can only weep at its arrival. The rabbi is impatient, he has no time for death, he cannot admit death's calmness into his living.

"R. Eleazar ha-Kappar says: Jealousy and greed and [the quest for] honor take man out of the world" (M *Avot* 4:21). Jealousy of what belongs to another, greed for more than one's basic needs, and the quest to arrest the attention of other selves in addition to one's own, drain man's energy and waste his time. He thus squanders the little bit of life that he has before death, he thus is taking himself willingly out of the world, bringing death closer than it already is, into his very living. Added to the rabbi's sense of the transience of time as living, which he shares with Ecclesiastes, is the sense of time as fleeting, reminding us of Jonah's "gourd." "R. Tarfon [around the turn of the second century] says: The day is short and the work is plentiful and the laborers are lazy and the reward is great and the Master presses. He used to say: It is not incumbent upon you to finish all the work, but neither are you free to avoid it" (M *Avot* 2:15, 16).

For one with such a consciousness there is never enough time. And, therefore, the perception of approaching death always tinges the present with a very vivid sense of urgency. And that sense of urgency gives the experience of performing the Law a quality of excitement and uniqueness.

> We repeat there (M *Avot* 2:10): "R. Eliezer [ben Hyrcanus] says: Repent one day before your death." R. Eliezer's students asked him, "But does one know on which day he will die!" He said to them, "Then certainly he should repent today lest tomorrow he will die; and he will thus be repentant all his life. And so, too, Solomon in his wisdom said, 'Let thy garments be always white; And let thy head lack no oil'."

Now, perhaps we may return to R. Eliezer ben Hyrcanus' teaching with some degree of understanding. His admonition indeed is grounded in the mood of Ecclesiastes and not merely in the imagery of "white garments" as indicating repentance.[33] For Ecclesiastes, the dimension of man's being is life. Man's biography is a worldly one, as evil as the world may be. He teaches man to embrace the here and now, the substratum of living, but with a sense of sadness. R. Eliezer sets out from this point, but goes further. Man can and must strive to better himself and the world. The way to do this is the way of the Law. That is an endless task, and man is very likely to lose himself and his time in the enormity of the task. Therefore, the sage warns his pupils not to be deluded by the infinity of time and task. Each man has his own completion. That is a subjective completion, limited only by death. One must always have a sense of trying to accomplish the most in the least amount of time. He must always transcend the achivements of the past, even to the point of examining them ever so critically, as painful as that may be. And he must attempt to achieve an excellence in the immediate present that will give him some feeling of accomplishment despite the tragedy of imminent death. In a sense, R. Eliezer is saying that one must, by constant self-criticism and improvement, always be prepared to accept the total end that is death. Living throughout one's years a life of repentance, then, means living with a sense of the utmost urgency of the present.

> The Rabbis repeated: One should always see himself as if[34] his moral debits and merits were of equal amounts: If he does a good deed, happy is he that he has tipped his scales towards merit; If he does a bad deed, woe for him that he has tipped his scales towards debit. As the verse says, "[Wisdom is better than weapons of war;] But one sinner destroyeth much good" (Ecclesiastes 9:18): On account of a sinner's one sin[35] he loses much good. (BT *Kiddushin* 40a,b)[36]

Here again, we have the urgency of the present moment. But this *Baraitha* takes things a step further. One should experience the present moment as if all of one's being turned on it. This is not merely a struggle to improve on one's past. This is a transcendence of the past, seeing the moment in which being is actuated as the central moment of life. Nor is this a withdrawal from the future because of impending death. Rather, it is a viewing of the present as unique because it is here and now and, as such, real, regardless of how long the past and future might be. "Wisdom is better than weapons of war" because wisdom is the only real light in a world being overcome by the darkness of absurdity. But, nevertheless, "one sinner destroyeth much good" because in that world so much depends on the dimension of action that even a sinner, or a fool, can determine fate.

And that dimension of action is viewed as the moment of a present. In the world of the 'I', too, past and future fade into the chaotic masses of remembered perceptions and unrealistic dreams. In memory and anticipation, the distinction between the self and the world, between the experienced and the vicarious, is never as vivid as in the present. But the action of the self in the present is an unequaled strength, a bastion before the absurd of world and man. In the dimension of the moment man makes himself, and his moral behavior now is his essence. In the present, the acting sinner may have more influence on events than all the world's wisdom; and in the present, religious man must act out what it is that he wants his own reality to be. The *Baraitha* continues:

> R. Eleazar ben R. Simeon [ben Yohai, second century][37] says: Since the world is judged according to its preponderance [of merits or debits] and the individual is judged according to his preponderance:[38] If he does a good deed, happy is he that he has tipped his scales and those of the whole world towards merit; If he does a bad deed, woe for him that he has tipped his scales and those of the whole world towards debit. As the verse says, ". . . But one sinner destroyeth much good": on account of a sinner's one sin he loses for himself and for the whole world much good. (Ibid.)

This sage goes even further. Not only for the lonely self does the vividness of the present make its action the "preponderance" of all his actions but for the world the self perceives as well. Man is the subjective center of the world he perceives, and his responsibility to that world should equal his vision.

The seriousness of living that is to result from the consciousness of the way of the Law reaches here its climax. The moment you stand in now, the decision you make, the action you take, now, is your fate and, for you, the fate of the world. And the student of the sages is to live his life this way. Here, precisely at this point, is the pivot of the dialectic of Law and martyrdom of which we have spoken. At the apex of rabbinic seriousness, the seeds of a different way are sown. Let us follow that path in order to follow out the myth of the holocaust of Isaac.

The way of the Law has brought us to the apex of seriousness in the present. Does there not lie in that awe of the present the very undoing of the way of the Law, an undoing that is shattering and terrible?

The *Baraitha* continues:

> R. Simeon ben Yohai says: Even if one were completely righteous all his life yet rebelled in the end, he shall have lost what was beforehand, as the

verse says, "The righteousness of the righteous shall not deliver him in the day of his transgression" (Ezekiel 33:12). And even if one were completely evil all his life but repented in the end, he is no longer reminded of his evil, as the verse says, "and as for the wickedness of the wicked, he shall not stumble thereby in the day that he turneth from his wickedness" (Ibid.) (BT *Kiddushin* 40a,b)

From the juxtaposition we can learn that R. Simeon ben Yohai's son, R. Eleazar,[39] states a view that is grounded in the rabbinic notion of *teshuvah*, repentance. This is implicit in the son's meaning, but reading the *Baraitha* as a whole makes the point sharper. The perception of the importance of the present is a perception of man's ability to repent, to escape the past and to master his essence anew. What effect can that escape into the becoming present have on the sense of the bindingness of the Law? We shall answer that with an extreme example.

It was repeated: It was said about R.[40] Eleazar ben Durdaya [=wine dregs] that there was not a prostitute in the world with whom he had not been intimate. Once he heard that there was a certain prostitute in some faraway place who took a bag of denars for her favors. He took a bag of denars and went, passing over seven rivers in order to reach her. During their intimacy she passed gas. She[41] said, "Just as this gas cannot return to its place, so too Eleazar ben Durdaya will not be enabled to repent." He went and sat among the mountains and the hills. He said, "Mountains and hills, beg compassion for me!" They said to him, "Before we could beg for you we would have to beg for ourselves—as the verse says, 'For the mountains may depart, And the hills be removed' (Isaiah 54:10)." He said, "Heaven and earth, beg compassion for me!" They said, "Before we could beg for you we would have to beg for ourselves— as the verse says, 'For the heavens shall vanish away like smoke, And the earth shall wax old like a garment' (Ibid. 51:6)." He said, "Sun and moon, beg compassion for me!" They said to him, "Before we could beg for you we would have to beg for ourselves—as the verse says, 'Then the moon shall be confounded, and the sun ashamed' (Ibid. 23:23)." He said, "Stars and constellations, beg compassion for me!" They said to him, "Before we could beg for you we would have to beg for ourselves— as the verse says, 'And all the host of heaven shall moulder away' (Ibid. 34:4)." He said, "It is dependent upon me alone." He put his head between his knees and wept bitterly until he died so. An Echo went forth saying, "R. Eleazar ben Duryada is elected for the life of the coming world." (BT *Avodah Zarah* 17a)

In this colourful story, the humor serves, of course, to make the sinner ludicrous, but this in itself has a deeper implication. It underlines the vast chasm the sinner must cross in repenting, a chasm between what is, for the Rabbis, an evil flimflam, tellable as humorous in its absurdity, and the way of the Law. The picture of a man who crosses seven rivers in order to be with a certain prostitute, one who is very expensive and no doubt equally exotic (but then Eleazar knows them all and can only be interested by the different), describes a man whose palate is jaded but his appetite ever more voracious. Deep inside him is a hunger that is far greater yet not at all jaded. The image he has of himself is empty and weak, so weak that he must prove himself time and again, yet each additional "proof" only shows up his weakness. The intimate familiarity of an impersonal prostitute brings a final confrontation with his gray self, and her intimation that what she knows about him is all there will ever be to him is an awakening. It is in these very moments of satiety and impotence that his hunger for the power of the self becomes unbearable. He must escape himself and find himself—or perish. His desperate call for help from the "mountains and the hills," the "earth and the heavens," signifies his sense of personal helplessness. Perhaps in communion with powers outside himself he can find salvation. But the power seemingly incarnate in matter, or impersonal nature, for Eleazar, is only an illusion—his whole life has been a grovelling before that illusion, and he knows it well.

> For the mountains may depart,
> And the hills be removed;
> But My kindness shall not depart from thee,
> Neither shall My covenant of peace be removed,
> Saith the Lord that hath compassion on thee. (Isaiah 54:10)

The vision seen by Eleazar's will is one of a godliness that stresses the transience of nature in all her might and solidity.

> Lift up your eyes to the heavens,
> And look upon the earth beneath;
> For the heavens shall vanish away like smoke
> And the earth shall wax old like a garment,
> And they that dwell therein shall die in like manner;
> But My salvation shall be for ever,
> And My favor shall not be abolished. (Isaiah 51:6)

For the man who is light-headed from the fragrance of inevitable death, even the splendor of the heavens is no more lasting than his own fleeting days. And the heavens, the eternity of poets, shimmer unreally in the light whereby they are like smoke.

Then the moon shall be confounded, and the sun ashamed;
For the Lord of hosts will reign in mount Zion, and in Jerusalem,
And before His elders shall be Glory. (Isaiah 24:23)

For the Lord hath indignation against all the nations
And fury against all their host;
He hath utterly destroyed them,
He hath delivered them to the slaughter.

And all the host of heaven shall moulder away,
And the heavens shall be rolled together as a scroll;
And all their host shall fall down,
As the leaf falleth off the vine,
And as a falling fig from the fig tree.
For My sword hath drunk its fill in heaven;
Behold, it shall come down upon Edom,
And upon the people of My ban, to judgment. (Ibid. 34:2, 4–5)

Before the wrath of the Almighty God of history, even heaven's hosts are as naught, as prosaic as a withered leaf fluttering off a vine and a wrinkling, overripe fig dropping from a browning fig tree. What can stand, then, before God? Is God, then, a negation of all being save his own terrible anger? Eleazar knows, very deeply, the answer to this, and his conclusion never is to embrace nothingness. There is a being as real as God, and that is the being of him who in his smallness knows the awesomeness of God. Finally, there is only his self. Eleazar cries not only because he knows God's greatness but because he knows that in his being as a man there is never an escape into oblivion, only eternal shame. Eternal shame, that is, for the sinner. Remember that we are speaking within the rabbinic tradition and man is never doomed to eternal shame before God; with God he always has the way of the Law. So, Eleazar is convinced of his own power to stand before God. But how can he, since he no longer has, if he ever had, the strength for the way of the Law? Eleazar, "son of the wine dregs," finds the answer in a different strength, a superhuman strength of heroism. He can storm Heaven, grasp the grandeur of salvation in his own arms—if he can find the strength to annihilate his past and his future, if he can stand before God in the dreadful responsibility of a lonely present whose unbelievable intensity is to determine all at once the essence of Eleazar's being. Eleazar has this strength; he finds himself, regains his own godly image; he mocks the prostitute; he saves himself, in the heroic sacrifice of his own life, as Abraham was ready to sacrifice his own in the body of his son Isaac, the son who was life and promise to him. Eleazar embraces the ultimate of being—a heroic being of complete immediacy, for nothing else remains for him—he shirks nothingness with loathing. He is a paradigmatic rabbinic martyr, who returns to the way of the Law through repentance but escapes from its awesomeness, recognized in the intensity of repentance itself, through the awesome heroism of martyrdom. He flees from before God to God himself!

Again, Rabbi Judah the Prince is said to cry: "Rabbi [Judah ha-Nasi] wept, saying, 'There is one who makes his world in years while another makes his world in a moment.'" And, furthermore, "Rabbi [Judah ha-Nasi] also said: It is not enough for the repenters that they are accepted, but they are even called 'Rabbi' [as R. Eleazar ben Durdaya]!" (BT ibid.). How incisive is Rabbi's perception that repentance that leads into martyrdom is not the epitome of obedience to the Law but rather the very undermining of rabbinic authority and an alternative to it. Is this merely the perception of genius, or is it an interpretation of a historical development that Rabbi Judah the Prince, in his dismay and fear of the development, only dared hint at?

So again, this time in the matrix of repentance, we see the dialectic of Law and martyrdom. Did this affect the rabbinic attitudes toward repentance? Yes.

> It was repeated: R. Eleazar says: It cannot be that He will "clear the guilty" (Exodus 34:7) for it is already said that He "will by no means clear the guilty" (ibid.); and it cannot be that He "will by no means clear the guilty" for it is already said that He will "clear the guilty".[42] How, then? He clears those who repent and does not clear those who do not repent. R. Mattiah ben Heresh asked R. Eleazar ben Azariah [when the latter was] in Rome, "Did you hear the four categories of atonement which R. Ishmael [early part of the second century] expounded?" He said, "They are three and repentance accompanies each and every one:[43] If one transgressed a positive commandment and repented, then before he has a chance to move he is already forgiven, as the verse says, "Return, ye backsliding children, [I will heal your backslidings.—'Here we are, we are come unto Thee; For Thou art the Lord our God']" (Jeremiah 3:22; also see 3:14). If one transgressed a negative commandment and repented, then repentance holds [his debit] in abeyance and the Day of Atonement atones, as the verse says, "For on this day shall atonement be made for you, to cleanse you; from all your sins shall ye be clean before the Lord" (Leviticus 16:30). If one transgressed those commandments for which the punishment is to be cut off (כריתות) or to be put to death by the court, and repented, then repentance and the Day of Atonement hold [his debit] in abeyance and sufferings complete his atonement, as the verse says, "Then will I visit their transgression with the rod, And their iniquity with strokes" (Psalms 89:33). But one who has profaned

the divine name [in public], then neither can repentance hold in abeyance nor can the Day of Atonement atone nor can sufferings complete his atonement, but rather all of them together hold in abeyance and death completes his atonement, as the verse says, "And the Lord of hosts revealed Himself in mine ears: Surely this iniquity shall not be expiated by you till ye die, Saith the Lord, the God of hosts" (Isaiah 22: 14) (BT *Yoma* 86a)[44]

According to R. Ishmael repentance helps unconditionally only for comparatively minor sins. For more serious transgressions, repentance helps only as part of a process which ends with the Day of Atonement. This means that the experience of repentance can no longer be a grasping of the present, because no matter how sincere or intense, it must stretch through the time–axis, reaching its conclusion only with the arrival of the tenth of Tishri. Furthermore, it is no longer the psychology of the repentant's stance vis-à-vis being that determines his escape from sin, but there is now the cultic factor of a holy day, whose meaning is set by the Law as for atoning. True, the individual partakes of the penitence of that day only if he repents, but once having repented, his forgiveness is sealed by his participation in a formularized cultic ritual. The fact that one day a year is set aside as the final date for atonement also encourages men to experience their own repentance coincidentally with the drama of the calendar, increasing the seriousness of their repentance with the approach of the awesome day. This takes away from the experience of repentance its sense of spontaneity and thus its immediacy. Repentance, then, is no longer a reaction to the fleetingness of living and, consequently, no longer a daring embracing of the present in its immediacy, a heroic being in the moment. Rather, it is a living out personally of a drama described in the progress of the calendar, experienced through the unfolding of the year, in time as a dimension of past, present, and future. We are speaking, therefore, of a neutralization of the notion of repentance in its potentially antinomian nature. The Law takes repentance into its order of things and so changes its essence. In the first of Tishri, as the beginning of the Days of Awe and as the first of the Days of Repentance, we have a further institutionalization of repentance and undermining of its spontaneity. Even in the case of the most serious offences, the rhythm of the calendar continues to be the frame for living one's life in penitence, though freedom from sinfulness comes to a person with such heavy guilt only in death. The *Tosefta* has the same material:

But one through whom the divine name was profaned [in public][45] and who repented, then neither can repentance hold in abeyance nor can the Day of Atonement atone, but rather repentance and the Day of Atonement atone for a third, and sufferings during the rest of the days of the year[46] atone for a third, and the day of[47] death completes his atonement[48] . . . (*Tosefta Yoma* 5[4]:8)

Death has lost its ability to lay its hand on man before its time; fear of death no longer stops the pulse of time, nor does the dread of guilt, as well deserved as it may be, bring man to heroically embrace death. And this neutralization of antinomian repentance is firmly established in the Mishnaic traditions:

One who says "I will sin and then repent [and again] I will sin and then repent" is not given the opportunity to repent. [If one says] "I will sin and the Day of Atonement will atone", the Day of Atonement does not atone. Sins that are committed as between man and God are atoned for by the Day of Atonement. Sins that are committed as between man and his fellow are not atoned for by the Day of Atonement until he placate his fellow. The following was expounded by R. Eleazar ben Azariah: ". . . from all your sins shall ye be clean before the Lord" (Leviticus 16:30): Sins that are committed as between man and God are atoned for by the Day of Atonement. Sins that are committed as between man and his fellow are not atoned for by the Day of Atonement until he placates his fellow. R. Akiva said: Happy are you, Israel! Before Whom are you purified, Who purifies you—your Father Who is in Heaven, as the verse says, "And I will sprinkle clean water upon you, and ye shall be clean" (Ezekiel 36: 25); and another verse says, "Thou hope of Israel" (Jeremiah 14:8 and 17:13):[49] Just as the ritual bath purifies the unclean, so does the Holy One Blessed is He purify Israel. (M *Yoma* 8:9)[50]

R. Akiva stresses the efficacy of repentance as coming from God as Israel's heavenly Father and, we might add from the mishnaic context, on the Day of Atonement. This is different from Ezekiel's conception of repentance, which we have analyzed earlier, where its efficacy is grounded in the very makeup of man's psyche. It is that experience of repentance which may be a way into martyrdom because there it is an experience of the power and freedom of the self. But, in R. Akiva's view, the repentant depends ultimately on God's grace. The roots of this view, too, go through the visions of Ezekiel, as is evidenced by the verse the sage quotes.

And I will sprinkle clean water upon you, and ye shall be clean; from all your uncleanlinesses, and from all your idols, will I cleanse you. A new heart also will I give you, and a new spirit will I put within you; and I will take away the stony heart out of your flesh, and I will give you a heart of flesh. And I will put My spirit within you, and cause you to walk in My statutes, and ye shall keep Mine ordinances, and do them. (Ezekiel 36:25–27)

But the difference is this. For Ezekiel the redemption of Israel must finally take place through God implanting in Israel "a new heart . . . and a new spirit" because until then they have possessed a "stony heart." Because of his demanding vision of repentance, Ezekiel despairs of Israel's ability really to repent by themselves; but he never questions for a moment the efficacy of that repentance, which is totally human. The "dry bones" must be raised up by God because they are dead and withered, otherwise man would have the power of life within himself by virtue of his humanity. Ezekiel never winces from his vision of the strength incarnate in man's embrace of the present in repentance. But R. Akiva and the authors of the view that institutionalizes repentance in a neutralizing calendrical framework are deeply sensitive to the potentially destructive power of man's heroic passage into the present. R. Akiva's homily calls the freeing from sin a cleansing before God and describes it as an immersion in a ritual bath, performed albeit by man but efficacious through the Law. This clearly makes the flight from guilt a reassertion of man's elevation through the ways of God and thus a reassertion of redemption through the Law. The cooptation of repentance and release from guilt into the way of the Law does not stem from a despair of Israel's power to repent but, quite the contrary, from a deep-seated fear that man's superhuman power of the self may be his very destruction. Perhaps, R. Akiva sensed that power and danger so sharply because of a personal predilection for martyrdom?

One may somehow live with the awesomeness of the Law without the flight to martyrdom, R. Akiva's martyrdom notwithstanding. The reading of the Binding of Isaac on the second day of *Rosh ha-Shannah* thus loses the original meaning that motif had in connection with the old fasts for rain and deliverance, which, as we saw, retained their spontaneous nature. Now it becomes a promise that the terror of martyrdom will not be again.

But the question is Does institutionalization of religious experience successfully retain its teaching grasp on the heart of man? The answer in this case is that once martyrdom has become so deeply a part of the historical Jewish phenomenology, it can no longer disappear. It returns, even through the syndrome of repentance, when yearning can no longer be contained. There are still congregations, and there will continue to be, where, despite adherence to institutionalized formulas, the reading of the Binding of Isaac on the second Day of Awe may cause one whose ear is attuned to shiver deeply. That may happen either where the terror of the Holocaust still defies the calmness of history and order, or where there still lives a vivid religiosity that transcends history and order or subverts them.[51]

Those who watch history and biography with concerned expectancy must surely fear the signs of that yearning when they appear.

Our discussion of repentance should end by stressing again that the consciousness of repentance may be a matrix both of return to the Law and the escape to martyrdom. It is a stage for acting out the dialectic of Law and martyrdom, a dialectic so important in the history of Judaism, as we yet shall see, that no amount of institutionalization could do away with it. Indeed, for all the implied reservations about, and institutional limitations of, repentance, its zealous defenders were always to be found throughout the history of rabbinic thinking.

We now may look to an answer to the question raised at the beginning of this chapter: What is it about repentance that makes it knowable through God alone and not through "Wisdom and Prophecy" (as we learned from the source in PT *Makkot* 2:6)? In repentance, religious man's ability to escape himself and find himself, to flee the wrath of God and return to God, depends on his superbly heroic strength to actualize his being completely in the present—to the point of embracing martyrdom, the ultimately tragic and thus ultimately heroic action. That man has this strength within himself cannot be known through "Wisdom," because the wise study of men's biographies, especially the biographies of the pious, generally does not indicate heroism of this form. Nor can the prophet's piercing vision of the future reveal the essence of repentance, because absolute repentance, as heroism, indicates precisely the denial of the time axis of past–future and leaves only the dimension of the present. To the martyr, or to the truly repentant man, the moment is far more transparent than to any prophetic seer.

> Rav Joseph son of R. Joshua ben Levi . . . [said], "I heard them saying [in the afterworld], 'Martyrs, no one can stand in their presence.'" (BT *Bava Batra* 10b and *Pesahim* 50a)

> R. Abbahu said: Where the repentant stand, [even] the completely righteous do not stand. (BT *Berakhot* 34b and *Sanhedrin* 99a)

The repentant and the martyr come together in a lonely and heroic meeting.

We may now sum up some of the things we have said. Man's sense of his smallness and sinfulness is the revelation of his standing before God. It is a tearing open of the vast heavens that are God's; man is no longer imprisoned in the closed world of his autonomy. He is rather a speck, a citizen, in the world of the infinite God. Not at one with the cosmos but an 'I' breathlessly gazing out and in. How inebriating is it to breath the vastness of the outstretching that becomes a belonging—always becomes. In the way of the Law, man climbs laboriously forward, guided along the way by the stars. In martyrdom, his breathlessness at vision is a consummation.

Man's spiritual biography may take place in a dialectic of his transcendental or metaphysical nature and his immanent nature. By the former is meant his sense of reality as stretching out into the past and the future. This is the way of the Law and of history. By the latter is meant man's sense of the reality of the present. This is no less spiritual than the former. Man's ability to focus in on the moment of being as unique among all others, despite his memories and anticipations, is a truly spiritual ability. Animals, perhaps, live mainly in the present; this is not a focus on something unique, it is mere blindness. All their presents are the same. How unique is man in his perception of the uniqueness of each moment! Man's immanent spiritual nature takes the way of repentance, always gazing at the light of today, never daring to glance back into the spent past, Orpheus ascending from Hell, nor awaiting tomorrow like Sisyphus impaled on the future. The way of the Law is in the perception of the terrible evil in the world; it brings man, finally, to tremble before God. The way of repentance is the way of inner light and strength, and may bring man to martyrdom and to embrace God. In the former, man bears the yoke of heaven; in the latter, he is free. Religious man, who follows profoundly the way of the Law to its end, may flee from being in awe *before* God to martyrdom and being in awe *with* God (as in Isaac's holocaustal offering), not in the mystical sense (though that, too, may follow) but in the sense of action, a *this-worldly* enactment of being with God. And the same religious man, having saved himself in his readiness to martyrdom, may recoil, at the very last moment, from the terrible need to do all in the present, back into the way of the Law. In the rabbinic consciousness, the way of the Law saves man, finally, from two extremes: the gnostic escape into otherworldiness and the martyrial flight into the immediate. This, despite the paradox that the way of the Law may bring man to the edge of those two temptations and beyond. Yet the vision and possibility of those two temptations are the very amelioration of the Law; they soften the temptations to seek the tyranny of the Law. The possibility of overlooking the evil that abounds in the world, either in the melancholy and pain of living as a self or in the suffering of others, simply does not exist for religious man in the tradition we are studying, Nietzsche's deprecation notwithstanding. Religious man, in his religiosity, does not have a sense of humor, as Satan must surely have.

Chapter Nine

Pangs of Messiah

W e have seen that the story of the Binding of Isaac is a myth of deliverance. By myth we do not mean a figment of the imagination; on the contrary, it is a true reality. It tells the story of religious man's odyssey through the awesome seriousness of living the way of the Law and history, into the awesome heroism of a totally realized being in the immediacy of martyrdom and, perhaps, back. It is acted out in the vividness of biography, a living drama of life and death, whether that of Honi the rain maker or that of the repentant Eleazar ben Durdaya. It is this acting out of the myth that makes it into a real myth, thus distinguishing it equally from a mere figment of the imagination and from history, which is not told as an acting out of something but rather as an acting out of itself. We shall now retell the story once more, this time in a guise where acting out the myth surpasses all others in grandeur and where, therefore, the myth is most likely to hesitate into fantasy, thus neutralizing potential action rather than fostering it. The hero of this story is the messiah.

> In the footsteps of the Messiah insolence will burgeon, and prices will soar,[1] the fruit of the vine will be plentiful yet wine will be expensive, and the government will become an object of worship, and there will be no remonstration, the meeting-house will be for prostitution, and Galilee will be destroyed, and the Gablan will become desolate, and people [refugees] from the borderlands will wander from town to town—yet welcomed nowhere, and the wisdom of the Scribes will stagnate, and those who fear sin will be despised, and truth will be absent,[2] youngsters will put the old to shame, the old will stand up before the children, "the son dishonoreth the father, the daughter riseth up against her mother, the daughter-in-law against her mother-in-law, a man's enemies are the

men of his own house" (Micah 7:6). The face of that generation is like the face of a dog, the son is not ashamed [even] before his father. On whom is there for us to lean? On our Father Who is in Heaven. (M *Sotah* 9:15)[3]

In the times when the messiah is on his way, men's respect for one another will fade; inflation will spiral despite sufficient supply, indicating a crumbling economic order; misplaced authority will be venerated; not only will evil reign but its usual counterweight in human togetherness, the feeling that misuse of power is objectionable, will not be felt by anyone; the meeting hall, where the power of togetherness is palpable, will be for whoredom; destruction, all too reminiscent of the Great Revolt where imperial power was animallike and the peoplehood of Israel was crushed, will be rampant; desolation will replace settlement; refugees will roam the country without hope of finding new homes; the very knowledge of the Law will partake of decay rather than build or sustain order; those few who still fear sin will be outcasts; truth will not be suppressed, it will disappear because of its weakness in the prevailing atmosphere; the natural authority of age and parents will be either perversely reversed, or dissolved; the family structure will collapse or worse, turn into a hell; trust will change to undermining. In short, the humanity of that generation will degenerate into the drooling, tongue-hanging gaze of a dog and there will be no shame before anyone, let alone before God. In whom can there still be faithfulness except in Israel's heavenly Father?

The Mishnah is describing a total breakdown of everything that crystallizes into polity. The forces that interact to make an ordered society out of the chaos of mob—viz., mutual respect, sense of value, sense of right and wrong, respect for togetherness, loathing of the rampaging power that is worse than anarchy, the drive to settle down and build, the sense of awe before a law that is beyond man, the sense of truth, the ability to look to one's elders if only out of gratitude for having arrived at the present through the past, even love based on intimacy and warm knowledge. All the things that constitute a societal structure of understandability and love of living as a human being will disintegrate. Underlying this passage is a vision of society as rooted in men's sensibilities and stretching into the realm of government, a vision of polity as part of the basic substance of society and men—a vision that must be negatively inferred from the picture of the abject terribleness of the age when that structure crumbles on its rotting foundations.

If such evils characterize the eve of the Messiah's coming, then the messianic redemption must entail the reconstitution of those crumbling sensibilities and their structures. That, in turn, means that messianic redemption must take place along the patient axis of time or, more correctly, of history. No one with such a worldly vision of man's fall could imagine his redemption as anything but a process in which man's self rediscovers itself, learns, grows, reaches out, heals moribund relationships (which took eons to evolve and were real for centuries before crumbling under the impact of massive forces), rebuilds with great effort forgotten structures and ancient awes. That regrowth is real only if it happens in the dimension where the things lost were once real, the dimension of history. The organic structure of self-society-polity, whose grandeur is concrete only in the flux and order of history, cannot be built in the dream dimension of time as an apocalyptic event or in a gigantic onetime maneuver by heroic leaders. This Mishnah says that the dimension for deliverance is the dimension of living together in all its worldly richness. Thus, history is the wheel and loom on which messianic redemption is spun and woven, albeit with the aid of tremendous messianic energy and even personality. Think of Zionism in its painful and slow unfolding as an example of such a grand vision of redemption.

If messianic redemption must take place through history, then the distance to that redemption is the distance of history. We then are separated from messianic redemption by history. The present order of the world has yet to evolve through the messianic process. Here is a grounding for a notion of the world as evil. Ironically, the same perception may be a matrix both for a vision of redemption as historical and for a vision of redemption as apocalyptic. It may even lead to denial of the possibility of this-worldly deliverance. If the messianic millenium is so far away that one must trek through human history to reach it, then one dreams of an apocalyptic outburst to storm history itself.

There is a parable which describes this situation very well: The Emperor, so it runs, has sent a message to you, the humble subject, the insignificant shadow cowering in the remotest distance before the imperial sun; the Emperor from his death-bed has sent a message to you alone. He has commanded the messenger to kneel down by the bed, and has whispered the message to him; so much store did he lay on it that he ordered the messenger to whisper it back into his ear again. Then by a nod of the head he has confirmed that it is right. Yes, before the assembled spectators of his death—all the obstructing walls have been broken down, and on the spacious and loftily mounting open staircases stand in a ring the great princes of the Empire—before all these he has delivered his message. The messenger immediately sets out on his journey; a powerful, an indefatigable man; now pushing with his right arm, now with his left, he cleaves a way for himself through the throng; if he encounters resistance he points to his breast, where the symbol of the sun glitters; the way, too, is made easier for him than it would be for any other man. But the multitudes are so vast; their numbers have no end. If he could reach the open fields how fast he would fly, and soon doubtless you would hear the welcome hammering of his fists on your door. But instead how vainly does he wear out his strength; still he is only making his way through the chambers of the innermost palace; never will he get to the end of them; and if he succeeded in that nothing would be gained; he must fight his way next down the stairs; and if he succeeded in that nothing would be gained; the courts would still have to be crossed; and after the courts the second outer palace; and once more stairs and courts; and once more another palace; and so on for thousands of years; and if at last he should burst through the outermost gate—but never, never can that happen— the imperial capital would lie before him, the center of the world, crammed to bursting with its own refuse. Nobody could fight his way through here even with a message from a dead man.—But you sit at your window when evening falls and dream it to yourself. (Kafka, *The Great Wall of China*, Muir translation)

Are the meanderings of history any more transparent than Kafka's "door-keepers" or closer than his "fallen angels"? One who lacks the courage to dream is liable to view this world in its evil as being so distant from God that only the Gnostic ascent beyond eons to another world where the present one is even unimaginable may bring deliverance. From out of Kafka's world, which is vastly, tortuously, humanly distant from the pos-sibility of redemption, eerily resounds the echo of despair and dreaming. Could the gnostic world be more distant from God than Kafka's?

In the view where messianism arrives along the axis of history, man relates to God by working out an orderliness through the dimension of time. God is transcendent here at least in the sense that an unfolding through time determines man's stance before God; man does not stand before, or with, God in an immediate fulfillment. There always is an incompleteness because not enough time has passed, that is to say, not enough has happened. And what has yet to happen is vast. True, in the way of the Law man is so deeply involved in redemption along the time axis that he experiences a dynamics that makes him feel very close to God. The beautiful vision that one is actually a partner to the working out of things brings the goal ever so palpably close. Thus, the Law fills the gulf of waiting, which is a chasm of meaninglessness, with a dynamics of action and achievement, a "bringing of redemption," however slowly, and thus a nearness of God in the movement forward. The Law is a conviction that redemption may take place through time, which sprawls through past deeds and sins and through present and future toil, both of the individual and of the People of Israel through history. The Law is a huge optimism that fills the void left by the gnostic despair and flight. Yet, its tremendous effort is a keen witness to the difficulty of the way through time and history, of the imperfection of this world. So that while the belief in the Law is a powerfully saving optimism, it may open the way to the gnostic flight just as much as it may close it.

Hence the messianic yearning finds out a different path as well.

". . . even the selfsame day it came to pass, that all the hosts of the Lord went out from the land of Egypt" (Exodus 12:41)—these ["the hosts of the Lord"] are angels. And so you find that whenever Israel are oppressed, the Divine Presence is, as it were, oppressed together with them, as the verse says, ". . . and they saw the God of Israel; and there was under His feet the like of a paved work of sapphire stone" (Exodus 24:10): And when they are redeemed what does the verse say? ". . . and the like of the very heaven for clearness" (ibid.).[4] And the verse says, "In all their affliction He was afflicted" (Isaiah 63:9). Thus, perhaps, only when the group suffers; What about when the individual suffers? The verse says, "He shall call upon me, and I will answer him; I will be with him in trouble" (Psalms 91:15). And the verse says, "And Joseph's master took him, and put him into the prison. . ." (Genesis 39:20), and it says, "But the Lord was with Joseph" (ibid. 39:21). And the verse says, "Thy people, whom Thou didst redeem to Thee out of Egypt, a nation and its God" (II Samuel 7:23).[5] . . . R. Akiva says: Were it not for Scripture it would be impossible to say it; as it were Israel said before the Holy One Blessed is He, "You have redeemed Yourself". And so you find that wherever Israel went into exile, as it were the Divine Presence went into exile with them. They went into exile to Egypt, the Divine Presence is together with them, as the verse says, "Did I [not] reveal Myself unto the house of thy father, when they were in Egypt in bondage to Pharaoh's house?" (I Samuel 2:27).[6] They went into exile to Babylon, the Divine Presence is together with them, as the verse says, "Thus saith the Lord, your Redeemer, The Holy One of Israel: For your sake I have been sent to Babylon" (Isaiah 43:14).[7] They went into exile to Elam, the Divine Presence is together with them, as the verse says, "And I will set My throne in Elam" (Jeremiah 49:38). They went into exile to Edom, the Divine Presence is together with them, as the verse says, "Who is This that cometh from Edom, With crimsoned garments from Bozrah?" (Isaiah 63:1). And when they will finally return, as it were the Divine Presence returns together with them, as the verse says, ". . . then the Lord thy God will turn thy captivity" (Deuteronomy 30:3)—it does not say "God will bring back" but rather "God will turn". And it says, "Come with me from Lebanon, my bride, With me from Lebanon" (Song of Songs 4:8) And does she [Israel, the bride] come from Lebanon [the Temple[8]], does she not go up to Lebanon, and what, then, is the meaning of "Come with me from Lebanon, my bride?" As it were "I and thee went into exile from

Lebanon, I and thee go up to Lebanon". (*Mekhilta* to Exodus 12:41 [pp. 51–52])[9]

One reads this text incorrectly if one hears only the suffering of exile. There is here a feeling of cosmic loneliness. How powerful must that feeling be if only the notion of an immanent divine presence can relieve it! Nor is it correct to speak merely of "an immanent Divine Presence." The point is *not* that the Divine Presence has exiled itself from the Land and gone out into the land of the heathen. This type of anthropomorphism is foreign to rabbinic thinking[10] and, in any case, is not in keeping with the sense of the text. The point is rather that the Divine is in a state of exile, to wit, He is suffering the anguish of exile to such an extent that one can say, anthropomorphically of course, that he *is* in a state of exile. How great must Israel's anguish be if God himself must share it!.

Israel's experience of exile is one of estrangement in the world. Not only is the barbarism of the heathen so absurd and cruel, but the heathen is not even able to comprehend the horror with which his behavior is viewed. Compounded by the heathen's view that the Jew is strangely different, the experience of exile becomes one of lostness and wandering in a bewildering and repelling world. If we describe this sense of estrangement as a "cosmic loneliness," we perhaps can understand the need for the exile of God. It is almost a gnostic estrangement, where the Jew questions the very congruousness of his being with the evil heathens. The Gnostic yearning to escape imprisonment in a world that thwarts man's attainment of what many souls consider to be their profoundest hunger and most elemental need is based on the conviction that what is sought must subsist staggeringly far away from the clutches of this-worldliness and the men who thrive in it. But if God himself is immersed in the darkest corners of the Exile, it is because the Jew cannot shake off the realness of this world, cannot even traverse it with some saving sense of lightness or humor. The greatest reality is always in the sharpest of experiences, be they ecstatic or tragic. The Jew would lose his sanity if he thought that his travails were an impulsive amphigory, if he thought that he had to face them in isolated loneliness from meaning or from existence in the cosmos. Israel's cosmic loneliness can be relieved only because their suffering is never trite, because God always suffers with them in the reality of Exile.

Religious man must always recognize his inadequacy. The People of Israel are unable to overcome their loneliness merely by strengthening the sense of 'we' as against the 'they'. The religious intensity with which the estrangement of exile is viewed says that man alone cannot cope with it. So it is that, in his great love for Israel, God also suffers the Exile and the exiles find strength and are not alone.

"It was repeated: R. Simeon ben Yohai[11] says: Come and see how dear are Israel before the Holy One Blessed is He, that wherever they went into exile the Divine Presence is together with them" (BT *Megillah* 29a).[12] Loneliness is not relieved merely by being in the presence of someone else. The alleviation of loneliness requires a breaking out from the sense of personal isolation and finding a common experience of being with another. So, too, cosmic loneliness is not lessened merely by the notion of divine presence nor even by a notion of divine suffering per se.

Before one can speak of divine suffering, one must understand something of religious man's intimation of the nature of God's very being. That being is not to be understood, in the rabbinic perception, in terms of a 'Thou' before whom 'I' stand and certainly not as a 'totally Other'. Liturgy speaks the words of *I* and *Thou* in prayer. But, in the proliferation of anthropomorphisms in the biblical lexicon and even more in early rabbinic literature, and certainly in the notion of God as suffering the Exile, we perceive a knowledge of God as welling up through man's knowledge of his own self, albeit a godly self. Man discovers God not in the power or order of nature or the world but rather in the essence of his own spiritual make up. This does not mean that God is a projection of man's self; it means that self-knowledge is the discovery of a great deal more than oneself.

Man knows the being of self by virtue of the "I am." In fact, statements about the "I am" such as "I know that I am" or "It is good that I am" dull the fact of the "I am". It is also true that other statements that I make can not have the same assertiveness as the statement "I am." We understand "being," when applied to something other than one's self, as a being of "that thing" "in the world." But we do not know "that thing" in itself, only its "in the world." While *I* and *am* are inseparable even in thought, *that thing* and *is* are separable, because we can always come up with some explanation for the perception or knowledge of something even if it "is not." As for persons, we sometimes, through the greatness of our humanity, take a "leap of faith" and another person becomes one whose being is essential to our awareness of them—though not necessarily, as people romantically suppose, because of love or hate. When we do make that leap it is a projection of "I am" to another. And that act of breaking out of lonely solipsism is a most religious and holy act because through it, and through the why and the how and the when we do it, we are involved in an act as wondrous as Creation. The ability to do that depends on the greatness of the "I am." And the ultimate feat of the "I am" is the knowledge that "God is." For since it follows from the above that another "am" can never be more real than "I am," then to say, in truth, that "God is" requires the greatest of awe toward the fact that "I am." But the being of "I

am" that I assert for another person is always limited, finally, by its ultimate "otherness," a limit of which my being does not partake—for me.
God is infinite and his being as "I Am" does not partake of the limit of
otherness.

Since Judaism involves the togetherness of God with man, man as "I
am," which means being in the world, it could never imagine God as a
man. This would mean God's total otherness, making togetherness, in our
sense, impossible. To speak of God in human terms is essential to the
relationship of God and man, but to speak of God as actually a man is the
cardinal sin of anthropomorphism, because it makes the otherness of God
final and He becomes even more distant than "the God of the philoso-
phers." The belief in the possibility of togetherness with God is the most
Herculean attainment of man's self.

In Jewish tradition, God does not become man; rather, through self-
knowledge (that is, what tradition sees as self-knowledge), man becomes
godly. My sense of being with other persons involves, always, an existential apartness from them, no matter how intimate and loving the relationship may be. My sense of being with God may enable, theoretically at
least, an ecstatic sense of oneness with him because he is *not* another man.
God is not Thou; he is the Infinite 'I' before which man stands as a self.[13]

Thus, God "suffers" with man, and the fact that man partakes of an
existence that can be a togetherness with God is a true alleviation of his
loneliness.

So we have a sense of Israel's terrible estrangement, a suffering so
profound that it can be relieved only by an experience of being with God.
We noted that "God is in Exile" not in the sense that he is there and not in
the Land of Israel, but rather in the sense that he is suffering the pain of
Exile. The notion of God sharing the suffering of an individual (*Mekhilta*
ibid.) means that even the smallest and blackest of moments has a wholeness to it, since it may be said that God is immanent in it; this is not to
detract from His omnipresence, but to view man's being before God as a
being with God. God suffers like man and with him. Man's being as a
conscious agent is always complete in the present. Man's psyche, his
"soul," exists not as a series of events strung along a linear axis of past,
present, and future, but rather as a single unitary event that forever is
totally present in the moment of consciousness—the now. Man's consciousness is always completely "here and now," even if he himself is not
self-consciously aware of it. To say God "suffers like and with man" means
that God is completely present in each and every human moment of
suffering, as man is. How different is the very notion of time itself here
from the notion of time in historically unfolding messianism. In the historical view, time always exists as a dynamic analyzable duration, a process.

There, time "makes sense" only when it is a more or less orderly process. And, man may be said to stretch out to God, and God to man, in the sense that man tries to "work things out," to make the flux of time into a striving forward toward God, to make time into "salvation history," if you like that term. God in turn draws man along that road of growth and development toward Himself. But here, where "God is in Exile," time is experienced as a present moment. Time does not have to stretch out in order to be real. Rather time is the experience of consciousness in which each now is an indivisible moment, even though it has a duration. The substratum of the psychological experience of time is always the present, and the present, as Augustine pointed out, is a unity, a moment in the sense that it is not numerically measurable nor divisible. Just as the psyche is always completely "here" in the immediacy of consciousness, so, too, the experience of time is one of unity and not of extension. The self would know to embrace a total completion in the present. Indeed it yearns for it because that is its own nature, even though the nonself world more often than not is a prolix and wearisome one. Thus, the time of self is a very different time from the time of history. And in the time of self, where the present moment is a complete unity (memory and anticipation only making that moment ever more vivid), God may be said to be present in the now.

So it is that God is immanent, with man, even in the darkest darkness. He descends with man to the depths of hell, this is his real omnipresence, Satan has no domain. Salvation, therefore, is always at hand, imminent. Godliness is inherent in all events experienced by man, ready to burst out immediately. When deliverance is to happen, God need not come down to man to lead him out; he is always with man and returns to the Land of Israel with him.

Salvation, as imminent, must be very different from the redemption through history. In line with what I have been saying all along, one cannot isolate elements from a religious consciousness, understand them, and then return them to their places. We must understand the consciousness we dare analyze as an organic, whole structure. If the notions of time and God's relation to the world mean something unique, then so may the concomitant notions of salvation and redemption. We will continue our line of investigation on through messianic vision, too, where it naturally leads us.

At this point we must stress something that should already have been evident. Consciousness is a living in the world. Therefore, a given consciousness is never a pure idea structure. Men live highly complex, colorful, and often chaotic lives, and that is the level at which consciousness is. Thus, although we speak of "religious" consciousness, or a consciousness of "Law" or of "martyrdom," or even of a "rabbinic" consciousness, we do so only for the sake of oversimplification and "clarity." The very idea of a dialectic, which we have discussed, should imply the adventure of living rather than philosophy. In any case, we must never lose sight of the fact that our rabbinic sources, by their very nature, are deeply grounded in living and in teaching as part of living and are not long, theoretical, literary tracts. Our rabbinic sources were composed as fragments, as part of the memory of a man's life, and not as autonomous and extensive literary productions that sustain and explain themselves. Thus, for example, although R. Akiva is undoubtedly a sage of the Law, we are not at all unsettled when we find in his words the basis for an unfolding that leads in quite a different direction. We have already hinted that while R. Akiva's martyrdom probably is *not* the result of a martyrial consciousness but rather of one that views history as the arena for a redemption which must be battled for, nevertheless even in him the dialectical swirlings swerve out at times, passing into the realms of heroism and, perhaps, even mysticism. We may, we must, try to understand a consciousness as an organic structure in order to be able to grasp it with our understanding. But, we do not expect the living of that consciousness to coincide with our idea structure. Biography may reveal, to us its interpreters, a consciousness; but living is never a slave, even to biography. I stress this point particularly now because we are entering ever deeper into a theme that becomes problematic in turbid moments of Jewish history, and the words and lives of the sages in which we find our theme expressed come down to us through varied and involved traditions.

So, let us continue. Where do we find a messianism that is in the dimension of imminence? The answer, already in some of the prophets, particularly, again, in Ezekiel.

We have already seen that Ezekiel focusses in on the innerness of individual man. Deliverance involves, therefore, a profound change in man's "heart" and "spirit":

> A new heart also will I give you, and a new spirit will I put within you; and I will take away the stony heart out of your flesh, and I will give you a heart of flesh. And I will put My spirit within you, and cause you to walk in My statutes, and ye shall keep Mine ordinances, and do them. And ye shall dwell in the land that I gave to your fathers; and ye shall be My people, and I will be your God. (36:26–28; also cf. 11:19–20; 37:14)

This "new heart" and "spirit" is the inner change which enables repentance. We already have seen how profound an affair repentance is for Ezekiel and have noted that, as an element of deliverance, it therefore takes place, finally, through the grace of God, by his gift of "a new heart" and his spirit entering man. This identifies an event that is real in man's deepest and holiest depths, an event of the "heart," with a godly event, that is, an event in which God is a partner or an agent. Like the notion of God in Exile, it draws the Almighty into the "smallest" of moments—"small," that is, in comparison with the events of the "salvation history" of Israel and the world. And it is here connected with the vision of a final redemption, where Israel will remain God's people and he their God. Thus, while for Ezekiel deliverance retains its connection, generally speaking, to the "salvation history," here it begins to take shape in a new dimension as well, the inner dimension of the self.

For Ezekiel, deliverance must still take place mainly along the historical axis. But in the awe-inspiring richness of his imagination he has a vision that implies the possibility of a quite different drama of deliverance.

> In the five and twentieth year of our captivity, in the beginning of the year, in the tenth day of the month, in the fourteenth year after the city was smitten, in the selfsame day, the hand of the Lord was upon me, and He brought me thither. In the visions of God brought He me into the land of Israel, and set me down upon a very high mountain, whereon was as it were the frame of a city on the south. (40:1–2)

In Chapters 40–43, Ezekiel walks through and caressingly measures the precincts of a noncorporeal Temple. Ezekiel's transportation to that "heavenly" Temple intimates a freeing from the space–time dimension; and the measurability of that Temple gives it a certain concreteness that transcends the need to await the rebuilding of the earthly Temple. While the message of the vision is the coming earthly rebuilding, the vision also makes the deliverance embodied in that rebuilding palpable in the immediate present. Whatever apocalyptic uses Ezekiel's vision may have been put to, in itself it is not apocalyptic. It is not a fantastic event that takes place when the time of history is "ripe." Its saving breath does not have to await the passage of time, it makes deliverance palpable now.

Thus, we have in Ezekiel the intimations of a deliverance that need not, that cannot, take the way of history. I am convinced that Ezekiel perceived this vision because he has connected the notions of repentance, deliverance, and the immanence of God, as we have seen. In such a scenario, the Temple may always be rebuilt in all its grandeur, albeit a heavenly Temple, in the immediacy of the present. Such a scenario, in any case, is deeply embedded in rabbinic thinking.

> R. Liezer [R. Eliezer ben Hyrcanus] says: If Israel do not repent, they are never to be redeemed, as the verse says, In repenting and rest shall ye be saved" (Isaiah 30:15).[14] R.Joshua [ben Hananiah] said to him: Is it

possible that if Israel will consistently refrain from repenting they are never to be redeemed! R. Eliezer said to him: The Holy One Blessed is He will raise up over them a harsh ruler like Haman and immediately they will be repentant, and they will be redeemed. Which verse is applicable? "Alas! for that day is great, So that none is like it; And it is a time of trouble unto Jacob, But out of it shall he be saved" (Jeremiah 30:7). R. Joshua said to him: But it is written in Scripture, "For thus saith the Lord: Ye were sold for naught; And ye shall be redeemed without money" (Isaiah 52:3). What does R. Eliezer do with this verse? [He interprets it to mean that through] repentance [they "shall be redeemed without money"], as the verse says, "He hath taken the bag of money with him; He will come home at the full moon" (Proverbs 7:20).[15] R. Joshua said to him: But it is written, "I the Lord will hasten it in its time" (Isaiah 60:22). What does R. Eliezer do with this verse? [Deliverance will come through] repentance [that will mark "its time"], as the verse says, "And now, Israel, what doth the Lord thy God require of thee, but to fear the Lord thy God, to walk in all His ways, and to love Him, and to serve the Lord thy God with all thy heart and with all thy soul . . ." (Deuteronomy 10:12). R. Aha said in the name of R. Joshua ben Levi: If you will be deserving, then "I . . . will hasten it"; and if not, then "in its time". When R. Joshua said to him [R. Eliezer]: "'How long shall it be to the end of the wonders?' And I heard the man clothed in linen, who was above the waters of the river, when he lifted up his right hand and his left hand unto heaven, and swore by Him that liveth for ever that it shall be for a time, times, and a half; and when they have made an end of breaking in pieces the power of the holy people, all these things shall be finished" (Daniel 12:6–7), R. Eliezer left. (PT *Ta'aniot* 1:1 [63d])[16]

The admonition of R. Eliezer ben Hyrcanus (end of the first century and beginning of the second century) that if the people of Israel do not repent they shall *never* be delivered forbodes the possibility of an endless blackness of exile. This implies a nonhistorical viewing of deliverance, where history by itself is not an ineluctable unfolding toward a millenium, indeed where Exile may transcend history in the former's permanence. And, thus, the converse should also be true. If Israel *does* repent, then deliverance should be immediate, not taking place along the historical axis. This is also implied by the way the sage interprets the verse from Isaiah 30:

> For thus said the Lord God, the Holy One of Israel:
> In repentance[17] and rest shall ye be saved,
> In quietness and in confidence shall be your strength;
> And ye would not.
> But ye said: "No, for we will flee upon horses";
> Therefore shall ye flee;
> And: "We will ride upon the swift";
> Therefore shall they that pursue you be swift. (15–16)

Rather than taking the way of history and bringing deliverance through armed struggle, Israel should take the way of repentance and thus bring deliverance through God. The latter way is "waiting for God": "Happy are all they that wait for Him" (verse 18). But it is a wait that depends on deliverance as resulting from repentance and not a wait for the progress of history. It thus is a wait in the dimension of the repentance–deliverance dynamic, a dynamic that is intelligible where deliverance comes through the very same yearning that drives to repentance. It is not waiting in the dimension of history where man is carried along, even if he is an active partner, in a great stream of unfolding events and a patient progress that transcends the individual. R. Eliezer continues this theme, in answer to his colleague R. Joshua's amazement. Should Israel not repent of its own accord, says R. Eliezer, then God will subjugate them under the yoke of an evil Haman, which will certainly cause them to repent "immediately," and through this they will be delivered.

> And these are the words that the Lord spoke concerning Israel and concerning Judah. For thus saith the Lord:
>
> We have heard a voice of trembling,
> Of fear, and not of peace.
> Ask ye now, and see
> Whether a man doth travail with child;
> Wherefore do I see every man
> With his hands on his loins, as a woman in travail,
> And all faces are turned into paleness?
> Alas! for that day is great,
> So that none is like it;
> And it is a time of trouble unto Jacob,
> But out of it shall he be saved.
> And it shall come to pass in that day,
> Saith the Lord of hosts,
> That I will break his yoke from off thy neck,
> And will burst thy bands;
> And strangers shall no more make him their bondman;
> But they shall serve the Lord their God,
> And David their king,
> Whom I will raise up unto them. (Jeremiah 30:4–9)

R. Eliezer interprets this prophecy to fit his own vision by resetting verse 7, which he quotes, in the context of deliverance through repentance. "And it is a time of trouble unto Jacob, But out of it shall he be saved" comes to mean that precisely through the advent of that suffering Jacob will be saved, because suffering draws man into the immediacy of deliverance. In great travail man cries for immediate deliverance and repents; that is, as we have seen before, he leaps into an intense righteousness of the moment, tearing himself from the past, and deliverance storms history— now. We remember that R. Eliezer ben Hyrcanus himself admonished his students to repent with the sense that death is imminent, with the sense of the uniqueness of the moment. Deliverance, as grounded in such repentance, is also a deliverance that transcends history into the present. Furthermore, we should remember that R. Eliezer ben Hyrcanus lived at a time when Israel's suffering in the clutches of the Roman Empire was unbearable; no "Haman" could have inflicted much worse pain. Thus, this sage, like his younger contemporary and pupil, R. Akiva, must have dreamed of a deliverance close at hand, though unlike R. Akiva it is unlikely that he supported the way of military struggle through history, as we shall see.

We should not take R. Eliezer's reference to Haman as a casual reference. I suspect that the drama of Mordecai and Esther is conjured up because it connotes something more than repentance and deliverance, namely Mordecai's scorning of Haman even to the point of complete readiness for martyrdom. We shall return to this theme, and its connection to messianic redemption, later.

R. Joshua then asks:

> For thus saith the Lord:
> Ye were sold for naught;
> And ye shall be redeemed without money.
> For thus saith the Lord God:
> My people went down aforetime into Egypt to sojourn there;
> And the Assyrian oppressed them without cause.
> Now therefore, what do I here, saith the Lord,
> Seeing that My people is taken away for naught? (Isaiah 52:3–5)

Israel's present suffering, says the prophet, is not "in exchange for money," it is not for immediate gain. It is part of Israel's long history, a history that entails both the Egyptian exile and redemption and the Assyrian oppression. Therefore, the final redemption, too, must come by way of that history not through repentance. Redemption through repentance would be redemption through a nonhistorical event, a redemption "for money"—for an immediacy. So R. Joshua reads the prophet's words, quite in keeping with Isaiah's view of "salvation history," even if that view is not readily perceptible in these opaque verses. But R. Eliezer gives the verses a very different melody, and they say just the opposite. "And ye shall be redeemed without money" means that only repentance can help! "He hath taken the bag of money with him" is apparently interpreted by R. Eliezer in line with a rabbinic tradition that we know as part of a later homily (*Korban ha-Edah*): "'He is gone a long journey' (Proverbs 7:19): [Though God 'is gone,'] He has the righteous who pray and bring Him. . . . 'He hath taken the bag of money with him' (ibid. 7:20)— 'money' means the righteous" (BT *Sanhedrin* 96b).

R. Joshua is not put off by this either; he rightly perceived how deeply the vision of redemption through history by the God of history is inherent in much of the biblical tradition. Is it not written that,

> The smallest shall become a thousand,
> And the least a mighty nation;
> I the Lord will hasten it in its time. (Isaiah 60:22)

"In its time"! That is the key—the "proper time" along the way of history. "R. Johanan ben Torta said to him [R. Akiva], 'Akiva, grass will sprout from your cheeks [in the grave] and yet the son of David will not have come!'" (PT *Ta'aniot* 4:8[68d]). Here, R. Eliezer turns the tables completely. Deliverance comes "in its time" indeed, but that is not the time of history. It is rather the time of repentance, that is, the present. R. Eliezer's meaning is not merely a play on the Hebrew letters that make up both the word for *its time* and the word for *now*, as in Deuteronomy 10:12. Rather this play on letters underlines the sage's sharp intent. The "in its time" of deliverance is identical with the now of return to the Law, of repentance, because the latter draws into the former, both subsisting in the same nonhistorical dimension. R. Aha in the name of R. Joshua ben Levi perceives two possible axes of deliverance and handles the verse in a more homiletical fashion. He distinguishes between deliverance through repentance, which God "hastens" into the present, and the deliverance that unfolds through history. One can sense in his words the unbearable distance between the two. We shall return to R. Joshua ben Levi on this subject later.

The difference between R. Eliezer ben Hyrcanus's perception of the messianic deliverance and the apocalyptic one of the book of Daniel is not to be bridged. In the apocalyptic view there is the terrible wait for the "proper time"; finally, history is so awesome that it must be stormed and shattered. R. Joshua may have read the imagery of Daniel as referring to the way of history and not as an apocalypse. However it is read, R. Eliezer ben Hyrcanus could react only with silence.[18]

That repentance draws into a deliverance in the dimension of the present, a *salvation*, is stated even more explicitly by some of the *amoraim*: "Rav said: All the 'Ends'[19] have ended and it depends on repentance and good deeds[20] alone. And Samuel[21] said: It is enough for the mourner that he continues to mourn" (BT *Sanhedrin* 97b). In Rav's words there is a clear ring of exasperation with the circumlocutions of history. It is difficult to say what is Samuel's meaning. Does he mean that the depressed state of Israel is in itself enough to bring the deliverance now, or are his words, perhaps, a prayer? Or does he mean that in the realm of deliverance nothing is to be done now—it is sufficient that Israel mourns as it does—until the "proper time"?

> Israel said to Isaiah, "Our teacher Isaiah, what will come to us of this night?" He said to them, "Wait for me until I ask." When he had asked, he returned to them. They said to him [again], " 'Watchman, what of the night?' (Isaiah 21:11b)—What sayeth the Watchman of the worlds?" He said to them, " 'The Watchman said: "The morning cometh, and also the night" ' (ibid. 21:12)." They said to him, "And also the night?" He said to them, "Not as you are thinking, but rather—morning for the righteous and night for the wicked, morning for Israel and night for the heathens." They said to him, "When?" He said to them, "Whenever you want, He wants. . . ." They said to him, "What [then] is holding back?" He said to them, "[There must be] repentance—'Return, come' (ibid.)." R. Aha said in the name of R. Tanhum bar Hiyya: If Israel would repent for one day, the son of David would come immediately. What is the applicable verse? "For He is our God, And we are the people of His pasture, and the flock of His hand. Today, if ye but hearken to His voice!" (Psalms 95:7). (PT *Ta'aniot* 1:1 [64a])

At this point we may be allowed an interim summation. R. Eliezer ben Hyrcanus and R. Joshua both flourished between the great revolt against Rome and the Bar Kokhba revolt. It is a time of destruction, chaos, terrible disappointment, unbearable persecution, and a regathering for a final desperate lunge. Yet, it is also the period in which united rabbinic activity reached its peak, and those rabbinic structures crystallized in which the Jewish nation flourished as the People of God down to the present day. If we remember that for R. Eliezer the Rabbinic activity at Jabneh meant personal tragedy—his excommunication because he profoundly opposed the Jabneh drive toward the centralization of Rabbinic authority and the standardization of the Law according to a majority ruling—then we may understand better his own reading of the events of the day. For him the period was marked by failure of man, whether exemplified by the Romans sinking to depths of depravity or by the Jews unable to continue in the old ways.[22] For him, the fall of the old order—which he may have idealized, but this always happens after destruction and holocaust—was a sign that something was deeply wrong with man as an individual. The yearning for deliverance was above all a yearning for the salvation of man as an individual. Schooled by his own bitter experiences with his colleagues, he must have perceived failure in himself no less than in others. This sage, whom R. Johanan ben Zakkai described as a "well-faced cistern that loses not a drop" (M *Avot* 2:8), must have felt more than anyone else how heavy was the burden of the past upon Israel and upon himself. We may understand, therefore, why his soul yearns for deliverance through repentance. Israel as an individual must find himself again, must renew his piety before God, must reembrace the Law with intensity. But all this must be done with a freshness, with a feeling that it has never been done before. The new devotion must be a break with the past, a transcendence of the past. In short, even the Sage of the Law himself must take the way of the present, the way of repentance. We misunderstand R. Eliezer completely if we think that he is addressing the sinful alone. He is really addressing the most pious of Jews, his colleagues, his beloved students, and even himself. Deliverance for him is a flowering into the present, by way of man living his intensest piety in the becoming now. Total self-realization in the present would create the reality in which messianic deliverance would be an unavoidable, immediate, concrete truth. But "total self-realization in the present" means, paradoxically for R. Eliezer, a break with the past. Thus one of the greatest of the sages of the Law, and one of the most conservative, voices the deep-seated yearning of many of his contemporaries for spiritual renewal. His intent, and there is not the slightest doubt about this, was the intensest possible upholding of the Law. But, did he know that precisely that and the yearning for it, when they explode into virile and actual messianism, are the matrix either of a vast antinomianism or, as we shall see, of a gigantic need for the heroism of martyrdom? The first of these possiblities he did not recognize; the second, as we shall see, he did.

R. Joshua read his generation differently. He saw in it not the failure of men but the tragedy of history. Israel was the crane that had dared poke its head inside the gaping jaws of the lion, Rome, and yet survived (*Genesis Rabbah* 64:10 [p. 712]). Roman rule was such a fearful historic reality that even the Chosen People must cower before it. The evil that was Rome existed and held worldwide power; Israel's tragedy was to have fallen into the clutches of that evil polity. What would repentance do to change that reality of conquest and unrelenting, harsh administration? And revolt was equally out of the question (ibid.) because history cannot be wrenched from its unfolding—an unfolding so powerful that it seemed that the Roman hordes would rule forever. For R. Joshua, the only way was the way of the Law, because it alone subsists in the same dimensions as history: the dimension of biography, which takes time; the dimension of peoplehood, which spreads over space and time; the dimension that spans the distant past and the vague future. The dimension of patience, patience,

patience. For R. Joshua, redemption is the constitution of polity according to the Law; obviously, this means freedom from Rome, but it can be realized only through history as an unfolding not as a wrenching.

However, we are gravely mistaken if we merely equate R. Eliezer's and R. Joshua's views with two readings of the events of their times. We have seen that deep in the rabbinic consciousness is a dialectic of Law and something else, something equally awesome. R. Joshua's perception is not merely a reading of events close to him, it is a deeply ingrained tendency toward seriousness, hope, and patience. Similarly, R. Eliezer's is a view that finds its concreteness in a reading of events yet wells up from perception of the awesomeness of being, regardless of the historical situation. Such perceptions, perhaps, never would be true if they did not find the proper historical constellation to interpret. But when they do find it, they interpret with a passion, and their virility is felt and understood only if we appreciate their source, which is the very being of religious man.

Chapter Ten

The Binding of Messiah: Messiah Ben Joseph

["In that day shall there be a great mourning in Jerusalem . . ." (Zechariah 12:11, and see context]: What is the context of this mourning? R. Dosa [ben Harkinas, flourished already during the first century, before the destruction of the Temple, until the second decade of the second century][1] and the Rabbis disputed the question. One of them said: It is for Messiah ben Joseph who was killed. And the other said: It is for the evil inclination which was killed. The view of the one who said, "It is for Messiah ben Joseph who was killed", is in order as that fits the verse, "And they shall look unto Me because they have thrust him through; And they shall mourn for him, as one mourneth for his only son" (ibid. 12:10). But according to the view of the one who said, "It is for the evil inclination which was killed", does this require mourning—it should require rejoicing! Why did they weep? As R. Judah expounded:[2] In the coming future The Holy One Blessed is He will bring the evil inclination and slaughter it in front of the righteous and in front of the wicked. To the righteous it appears like a high mountain while to the wicked it appears like a hairbreadth. These will weep and these will weep: The righteous will weep, saying, "How were we able to conquer such a high mountain!" And the wicked will weep, saying, "How is it that we were unable to conquer[3] this hairbreadth!" And the Holy One Blessed is He, too, will wonder with them, as the verse says, "Thus saith the Lord of hosts: If it be marvelous in the eyes of the remnant of this people in those days, should it also be marvelous in Mine eyes, saith the Lord of hosts" (ibid. 8:6). (BT *Sukkah* 52a)

Two *Amoraim*, one said: This (Zechariah 12:11) is the mourning for Messiah. And the other said: This is the mourning for the evil inclination. (PT *Sukkah* 5:2 [55b])

207

Without getting involved in the intricate story of Messiah ben (the son of) Joseph as it is rooted in early apocalyptic visions and as it develops in later apocalyses, we shall try and understand his meaning for early rabbinic thinking. Suffice it to say that Messiah ben Joseph will appear before the advent of Messiah ben David and that he must die in battle. His descent from Joseph through the house of Ephraim apparently implies that he does not merely precede ben David chronologically, he is the incarnation of an aspect of messianism different from that of the Davidic scion. The prophecy of two messiahs suggests a highly developed messianic vision that, if uncovered, no doubt would be fascinating. But the wholeness of such a vision is beyond our grasp here, since it is no more than hinted at in the literary remains of early rabbinic thinking. We shall concentrate on two questions: Why is the death of a messiah necessary for deliverance? How is this connected with the notion of the destruction of the "evil inclination"? That the two notions are indeed connected is evidenced by the fact that, as the Babylonian Talmud itself points out, the thought of "mourning" over the death of the evil impulse seems absurd in a rabbinic context, the Talmud's answer notwithstanding. And, if the negation of the evil impulse is, for some reason, to be mourned, then why, indeed, negate it? It is clear that both opinions grow out of a common matrix where mourning is essential to the messianic advent, and each opinion lights up that same theme from a different angle.

The notion that a messiah must die for the advent of the deliverance is tied up with the notion of the "pangs of Messiah," that deliverance must come through cataclysmic suffering and even death.

> R. Johanan said: In the generation during which the son of David comes, the students of the Sages will dwindle in number and the rest—their eyes will fail with sorrow and anguish. And many troubles and harsh decrees will wax anew: Before the first will have waned the next will already be rapidly approaching. (BT *Sanhedrin* 97a)

That the "students of the Sages dwindle in number" is apparently a gentle way of saying that they die, and this is said explicitly in the parallel: "The Rabbis say: In the generation during which the son of David comes, the Sages of the generation will die" (*Song of Songs Rabbah* to 2:13).[4] About those events it is said: "Ulla said: Let him [the Messiah] come but may I not see him. And so, too, Rabbah said: Let him come but may I not see him. . . . And so, too, R. Johanan said: Let him come but may I not see him" (BT *Sanhedrin* 98b).

Deliverance does not unfold through historical events that may or may not affect the individual. That people experientially suffer those events is at least of equal importance. In the last passage quoted, suffering cannot be avoided unless one avoids being present in the generation of deliverance altogether. If suffering is so important for the advent of deliverance, then we are speaking of a deliverance that does not come along the historical axis but unfolds in the subjective experience of men—not a redemption, then, but a salvation. The dying Messiah ben Joseph seems to epitomize this happening of messianic deliverance. It is not "merely" his suffering and death but the fact that he stands heroically in "battle" where it is *clear beforehand* that death *must* be the result. In other words, his death is a martyrdom, not a vicarious martyrdom, as we shall see from our analysis of the "death of the evil impulse," but a heroic death suffered by the messiah along with others.[5]

If we understand the death of Messiah ben Joseph as martyrdom for the sake of deliverance, then we can understand the death of the evil inclination similarly. The mourning over the death of the evil inclination means that that inclination is a part of man himself, and its "death" is the death of part of man, of part of the human activity.

> ["And God saw every thing that He had made, and, behold, it was very good" (Genesis 1:31)]. Nahman said in the name of R. Samuel: "behold, it was very good"—this is the good inclination. "*and*, behold, it was very good"—this is the evil inclination. But is it conceivable that the evil inclination is "very good"? [It is good] in the sense that if not for the evil inclination nobody would build a house or marry a woman nor have children. And likewise Solomon says, "Again, I considered labor and all excelling in work, that it is a man's rivalry with his neighbor" (Ecclesiastes 4:4). (*Genesis Rabbah* to 1:31 [9:7, pp. 71–72])

This is in keeping with rabbinic thinking where the evil inclination is rarely personified, and even when personified, it is done metaphorically for the most part. The death, then, of the evil inclination, as part of man's self, must mean that it is to die in each and every man.[6]

An individual's overcoming of his evil inclination is referred to as a "killing" of that inclination, in the following:

> Abraham our father made the evil inclination good, as it is written, "Thou . . . didst choose . . . Abraham; and foundest his heart faithful before Thee" (Nehemia 9:7–8). . . . But David could not withstand it so he killed it in his heart. What is the applicable verse? "[For I am poor and needy,] And my heart is wounded within me. [I am gone like the shadow when it lengtheneth; I am shaken off as the locust. My knees totter through fasting; And my flesh is lean, and hath no fatness]" (Psalms 109:22–24). (PT *Berakhot* 9:7[14b])

And the death of that inclination in the individual can mean only a final overcoming of one's own will by one's self, a "conquest" of the will: "Who is mighty? He that conquers his inclination" (M *Avot* 4:1). Here, too, in the internal realm, the evil inclination is not personified; it is not even dissociated from man's personality, certainly not to the extent that one could speak of its death as anything but an act of will. The context of the verse quoted from Psalm 109, interpreted as referring to David's own struggle with his evil inclination, implies that the death of the inclination has to do with the experience of repentance. And it is exactly in this context that we find this notion again:

> R. Joshua ben Levi said: Whoever slaughters his inclination and con-
> fesses for it [its deeds], Scripture considers him as if he had honored the
> Holy One Blessed is He in two worlds—this world and the coming
> world, as it is written, "Whoso offereth the sacrifice of thanksgiving
> honoreth Me; And to him that ordereth his way aright Will I show the
> salvation of God" (Psalms 50:23).[7] And R. Joshua ben Levi said: When
> the Temple is intact, a person who sacrifices a burnt-offering—he has in
> hand the reward for a burnt-offering; a meal-offering—he has in hand
> the reward for a meal-offering. But one whose psyche is humble, Scrip-
> ture considers him as if he had sacrificed all the sacrifices together, as the
> verse says, "The sacrifices of God are a broken spirit" (Psalms 51:19).
> And what is more, his prayer is not rejected, as the verse says, "A broken
> and a contrite heart, O God, Thou wilt not despise" (ibid.). (BT
> *Sanhedrin* 43b)[8]

The context of confession is undoubtedly the context of repentance.[9] A repentance that is a "slaughtering" of the evil inclination is of such import for the individual's nature that it has meaning for him even in his being as overcoming death (thus, its meaning for "the coming world" as well). It is a veritable sacrifice, the sacrifice of part of one's very self. And it always remains a psychic experience, a humbling of one's spirit and not the van-quishing of a dissociated, evil reality, of a "Satan." What power does such a person evince that even the Almighty does not disdain it but even succumbs to it! Repentance is a sacrifice of part of the self furthermore because, as we have seen, it is a total wrenching from one's own past, from the dimension of the past in one's being. Repentance, then, is a partial martyrdom. And the "killing" of the evil inclination as ushering in the messianic era thus is parallel to the martyrdom of Messiah ben Joseph.

But, before we complete this scene in the messianic drama and look upon it, let us return to R. Eliezer ben Hyrcanus, in whose perceptions as drawn by tradition we discerned the essential connection between repen-tance and deliverance.

"It was repeated: The students of R. Eliezer [ben Hyrcanus][10] asked him, 'What should a person do in order to be saved from the pangs of Messiah?' [He answered,] 'Let him busy himself with Torah and with acts of compassion'" (BT *Sanhedrin* 98b). The prophecy of the "pangs of Messiah" says that the messianic deliverance must arrive through cataclysmic suffering and death. Either this is an apocalyptic vision, where for deliverance to take place history must be shattered, or else, in the context of a deliverance that takes place through repentance, as R. Eliezer ben Hyrcanus has it, it means that without martyrdom deliverance cannot penetrate into the dimension of the present. We shall see this point again, soon. For R. Eliezer, the only alternative to the pangs of messiah is the way of the Law, because that is the way through patient history. But does the sage believe that that actually is the way deliverance will happen?

> R. Eliezer [ben Hyrcanus][11] says: If you will be worthy and keep the Sabbath, you will be saved from three tribulations: i.e. from the day of Gog and Magog (Ezekiel 38:39), and from the pangs of Messiah, and from the great judgment day. Therefore the verse says, "Eat that [the manna] to-day; for to-day is a sabbath unto the Lord" (Exodus 16:25). (*Mekhilta* to Exodus 16:25 [p. 169])[12]

Though couched in apocalyptic imagery, R. Eliezer's view here is the same. One may avoid the escape from history, with the terrible price that escape involves, only through the way of the Law. This is particularly true in the keeping of the Sabbath, where the profound significance of time's unfolding becomes explicit. However, the sage is quoted as ominously introducing his remark with the words "If you will be worthy," which intimates a deep scepticism as to the ability of man to properly keep the Sabbath. If the Law is not to be kept properly, then the Day of Judgement is a cataclysm. The alternative to the way of the Law is terrifying, but it *does* bring deliverance; as apocalypse, here, it is an escape from history.

> It was repeated: When R. Eliezer [ben Hyrcanus] fell ill, R. Akiva and his colleagues entered to visit him, he sitting in his canopy and they sitting in the main room. And it was Friday, and Hyrcanus his son came in to remove his *tefillin* [before the beginning of the Sabbath]. He [R. Eliezer] scolded him and with that he [the son] left, saying to the colleagues, "It seems that father's mind is affected." He [R. Eliezer] said to them, "It is his mind and his mother's that are affected: How do they ignore serious prohibitions [by not preparing in time for the Sabbath] and busy themselves instead with a minor prohibition [the wearing of *tefillin* on the Sabbath]!" Upon seeing that his mind was clear the Sages entered and sat before him, keeping a distance of four cubits [because he was in excom-

munication]. He said to them, "Why have you come?" They said to him, "We have come to learn the Law." He said to them, "And till now why have you not come?" They said to him, "We did not have time." He said to them, "I will be surprised if they die a natural death." R. Akiva said to him, "What [death] shall be mine?" He said to him, "Yours will be harsher than theirs." He lifted both his arms and placed them on his heart. He said, "Woe for you my two arms that are like the two rolls of the Scroll of the Law that are being folded together [for the last time]. I have learned much Torah and I have taught much Torah. I have learned much Torah and yet I have not emptied out my teachers even as a dog lapping at the sea. I have taught much Torah and yet my students have not emptied me out—only as a paint-brush dipping into the vial. And what is more, I repeat [from tradition] three hundred *Halakhot* concerning the intense *baheret* [which may indicate a leprous syndrome], and yet there was never anyone who asked me something about them. And what is more, I repeat [from tradition] three hundred *Halakhot*, and some say "three thousand *Halakhot*", concerning the [magical] planting of cucumbers, and yet there was never anyone who asked me something about them, except for Akiva ben Joseph. Once I and he were walking along: He said to me, 'Rabbi, teach me concerning the planting of cucumbers.' I said something and the whole field filled up with cucumbers. He said to me, 'Rabbi, you have taught me their planting, teach me their uprooting.' I said something and they were all gathered in to one place."[13] They said to him, "A stuffed ball, a last, and an amulet pouch, a sealed bag of pearls, and a small covered weight, can they become ritually unclean?" He said to them, "They can become ritually unclean, yet they can be ritually cleansed as they are (without emptying them)." "A shoe which is still on the last, can it become ritually unclean?" He said to them, "It remains ritually clean."[14] And he died on the note of "ritually clean". R. Joshua stood up and exclaimed, "The excommunication is undone, the excommunication is undone!" After the Sabbath R. Akiva joined the funeral procession on the way from Caesarea to Lydda. He was beating his breast till the blood dripped to the ground. He began to eulogize him and said. 'My father, my father, the chariots of Israel and the horsemen thereof' (II Kings 2:12): I have many coins, but I have no one to break them down for me." (BT *Sanhedrin* 68a)[15]

R. Eliezer ben Hyrcanus is on his deathbed. He is under a ban placed on him by the scholars at Jabneh, who felt that his refusal to accept the centralized rabbinic authority was too dangerous to be tolerated in those precarious times.[16] Until now, his colleagues and students have respected the ban and kept away. But, now that his end is near, they can no longer bear the separation. Nevertheless, they are careful to obey the letter of the ban; they maintain a distance of at least four cubits from the sage. At first they dare not enter the room, aware of the charged atmosphere engendered by their very belated visit and afraid to upset the dying man. R. Eliezer, very much in character, berates his son and wife for not handling properly the laws concerning the Sabbath approaching through his waning last day. When the solemnly gathered visitors see that the fading man appears to have lost none of his sharpness, they enter the room and sit down, still keeping their distance from him very correctly. R. Eliezer does not mince words, he asks them why have they come, he does not enjoy being visisted as a dying man. Their answer shows their clumsy discomfort, their inability to face the situation that they themselves have been partner to. They come "to learn the Law" indeed! For R. Eliezer this ironically emphasizes what he considers to be their failure in their way through the Law. "And so why have you not come till now?" he demands. "We have not had time," comes the answer. He has been right! The greatest scholars of the day and of tomorrow fail in the way of the Law! Is there any alternative left to them except the way of martyrdom, he wonders, half to himself, half out loud. For R. Eliezer ben Hyrcanus events have turned out in such a way that he can interpret them in light of what for him has always been a deeply harbored suspicion. The way of the Law is to be failed, and by those most faithful to it; and the alternative to it will be no less awesome. One man is there whose ears are attuned to all the chords. "And what shall be my death?" he asks. R. Eliezer knows his beloved pupil R. Akiva, he knows his rippling soul. "Yours will be worse than theirs," he answers.

And here the dying sage turns inward. He is like the scroll of the Law being rolled closed for the very last time. He has learned ever so much of the Law throughout his intense life, yet he has been "not even like a dog lapping at the sea"! And even his most faithful of pupils have been only like a brush darting into the rich colors of tradition. There has been no one at all to wonder about the myriad details of the Law concerning the "intense *baheret*." But there was one man who wondered about the ways beyond waiting. R. Akiva, the son of Joseph, was fascinated, says R. Eliezer ben Hyrcanus, by the possibility of ways that did not pass through patient time. And, it is on this subject that the great sage's mind hovers now, so close to the end.

However, his colleagues and students interrupt his reveries. They want to know if he has changed his old views on controversial points in the Law. But, he has not budged a bit. And his soul passes out in purity. Who feels his loss more than R. Akiva, the son of Joseph?

R. Eliezer ben Hyrcanus envisioned the deaths of his colleagues and students as martyrdoms, as the only alternative to the way of the Law, in which, to his view, they had failed. He must have sensed the impending Bar Kokhba war (perhaps he even lived through it);[17] he must have viewed it as a drive toward martyrdom, not as a struggle through history. If the greatest scholars of the day fail in the way of the Law and can only go the way of martyrdom, is deliverance possible without martyrdom? Is not R. Eliezer ben Hyrcanus's vision of deliverance through repentance, a vision of repentance through martydom? Is not that martyrdom itself the deliverance, the salvation?

The deathbed scene of R. Eliezer ben Hyrcanus is shot through with cryptic meaning. He views his death as a closing of a scroll of the Law for the last time, a perception that was not at all only a subjective one. "The Rabbis repeated: With the death of R. Eliezer [ben Hyrcanus] the Scroll of the Law was hidden away"[18] (BT *Sotah* 49b). His mind wanders to a scene of magical planting and ingathering that defies time. The very different subject that his visitors bring up also indicates another layer of meaning: "They can become ritually unclean, yet they can be ritually cleansed as they are" says the sage; and his final teaching, "It remains ritually clean" clearly is being taken symbolically: "And he died on the note of 'ritually clean.'" The opposition *unclean/clean* is juxtaposed with the opposition *excommunication/excommunication undone*, and the two together are colored by the drama of life and death. Finally, although R. Akiva's repetition of Elisha's exclamation at Elijah's ascent to heaven in the fiery chariot is the tribute of a pupil to his teacher and the teacher of Israel, it also throws open the door to a messianic context. In sum, we have a sharp sense of cryptic contrasts within a frame of R. Eliezer's tarrying in a field where "cucumbers" are magically sown and timelessly reaped and a flickering reference, perhaps, to Elijah as the messianic herald.

> R. Jacob bar Idi said in the name of R. Joshua ben Levi: R. Johanan ben Zakkai, just before his death, instructed, saying: "Clear out [the utensils from] the entire enclosure because of the ritual uncleanliness [that will be caused to them by the presence, under the same roof, of a dead person] and prepare a chair for Hezekiah king of Judah."[19] R. Liezer [R. Eliezer ben Hyrcanus] his student, just before his own death, instructed, saying: "Clear out the entire enclosure because of the ritual uncleanliness and prepare a chair for R. Johanan ben Zakkai." And some say: He [R. Eliezer] saw the same that his teacher saw [i.e., Hezekiah king of Judah]. (PT *Sotah* 9: 17 [24c]; *Avodah Zarah* 3: 1 [42c])

As in the Babylonian Talmud's treatment of unclean/clean, instruction to clear the house of utensils lest they become ritually unclean is associated here with the meaning of the sages' dying. R. Johanan ben Zakkai was apparently a priest[20] and his concern with the laws of ritual cleanliness could be explained as appropriate to that function. But R. Eliezer was apparently not a priest,[21] so that here the explanation does not apply. It may be that both men belonged to those who ate their regular meals with scrupulous adherence to the laws of ritual cleanliness that pertained to the eating of consecrated food such as *Terumah*, even when the latter was not involved, whether the Temple was intact or not.[22] But it is difficult to see this as justifying their final deathbed exclamation, as if to say: See how great these men were! On recognizing that the moment of death was approaching, their first concern was that others should not overlook the danger of ritual uncleanliness to their utensils. Even if we choose this line of interpretation, we must take notice of the meaning of such ritual practice, a meaning that lends a special appropriateness to the mention of such practice in a deathbed scene.

"It was repeated in the name of R. Meir: Whoever is permanently settled in the Land of Israel, and speaks Hebrew, and eats his meals in ritual cleanliness, and recites the *Shema* morning and evening, let it be known to him that he is an initiate of the coming world" (PT *Shekalim*, 3: 4 [47c]). The significance here of permanent residence in the Land of Israel may be appreciated in light of the situation there, from the devastating suppression during the Bar Kokhba revolt to the end of Hadrian's rule in 138 C.E. and on through the reign of Antoninus Pius, when the oppression only gradually lightened. A Babylonian contemporary of R. Meir gives a frightening description of the time and voices the same attitude:

> ". . . them that love Me and keep My commandments" (Exodus 20:6): "them that love Me"—this is Abraham our father and those like him; "and keep My commandments"—these are the prophets and the sages. R. Nathan says: . . . these are the Jews who live in the Land of Israel and give their very lives for the commandments: "Why are you being taken out to be killed?" "Because I circumcised my son." "Why are you being taken out to be burnt?" "Because I read the Torah." "Why are you being taken out to be crucified?" "Because I ate the unleavened bread." "Why are you being flogged?" "Because I lifted the *lulav*." And the verse says, "And one shall say unto him: 'What are these wounds between thy hands?' Then he shall answer: 'Those with which I was wounded in the house of my Lover'[23]" (Zechariah 13:6)—these wounds caused me to be loved by my Father Who is in Heaven. (*Mekhilta* to Exodus 20: 6 [p. 227])

Under such circumstances to live in the Land of Israel, to speak its language which is the language of the holy and is spoken by the angels,[24] to eat one's food in accordance with Temple laws,[25] despite the destruction of the Temple, and to recite twice daily the *Shema*, where the love of God is paramount and his dominion palpable[26] and where he promises the fruitfulness of his Land to those who follow His way—all this is to balk the monstrousness of history. One who does so is indeed an initiate of the coming world, because his living in the world already partakes of a heroism that is itself a salvation. And so R. Eliezer's concern with the laws of ritual cleanliness at the moment before death, even if we suppose it to be a continuation of a lifelong concern, is to be seen in the light of the connection between facing death and embracing a Temple religiosity: there is a Temple immanence despite history,[27] just as the sage perseveres despite death. Indeed, as we shall see, salvation from history and salvation from death meet here.

If we have any doubts about the implication of personal salvation in the story of R. Eliezer's dying, the Palestinian Talmud dispels them. At the moment of death preparation is to be made for the coming of R. Johanan ben Zakkai. This is surely to be read *at least* as a sign of R. Eliezer's following in the way of his teacher, whose coming now manifests the meaning of the teacher's own death.

A structure of contrasts thus becomes visible in the Palestinian Talmud, as in the Babylonian Talmud. In front of the contrast of ritual uncleanliness, which is imminent with death, and ritual cleanliness, which is to be achieved by clearing out the utensils from the house, a movement away from death, there is a more resonant contrast: death and salvation from death. If we go to the Babylonian Talmud, we find that the imagery of ritual uncleanliness and cleanliness there has become richer for us. R. Eliezer's death on the note of ritual cleanliness echoes the Palestinian Talmud's note of salvation from death. Death brings ritual uncleanliness but R. Eliezer's death is a conquest of death and thus of ritual uncleanliness, just as his teacher, in the Palestinian Talmud, comes to meet him beyond death. In the Babylonian Talmud, there also is an echo of this in the contrast of excommunication and excommunication undone.

We saw that in the Babylonian Talmud, in the story of the marvelous cucumbers, there is a hint of something beyond the narration of R. Eliezer's death. This helps to point up the meaning of the continuation in the Palestinian Talmud and that, in turn, again clarifies the Babylonian Talmud. The organicism of the tradition feeding both Talmuds, diffusing into their respective foliations, becomes increasingly manifest. A second opinion in the Palestinian Talmud states that, before dying, R. Eliezer saw the same vision his teacher saw before his death, King Hezekiah of Judah. The choice of the Davidic scion Hezekiah is not to be taken lightly.

> R. Tanhum told that Bar Kappara [beginning of the third century], when in Sepphoris, expounded: . . . The Holy One Blessed is He wanted to make Hezekiah Messiah and Sennacherib Gog and Magog. The Way of Justice said before the Holy One Blessed is He, "Master of the World, but if David, king of Israel, who said so many songs and praises before You, You did not make him Messiah: Hezekiah, for whom You did all these miracles yet he did not say a song before You, him will You make Messiah! . . ."

And when God is pressed to nevertheless appoint Hezekiah as the messiah, He answers, "My secret is with Me, My secret is with Me!" To which the prophet Isaiah exclaims, "Woe is me (Isaiah 24:16), woe is me, till when?" Whereupon an echo went forth saying, "[When] 'the treacherous deal treacherously; Yea, the treacherous deal very treacherously' (Isaiah ibid.)" (BT *Sanhedrin* 94a). And yet another Rabbi, R. Hillel, said, "Israel will not have Messiah because they used him up in the time of Hezekiah" (ibid. 99a). So that there is in tradition, even if peripherally, an aura of messianism around the character of Hezekiah.[28] This is not to say that he is actually thought of as the messiah; rather it means that for that tendency in tradition Hezekiah adumbrates the prayed for messiah in his personality and actions. Thus, when the great king of Judah appears at a sage's death, his appearance has to do with messianic yearnings and hopes. To put this together with our previous perceptions, R. Eliezer's drama of "ritual uncleanliness and cleanliness," that is, of death and salvation, reaches beyond the bounds of a personal deathbed scene in a messianic yearning.

The tradition that R. Eliezer announced the coming of R. Johanan ben Zakkai is in form and content strikingly similar to, though not identical with, the tradition describing the older sage's own final moments. R. Eliezer, before his death, called for evacuation of all utensils in order to retain their ritual cleanliness and preparation of "a chair," in just the same way his teacher did. But whereas his teacher ordered the "chair" for Hezekiah, R. Eliezer ordered the "chair" for the sage who earlier had announced the coming of that king of Judah. The later predeath pronouncement thus retains the messianic symbolism of the earlier one except that, for the sage of the next generation, messianism is alluded to through the mediation of his teacher, who appears as the one who earlier had announced the coming of Hezekiah. For both versions, then, the first in which R. Eliezer announces the coming of his teacher and the second in which he announces the coming of Hezekiah, the symbolism of the coming of the king of Judah points the drama of personal salvation in the direction of a messianism. This element of messianism finds its echo in the Babylonian Talmud's tradition where a student of yet another generation, R. Akiva, who believed Bar Kokhba to be the messiah, refers to his teacher R. Eliezer as Elisha did to his teacher Elijah, the herald of the messiah.[29]

In the Babylonian Talmud, R. Eliezer's mind wanders before his death to a walk he took with R. Akiva, of whose martyrdom he was certain, through a field where he sowed and reaped without time or bending down. The great sage of the Law, who perceived salvation as happening through repentance, despaired of his colleagues' ever passing through that way and foresaw their martyrdom as the only alternative way of breaking through to salvation, that same sage on his deathbed dreamed that time and bending down could be overcome, that the terrible impending martyrdoms would usher in a messiah. How much did his sensing of a hurrying influence his greatest pupil, R. Akiva, who thought that Israel could fling herself through Roman might toward the Kingdom of God?

R. Akiva and many of his colleagues viewed their own fate quite differently. They fought the gigantic imperial polity as the only way to make room for the polity of God in the same dimension, not for the purpose of martyrdom. They attempted, albeit hopelessly, the vast way of history—as the Romans wrote it, by war. Had they succeeded, we would have called them pragmatic freedom fighters (because even freedom we are capable of justifying only as "pragmatic") and men with a grand yet realistic vision of history (as if only "realism" were real). Does their failure make R. Eliezer ben Hyrcanus right?

We may now adumbrate our messianic scenario as crystallized in the prophecy of a Messiah ben Joseph, as revealed by the sayings of R. Dosa ben Harkinas and his colleagues, as recorded in tradition. This scenario of Messiah ben Joseph takes place in the dimension of the self and the present. That Messiah ben Joseph must die a heroic death means an event of salvation in the dimension of the present through martyrdom. This is not a vicarious martyrdom, it is bound up with the notion of the "pangs of messiah," which says the ushering in of deliverance through a cataclysm that is not vicarious. In fact, in this messianic drama, salvation may be coincidental with destruction. Martyrial heroism is a salvation for the heroic self, as we have seen where martyrdom is the culmination of repentance. The deliverance of Messiah ben Joseph, coming through the "slaughtering of the evil inclination," is no less martyrial a scenario, although it may seem to be. It means that salvation, in the dimension of the present, happens through repentance. The fantastic notion of the death of the evil impulse has a foothold in reality in the experience of zealous repentance, where the past is fled from and the reality of the future does not stand up to the vivid determination of the self in the present. The death of the evil inclination is, as it were, a perpetualization of that intense penitential stance. That the evil impulse is slaughtered "before the righteous" as well as the wicked, and that the righteous as well as the wicked cry means that messianic repentance is a wrenching away from the very nature of man, regardless of whether he has sinned. This is such a profound wrenching that "mourning" must take place, mourning for the death of part of man's very humanity, a veritable martyrdom. This is a total break with the nature of man as it has unfolded through the dimension of history, a complete infatuation with man in his repentant state in the present. It is man as he wants to be in his repentant and passionate embrace of God in the present without any regard for the reality of human nature as it stretches out over the difficult road through time. It is an illusion of completeness in the present, the same as martyrdom. These two visions of messianic salvation are one, or they conflate into one. The "death of the evil inclination" evidences a drive leading irresistibly into the salvation abyss of martyrdom, the ultimate conquest of the present.

This is altogether too extravagant a messianism, nay, it is a nihilistic one. Perhaps it is acted out, very imaginatively, in the grotesque Sabbatean apostasies. That we find it at all perhaps may be the reason for the unrelenting rejection of messiahs by rabbinic Judaism, with few exceptions. If redemption is to come along the way of history, then it is too far away to be now, and the prospect of a deliverance "now" conjures up a frightening nihilistic price that, thank God, we as a people do not hurry to pay. It is in the recognition of the profundity of the messianic deliverance that the rabbinic rejection of it is grounded. It is not surprising that the fantasy of a Messiah ben Joseph is hardly mentioned in early rabbinic sources, and when it is, it is part of a longer scenario.[30] Even in the material centering around R. Eliezer ben Hyrcanus, we perceived a structure of repentance, martyrdom, and messianism but not a scenario identical with that of a Messiah ben Joseph.

> The Rabbis repeated: Messiah ben David who is to be revealed in the future, speedily in our day, the Holy One Blessed is He says to him, "Ask of Me something and I will agree", as the verse says, "I will tell of the decree: The Lord said unto me: 'Thou art My son, This day have I begotten thee. Ask of Me, and I will give the nations for thine inheritance, And the ends of the earth for thy possession'" (Psalms 2:7, 8). And having seen Messiah ben Joseph, who was killed, he says before Him, "Master of the World, I ask only for life." [God] says to him, "As for life, before you asked—David your father already prophesied concerning you, as the verse says, "[O Lord, in Thy strength the king rejoiceth; And in Thy salvation how greatly doth he exult! Thou hast given him his heart's desire, And the request of his lips Thou hast not withholden. . . . Thou settest a crown of fine gold on his head.] He asked life of Thee, Thou gavest it him; Even length of days for ever and ever" (ibid. 21:2–5). (BT *Sukkah* 52a)

When the Messiah ben David understands the extremes to which the messianic yearnings have driven his predecessor, the entire messianic fantasy seems to crumble in holocaust. The drive for life seems to preclude deliverance! But the scion of David is reassured. The messianism of David is predetermined to be one of living. The messianism of David is through history not instead of it.

Messiah ben Joseph must precede Messiah ben David. It is the readiness to martyrdom, the nearness of salvation through repentance that enables the redemption through history. It is the inner strength of individuals, their readiness for total sacrifice, and the concomitant conviction that the salvation for which the individual yearns is powerfully imminent that sustains Israel through the patience of history. The consciousness that within his grasp he has a fulfillment that can bypass peoplehood and its ever-so-long story of descent into Exile and Return to the Land gives the individual a conviction of confidence and power. The yearning that wells up inside the individual drives him to repentance and beyond; it knows a salvation that may be complete in the dimension of the self in the present alone. This messianic yearning leads into martyrdom; but it redeems from the despair brought on by the endless waiting for Messiah ben David.

Messiah ben David will inevitably come. Therefore, man need not take the way of the martyrial immediacy and finality. Messiah ben David does not redeem from the external exile alone. He delivers man from his uncontrollable inner drives, which well up from the oversensitivity of the religious soul to the suffering of the Exile. Never is the Exile as black as the inner vision of the religious man sees it; yet we must thank God for the passion of the religious souls. Without it, we would be callously unaware of the pain of man's Exile, in which God himself suffers too. As historical beings, coming into being through the circumlocutions of history, we are inured to suffering, certainly to that of others. The religious vision alone refuses to accept suffering as an inescapable historical reality. The religious soul rebels with all its holiest being against the eternal fatality of evil. The genesis of religion is in the love of the religious soul for man and the fact that she cannot sleep as long as he suffers. Messiah ben David is the grand promise to the religious soul that she need not be driven into martyrdom in the quest for deliverance because deliverance can happen in another dimension, a dimension in which the individual is not so terribly alone. True, the messianic redemption through history is a very different deliverance, but through its promise the religious soul may return to her rest, reassured that evil is not eternal. The messianic yearnings represented by Messiah ben Joseph and Messiah ben David both well up from the religious shuddering before the reign of evil. But, in the prophecy of a Messiah ben Joseph, religious man must break himself on the rocks of the opaqueness, the insensitivity, of humanity in the present in order heroically to conquer evil for an immediate salvation. In the prophecy of a Messiah ben David, on the other hand, the conquest of evil will take the time and energy of history.

With this, we return to our myth of the Binding of Isaac. In the messianism of Ben Joseph, as in the binding of Isaac, salvation comes through a true readiness to martyrdom, a readiness concretized in the actual martyrdom of some, such as that of Messiah ben Joseph. But, as in the Binding of Isaac, the dialectical drawing back of the plunging hand into the way of Law and history retrieves man from the edge of the abyss to which the messianic yearning brings him. That which drives religious man to the abyss is the only power in the world that can save him, if he is to remain himself. The Law and history deliver, but so does the martyrdom of Messiah ben Joseph. That the immediacy of martyrial salvation is really available makes the yoke of Law and history bearable, it delivers from that yoke. Messiah ben David delivers from Messiah ben Joseph, but so does Messiah ben Joseph deliver from Messiah ben David.

Thus, it is that the myth of the Binding of Isaac becomes a myth of messianic deliverance. However, in order for the myth to be palpably true, it must be acted out in the life of the individual, just as Abraham and Isaac acted it out themselves. Does this happen? How does it happen? What are its implications for the notion of messianism? These questions can be dealt with only in the context of biography, which is the subject of the final chapter.

Chapter Eleven

When the Messiah

R. Joshua ben Levi (Palestine, first half of the third century) comes alive to us richly through tradition, and yet in such a way as to reveal the adumbration of a messianic myth that is deeply a part of rabbinic consciousness. That we must await a particular biography for such illumination is liable to create a historical illusion. We may easily conclude that the myth is very young in the period in which we first uncover its clear outline. But the fact that it is fully blossomed, as we shall see, should be sufficient warning as to the illusion of youth. I suspect that we might consider personalities like R. Akiva and his impatient colleagues in the Bar Kokhba struggle, by taking the biography of R. Joshua ben Levi as our starting point. If we, the distant generations, seek illumination of the myth in biography, then we must wait patiently for tradition to give us the biography that not only lives out the myth but also, a much rarer thing, embodies it in a form and meaning that *we* can hear as authentic. However, the development of ideas itself need never await that degree of transparency we demand.

A biblical formulation of yearnings that come to be centered around the figure of a messiah is present in the following sentences from Isaiah. These passages are read as one of the seven *Haftarot* of consolation after the mourning of the fast of the Ninth of Av, which commemorates the destruction of both Temples.

> For brass I will bring gold,
> And for iron I will bring silver,
> And for wood brass,
> And for stones iron;

I will also make thy officers peace,
And righteousness thy magistrates.
Violence shall no more be heard in thy land,
Desolation nor destruction with thy borders;
But thou shalt call thy walls Salvation,
And thy gates Praise.

The sun shall be no more thy light by day,
Neither for brightness shall the moon give light unto thee;
But the Lord shall be unto thee an everlasting light,
And thy God thy glory.
Thy sun shall no more go down,
Neither shall thy moon withdraw itself;
For the Lord shall be thine everlasting light,
And the days of thy mourning shall be ended.

Thy people also shall be all righteous,
They shall inherit the land for ever;
The branch of My planting, the work of My hands,
Wherein I glory.
The smallest shall become a thousand,
And the least a mighty nation;
I the Lord will hasten it in its time. (Isaiah 60:17–22)

This passage is ambiguous to the point of enigma. It may be understood simply as a vision of redemption in the historical dimension, of the reconstruction of polity. But even if the imagery appearing here is metaphorical, it implies straining the historical dynamics and their meaning beyond recognition. Does not this chapter in Isaiah already offer more than an intimation of that deep yearning for deliverance that is rooted in the experiences of history but gazes beyond it?

The words of the final verse of the chapter—"The smallest shall become a thousand, And the least a mighty nation"—seem to be echoed in the words of R. Joshua ben Levi:

> R. Joshua ben Levi said:[1] In the future the Holy One Blessed is He will give in perpetuity to each and every righteous person three hundred and ten worlds, as the verse says, "That I may cause those that love me to inherit substance,[2] And that I may fill their treasuries" (Proverbs 8:21). (M *Ukzin* 3:12)[3]

Both passages seem to promise a deliverance that will be a bursting of the boundary between small and great. In the passage from Isaiah, this impression is contrasted by the end of the verse, "I the Lord will hasten it in its time," which sets up a tension between impatience and patience, between a "hastening" and a "ripening of the time": here deliverance must bear the tension and not burst it. R. Joshua ben Levi unravels Isaiah's vision into his own perception of things: "R. Alexandri said that R. Joshua ben Levi juxtaposed the two parts of the verse, 'I the Lord will hasten it' and 'in its time' (Isaiah 60:22): If they are worthy, then 'I the Lord will hasten it', if they are not worthy, then 'in its time'" (BT *Sanhedrin* 98a).[4] Isaiah is understood as referring to two different unfoldings of deliverance. Yet distant as the two are—one close at hand, "hastened" by the Almighty, the other happening through the grandeur of a ripening history—they are essentially linked through Israel, who hovers uncertainly between both. For R. Joshua ben Levi, the move from the "small" to the "great," from the "I" to the "we," from the "now" or "soon" to the "end of the days," and back again, is not a "bursting." The seeming poles lie close together in the sage's perception of the messianic myth.

A study of R. Joshua ben Levi will show us, I think, the nature of that proximity. We shall first discern what in tradition points, or is connected, to the sage's perception of each kind of messianism, and then we shall try and tell the messianic myth as a whole as he lived with it.

> It was repeated: A group of people who were traveling on the way and were accosted by heathens who said to them, "Give us one of you and we will kill him, and if not, we will kill all of you": Even if they are all to be killed they should not give over one Jewish life. If they [the heathens] singled out one particular person, like Sheba the son of Bichri,[5] they are to give him over and not to be killed.[6] . . . Ulla bar Kushav was sought after by the authorities. He fled and came to Lydda where R. Joshua ben Levi lived. They [the authorities] came and besieged the town, saying to them, "If you do not give him to us, we will destroy the town." R. Joshua ben Levi went to him and talked him into giving himself up. And Elijah of blessed memory was wont to reveal himself to him [R. Joshua ben Levi], but he did not reveal himself to him [after that]. So he fasted several times and he [Elijah] revealed himself to him. He [Elijah] said to him: "But do I reveal myself to informers?" He [Joshua] said to him, "But did I not follow a Mishnah?[7]" He said to him, "But is that a Mishnah of the *hasidim* [pietists]?" (PT *Terumot* 8: 10 [46b])

R. Joshua ben Levi has followed the Law's unflinching calculations, which rule out heroic martyrdom for the sake of a marked man whose death is unavoidable. But struggling inside the sage's person is a facet of his being that knows the revelation of a reality unperceivable to those who choose life over martyrdom. That facet of R. Joshua ben Levi reasserts itself, not through righteousness according to the Law but through self-sacrifice.

When Elijah finally reappears to the unhappy sage, the dilemma of the sage's personality is sealed as unrelievable: He has behaved in accordance with the Law, but in his loyalty to his calling as the rabbi of his flock he has contradicted his being as a *hasid* (pietist), a being which would choose martyrdom.

R. Joshua ben Levi's martyrial tendency is evidenced again in the following:

> R. Johanan used to warn, "Beware of the flies around the *ba'alei ra'atan* [sufferers of some dreaded, festering disease[8]]." R. Zeira was careful not to sit where a breeze that had fanned one of them would pass over him. R. Eleazar would not enter into the same house with one of them. R. Ammi and R. Assi were careful not to eat eggs that came from that alley [where the sufferers lived]. R. Joshua ben Levi huddled together with them and learned Torah. (BT *Ketubbot* 77b)

We shall soon return to this story and especially to the entire context in which it appears, a context that infuses it with meaning. But, for the moment, it is sufficient to point to R. Joshua ben Levi's martyrial heroism and compassion, which conjure up for us themes we have already discussed.

> R. Joshua ben Levi said: Whoever is happy with the sufferings which come upon him brings salvation to the world, as the verse says,

"[Thou didst take away him that joyfully worked righteousness,
Those that remembered Thee in Thy ways—
Behold, Thou wast wroth, and we sinned—]
Upon them have we stayed of old, that we might be saved" (Isaiah 64:4) (BT
   Ta'anit 8a)

R. Joshua ben Levi identifies the *them* of "Upon them have we stayed of old, that we might be saved" as the those who embrace their own suffering. The verse as a whole is understood to mean: we, who have sinned and brought God to anger, rely for our salvation on those who "joyfully worked righteousness", on "those that remembered Thee in Thy ways" and were "taken away by Thee" or were made to suffer. The one who embraces his own suffering thus is likened to the one who dies despite his righteousness, which is understood to mean a martyrial heroism of self-sacrifice, and "that we might be saved" is understood to mean that salvation comes through their self-sacrifice. It should be pointed out already at this juncture that this is *not*, strictly speaking, a notion of vicarious atonement. The sage's reading of the verse calls on all who suffer to interpret their own painful experience. This is a call that may be answered by anyone who is sensitive enough to suffer.

R. Joshua ben Levi's sense of deliverance comes out further in the following: "A certain man was eaten by a lion within three parasangs of R. Joshua ben Levi, and for three days Elijah did not come to speak to the Rabbi" (BT *Makkot* 11a). It was considered an affront to R. Joshua ben Levi's vision of the imminence of divine intervention that within his sphere human life should be cheap. The same sage was reputed to have actualized that imminence of the divine ways in the bringing of the rains; "R. Joshua made a fast-day in the South and it rained, and the people of Sepphoris were saying, 'R. Joshua ben Levi brings the rain to the Southerners'" (PT *Ta'aniot* 3:4 [66c]). The figure of the rain maker has already been interpreted within the context of our themes (earlier, in Chapters 4 and 5).

In short, we may say that R. Joshua ben Levi's vision of a messianic deliverance that may be "hurried" is bound up with his notion of the martyrial figure as driving the happening of deliverance into the dimension of the imminent, of the "now," along the lines discussed.

However, there is another side of R. Joshua ben Levi.

> It was said to R. Johanan, "There are some very old men in Babylonia." He answered in wonderment, "It is written in Scripture, '. . . that your days may be multiplied, and the days of your children, upon the land which the Lord swore unto your fathers to give them' (Deuteronomy 11: 21),⁹ but not outside the Land!" When he was told, "They come to the synagogue early in the morning and stay there till late at night", he said, "That is what helps them, as R. Joshua ben Levi said to his sons: Come to the synagogue early in the morning and stay there till late at night so that you will live long." (BT *Berakhot* 8a)

Here individual deliverance in the form of longevity happens through rising early to go to the synagogue and leaving it only late in the darkened evening. One conquers the dimension of time, the long hours that stretch from dawn till tiredness, by ordering it according to a rhythm steeped in the study of the Law. Death, which follows upon the ineluctable entropy of time, is overcome only when the passage of time as it stretches through man's waking day and days is changed into an unfolding through and about the Law. But R. Johanan understands R. Joshua ben Levi to be saying even more than this: his promise refers not to simple longevity but to the conquest of death that has to do with living in the Land of Israel.

This longevity means a different quality of living, not only a greater quantity. It has to do with man's deliverance, and it happens in the dimension of time unfolding through the order of a biography steeped in the Law. As R. Johanan puts it, the religious individual's way of the Law through long, exhausting days is equivalent to the vast way of a people and their Law and their land, that is, the way of history. For the individual, the long daily religious toil replaces the grandiose way of history.

R. Joshua ben Levi's perception of the importance of the way of the Law and of its meaning comes out in the following as well:

> R. Joshua ben Levi said: One who is going along the way without anyone accompanying him should occupy himself with the study of Torah, as the verse says, "[The fear of the Lord is the beginning of knowledge; But the foolish despise wisdom and discipline. Hear, my son, the instruction of thy father, And forsake not the teaching of thy mother;] For they shall be a chaplet[10] of grace" (Proverbs 1:7–9). If one feels pain in his head, he should occupy himself with the study of Torah, as the verse says, "For they shall be a chaplet of grace unto thy head" (ibid.). If one feels pain in his throat, he should occupy himself with the study of Torah, as the verse says, "And chains about thy neck" (ibid.). If one feels pain in his bowels, he should occupy himself with the study of Torah, as the verse says, "It shall be health to thy navel" (ibid. 3: 8). If one feels pain in his bones, he should occupy himself with the study of Torah, as the verse says, "And marrow to thy bones" (ibid.). If one feels pain in all his body, he should occupy himself with the study of Torah, as the verse says, "[For they are life unto those that find them,] And health to all their flesh" (ibid. 4: 22). (BT *Eruvin* 54a)

If a man is alone and away from home, heading toward a distant destination or following the long way homeward, a stranger without a partner to his wayworness, his relief from limbo is to be found in immersion in the Law. The Law is a wisdom, a gnosis, but a gnosis that instead of underlining man's foreignness to this world makes him at home even in his wanderings. The way of the Law is a way through the long meanderings of living, not a contradiction or alternative to them. So, too, if one senses a tension in the unity of his person, if he experiences a seeming estrangement from his imperfect, unsymphonic body, and certainly if he experiences an estrangement within the melodies of his psyche. Deliverance lies not the distillation of a true inner self or of a divine spark that is the essential man but rather in the retuning of the chords of being, those chords that run up from man's frailest humanity into his loftiest spirituality. If compared to a salvation where the shadow of martyrdom darts, this means an unfolding rather than a wrenching, a patience rather than a now.

A Song of Ascents; of David

I rejoiced when they said unto me:
"Let us go unto the house of the Lord."
Our feet are standing
Within thy gates, O Jerusalem;
Jerusalem, that art builded
As a city that is compact together;
Whither the tribes went up, even the tribes of the Lord,
As a testimony unto Israel,
To give thanks unto the name of the Lord.
For there were set thrones for judgment,
The thrones of the house of David.

Pray for the peace of Jerusalem;
May they prosper that love thee.
Peace be within thy walls,
And prosperity within thy palaces.
For my brethren and companions' sakes,
I will now say: "Peace be within thee."
For the sake of the house of the Lord our God
I will seek thy good. (Psalms 122)

This psalm, upon which, as we shall see, R. Joshua ben Levi comments, expresses an organized theology in succinct form. The first and the last verses emphasize the importance of the "house of the Lord." This sets the frame and the meaning of the psalm. The Temple stands in Jerusalem in a double sense. It stands there in the simple, physical sense; and it stands there as focal point of the "capital" of the Davidic realm. Jerusalem is not holy merely in the sense that it is chosen by God. That it is "builded"— built up, enlarged, glorified by the People of Israel—is no less a part of its essence as the Holy City. It is the place "Whither the tribes went up, even the tribes of the Lord." It is the spiritual center of the Land of Israel where the People actually congregate and experience a togetherness that far exceeds their sense of unity as grounded in mere country and even ancestry. Israel is a People first and foremost because it is the People of God. And the epitome of their being as such is concrete in the Davidic monarchy, called by God to shepherd the monotheism of Israel down through history. This, then, is the thread of the psalm: "David" (as R. Joshua ben Levi reads it) prays for the peace of Jerusalem which is the concretization of the togetherness of the People of God, in which the "house of the Lord" is "builded" thus expressing the essence of Israel; and over all is the house of David that assures the rule, the order, which is the historical expression of the essence of God's People as the psalmist conceives it.

Thus, Israel, its polity, and their rulership, that is to say the People and their history, are united in the theological structure framed by the Temple. Thus, the meaning of the Temple is perceived as far exceeding the Temple's looming as a holy place.

Having understood Psalm 122 in this sense, we are able to interpret R. Joshua ben Levi's comments on it:

> R. Joshua ben Levi said: What is the meaning of that which is written in Scripture, "A Song of Ascents; of David. I rejoiced when they said unto me: 'Let us go unto the house of the Lord'"? David said before the Holy One Blessed is He, "Master of the World, I heard people saying, 'When will this old man die already so that his son Solomon may come and build the Temple and we may go up there for the festival!' and I rejoiced." The Holy One Blessed is He said to him, "'For a day in Thy courts is better than a thousand' (Psalms 84:11)—one day in which you occupy yourself with Torah before Me is better to Me than a thousand burnt offerings which your son Solomon will sacrifice before Me on the altar in the future." (BT *Makkot* 10a)[11]

The people yearn for the unfolding that will bring the building of the Temple. David, though he himself will not be alive to enjoy that ripening time, is happy with the hope of those who will. After all, the house of David will be intimately associated with the caretakership of the House of God; its very legitimacy will be bound up with this function. The divine perception of these things is expressed through a verse from Psalm 84, which reads in full:

> How lovely are Thy tabernacles, O Lord of hosts!
> My soul yearneth, yea, even pineth for the courts of the Lord;
> My heart and my flesh sing for joy unto the living God.
> Yea, the sparrow hath found a house, and the swallow a nest for herself,
> Where she may lay her young;
> Thine altars, O Lord of hosts,
> My king, and my God—.
> 5   Happy are they that dwell in Thy house,
> They are ever praising Thee.   Selah
> Happy is the man whose strength is in Thee;
> In whose heart are the highways.
> Passing through the valley of Baca they make it a place of springs;
> Yea, the early rain clotheth it with blessings.
> They go from strength to strength,
> Every one of them appeareth before God in Zion.
> O Lord God of hosts, hear my prayer;
> Give ear, O God of Jacob.   Selah

10 Behold, O God our shield,
And look upon the face of Thine anointed.
For a day in Thy courts is better than a thousand;
I had rather stand at the threshold of the house of my God,
Than to dwell in the tents of wickedness.
For the Lord God is a sun and a shield;
The Lord giveth grace and glory;
No good thing will He withhold from them that walk uprightly.
O Lord of hosts,
Happy is the man that trusteth in Thee.

The subject of this psalm is the relationship between man and the Temple and the meaning of that relationship. The configuration that is the Temple undergoes a change that is subtle in its language but effective in its implications. The word *tabernacles*[12] in the opening verse refers ostensibly to the Temple building, just as "the courts of the Lord" in verse 3 refers to parts of its complex. But the use of the plural *tabernacles* enables a more resonant meaning. Verses 5 and 11 explain why the suggestive *tabernacles* is chosen. "They that dwell in Thy house" are the righteous whose heart is in "Thy house" though they do not actually "dwell" there. When verse 11 sets "a day in Thy courts" and to "stand at the threshhold of the house of my God" against "to dwell in the tents of wickedness," we understand that one way of life is being contrasted to another. Thus, "Thy tabernacles" is to be understood as meaning both the Temple proper and the indwelling of God that enables man to sense His immanence outside the Temple proper. We have here a metaphorization of the Temple: the Temple as a building says the possibility of standing before God and experiencing his closeness in any place. This reading of the psalm is borne out by the rest of its content as well.

This reinterpretation of the Temple is inseparably connected to the way religious man's living, or "dwelling," is perceived. The psalmist yearns terribly for "the courts of the Lord," a yearning rooted in his "heart" and "flesh" that "sing for joy unto the living God" (verse 3). In finding a home in God's house, like "they that dwell in Thy house" (verse 5), the psalmist is like the free-flying bird[13] that finds a nest for herself and her young, a place where they may find sweet rest and shelter. Religious man's stance with God is not merely the stance of a subject before his king. It is rather a total living with God, as essential to religious man as nest building to the sparrow and the swallow. That the psalmist seeks a dwelling place with God means, then, that everything involved in the home proper—shelter, warmth, relief from loneliness, quiet and knowability, familiarity of belonging—is deeply colored by the being with God. The Temple becomes a home for man as well, it assures that he is not a confused stranger in a cold and foreign world; and living in general becomes equally the domain of being with God and is transformed: "For the Lord God is a sun and a shield; The Lord giveth grace and glory; No good thing will He withhold from them that walk uprightly. O Lord of hosts, Happy is the man that trusteth in Thee"(12–13). The living of the righteous is in the Temple, and the Temple is in the living of the righteous. The visions of Temple and religious man are interdependent.

That this is indeed the sense in which R. Joshua ben Levi reads Psalm 84 may be gathered from his comments on verse 5 of that psalm:

> R. Joshua ben Levi said: Whoever enters the synagogues and houses of learning will worthily enter the synagogues and houses of learning in the coming world, as the verse says, "Happy are they that dwell in Thy house, They are ever praising Thee. Selah". (*Midrash Shoher Tov, Tehillim* to Psalm 84:5 [pp. 370–71, also see note 5])

R. Joshua ben Levi equates "they that dwell in Thy house" with those who frequent the synagogues and houses of learning. This equation makes sense not only because the synagogues and houses of learning replaced the Temple in the course of history but because the sage understands the essence of the Temple in terms of that which happens in those places of prayer and study. "R. Joshua ben Levi said: Whoever praises God in this world will worthily do so in the coming world, as the verse says, 'Happy are they that dwell in Thy house, They are ever praising Thee. Selah'" (BT *Sanhedrin* 91b). Here it is clear that R. Joshua ben Levi is referring to an *event* of religious man's standing with God. The "dwellers" in "Thy house" are such, therefore, by virtue of their living and doing and not by virtue of their location.

> R. Joshua ben Levi said: Where is the resurrection of the dead alluded to in Scripture? The verse says, "Happy are thy that dwell in Thy house, They are ever praising Thee, Selah". It does not say, "They have praised Thee", but rather, "They are ever praising Thee"—so here is an allusion in Scripture to the resurrection of the dead. (Ibid.)

That event, that doing, which is a "dwelling in the house of God" has to do with the very nature of religious man as one who finally overcomes death.

We may get some feeling of how deeply a part of the rabbinic consciousness these perceptions are from the fact that this verse is prefixed, together with verse 15 of Psalm 144, to Psalm 145 and said three times a day by religious Jews, twice as part of the morning prayer and once as the introduction to the afternoon prayer. About this daily repetition of Psalm 145 it is said, "R. Eleazar bar Avina said:[14] Whoever says 'A Psalm of praise; of David' [i.e., Psalm 145] three times every day is assured that he is an initiate of the coming world" (BT *Berakhot* 4b). The religious Jew whose religiosity orchestrates around the crystallized format of praying experiences in that praying, if he takes it seriously, what rabbinic tradition would call sitting in the House of God. And those for whom religiosity is a daily, daylong toil in heart, word, and deed, they veritably "dwell" in the House of God.

Through this reading of Psalm 84 we may grasp R. Joshua ben Levi's reading of Psalm 122. The first part of verse 11 of Psalm 84 is attributed to God himself: "The Holy One Blessed is He said to him, '"For a day in thy courts is better than a thousand"—one day in which you occupy yourself with Torah before Me is better to Me than a thousand burnt offerings which your son Solomon will sacrifice before Me on the altar in the future.'" Here, R. Joshua ben Levi adopts the definition of the Temple given in Psalm 84 for understanding the theological structure in Psalm 122. A day of David's immersion in the Law is preferable to countless animal sacrifices because it is not merely a delivery of substance to the altar. It is a day of living, involving David, Israel, the Law, and God in an organic, dynamic structure in which each is "real" and makes sense: David as the anointed, the "messiah" in the strict sense as well as much more; the Law as the perceived order of things; Israel as the one who perceives and acts upon and who thus is the real substratum of reality; and God who is an objectified reality in the bounds of this all-encompassing world of Israel's living-experiencing. Such an *event*—not merely a place, a thing, a time, or a person—is much closer to the notion of Temple in Psalm 84 than any Temple proper. When the psalmist says "For a day in Thy courts is better than a thousand"(verse 11), he has something like this notion in mind, certainly to the ear of R. Joshua ben Levi. And, thus, the ironic switching of the identity of the sayer of verse 11 from man, as in the psalm itself, to God, as the sage reads it, means the most brazen statement of their truth. The Temple reality must be grounded in a scenario centered around the living of man and not around God. For Psalm 84 to be "true," the Temple must mean a stretching out in the direction of man (with God certainly but man nonetheless) and not man's mere yearning for what is remote from him.

Thus, for R. Joshua ben Levi, it is not that the Law takes the place of the Temple. Rather, the Temple is understood in the sense defined in Psalm 84, and this new sense determines the meaning the Temple holds in the theology of Psalm 122. "R. Joshua ben Levi said: What is the meaning of that which is written in Scripture, 'Our feet are standing Within thy gates, O Jerusalem' (Psalms 122:2)? What enabled our feet to stand up in battle—the gates of Jerusalem, that they occupied themselves with the study of Torah"[15] (BT *Makkot* 10a). R. Joshua ben Levi interprets verse 2 of Psalm 122 in the light of the ideas of Psalm 84: rather than the Temple as a mere cultic center, the preoccupation with the Law, which is the living of the righteous, becomes central to the configuration of People and polity. With this new understanding of the relationship between Temple and man, the former as more than a holy place and the latter as partner to the event of holiness, "David" may indeed say "I rejoiced when they said unto me: 'Let us go unto the house of the Lord'" (122:1). Man becomes ever more central in a view where the Temple really "is" only if it subsists in the dimension of humanity as well. And, in that case, the relationship between man and Temple says something far-reaching about Israel, who alone can build and sustain the Temple and whose righteous, therefore, are "they that dwell in Thy house" (84:5). David, as the anointed who like the righteous is steeped in the Law, indeed has reason to rejoice. Thus, R. Joshua ben Levi's interpretation of Psalm 122 is not at all contradicted by the final verse of that psalm, "For the sake of the house of the Lord our God I will seek thy good." The "house of the Lord our God" remains central, though what is meant is not the Temple that is built of stone and wood but rather the Temple in which the righteous of Israel live. Actually, this interpretation is not at all foreign to Psalm 122, and it is a true insight that brings the two psalms together. For we have already seen that the theological structure of Psalm 122 perceives the Temple as something more than a mere holy building, as part of that structure, as its very frame.

Our interest here in a psalmic theology is for the sake of providing our understanding of rabbinic consciousness with the depth of history in which alone ideas are real. We must, therefore, not limit our vista only to the historical roots of the rabbinic perception in question. We must also, particularly at this juncture, begin to lend a sensitive ear to the difference between the psalmic theology in which R. Joshua ben Levi's view is so deeply rooted and the new nuances, or what at this point in our argument seemingly is nuance alone, in the words attributed by tradition to him; all the while remembering that a fully developed structure of thinking, such as we shall yet discern in the biography of that sage, cannot reasonably emerge suddenly but results from a long historical development in the domain termed *rabbinic*.

R. Joshua ben Levi's statement, although it does not contradict any-thing in either Psalm 84 or 122, nevertheless has a dissonant ring. With all their stress on personal piety, the psalms are almost never entirely free of the deep tinge of prophetic grandeur involving notions like the house of

David, the "salvation history" of Israel, the Land of Israel and the city of Jerusalem, and so on. While R. Joshua ben Levi, too, speaks of David, Israel, and the Temple, his words unmistakably conjure up a different picture. The divine "one day in which you occupy yourself in Torah before Me" is spoken to David the king, but what flashes before our eyes? Not the warrior and statesman, who in the psalms, according to tradition, reveals his own inner religiosity yet always remains David the king, but rather an individual whose life is steeped in the "four cubits" of a personal preoccupation with the Law. In the psalms, David finds time, sometimes, to be alone with himself and his God in moments of deep trouble and anguish and also of joy. In this sense the psalms lift a plush curtain, allowing us to glimpse a dazzling inner world that, outside of the psalms, would remain mostly opaque to us through the history of Israel and the biography of the king. But the David that R. Joshua ben Levi is speaking about is quite different. He is a deeply pious, almost retiring person who darts out into the historical arena occasionally. Put differently, in the psalms David is the hero-king who also writes psalms; in the rabbinic telling, David is the pious and learned man who also leads Israel.

In short, if in the old tradition connecting David to the psalms he is, as has often been pointed out, a micro-Israel of the Israel of "salvation history," then in the rabbinic telling of things he is first and foremost the epitome of the pious and learned Jew. This is evident in R. Joshua ben Levi's comments on verse 2 of Psalm 122:

> R. Joshua ben Levi said: What is the meaning of that which is written in Scripture, "[A Song of Ascents; of David. I rejoiced when they said unto me: 'Let us go unto the house of the Lord.'] Our feet are standing Within thy gates, O Jerusalem"? What enabled our feet to stand up in battle— the gates of Jerusalem, that they occupied themselves with the study of Torah.

The transition from the centrality of David, whom R. Joshua ben Levi takes to be the subject of the first verse, to the major importance that the second verse, in the sage's reading, ascribes to those individuals preoccupied with the Law, is not at all unsmooth. David is important as one who is steeped in the Law, and as such he is worthy of being God's anointed; therefore, his chosenness means the chosenness of each and every individual about whom it can be said "one day in which you occupy yourself with Torah before Me is better to Me than a thousand burnt offerings."

R. Joshua ben Levi's reading of Psalms 84 and 122, then, winds out from a view that has deep historical and interpretive roots in an old theology into a rabbinic consciousness. The older psalmic thinking, which in Psalm 84 sees the meaning of the Temple as centering around the living of the righteous but which in Psalm 122 still sees the essence of righteous living expressed in the theological and historical structure of people, land and polity, gives way, no doubt slowly, to a structure whose base is the pious learned individual rather than the People of Israel. The old theology has more than set the scene by drawing together holiness of place and human righteousness, history and the chosenness of Israel. The result is an unfolding of events where there is no longer a story of God as creating the world and man as worshipping him but rather a history in which order and meaning are discerned only through the adventure of God's People, the Jews. In the rabbinic theology, a further step is taken in the direction of man. Even while the traditions concerning R. Joshua ben Levi convey a clear vision of a redemption that unfolds along the historical axis, a new element comes colorfully into play in the perception of the historical dimension; *personal biography*. The biography not of a patriarch or of a king, nor even of a prophet who is God's messenger to Israel, but of an individual. We shall see this more manifestly in the following discussions.

> "And it shall come to pass in that day, that there shall not be light, But heavy clouds and thick" (Zechariah 14:6). . . . R. Joshua ben Levi said:[16] These are people who are heavy and dear in this world but are light and insignificant in the coming world.[17] Like that [which is told], that Rav Joseph son of R. Joshua ben Levi[18] became ill and fell into a coma. When he came out of it, his father said to him, "What did you see?" He said to him, "I saw an upside-down world, the lofty were down below and the lowly were on top." He said to him, "My son, you saw a clear world. And what is our position there?" "Our position there is the same as our position here. And I heard them saying, 'Happy is the person who comes here with his learning intact.'[19] And I heard them sayng, 'No one can stand within the pale of the martyrs.'" Who are they [the martyrs]? If it is R. Akiva and his friends, is their position [so lofty] as martyrs only and nothing else? It is, rather, the martyrs of Lydda.[20] "In that day shall there be upon the bells of the horses: HOLY UNTO THE LORD" (Zechariah 14:20): What does ". . . the bells of the horses . . ." imply? R. Joshua ben Levi said: In the future the Holy One Blessed is He will extend the city of Jerusalem as far as a horse can run . . . (BT *Pesahim* 50a)

Chapter 14 of Zechariah contains dramatic elements that, if appearing at a later period, would be termed *apocalyptic*:

> Then shall the Lord go forth,
> And fight against those nations,
> As when He fighteth in the day of battle.

And His feet shall stand in that day upon the mount of Olives,
Which is before Jerusalem on the east,
And the mount of Olives shall be cleft in the midst thereof
Toward the east and toward the west,
So that there shall be a very great valley;
And half of the mountain shall remove toward the north,
And half of it toward the south. (verses 3–4)

And it shall come to pass in that day, that there shall not be light,
But heavy clouds and thick;
And there shall be one day
Which shall be known as the Lord's,
Not day, and not night;
But it shall come to pass, that at evening time there shall be light.
(verses 6–7)

The prophet here envisions wrenching change in the historical process, which requires him to describe the divine interference in the world in terms of a quaking earth and a shaking of the sense of time, however metaphorically those things may be intended. This can be read as an expression of the apocalyptic view that history must be transcended, even shattered, and the this-worldly order of things must be violently deranged so as to make room for the happening of a deliverance that is an altogether different order of things. In the light of this, R. Joshua ben Levi's comments and the story about his son are very suggestive.

That R. Joshua ben Levi's son, Rav Joseph, "dies," glimpses the "world of truth" that is after death, and returns to life, already sets the stage for our story. The son has "overcome" death (we shall see this more clearly later on when we discuss the story where R. Joshua ben Levi himself is the protagonist). The father seems to be unperturbed by the events; at least, he gives the impression of being not at all surprised by his son's experience and of understanding it more fully than his son does. The son tells the father, with a sense of wonderment, that upon dying he saw a topsy-turvy world: the upper class were suddenly on the bottom and the lower class were the aristocrats. The father gently explains to his son that his vision is not a deranged one but rather a clear vision of this world. And in what state are the sages and their students in that world the son has seen? Again the answer returns us to the present world: the same as now.

R. Joshua ben Levi's grasp of things has, for us, four important points. First, the world of after death is a configuration of the world we live in. Second, its configuration is not a wrenching away from this world but rather a "clear" vision of this world. Third, nevertheless something must "happen" in order for that vision to be actualized completely.

Fourth, whatever must "happen" is not an event of the distant future, since his son, in a state of "temporary death," could perceive it. That the rabbis are in the "same state" in both "worlds" means that the preoccupation with the Law is the meaningfulness around which deliverance is achieved and kept within that context of personal familiarity and reachableness which bridges the two "worlds."

The juxtaposition of this story with Chapter 14 of Zechariah gives us a model through which we may understand the sense that lies behind the story. Zechariah's vision, as we have said, is capable of being read as apocalyptic, though it actually is only semiapocalyptic. In an apocalypse, the world of history is replaced by an altogether alien reality; whereas in Zechariah history continues after the cataclysm, though in a purified form. Similarly, the present story hovers on the borderline between the two main concepts of deliverance examined up till now. For R. Joshua ben Levi, the final redemption has to do with personal salvation. That is to say that the final deliverance of Israel is meaningful not only in the long history of God's People, but it is also, perhaps primarily, meaningful in the biography of the individual. It has to do with the most intimate yearnings of the individual for salvation. For that reason, it must be *within reach of personal biography*. But this does not mean the total rejection of history, it is not the martyr jumping into the dimension of the immediate only. For deliverance is brought about, according to the sage, by what amounts to a reconstitution of polity, a reordering of human power and relationships. This is not yet the complete deliverance because, as we have said and shall see more manifestly later on, there must be a personal salvation as well. However, the realm of polity is deeply involved with the occurrence of deliverance, and this means an occurrence that is real in the dimension of history as well. In short (and we shall see this, too, more clearly later), *personal biography becomes the timetable of history and personal salvation becomes an unfolding in time and not only a reality of a sudden moment.*

We have said that apocalypse means the breaking away from history and a this-worldly order to an alien or otherworldly order of things. People begin thinking in apocalyptic terms when they feel they have waited altogether too long for history to bring deliverance, so that they abandon history. Here, the opposition is not between a this-worldly order and an otherworldly order but between a historical and a nonhistorical dimension, which become conflated. Thus, this solution is not really apocalyptic because history is never totally abandoned, although here, too, there is a feeling of having waited far too long . I suggest this model in order to get some sense of the tensions handled here, not to imply that we are dealing with some kind of compromise or syncretism. The juncture in history at which apocalypse seems reasonable is similar to that at which the fantastic story about Rav Joseph ben R. Joshua ben Levi makes sense, although the latter demands a more subtle intellectual energy in order to conjure it up. I stress that I mean this as a model for the purpose of understanding and have no intention at this point of attempting the history of such fascinating and important notions. I will risk only one historical suspicion. It is not surprising that apocalypse sometimes does enter the stage in close proximity with a rabbinic consciousness.

The interplay of the two tendencies of patience, which is the way of history, and impatience, which demands an imminent salvation, is evidenced in the two fragments of knowledge that Rav Joseph "hears": "I heard them saying, 'Happy is the person who comes here with his learning intact.' And I heard them saying, 'No one can stand within the pale of the martyrs.'" The Talmud's conclusion that it is the "martyrs of Lydda" to whom reference is made and not "R. Akiva and his colleagues" because the latter were not "only" martyrs shows that tradition understood the second fragment to imply a salvation that manifestly springs from the heroism of martyrdom. The second fragment reminds us of the salvation of "one who makes his world in a moment" (earlier, Chapter 6). On the other hand the first fragment clearly refers to the cumulative labor of a student of the Law throughout a lifetime. The dialectic of Law and martyrdom again appears before us, yet in a new perspective, as we shall see.

> R. Johanan used to warn, "Beware of the flies around the *ba'alei ra'atan*." R. Zeira was careful not to sit where a breeze that had fanned one of them would pass over him. R. Eleazar would not enter into the same house with one of them. R. Ammi and R. Assi were careful not to eat eggs that came from that alley [where the sufferers lived]. R. Joshua ben Levi huddled together with them and learned Torah. He said, "'A lovely hind and a graceful doe' (Proverbs 5:19)—If she [the Torah] graces those who learn her, does she not protect them?" (BT *Ketubbot* 77b)

The *ba'alei ra'atan* suffer a disease so repulsive that it made them outcasts from society, living in an alley of their own where some feared even to enter. To keep one's distance from them was to cherish one's life. But R. Joshua ben Levi sits in their wretched alley, and he huddles together with them in warmth and studies the Law with them. An act of love and kindness and a flaunting of danger, a true act of self-sacrifice. It is not the behavior of the student of the Law who must guard his health and strength for a life that is a labor of love. It is the behavior of the martyr who is so taken up with the compassion of the moment that he shirks prudence and lives his essence in the heroism of those warm moments with the lonely. But, ironically, in that very martyrial embracing R. Joshua ben Levi finds the conviction that he need not suffer the trauma of death at all.

> Let thy fountain be blessed;
> And have joy of the wife of thy youth.
> A lovely hind and a graceful doe,
> Let her breasts satisfy thee at all times;
> With her love be thou ravished always. (Proverbs 5:18–19)

The Law is a gently yet demandingly embracing wife with whom familiar intimacy is a comfort even to the deepest passions (as the sage reads these verses). Martyrdom is a passion and draws into the abyss. Yet, if one so thirstily embraces the Law, who is a "graceful doe" and who caresses her lover, making him graceful as well, then she gently draws him out and away from the danger he is to himself; she saves him from self-destruction. So R. Joshua ben Levi finds in his martyrially reckless embrace that the Law saves him from dying. Put more directly, R. Joshua ben Levi sits in comradeship with the leperlike in a martyrial flaunting of danger. He says that he does not fear death because his preoccupation with the Law will protect him. What this amounts to is a martyrial tendency mingling with a conviction that God cannot want the death of those who are righteous in the Law. The continuation of this story provides the key for its understanding, but first we must linger on R. Joshua ben Levi's conception of the role martyrdom plays in religiosity. Later, we shall return to our story.

> R. Joshua ben Levi said: Come and see how great are the humble-minded before the Holy One Blessed is He: For when the Temple is intact, a person who sacrifices a burnt-offering—he has in hand the reward for a burnt-offering; a meal-offering—he has in hand the reward for a meal-offering. But one whose psyche is humble, Scripture considers him as if he had sacrificed all the sacrifices together, as the verse says, "The sacrifices of God are a broken spirit" (Psalms 51:19) (BT *Sotah* 5b)[21]

The sage makes his comment on Psalm 51, which expresses David's repentant yearnings after his sin with Bath-Sheba.

> A Psalm of David; When Nathan the prophet came unto him, after he had gone in to Bath-Sheba.

> Be gracious unto me, O God, according to Thy mercy;
> According to the multitude of Thy compassions blot out my transgressions.

> Wash me thoroughly from mine iniquity,
> And cleanse me from my sin. (51:3–4)

The sinner wishes for a total freedom from his sinful actions, an escape from his past.

> Create in me a clean heart, O God;
> And renew a steadfast spirit within me.
> Cast me not away from Thy presence;
> And take not Thy holy spirit from me. (51:12–13)

A total remaking of the self is the only alternative to what is the cruelest fate for religious man, to be brushed aside by the Divine Presence.

> O Lord, open Thou my lips;
> And my mouth shall declare Thy praise. (51:17)

David's sense of guilt renders him speechless before God. His salvation must be a new beginning, a new "opening of the lips" so that the praise of God may again well up through his mouth.

> For Thou delightest not in sacrifice, else would I give it;
> Thou hast no pleasure in burnt-offering.
> The sacrifices of God are a broken spirit;
> A broken and a contrite heart, O God, Thou will not despise. (51:18–19)

Here a finger is put on the very essence of the meaning of self-sacrifice. It is not the sacrifice in which God "delights not," that which is a giving away and remaining empty. The psalmist is not speaking about the humility that is a lethargy of spirit, a resignation, a passivity, an impotence. One could hardly imagine a more inept description of King David even in his deepest contrition. The very fact that tradition ascribes to David the composition of a psalm in this state indicates quite the contrary. The psalmist rather is speaking of that greatness of spirit that is "broken" in the sharpness of keen self-knowledge, which senses its standing before God in the introspective realization of what one could have been and what one is. It is the stance of a spirit that knows how great is the sacrifice of its own humbling before God, that knows what is the power of one who feels lowly before God. There is no greater freedom and power of spirit than that possessed by one who feels humbled before God, since what or who can perturb him whose shame is before almighty God? The sacrifice that is a "broken spirit" and a "contrite heart" before God is an uplifting, a sense of catharsis, and a resulting sense of the integrity and completeness of being that allows forgetting the past and gathering strength for renewal. It is a sacrifice of self in the sense that martyrdom is, where completeness is achieved in the moment of seeming, but only seeming, self-denial. Like the martyr, David knows very well how striking is his stance. This does not detract from its sincerity; on the contary, it is quite in keeping with the nature of the personality behind it. The resulting psychic state comes out in the way R. Joshua ben Levi puts verse 19, in the continuation of the passage quoted earlier, "And what is more, his prayer is not rejected, as the verse says, '. . . A broken and a contrite heart, O God, Thou wilt not despise'" (BT *Sotah* 5b). Could a prayer grounded in such an attitude be unanswered! And now we catch the irony in the Sage's opening words, "Come and see how *great* are the humble-minded before the Holy One Blessed is He."

Humbling oneself, then, partakes of martyrdom in three ways. It is a self-sacrifice, a denial of the greatness that is the true birthright of the self (the denial of undeserved aggrandizement is merely a recognition of the truth and not a humbling). It is a self-confidence, and as a stance before God it brings a sense of completion as well as freedom vis-à-vis the world. Finally, in its foundation in guilt feelings, it is a renunciation of the past and an embrace of the present wherin, alone, the experience of humility before God is saving (as an experience and not a fact, it is real only in the present, when one "feels humble").

This perception of humility as a sacrifice of self enables the acting out of martyrdom as part of the religious life rather than as its finale. The stance with before God where man finally reaches the self-confidence appropriate to one who would be with God, the supreme *imitatio Dei* where man experiences ultimate power, completion, and perfection in the very dimension in which he is most human, the present—this is the stance of martyrdom. Religious man craves that stance because, in his knowledge of God, he knows to what heights he can aspire and he experiences the hopelessness, at times at least, of the long way through the twisting, turning roads that make up this world. Religious man is willing to pay the price for the achievement of that for which he yearns because that achievement is—let us say it—is worth the price, otherwise who would pay it? As long as the fulcrum of religiosity is an action or an event where man is an onlooker, passive, or merely imitative—an actor acting out a pageant he has no part in writing nor directing, that is not a part of him—then when he does take the brazen step into the power and freedom of self which is martyrdom he takes it as a onetime, terrible action. But, in rabbinic religiosity, a new arena for acting out religiosity comes into focus, although in biblical thinking it already had been marked out. That arena, that new frame within which things are now to happen, is the biography of the individual. Not the "inner man", the soul, the psyche, the self, the "divine spark", but the story of each man's life, the story that is man's very being in the world. For martyrdom still to happen, then, it must now happen as part of biography. It is no less serious, nor is it easier; on the contrary, it is probably more difficult, because the sustaining of a serious biography is no easy matter. Now martyrdom must be diffused through an entire life, and this is done, among other ways, through this perception of humility and its performance.

Having discerned this diffusion of the event of martyrdom throughout biography, we can now see a new dimension in a passage we have already quoted:

> R. Joshua ben Levi said: Whoever is happy with the sufferings which come upon him brings salvation to the world, as the verse says,

> "[Thou didst take away him that joyfully worked righteousness,
> Those that remembered Thee in Thy ways—
> Behold, Thou wast wroth, and we sinned—]
> Upon them have we stayed of old, that we might be saved" (Isaiah 64:4)
> (BT *Ta'anit* 8a)

Interpreting the beginning of the verse[22] to mean "Thou didst smite" rather than "Thou didst take away," R. Joshua ben Levi reads the verse as describing the saving nature of the sufferings of the righteous. The rejoicing in suffering that brings salvation is something other than the way of the Law; it adds another aspect to the quality of being righteous that is not "just" righteousness itself. The righteous are not only joyful in their working of righteousness despite their sufferings, they are joyful because of their sufferings. The righteous rejoice at their relinquishing of themselves, at their self-sacrifice. In it, they plunge beyond the day-to-day orderliness, a plunge in which their very being and sensing is clutched in the awareness of evil and suffering in the world. In their joy, that clutching awareness becomes all the more self-conscious, drawing man into the deliverance, the conquest of the world and evil that must be rooted in an embrace and knowledge of the world. The rejoicing in suffering that brings deliverance is a heroism that bypasses the way of creeping time and is potent beyond the way of the Law; it is a martyrdom in its intensity of self-sacrifice and in its power. Yet, it is entered upon by way of the Law; and it is not a martyrdom that ends the story of life but is a part of it.

Let us sum up, for the moment, what we have been discussing. The more we examine the traditions clustered around the person of R. Joshua ben Levi, the more it becomes clear that the way of the Law and history and the way of martyrdom conflate. They both have more and more to do with the biography of an individual person. The length of history is powerfully condensed into the length of man's life, or at least, for the moment, we may say that the redemption of the historical dimension must somehow happen in connection with, within reach of, the story of one's life. And martyrdom diffuses throughout one's biography, marking one's life with a struggle for the salvation that is a self-realization in the present. Not contented with the elaboration of ideas, let us now return to the biography of R. Joshua ben Levi as understood in tradition.

In continuation of the story of R. Joshua ben Levi's heroic embrace of the *ba'alei ra'atan*, the Talmud tells the following:

> As he [R. Joshua ben Levi] was dying, it was said to the angel of death, "Go do as he wishes." He went and revealed himself to him. He [the sage] said to him, "Show me my place." He said to him, "Fine!" He said to him, "Give me your knife, lest you frighten me on the way." He gave it to him. When he arrived there, he [the angel] picked him up and suspended him, showing him [his place]. He jumped and fell onto that side. He [the angel] grasped him by the tail of his cloak. He [the sage] said to him, "On my oath, I shall not return!" The Holy One Blessed is He said, "If he ever cancelled an oath [by legitimate means], he should return; if not, he need not return." He [the angel] said to him, "Give me my knife." He refused to give it to him. An Echo went out, saying to him, "Give it to him because it is needed for the living." Elijah heralded him, "Make room for the son of Levi, make room for the son of Levi."

> R. Hanina bar Papa was his friend.[23] When he was dying, it was said to the angel of death, "Go do as he wishes." He went to him and revealed himself to him. He [the sage] said to him, "Leave me for thirty days until I review my learning. For it is said, 'Happy is the person who comes here with his learning intact.'" He left him. At the end of thirty days he [the angel] went and revealed himself to him. He [the sage] said to him, "Show me my place." He said to him, "Fine!" He said to him, "Give me your knife, lest you frighten me on the way." He said to him, "You are are trying to do to me the same thing your friend did?" He said to him, "Bring a Scroll of the Law and see if there is anything written in it that I did not uphold." He [the angel] said to him, "Did you huddle together with the *ba'alei ra'atan* and learn Torah?" (BT *Ketubbot* 77b)

R. Joshua ben Levi's deathbed wish is to see his place in the hereafter. That is to say that his deep yearning is to know his own personal salvation as a concrete and imminent reality. In order to know that salvation now, he has the terror of the angel of death suspended. Note the following description of the fear-instilling angel:

> It was said about the angel of death that he is all eyes.[24] When the time comes for a sick person to die, he stands over him, at his head, with his unsheathed sword in his hand—a drop of bitter poison at its tip. Upon seeing him the sick man opens his mouth in horror, and he [the angel] throws it [the drop] into his mouth. From that he dies, from that he rots, from that he decomposes. (BT *Avodah Zarah* 20b)

The angel of death is a total and glowering awareness of every detail. Standing before death, man knows the absolute inescapability of its omnipresently suspended sword. Is there a greater fearfulness than that of death? But it is not the fearfulness itself that kills man; it shatters him so that he succumbs to the bitterness of death, a bitterness of degeneration and decay. From the story of R. Hanina bar Papa, we may be certain that R. Joshua ben Levi's heroic behavior with the *ba'alei ra'atan* is understood as bringing about the suspension of that terror. The same R. Joshua ben Levi who embraced the danger of that dark alley of the *ba'alei ra'atan* is inured to dying, it can hold no terror for him. So he heroically "jumps" through death, he dies without the fearful blow from the angel of death. But, even for R. Joshua ben Levi, the darkness of death clings threateningly to the edge of the cloak he draws after him. Finally, he is able to conquer the fear of dying by his readiness for death because he has stringently followed the way of the Law (scrupulous adherence to the serious bindingness of oaths), and he need not succumb to death's terrifying sword.

This story means that R. Joshua ben Levi's martyrial readiness is a conquest of the fear of dying. That he "jumps" into the hereafter means that his heroism has been so complete that it could not have been more so even had his martyrial readiness ended in actual martyrdom. That finally he overcomes the terror of death because of his adherence to the way of the Law means that, because he has the alternative of the way of the Law and is not forced into martyrdom, he can approach martyrdom fearlessly. But note that that way of the Law that saves the sage from the total need for martyrdom is not a simple way but rather one in which he finds himself by going beyond the Law. He has never undone an oath even though he could have done so rightfully through the Law.[25] *The Law neutralizes the need for actual martyrdom, but the one ready for martyrdom retains his freedom even while walking the way of the Law, by going beyond it.*

R. Joshua ben Levi overcomes the fear of death by embracing death. He is a martyr not in a onetime heroic act of dying but rather in his readiness to die. He must return the sword of death to its angel, most men are incapable of dying fearlessly. R. Joshua ben Levi does not die one moment before his time has come, his martyrdom does not hurry death. Martyrdom becomes part of his long and arduous biography in that for him death loses its fearfulness. Again, we see that biography is the dimension of meaning, the medium in which even martyrdom is acted out. Integrated in the lifehistory, martyrdom is no longer an event outside the organic whole of man's being in the world, not even as its seal or closure. Such men may frighten us. Did not R. Akiva and his friends who plunged into war with the Romans partake of that fearlessness, mingled with the faith that the redemption through history may be hurried into our quick lives?

The connection between martyrdom and redemption-salvation returns us to our essential theme. But the role they play in the meaning of R. Joshua ben Levi's biography is not yet fully manifest. For this, we must turn to still another story concerning the sage, a story rich in myth and, thus, truth.

> R. Joshua ben Levi met Elijah who was standing at the entrance to the cave of R. Simeon ben Yohai.[26] He said to him, "Will I come to the coming world?" He said to him, "If this Lord will want." R. Joshua ben Levi said, "Two were visible[27] yet I heard a third voice." He [R. Joshua ben Levi] said to him [Elijah], "When will the Messiah come?" He said to him, "Go ask him himself." "And where does he sit?" "At the gate of Rome."[28] "And how will I recognize him?" "He sits among those poor who suffer disease. While they all unbandage all their sores at the same time and then rebandage them, he unbandages and rebandages only one at a time, saying, 'Perhaps I will be needed, I should not be delayed.'" He went to him. He said to him, "Peace upon you, my Rabbi and my teacher."[29] He said to him, "Peace upon you, the son of Levi." He said to him, "When are you, sir, coming?" He said to him, "Today." He [the sage] came back to Elijah. He [Elijah] said to him, "What did he say to you?" He said to him, "'Peace upon you, the son of Levi.'" He said to him, "He has assured you and your father for the coming world." He said to him, "He lied to me, for he said to me, 'Today I am coming' but he has not come." He said to him, "This is what he said to you: 'Today, if ye would but hearken to His voice' (Psalms 95: 7)."[30] (BT *Sanhedrin* 98a)

Let us begin with an analysis of the nature of the salvation or redemption, or both, which are referred to here in connection with a messianism and a world to come. Our starting point will be the scene of the messiah sitting at the "gate of Rome."

> R. Joshua ben Levi said: If someone should say to you, "Where is your God?" say to him, "In the metropolis of Rome." What is the appropriate verse? "One calleth unto me out of Seir" (Isaiah 21:11).[31] It was repeated: R. Simeon ben Yohai [said]: Wherever Israel went into exile the Divine Presence went into exile together with them . . . . They went into exile to Rome, and the Divine Presence went into exile together with them. What is the appropriate verse? "One calleth unto me out of Seir: 'Watchman, what of the night?'" (ibid.) Israel said to Isaiah, "Our teacher Isaiah, what will come to us out of this night?" He said to them, "Wait for me while I ask." When he had asked, he returned to them. They said to him [again], "'Watchman, what of the night?' (ibid.

21:11)—What sayeth the Watchman of the worlds?" He said to them, "'The Watchman said: "The morning cometh, and also the night"'" (ibid. 21:12)." They said to him, "And also the night?" He said to them, "Not as you are thinking, but rather—morning for the righteous and night for the wicked, morning for Israel and night for the heathens." They said to him, "When?" He said to them, "Whenever you want, He wants. . . ." They said to him, "What [then] is holding back?" He said to them, "[There must be] repentance—'return, come' (ibid.)." R. Aha said in the name of R. Tanhum bar Hiyya: If Israel would repent for one day, the son of David would come immediately. What is the appropriate verse? "For He is our God, And we are the people of His pasture, and the flock of His hand. To-day, if ye would but hearken to His voice!" (Psalms 95:7). (PT *Ta'aniot* 1:1 [64a])[32]

The thematic construction common to this pericope and that quoted earlier is manifest. The passages interpret Isaiah as saying that God, or the messiah, is in Rome. In both cases this idea is connected to the deliverance of Israel now, a deliverance that must come through repentance. Within the material in the Palestinian Talmud, we discern what seems to be an older source for R. Joshua ben Levi's vision of God in Rome, but with different nuances that uncover for us the amora's real intent. R. Simeon ben Yohai, the famous tanna who flourished during the aftermath of the Bar Kokhba revolt, is speaking about God going into exile with Israel. As we have seen earlier (Chapter 9), this implies that the immediate moment is pregnant with deliverance because God himself suffers the exile. Time need not stretch out over the unfolding of history in order to contain the immanence of God; he is with man even in the suffering of the present, in which he partakes. God need not reenter history to redeem man, he is with man in his very consciousness of Exile. In other words, Israel's being with God does not happen in and through the reality of history but rather despite it, or beyond it, or if you will "below" it, in the intimate, personal dimension of the present. R. Joshua ben Levi relies on the older material. But, through careful choice of words, he actually brings quite a different notion to the forefront. God is not with Israel despite the Exile, he "is" in Rome because it is a "metropolis." If a man demand of you, Where is your God? point toward the sprawling environs of Rome and say, "There!" God "is" in the great power of Rome, in its ruling multitudes, in its hustle and bustle, in its teeming courtyards and squalor, in its richness and its poverty, in its order and its chaos. God "is" in the towering dimension of polity, its great construction can be said to contain the "happening" of God or godliness. And, should one ask How could He "be" in such evilness? the answer will be found in R. Joshua ben Levi's wise insight into his son's deathlike vision, which we have already read:

> Rav Joseph son of R. Joshua ben Levi became ill and fell into a coma.
> When he came out of it, his father said to him, "What did you see?" He
> said to him, "I saw an upside-down world, the lofty were down below
> and the lowly were on top." He said to him, "My son, you saw a clear
> world." (BT *Pesahim* 50a)

Our this-worldly polity is indeed the dimension of deliverance, but its
present construction of relationships is an illusion. It hides the barrenness
of the rich and the grandeur of the pious. If one could but see the real
order of society and know where true power is, perceive what is really
lasting and thus concrete and what is mere vanity and passing fancy or evil,
then one would really see the greatness and grandeur of polity in which
God may be said to "be". (And, we may add, if the redemption in polity
may be truly so hurried into the present, is it at all brash to jump history?)
Thus, R. Joshua ben Levi's vision of the messiah sitting at the gate of the
city of Rome no doubt says that this redemption through and in polity is
at least one aspect of his mission.

However, R. Joshua ben Levi's messianic yearnings are never only for
an unfolding in the realm of polity. That his first question is "Will I come
to the coming world?" (without going into the concepts involved in that
short question) intimates a yearning for a personal salvation that is not
transparently dependent upon polity. That the messiah is to come "today"
says anything but a messianism that happens in the dimension of polity
alone, which is the dimension of history. We have seen that the timetable
of "today" is rooted in a messianism that happens in the dimension of the
self and that the messiah's coming through repentance likewise is an event
of the self not an unfolding in polity.

In fact, the yearnings that disturb R. Joshua ben Levi at the cave of R.
Simeon ben Yohai and send him to search out the messiah at the gates of
Caesar's Rome are compound. He goes to Rome where the greatness of
polity is manifest, but his messianic yearnings there are drawn toward the
quickness of life, away from the intransigent slowness of history. And yet,
again, he doubts the veracity of a Messiah who promises to come "today."
He seeks his own personal salvation, yet wanders the streets of the metropolis; and when he doubts the messiah who is to emerge from the gutters of
the Imperial City, he doubts the tidings of his own salvation as well.

The key to the strange story of R. Joshua ben Levi lies in the meaning
of the messianic figure here. Rashi has already pointed out that it is the
figure of the suffering servant of the Lord, that is, an interpretation of
Isaiah 52:13–53:12.

> He was despised, and forsaken of men,
> A man of pains, and acquainted with disease,

And as one from whom men hide their face:
He was despised, and we esteemed him not.
Surely our diseases he did bear, and our pains he carried;
Whereas we did esteem him stricken,
Smitten of God, and afflicted.
But he was wounded because of our transgressions,
He was crushed because of our iniquities:
The chastisement of our welfare was upon him,
And with his stripes we were healed. (53:3–5)

He was oppressed, though he humbled himself
And opened not his mouth;
As a lamb that is led to the slaughter,
And as a sheep that before her shearers is dumb;
Yea, he opened not his mouth. (53:7)

In endless exegesis, the identification of the suffering servant has varied from the People of Israel through the righteous to the messiah. R. Joshua ben Levi not only identifies the messiah as the sufferer, his vision adds a depth of meaning that throws open the nature of the messianic mission as the sage sees it.

The suffering messiah unbinds and binds each of his festering sores one by one, because he wants to remain forever immediately ready for his mission. Imagine that man: his nerves continuously tensed in listening for the call to deliverance; his weathered body ready to spring into the moment. His wretchedness is as much a part of his nature as is his anxiety for the call. He sits in the filthy gutter of the sickly poor, none of the greatness of that city for him. He has not burdened himself, over the ages, with any possessions, nor does care for his own welfare in even the near future arrest his attention, other than the care of the particular point of pain that he tends at the moment. He has none of the leisure and time of the other poor. The totality of the passion of his being is centered on the present, on the thought that this will be the moment that God bursts with the fullness of the delivering call. The messiah is a true martyrial figure in his absolute desire for deliverance in the immediate moment, not only without regard to cost but with the sense that the greater his self-sacrifice the more imminent deliverance will be. The messiah is an Abraham sacrificing his son Isaac, the promise of the future, in the conviction that a heroic embracing of the present is an embracing of God and His deliverance. His is a terrible struggle for freedom from past and future, a lustful quest for fulfillment in the present. Yet, his martyrdom is not a finale of dying but a living out—a living out at least as long as the Exile!

The messiah suffers the pain that is Israel's. He does not provide a vicarious passion and atonement for Israel; his living says, rather, the imminence of deliverance potentially implicit in the suffering of each and every Jew, thus combining the different interpretations of Isaiah's prophecy. This is the real secret of our story. For, is it not evident by now that R. Joshua ben Levi's fantastic vision of the messiah is the vision of his own life?

R. Joshua ben Levi sits closely with the outcast, festering *ba'alei ra'atan* in that dark alley shunned by men—how like the messiah who sits among the wretched poor on the periphery of the Roman metropolis! The messiah suffers the torments of his destitute friends with the festering sores—how like R. Joshua ben Levi who ignores his own welfare in his desire to break the loneliness of the *ba'alei ra'atan* by embracing togetherness with them in the midst of their wretchedness! In his grasping of the warm nowness of being with the *ba'alei ra'atan*, R. Joshua ben Levi embraces his own personal danger—how like the messiah of the gutter whose life is held in abeyance, waiting with bated breath for salvation, convinced that his own self-sacrificing readiness will help to speed the redemption to his People. Both the messiah and the sage live every moment as if now were the moment of redemption-salvation, forgiving the past and anticipating the future's deepest hope while ignoring the future's warning. When the messiah leaps out into the event of redemption, he finally will have that personal salvation, the yearning for which has driven him through the years of the exile, and in the redemption of Israel he will be saved from his terrible need for self-sacrifice. How like R. Joshua ben Levi who by virtue of his lifelong heroism and readiness for self-sacrifice and fearlessness before death finally achieves the salvation he has sought so forcefully! R. Joshua ben Levi's life is that within and through which that which he yearns for is to happen, and he embraces not the end until the end itself. How like the messiah whose story does not end a moment before the end of the Exile! R. Joshua ben Levi and the messiah enter their edens through a fearless embrace of their fates. Is not R. Joshua ben Levi surely the messiah? Or much rather say, Has not R. Joshua ben Levi lived out a messianic myth of truth in his own biography?

The messiah impatiently awaits the moment of deliverance that is to come through repentance. While repentance is an embracing of the present, compared to the messiah's need for self-sacrifice it is a retreat into the Law. In a way that seems paradoxical, repentance here represents *both* the heroism of embracing the present ("For He is our God, And we are the people of His pasture, and the flock of His hand, *today*", as the messiah is said to have said) *and* the dialectical return from the abyss back into the way of the Law ("if ye would but hearken to His voice!", as Elijah completes the messianic tiding). How much are the Law and martyrdom intermingled in the stories of the messiah and the sage!

The paradox is resolved in life. Martyrdom has elevated the being of individual to the pinnacle of centrality; and the infusion of history into the story of a man's life has made biography the stuff of the significance of being. In turn, the story of a man's living draws out the martyrial nihilism into a heroic lifelong performance, and quickens the ever-so-long way of the Law and history into an embraceable biographical unfolding. Thus is formed a rabbinic notion of deliverance that partakes of both the historical redemption of people and personal salvation, blurring the boundary between the two and replacing the clarity of their bifurcated meaning with the far more arduous meaning that "makes sense" in the existential living of life alone. The importance of this perception is not that of an analytical concept new to the history of ideas; it is that of a new and unique existential awareness of biography as the arena of meaning. And we remember that, while this sensibility comes to full flower in the form and content of the traditions centering on R. Joshua ben Levi, its roots are in earlier rabbinic religiosity. The perception of these roots can help to make the lives of R. Akiva and others of his and even earlier generations more transparent to us.

The great myths of man are true, as long as they are alive, in two different ways. On the one hand, they may neutralize potential behavior. Here, the listener to the myth is a spectator; he lives through the scene in vicarious participation. If the myth is a true one then the drama will be so intense for the listener that he will stand up and follow the actors back and forth with all his energies. He will root them on, sweat their effort, laugh their laughter, cry their tears, mourn their vanquishment, and celebrate in their victory. He will live out a part of himself by listening, the blood rising to his head. Afterward, he will return home, ready again for the tediousness of his own life. Listening to the myth will take the place of acting it out, the myth will have neutralized the need to act it out. This will have been a true catharsis.

On the other hand, a myth may be true not in the intenseness of the vicarious listening but rather in the acting out of it. Here, listening to and understanding the myth are only part of its telling. It really is told most fully when its listeners enact the myth. If their enactment is a virile one, then the myth is powerful. Otherwise, it is a flat story, disappointing and even boring. Here the myth is vibrant in that it awakens men to action, in that it is the animus of their living. The story says the meaning of their actions, it is the thunderous tremors according to whose beats they step and plunge. Here, the genius of man is not merely mythopoeic, it is self-creating. Only when you watch the listeners of this myth as they live and die can you fully know the myth.

In either case, a true myth is no mere product of a genius for storytelling. The myth is conceived deep inside the world view of a society and the truths perceived by the members of that society. A true myth emanates from the revelations of the very being of a group, it is not merely handed down from mountains. The myth-teller is a genius in his attention to the heartbeats of his listeners. It is a great age that has its giants who prophetically glimpse the true myths and are able to tell them, if even partially.

The myth of the Binding of Isaac is a true myth in both senses. One may yet visit synagogues where, on the second day of *Rosh ha-Shannah*, the congregation trembles when the Binding of Isaac is chanted before the community. Its tune is a piercing one, a waiting, a wondering, a weeping, a strength, a knowledge, a prayer, a demanding. This is a community whose members survived, if survival is possible, the Holocaust. They know the ineluctability of martyrdom for being Jewish, they know the command to *Akedah*; Abraham's vision comes as no surprise to them. They listen in hushed, sweating silence to the chanting. Their eyes fill with tears at the frightening truth of the myth. Their crying is the plea that the *Akedah* should no longer be demanded, that Abraham may draw back the knife; that history should be sufficient, that the Bindings of Isaac they have seen and know should obviate the need for further martyrdom. For them Isaac's blood is truly shed, and they pray for it to be a vicarious deliverance, though it can be vicarious only in the sense that the survivors are spared, not in the mitigation of tragedy—for they have partaken of it. They will return home with a sense of relief, with a conviction that they have received a sanction for their quietism and passivity.

But there are other communities in which the reading of the *Akedah* is not satisfyingly cathartic. There, the chanting may seem to lack a certain seriousness, or even authenticity; or again it may be more serious because the assembled listeners know that it is not all, it is not finished. The chanting for them will be a sparking, a foreboding—a beginning, never an end—an exciting knowledge of strength, a palpable expectancy and fear. These listeners themselves may be overcome, as Abraham was, by the command to ascend Moriah, children in hand. They, too, will struggle with the angel in the withdrawal of the knife. They will return home from the synagogue, not relieved but ready or wary. They or their children, or both, may be caught up in the acting-out of the myth, in the ascent to Moriah and, or perhaps not, the descent from it. The ascent and descent may mingle together in dialectic; the patient way, which is the way of the promise, may slow down the ascent to the mount, draw out the sacrifice to a story of living on; or the drive to strike a swift and perfect, heroic, blow may fire the conviction that the way of history can be hurried closer to the present; or one way may overtake the other. The result must be rich in meaning and trembling. Must the blood of Isaac be truly shed?

In the story of R. Joshua ben Levi the significance of individual biography reaches out to encompass an acting-out of the vast and multifarious messianic myth, as that myth is a retelling of the ascent to Moriah and the promised descent. Are we not awed by such power of the individual? Is that not the greatness of the 'I' that we seek? Do we not fear him who would gulp all in the quickness of his own being? Will not such individuals surely hurry the Redemption?

However, it is the fate of such men to be doubted.

Elijah heralded him [R. Joshua ben Levi, in the afterlife], "Make room for the son of Levi, make room for the son of Levi." He went, meeting R. Simeon ben Yohai who was sitting on thirteen stools of gold. He said to him, "You are the son of Levi?" He said to him, "Yes." "Was a rainbow seen during your lifetime?" He said to him, "Yes." "If so, you are not the son of Levi!" But that is not so—there was nothing [no rainbow was seen during his lifetime], it was rather that he [R. Joshua ben Levi] thought, "I shall not credit myself with such favor." (BT *Ketubbot* 77b)[33]

One who sees the rainbow in the clouds says: Blessed are Thou God Who remembers the covenant. R. Hiyya [said] in the name of R. Johanan: [One says, rather: Blessed are Thou God] Who is faithful in [the promising of] His covenant and Who remembers the covenant.[34] R. Hezekiah [said] in the name of R. Jeremiah: During the whole of R. Simeon ben Yohai's lifetime the rainbow in the clouds was not seen. R. Hezekiah [said] in the name of R. Jeremiah: If R. Simeon ben Yohai would say, "Valley, valley, fill up with gold coins" then it would indeed fill up. R. Hezekiah [said] in the name of R. Jeremiah: R. Simeon ben Yohai used to say: I have seen the initiates of the coming world and they are few. If there are three, I and my son are among them. If there are two, I and my son are they.[35] R. Hezekiah [said] in the name of R. Jeremiah: R. Simeon ben Yohai used to say: Let Abraham draw in [all those] from his time till mine, and I will draw in [all those] from my time till the end of all generations. And if not, let Ahijah the Shilonite join me and I will draw in all the people.[36] (PT *Berakhot* 9:3 [13d])

Elijah himself (the messianic herald!)[37] announces the coming of R. Joshua ben Levi. But, the towering figure of R. Simeon ben Yohai, the same one at whose cave R. Joshua ben Levi wondered about salvation and redemption, casts its shadow over the sage of a later generation. R. Simeon sits on thirteen golden stools, who dare be compared to him! In the days of R. Simeon ben Yohai, the rainbow was never seen because there was never any need to remind of God's covenant with man. Salvation and redemption must have seemed so real around that great tanna who escaped the vast Roman power in his flight to that wonderful cave, together with his son (BT *Shabbat* 33b). Is there a need for the messiah in those days when a man of such strength arises above the post-Bar Kokhba destruction and despair strewn around him? Compared to what was in the past and what, therefore, cannot be in our generation, R. Joshua ben Levi's very identity is doubted. The loss of self-identity through a generation that doubts itself is the tragedy of a messiah who cannot come. The greatness inherent in some men of some generations may be intimated by those men themselves but not by their generation, who have a tradition of perhaps too much greatness. It is only recognized by later generations, when it is too late to do anybody any good, and then only to cast shadow on seeming pretenders.

But we remember always that those seeming pretenders draw their strength from the very same wells wherein their scoffers drink. So, when we read the stories with our children, we will take care how we tell them to the poised listeners. We will tell them how great were our forebears and how small are we. We will tell them how long is history and how patient our People. We will tell them how much we and our fathers have done and how little that is in the vast sea of what is to be done. We will tell them these things with the greatest of care and seriousness. Lest they hear the stories and not what we tell. Lest those stories come alive in our children's ears. Lest the giants of those stories hold our children's warm hands. For then they will leave us and wander out in the inebriation of self-knowledge. They will act out their parts in those myths, those myths that are yet vaster than history and greater than our fizzled dreams. They will act out their own parts, God help us, in a knowledge that we could not contain. Then we will feel old and impotent. Then we will be an unwilling Abraham leading his sons to their self-binding. Then their strength will frighten us and we will draw back from them. And "your little ones, that ye said would be a prey, them will I bring in, and they shall know the land." They will drive the messiah bound before them; and through them our dried bones will be quickened.

Notes

Introduction

1. I have altered the verse's translation slightly in order to fit the sense of the homily. Rava's statement apparently is an exegesis of the whole verse in Isaiah, following upon a previous homily on the same verse in BT ibid. Rashi reads it that way and the variant readings bear it out. But I have refrained from that complication in my translation.

2. See continuation of *G.R.* and BT *San.* 89b for different versions and where it is clearly amoraic.

3. "The sound of birth" is missing in most variants.

4. The angel of the sweet waters, cf. BT *Taanit* 25b. And see Louis Ginzberg, *The Legends of the Jews*, vol. 5 (Philadelphia 1925); pp. 38–39, note 107.

5. See also *G.R.* Chapter 6 (Genesis 1:17), pp. 47–48 and note for parallels.

6. Translation of E. A. Speiser in *The Anchor Bible: Genesis* (New York 1964), p. 356; also see note on p. 358.

7. Joshua 10:12–14.

8. *G.R.* 97 (Genesis 48:19), p. 1247, reads, anonymously, "Is it possible? But this is Joshua that he halts the wheel of the sun and the moon, both of which rule" etc.

9. See Chapter 11 of this book.

10. R. Joel Sirkes in *Haggahot ha-Bah* records "other texts" as reading "is greater than".

11. Compare Chaim Bloch, *Gemeinde der Chassidim*, Vienna, 1920, p. 325.

1. The Mother of the Sons

1. *Sefer Josippon*, Constantinople 1510, 4:18–19 (based, apparently, on I Samuel 2:1–10). In some rabbinic versions the mother is called Miriam bat Tanhum, or bat Menahem, influencing some Christian accounts, while in Maccabees II and IV and in the Talmudic version she is anonymous, to be discussed later.

2. For the historical settings of the story see Gershon D. Cohen, "The Story of Hannah and Her Seven Sons in Hebrew Literature" in *Mordecai M. Kaplan Jubilee Volume*, Hebrew section (New York 1953), pp. 109–22.

3. Dropsie College Edition of Jewish Apocryphal Literature, ed. Solomon Zeitlin, translated by Sidney Tedesche (New York 1954), pp. 159–69.

4. Loeb Classical Library, The Apostolic Fathers, translated by Kirsopp Lake, (London 1976), Vol. 2, p. 315.

5. Penguin Classics, translated by A. J. Krailsheimer (1979), p. 134.

6. Dropsie College Edition of Jewish Apocryphal Literature, *The Third and Fourth Books of Maccabees*, edited and translated by Moses Hadas, (New York 1953), pp. 145–47.

7. Ibid. pp. 235–37.

8. Translating the Hebrew אל תזוח דעתך עליך with the English metaphor so as to retain some semblance of the biblical meaning of the verb as in Exodus 28:28. Cf. M. Moreshet in *A Lexicon of the New Verbs in Tannaitic Hebrew* (Ramat-Gan 1980) [Hebrew], p. 147 and notes.

9. Like all such midrashic sermons this is a weaving together of various ideas and motifs that can be found scattered throughout rabbinic literature. A comparative study of those individual parallels shows that the final editing process of each version gives the elements its own peculiar accentuation, even, at times, to the point of a change in their significant content. Despite the complexity of the process of literary crystallization the version quoted has a definite, organic structure even if the strains of its literary archeology are evident, as I point out in my analysis of the text and comparison with the talmudic version.

A short description of the highlights of what I have called rationalization, in the prominent versions other than those just mentioned, is as follows.

Lamentations Rabbah, ed. Buber (Vilna 1899), pp. 84–85, and the *Seder Eliahu Rabba*, Chapter 28 (in some editions, Chapter 30), ed. Friedmann (Meir Ish-Shalom) (Vienna 1904), pp. 151–53, while basically similar to those cited, do not read the notion of the eternity of God versus the transience of man (in both of them, Caesar's taunt about the fullness of the older brothers' lives contrasted with the brevity of the life of the youngest does not appear either, and these two pieces, of course, are one unit). The latter does not contain the promise of future retribution for Caeser (nor does it record the mother's statement that her *Akedah* is actual whereas Abraham's was a trial), but it adds the notion that the sons have been placed in this world for the very purpose of sanctifying God's name through martyrdom. *Lamentations Rabbah*, on the other hand, adds to the mother's words to her youngest son the reminder that he will soon join his brothers in the embrace of Abraham the Father and that, therefore, he should be fearless.

The redactor of the *Pesikta Rabbati* Chap. 43, ed. Friedmann (Vienna 1880), p. 180b, brings a short version within the context of the notion of suffering in the present as a preparation for happiness in the future, and the mother, Miriam bat Tanhum, is quoted as admonishing her youngest son, "Oh my son! What do you want, that [only] your brothers will all be embraced by Abraham in the coming future?"

The *Midrash Zutta*, ed. Buber (Berlin 1894), p. 69, and *Yalkut Shimoni* (no. 1029) to Lamentations 2:17 read like an unfaithful copy of the short talmudic version, which will be quoted and discussed in detail later, except that it adds some details—probably under the influence of the other versions—and weaves into the youngest's refusal to lift the sovereign's ring and assertion of the glory of God's rulership against the humbleness of Caeser's (which appears in all the rabbinic versions), the notion of the eternity of the former.

For a more complete list of parallels see Gershon D. Cohen, op. cit., p. 109, note 3. See also Zvi Meir Rabinowitz, *Ginzei Midrash* (Hebrew) (Tel-Aviv 1976), p. 143, for a fragment of *Lamentations Rabbah* (the mother is named Martha bat Tanhum) and note 58.

10. The woman's insanity is not introduced as an apology for her death. See *Semahot* 2:2 where one who "climbed to the top of a tree" or "to the top of a roof and fell to his death" is not to be treated as a suicide, unless he clearly states his intent before so doing and is faithful to the letter of his statement. In our story of the mother, her madness is the shuddering of one for whom the garish sanity of the realists is an obviation of man's ability to see; it is the climax to a story of forced and tragic exile from day to dayness.

11. See note 16.

12. The mention of Caesar here and in reference to the second son is missing in some manuscripts but appears in them, nevertheless, in the conversation with the seventh son. See M. S. Feldblum, *Dikduke Sopherim* (New York 1966) [Hebrew].

13. There are some variations in the quotations of the different verses as recorded in the manuscripts (see ibid.) and the commentators, but I have not discerned any significance therein for our purposes.

14. For the homiletical identification of Esau's descendants with Rome see, among many others, the following: *Sifre* to Deuteronomy 33:2 (343, ed. Finkelstein, p. 395); PT *Ta'aniot* 1:1 (64a); BT *Megillah* 6a.

15. Italics mine.

16. The *Akedah* motif, therefore, is an integral and central part of the talmudic version. Since, in the *Lamentations Rabbah* version, however, eschatology and

theology take the place of the *Akedah*, the latter remains somewhat out of place. It thus is not surprising that the homilist in *Lamentations Rabbah* develops the *Akedah* motif in a direction that definitely dulls the identification of the mother with Abraham, as that identification is no longer germane to the power of the sermon as a whole.

2. Martyrdom and the Law

1. See M *Yadayim* 3:2, 5; *Eduyyot* 5:3; BT *Shabbat* 3b, 4a.

2. Variants: Rav Judah in the name of Samuel, see *DDS*.

3. See also BT *Yoma* 29a.

4. "Esther does not render the hands unclean" is said by the Talmud to be in accordance with the view of the tanna R. Joshua (ben Hananiah, first and second centuries); and it quotes "Esther was said through the Spirit of Holiness" in the name of the tanna R. Eliezer (ben Hyrcanus, a contemporary of R. Joshua), among other tannaim.

5. M *Megillah* 1:3, 4; BT *Megillah* 7a,b; *Rambam, Yad, Megillah* 2:13–17; *Tur and Shulhan-Arukh Orah Hayyim* 694–696; and see also BT *Hullin* 139b and Rashi.

6. See *Tosefta* 1:8 for other examples.

7. Following the reading of H. Malter in *The Treatise Ta'anit* (New York 1930), p. 53. Malter correctly assumes that the homilists did not merely quote fragments of verses, unless removing them from their respective contexts. In fact, as I have shown elsewhere in this book, it happens, perhaps quite often, that one must read the entire section from which a particular verse is quoted to understand a homilist's message. It is not at all unlikely, therefore, that the homilists actually did read long sections of Scripture before their audiences as part of their sermons. The amoraic collections of *Midrashim* generally are organized around the weekly portions as read in the synagogue, and we can assume that the turning of the homilist's attention to the whole portion in one way or another is rooted in old custom. We tend to lose sight of that because the rabbinic homilies come down to us as based on fragments of verse; this is the fault of both redactors and copyists. In short, whether we are dealing with the popular public sermons or with the more esoteric homilies of the *Yeshivot*, we should pay far more attention to the broader contexts of quoted Scripture than generally is the practice.

8. Cf. the list in I Kings 8:37.

9. I have preferred the reading of the printed texts, adding the word *immediately* from the Munich manuscript (see *DDS*) although rejecting its reading as a whole. The text thus is to be understood as follows: The ram's-horn is sounded immediately when bands of armed men cross the country, even if their intent is, at

the present, manifestly peaceful ("and even because of a peaceful sword," *Tosefta Ta'anit* 2:10). Their predilection for violence is a warning to be ready for the worst and not to sit by idly waiting for a change of mood (["like] the sword [of peace] of Pharaoh Neco which nevertheless engulfed the righteous man, that is to say, Josiah," *Tosefta* ibid., see II Chronicles 35:20–24). Nor should one expect the danger to be contained entirely in one local area because of the soldiers' tendency to wander off their appointed path in search of adventure and booty, very much like the other evils mentioned in the Mishnah because of which the alarm goes out, "everywhere." Cf. Rabbinovicz's comments in *DDS*, and contrast Malter, op. cit. p. 73.

10. Following the printed texts (except M Pesaro) and several of the medieval commentators, DDS and Malter notwithstanding. Accordingly an extremely small extent of blight was sufficient to raise alarm.

11. Instead of "another time," some read "on the morrow."

12. *Rambam, Yad, Ta'aniot* 1:6: "they are to be fasted for [even] on the Sabbath. . . . But the ram's-horn is not sounded unless it were sounded in order to gather people together for the purpose of helping and saving them." R. Joseph Caro in his *Kesef Mishneh*, on analytical grounds, denies the reading, "to be fasted for on the Sabbath," but *Rambam* himself writes in his commentary on this Mishnah, "they are pleaded for [before God] and fasted for [even] on the Sabbath, without the sound of the ram's-horn."

13. Cf. BT 16a and *G.R.* to Genesis 18:27 (49, p. 513).

14. That is to say, "to the first blessing" of the "eighteen," i.e., the first blessing from among the daily ones which on a fast day introduces the extra order of blessings (namely, the blessing ending with "Redeemer of Israel"), he adds the following. Thus, besides the adding of "six" blessings, the seventh of the daily "eighteen" also is expanded.

15. Cf. *G.R.* ibid. and *Tosefta Ta'anit* 1:9 and 14.

16. The material that follows has many parallels, for lists see *G.R.* ed. Theodor-Albeck, pp. 603–607 and *L.R.* ed. Margulies, pp. 682–84. And see S. Spiegel, *The Last Trial* (New York 1969), pp. 86–100.

Some of the images and ideas that I painstakingly read, through the following discussions, in the material I quote, are stated more manifestly in various parallels. However, I have chosen the PT version for two reasons.

First, the Palestinian Talmud and the Babylonian Talmud are our most important sources for an understanding of amoraic rabbinic thinking. The former, in fact, is more important than the latter in certain respects, because it did not pass through the very long literary development that molded the latter, and therefore we have in PT a more pristine form of amoraic material, generally speaking (cf. L. Ginzberg, *A Commentary on the Palestinian Talmud* [New York 1941], vol. 1, pp. xxxvi–xli; A. Weiss, *The Literary Development of the Babylonian Talmud* [Hebrew, Warsaw 1939], vol. 2, p. 132 ff.; M. S. Feldblum in the *Abraham Weiss Jubilee*

Volume [New York 1964], Hebrew section, pp. 34–35, English section pp. 32–33; J. N. Epstein, *Introduction to Amoraitic Literature*, [Jerusalem 1962] [Hebrew], pp. 273–75; J. E. Ephrati, *The Sevoraic Period and its Literature* [Jerusalem 1973] [Hebrew], pp. 82–88). Both talmudim surpass the other sources for amoraic material, both because of their comparative faithfulness in reporting and, more so, because their level of seriousness is determined primarily by their growing out of study in the *yeshivot* and not directly out of the popular rabbinic lectures given to the public. Throughout this work, therefore, I have preferred talmudic material as my source for the words of the amoraim, whenever possible. As for tannaitic traditions, one must take into no less serious consideration the various collections of patently tannaitic material (remembering, however, that they are not all of the same caliber, some even being spurious).

Second, the PT version has preserved, in this case, the best evidence of the underlying structure that I am searching out, within the context of the subject matter of the present work.

It is my intention to uncover themes that, although they do not at all necessarily constitute a generally accepted rabbinic point of view, are far more than the whim of a particular homilist. I am looking for what constitutes a viewing, a perception, of experienced reality, be it a historical experience of Israel or an existential experience of some religious men. That is to be found deeply embedded in the sources, sometimes even unnoticed by the particular author of the pericope. Thus, the age of a source indicates the depth of its roots, and an underlying or implicit structure or pattern or motif, at times, is more significant than abstractly stated comments, views, or ideas.

17. Unidentifiable *Amora*, see A. Hyman, *Toldoth Tannaim Ve'Amoraim* (London 1910) [Hebrew], p. 264 and C. Albeck, *Introduction to the Talmud Babli and Yerushalmi* (Tel-Aviv 1969) [Hebrew], p. 230. And see *Leviticus Rabbah* ed. Margulies p. 682, note, for confusion among the parallels in recording the name of this *Amora*.

18. Translating אלוהים יראה לו השה לעולה literally, "God will see for Himself the lamb for a burnt-offering." Later on in Genesis 22:14, the phrase ד' יראה, meaning literally "The Lord will see," is found. But here the homilist is referring to verse 8, as is evidenced by the continuation in PT, or at least that is the meaning of the homily in the context of PT. However, in any case, in the upshot of the PT homily as a whole, as we shall learn, "The Lord will see" of verse 14 comes to have the meaning that the homilist here imbues verse 8 with so that we should read "God will see" here as actually a homily on both verses, extracting them from their individual isolation because of their manifest parallelism and grounding the meaning of each in the other. The meaning within the temporality of the story in verse 8 gives a very specific content to verse 14 and the latter in turn draws the meaning of both into the realm of the history of Israel. This will become clear in the following discussions. Also see note 21.

19. The Leyden manuscript reads בשופר, "with the horn," but the scribe himself corrected it to בקרניו, "with the horns."

20. Literally, "this ram," but meaning any ram like the original. I do not think that there is any hint here of the efficacy of the original horn for the redemption.

21. The text does not read this first part of the verse, but only its continuation. I have nevertheless included it because I am convinced that the stress on the words *The Lord shall be seen*, which I have italicized, is part of the homily, recalling Genesis 22:14 where ד' יראה means, literally, "the Lord shall be seen" (or "is seen," but understood no doubt by the Rabbis as "shall be seen"). See earlier note 18.

22. בכל נפשך probably should be translated best as, "with all your life," "man should carry the whole living force of his wishes and all his longing desire into his love for the one God of Israel" (H. W. Wolff, *Anthropology of the Old Testament* [London 1974], p. 17 [trans. of German, *Anthropologie des Alten Testaments* (Munich 1973)]). In rabbinic Hebrew, too, נפש often may be translated as "life," cf. M *Yoma* 8:6; *Tosefta Sabbat* 16 (Zuckermandel 15):11, 16, 17; PT *Ketubbot* 5:7 (30b); BT *Sanhedrin* 74a. And here, too, *life* would be better than *soul*, but I have followed the JPS and adjusted the homily accordingly.

23. אֹהֲבִי.

24. *Targum Pseudo Jonathan* reads, on *this* verse, "Isaac said to his father, 'Bind me well'," and so, too, *Targum Yerushalmi* and the *Neofiti*. And *Targum Yerushalmi* to Leviticus 22:27, "[Isaac] bound himself upon the altar and stretched out his neck." However, most manuscripts of the *Sifre* do not read this quotation of Genesis 22:10.

25. "two camps" being Jacob's "might."

26. It was Roman practice to have the condemned man himself carry the instruments of his execution to the place of execution, see S. Lieberman, "Roman Legal Institutions in Early Rabbinics and in the Acta Martyrum", *JQR* 35 (1944–1945): 36–38, and see also pp. 35–36.

27. This being preferred, according to the accepted custom, though it is not the unanimous opinion in the old Halakhah, see M *Rosh Ha-Shanah* 3:2–5; BT ibid. 26b; *Rambam, Yad, Shofar* 1:1 and *Rabad; Tur* and *Shulhan-Arukh Orah Hayyim* 586:1; and see *Mishnah Berurah* ibid. 4, for an interesting comment.

28. The context in BT would indicate that the reference is to the New Year's festival, and so, too, from the statement of R. Levi in BT ibid. 26b. However, see M ibid. and *Rashba* to BT ibid. 26b.

29. Following the texts that do not read "and so forth" (see ed. Horovitz-Rabin).

30. The quotation of this final verse is missing in some printed editions.

31. Cf. BT *Berakhot* 62b: "Samuel [Babylonia, third century] says [on I Chronicles ibid.]: He 'beheld' the ashes of Isaac, as the verse says 'God will see for Himself the lamb for a burnt-offering'".

32. Translating with the future tense in order to underline the eschatological depth that the homily reads in the verse.

33. On the difficulty of this biblical *midrash*, cf. G. Von Rad, *Genesis* (London 1961), p. 242, and E. A. Speiser, *The Anchor Bible*, Genesis (New York 1964), p. 163, note 14.

34. See earlier note 18.

35. The name of God, that is, that by which man calls to God, became central in the rabbinic phrase for martyrdom, i.e., קדוש השם, "sanctification of the name," cf. *Tosefta Berakhot* 4:18, *Sifra* to Leviticus 18:5, BT *Zevahim* 115b.

36. The pertinence of the verses I have added, in brackets, is manifest, since only in them is the notion of the expiation of sin expressed. Thus, again, whereas our text quotes only a small part of a biblical chapter (except for *Midrash Tannaim*, p. 204, which adds, "And with what does Scripture close the subject? 'Help us, O God of our salvation'"—but that is clearly a later gloss), its broader context is clearly referred to.

In BT *Sanhedrin* 47a, "Thy servants" of verse 2 is contrasted to "Thy saints" of the same verse and, based on the "redundancy," the former is interpreted to mean those who are privileged to be so called by virtue of their martyrdom, which expiates their sins. The *Sifre* text hints at no such allusion and the BT homily is clearly a later "explanation" of an earlier tradition. The BT text cannot be dated closely because it is not clear if it is amoraic or anonymously saboraic, and does not help us, therefore, in conclusively dating the above *Sifre* beyond a relative chronology. On the problem of dating the *Sifre* and the *Midrashei Halakhah* in general see C. Albeck's discussions in his *Introduction to the Talmud* (Tel-Aviv 1969) [Hebrew], pp. 102–43, esp. pp. 102–106, 122, 129–34, 141–43. On the problem of distinguishing saboraic from amoraic material within the context of the *memra* see A. Weiss, *The Talmud in Its Development* (New York 1954) [Hebrew], pp. 141–43, 151–54; and M. S. Feldblum in the *Abraham Weiss Jubilee Volume* (New York 1964), English section, pp. 18–19.

37. *Yalkut Shimoni* (Genesis, 102, p. 456) reads, "in order that the evil eye should have no sway over him."

38. *Yalkut Shimoni* ibid. adds, "For the nations of the world were spitting at them and saying, 'You [Israel] have such a God and you worship pagan rites!'" And see BT *Sanhedrin* 93a and *Rashi*.

39. See BT ibid., where the question of the three's fate is recorded as a tannaitic controversy.

40. See Lieberman's discussion in *Greek in Jewish Palestine* (New York 1942), pp. 106–10. Even if we grant Blau's interpretation of the Adrumentum love charm (ibid. pp. 108–109) as alluding to Daniel, among others, it does not establish any essential connection between Daniel and his three friends and Abraham, Isaac, and Jacob, who appear at the beginning of the charm only as part of the formulistic

turning to the God of the Fathers. Furthermore, Lieberman's interpretation of our midrashic pericope on the basis of that charm is purely conjectural. In any case, the Rabbis would not have enjoyed a homiletical juxtaposition of the three Fathers with the three martyrs or an identification of the latter with the "pillars of the earth" merely on the basis of the context of a love charm, unless that was justified within rabbinic associative thinking itself. The identification in *Midrash Shoher Tov* (*Midrash Tehillim* to Psalms 1:3, ed. Buber, p. 8a) of the "three pillars" as the sons of Korah is based on the image conjured up by the story in Numbers 16. Korah's entire congregation is swallowed into the earth's "mouth" (verses 31–33) while his own sons stalwartly survive the earthshaking incident (ibid. 26:11) "like the mast of a ship. . . . Rabbi says: All the ground around them was torn away while that ground which stood underneath them was not torn away. R. Samuel bar Nahman says: They were not standing all in the same place but rather each was standing by himself so that [afterwards] they remained standing like three pillars, and that is what people mean when they say 'On whom does the world stand, on three pillars', some say 'Abraham, Isaac and Jacob', and some say 'Hananiah, Mishael and Azariah', and some say 'the three sons of Korah' (ibid., pp. 7b–8a). Cf. also BT *Megillah* 14a and *Sanhedrin* 110a.

41. A. Hyman, *Toledoth Tannaim Ve Amoraim*, p. 1242, suggests the possibility of identifying this amora with R. Tanhum ben Hanilai, who belongs to the second generation of Palestinian amoraim. C. Albeck, however, in his *Introduction to the Talmud*, p. 270, identifies him separately, placing him in the third generation.

42. Assuming him to be the later of the two tannaim of the same name. Other manuscripts and editions do not read "ben Jacob" and perhaps, then, we would read R. Eleazar [ben Pedat] of the third century, Palestine.

43. ילדים, corresponding, for the homilist, to ילדיו, "his children," of the verse from Isaiah.

44. Saying, for the homilist, that the three martyrs were initially perfect for their ordeal of holocaust, cf. *Genesis Rabbah* to Genesis 22:9 (56, p. 600, and see note for similar material) concerning the perfection of Isaac.

45. Cf. Rashi to Isaiah 29:23.

46. The real justification of R. Johanan's understanding of "the myrtle-trees" as the righteous martyrs Hananiah, Mishael and Azariah lies in the following identification of "the bottom" as Babylon, which in turn makes sense, as does the essential meaning of the homily as a whole, within the redemptive message that Zechariah, this first chapter as well as the entire book, had in its historical setting as well as his eschatological message as read by the Rabbis (cf. *Deuteronomy Rabbah*, the end of *Re'ei* [end of 4, 148d] and BT *Sanhedrin* 98a).

47. The *Targum* likewise translates "Babylon" in both Zechariah and here.

48. In BT *Megillah* 13a interpretation of "the myrtle-tree" as symbolizing "the

righteous" within the context of both Esther and Zechariah is recorded in the name of the second century tanna R. Meir, but without any justification for such an interpretation. This would seem to indicate that R. Johanan's homily, identifying "bottom" as "Babylon" and, through that, pointing to the three martyrs, is rooted in an older tradition that R. Meir could rely on without manifestly referring to. The fact that the *Targum* to Zechariah shares the identification of "Babylon" but does not follow through with anything but a literal translation of "the myrtle-trees" gives us, it seems to me, another fragment of the older homily as the geographical identification by itself is pointless. That the *Targum* to Isaiah 44:27 understandably translates צולה as "Babylon" is not a serious reason for doing the same to מצולה in Zechariah 1:8, just as R. Johanan would not have bothered with that unless his interest was the identification of the martyrs. Actually, the whole subject of how and why the Rabbis "clarified" the identification of persons and places in the Bible must be reviewed with less glibness than usually is done; for examples of the many problems involved see Y. Heinemann, *Darkei HaAggadah* (Jerusalem 1954), pp. 21–24, 27–31. In the present case, if we assume a serious reason for the information in the *Targum* on Zechariah and if we tend towards the early dating of the Haggadic material in the *Targumim* as by G. Vermes, *Scripture and Tradition in Judaism* (Leiden 1973), e.g., pp. 38–39, 183±84, and 228–29 (and see Y. Komlosh, *The Bible in the Light of the Aramaic Translations*, [Tel-Aviv 1973] (Hebrew), pp. 57–61, for a survey of datings), then we can conclude that R. Johanan is reviving a homily whose essential idea as part of that homily was already dulled with age at least as early as R. Meir's time and probably earlier.

49. See Daniel 3:1. This identification of the valley of the dried bones (Ezekiel 37:1–14) with the place wherein the Babylonian king set up his impressive golden idol is meant to underscore the connection between the two stories as the homilist sees it.

50. The homilist thus sees this second of Nebuchadnezzar's two declarations about God, which both follow the miraculous saving of the three martyrs, as differing from the first (verses 28–30). The second, which speaks of God's "kingdom" and "dominion" as "everlasting" is grounded, for the homilist, in the astonishment over the event of the revival of the dead because, no doubt, that is taken as an event of eschatological dimensions.

51. Although the pericope is followed by an identification of the "four kingdoms" in the functionaries enumerated before the drama in the furnace (verses 2, 3) and after (verse 27), it is quite plausible that this is meant to allude symbolically to the downfall of the "four kingdoms" in whose empires the Exile stretches out— a motif that is more than adumbrated already in Daniel: 2:37–45, 7:17–27; and see, too, 8:20–26. The rabbis further developed the rich and fertile imagery that these interpretations, and the dreams and vision they purport to explain, have captured from and bequeathed back to the eschatological imagination. Under the vast Roman rule, the "four" were identified as Babylonia, Persia, Greece, and Rome, see, e.g., PT *Ta'aniot* 1:1(64a) in the name of R. Simeon ben Yohai (cf. *Mekhilta* to Exodus 12:41 [pp. 51–52] and *Sifre* to Numbers 10:35 [84, p. 83])

and *Gen. Rabbah* to Genesis 15:12 (44, pp. 439, 440). The "fourth kingdom," the "evil kingdom," is seen, in later perceptions, as continuing far beyond the waning of imperial Rome.

52. Some variants of *Gen Rabbah* 56 (p. 607) read similarly and we are dealing with a turn of phrase that is established as liturgy, discussed later. The *Pesikta de Rav Kahana* for *Rosh ha-Shanah* (p. 342) reads, "[You] will change the measure of judgement into the measure of compassion."

53. Compiled by R. Tobias ben Eliezer in the eleventh century from older material.

54. On the problem of dating this prayer see S. Spiegel, *The Last Trial* (New York 1969), pp. 95–96 and notes 77–78. If the liturgical literary crystallization precedes the midrashic ones, then we are to recognize the tenacity with which amoraic traditions, themselves of a sufficiently independent nature to withstand liturgical formularizations, were preserved in some works, particularly, in this case, PT, whereas in other works the liturgical phrasing influenced the recording of traditions, as, in this case, the version of *Midrash Lekah Tov*.

55. I have rejected the JPS division of the psalm into paragraphs as irrelevant.

56. נפשי.

57. כל–קְרָבַי, which would be translated best as "all my innards," cf. Isaiah 16:11.

58. Cf. H. W. Wolff, *Anthropology of the Old Testament*, p. 25.

59. Translating מְעַטְּרֶכִי as in Psalms 8:6 and Song 3:11, rather than "encompasseth thee."

60. Some variants read "and waited for me at the door" (*Rashi* apparently reading only ושמר לי without על הפתח, and, as *DDS* points out, rather than והמתין לי, which is probably a gloss). The *editio princeps* of the *Ein-Ya'akov* does not read "until I finished my prayer" (see *DDS*) but this does not succeed in blurring the subtly expressed deference the prophet shows for the sage.

61. See *Tosafot* to BT *Berakhot* 27b ד״ה והנותן שלום לרבו.

62. This is undoubtedly the correct reading. The variants reading without "for Me," in one way or another, are either moved by deference or inadvertently influenced by censorial tampering with texts, see *DDS* p. 4 and note 5.

63. ביתי . . . היכלי could be translated literally as "My temple . . . My sanctuary." My preference for "My house . . . My temple," allowing a more encompassing implication, seems to be more in keeping with the context of the pericope and is borne out further by the use of ביתו, "His house," as referring to "the synagogues and the houses of learning."

64. From the *Kaddish*, discussed later.

65. Following the Munich MS, see *DDS*, and note 62.

66. The day being *Rosh Hodesh*, they prayed the *Musaf Amidah* as well, thus delaying Elijah even more than usual. The all too human description of the lumbering fathers being helped up to pray and the vision of them lingering deeply in prayer, altogether a scene of old age yet gathering profundity, together with the intense compassion of their concentration and its fearful aura of immediate efficacy rooted in that same careful and knowing slowness, is what brings Rabbi to blurt out the thought that perhaps there are such men in this world. Elijah thus truly is partner to the following messianic outburst. That R. Hiyya is called together with his sons underlines his fatherliness and so strengthens the parallelism between him and the three fathers.

67. See *Tosafot*, BT *Bava Mezia* 86a, ד"ה אוקמינהו, on the custom of having more than one person lead the congregation in prayer on a fast day.

68. This description of the efficacy of the quoted prayer in the mouth of a certain individual is found, word for word, in BT *Ta'anit* 24a (twice) and 25b (and see *DDS*). The fact that it is found in the former in two separate but similar stories, while it is a necessary and integral part of both those stories, shows that it at least subsisted—as a literary formula (or a popular one)—outside either of the two stories. But it also probably shows that they are the source both for *Ta'anit* 25b, where the sentence is anonymously used to explain the view of an earlier sage (an unnecessary explanation at that because Samuel ha-Katan may simply have felt that the very need for the declaration of a public fast day for rain was already an inauspicious sign as the proper rainfall should be a natural event), and for our pericope, since here the storyteller's interest is the drama concerning the blessing for the quickening of the dead and not the need for rain (the latter motif entering through the patent reason for the declaration of the fast day). However, in a later chapter, we shall perceive an essential connection between the attitude of the rain maker and a certain conception of the deliverance of eschatological import. Besides, the connection, as here, between the rain and the quickening of the dead has very ancient roots in the crystallization of the promise of triumph over death around the dying and rising fertility gods who, in the areas in the Near East dependent on rain, were wont to be identified with the rain or storm deity, as in the case of the West Semitic Baal. The one God of Israel is the God both of the creativity inherent in nature's rebirth and that which wells up through man's search for his own rebirth; the two are not separated in the *Amidah* prayer because the possible intellectual connection of the two makes it unnecessary to deny the fossil of their history. And in our story, too, perhaps that connection has been somehow retained—and not necessarily through the influence of BT *Ta'anit* 24a, albeit through the use of a formula. Cf. ibid. 2a and 2b for further examples of the vitality of the ancient connection.

69. So great is his own yearning for the bursting forth of the messianic deliverance!

70. Variants do not read "fiery," see *DDS*.

71. I Kings 19:10,14. And see *Yalkut Shimoni* to Numbers 25:11, where Elijah is identified with Phinehas because, probably, the latter was also jealous for the sake of God (*Rashi* to BT *Bava Mezia* 114b ד"ה לאו כהן מר) and see BT *Sanhedrin* 82a,b concerning Phinehas.

72. II Kings 2:11, 16–18.

73. It is not clear if the "short prayer" referred to in the story of Elijah and R. Yose is either this prayer, or the "highlights of the 'Eighteen,'" or perhaps something else (see BT *Berakhot* 29a for the content of the "highlights" and ibid. 29b and 30a for other "short prayers" (and following note), and *Tosafot* ibid. 3a ד"ה היה for a discussion of the problem). However, in any case, Elijah's teachings on the subject clearly would not be, to a student of Jabneh, anything outside what a contemporary sage might have said.

74. *Cf. Tosefta Berakhot* 3:6, 7, 11, 16, 18, and see PT *Berakhot* 4:4 (8b).

75. On the same R. Yose, and gnosticism, see my "Some Early Rabbinic Thinking on Gnosticism", *JQR* 71 (1) (July 1980):18–30.

76. Both these liturgical pericopes are said in Hebrew and Aramaic or else only in Aramaic, the language of the masses at that time. The former has its source in the finale to the popular community study of Torah, which seems already to have been connected at the outset with the regular orders of prayer, especially the daily morning prayer (see I. Elbogen, *Der Jüdische Gottesdienst in Seiner Geschichtlichen Entwicklung*, [Leipzig 1913], Chap. 1, 10, 9 [התפילה בישראל (Tel-Aviv 1972), pp. 62–63] and J. Heinemann, *Prayer in the Period of the Tanna'im and the Amora'im* [Jerusalem 1978] [Hebrew], pp. 166–67 and note 23). The latter is to this day a part of the *Kaddish de-Rabbanan* and as such is said, like the former in its historical source, after the study of Torah by the community (as well as being part of the other forms of *Kaddish*) (see *Tosafot* to BT *Berakhot* 3a ד"ה ועונין).

77. "in the world which He has created according to His will" gives the rabbinic echo of Ezekiel 38:23, the latter having a decidedly apocalyptic context (see, for example, 18–22), quite a different turn.

78. This sentence is almost identical with Psalms 113:2 and Daniel 2:20. The context of Daniel 2 (see verse 19) and of Psalm 113, especially the latter's inclusion as the opening portion of the *Hallel* (which includes Psalms 113–18 and is recited and sung on the holidays of happiness and redemption), give the words a marked sense of praise for an achieved deliverance. For that reason, the opening sentences of the *Kaddish*, which are a prayer for a close and speedy redemption (underlined in the Sephardic version that adds, after the words "ordain His kingdom," "and may He cause His deliverance to burgeon and may He hasten His Messiah"), together with this sentence bring out a sense of darkness and light: In a world "created according to His will," there is yet a vision of a very untedious redemption, the swiftness and glory of that redemption, as yearned for, being deeply indicative of the condition of that world. As such, the addition in the *Kaddish* of the adjective *great* to his "Name" is an expression of the visionary nature of the

Kaddish rather than as a hymn of praise. For this reason, custom has it said by mourners, besides its other functions.

79. Indeed "the angels do not [even] recognize Aramaic," BT *Shabbat* 12b and *Sotah* 33a in the name of R. Yohanan, and see *Tosafot* to BT *Berakhot* 3a ד"ה ועונין.

80. קונה, which could also be translated as "acquire."

81. Referring to the "coming world."

82. Some variants reverse the order, but this seems more apt and this apparently was the reading before R. Hananel (10b).

83. BT *A.Z.* 17a and 18a are undoubtedly martyrial contexts, the former probably being the source of the statement. If 10b is not a martyrial context (but see *Rashi* ד"ה בלא מיכסא and R. Hananel) then our statement appears there as a gloss, since "in a moment" does not fit in.

84. *This-worldly martyrdom* is an epitomization of the seriousness of being in the world, a point that, I hope, will become manifest in this book. *Otherworldly martyrdom* is a flight.

85. PT *Berakhot* 9:7 (14b) and *Sotah* 5:7 (20c) tell the story with Tinneius Rufus as inquisitor.

86. Quoted before our pericope as the way R. Akiva was wont to interpret the verse. But, in M *Berakhot* 9:5 and *Sifre* to Deuteronomy 6:5 (p. 55), it is anonymous whereas in *Tosefta Berakhot* 7:7 it is in the name of R. Akiva's pupil, R. Meir.

87. PT ibid: "The time of the reading of '*Shema*' came. He [R. Akiva] began to read the '*Shema*' and smiled. He [Tinneius Rufus] said to him, 'Old man, either you're deaf or you scoff at suffering!' He said to him, '. . . I am neither . . . but all my life I read this verse and was distressed, saying, "When will I have had the opportunity of all three: . . . I have loved Him with all my heart, and I have loved Him with all my wealth; and yet in loving Him with all my soul I have not been tried." And now that it has come to loving Him with all my soul, and the time of reading *Shema* coincides with it, I succeed in uniting my consciousness [in reading and acting]. Because of that I smile now as I read.' He did not succeed in finishing before his soul took flight." In the continuation of BT the motif of unity has an overtone of completion and even perfection. In both versions the martyr's partaking of unity (see my discussion of BT) infuses his reading of the *Shema* with a sense of togetherness with God whose Unity is understood as the final subject in the verse "*Shema* . . ."

88. Many variants contain neither "He drew out the word 'one'" nor this "Echo"; but some of those same include the latter as part of the continuation of the pericope (which I have not quoted). All variants include the coincidence of death with the word *one* (see, however, *DDS*). The custom in the synagogue indeed is to draw out the word *one*, see BT *Berakhot* 13b and the *Posekim*.

89. His, therefore, is a this-worldly martyrdom.

90. Contrast the discussions in this chapter with S. Spiegel, *The Last Trial*, pp. 114–17; E. E. Urbach, *The Sages—Their Concepts and Beliefs* (Jerusalem 1971) [Hebrew], p. 448; and G. Vermes, *Scripture and Tradition in Judaism*, pp. 193–227.

3. The Binding of Isaac

1. Cf. *Genesis Rabbah* to Genesis 22:20 (57, pp. 612–614).

4. Honi ha-Me'aggel

1. שאני כבן בית לפניך.

2. Following the overwhelming evidence (see Malter) for the reading אבן הטועין (allowing minor variations), which translates literally "the stone of those who have mistaken their way." It, no doubt, was impressive and conspicuously situated in a high place, above any flooding. PT *Ta'aniot* 3:11 (66d) and BT *B.M.* 28b, which identify the place to which lost objects were brought, in order to be publicized, with the same stone as here are to be understood in terms of this particular stone serving as a gathering place because of its conspicuousness for travelers even at a distance, thus there, too, the correct reading, as in most variants, is אבן הטועין and not אבן הטוען (see *DDS*).

3. Rejecting, with Malter, the printed readings as influenced by the *Baraitha* quoted in BT 23a.

4. מתחטא. Cf. M. Moreshet, *A Lexicon of the New Verbs in Tannaitic Hebrew* (Ramat Gan 1980) [Hebrew], pp. 162–63. Also see note 7.

5. The phrase "and He does your will for you" is missing in the variants and Malter accordingly has erased it, assuming it to be merely the influence of the continuation. I have retained it because it so sharply points up what is, to me, the reason for Simeon's discomfort, too sharply, perhaps, for the readers of the story of the righteous Honi.

6. Malter wrongly prefers here the reading "before" as in the previous statement that refers to God. I have chosen those variants reading "with," or, literally, "on," because what is being gotten across is a feeling of immanency and imminency in Honi's relationship with God, an intimacy (see the next note); *before* is used earlier in the deference of rabbinic thinking and, thus, language, concerning God, but here in the metaphor of child and father the warm sense is allowed more freedom of word.

7. The *Baraitha* quoted in BT 23a adds here, "When he says to him, 'Wash me

with warm water', he washes him, 'Rinse me with cold water', he rinses him, 'Give me nuts, peaches, almonds and pomegranates', he gives him" (following Malter).

8. Cf. besides later material, *Tosefta* 3(2):1 and BT *Berakhot* 19a.

9. Malter, on the basis of variants, thinks the word *nevertheless* to be a gloss, although he refrains from erasing it. If so, then in the original reading, the contrast between Honi's tradition, which is that of the Mishnah, and his praying for the cessation of the rain would sound sharper.

10. לקבל in most variants. In any case, *cope* fits the context best as a whole.

11. ריוח, which could be translated more literally as "relief." PT ibid. (67a) reads: "and he said, 'My Master, You brought evil upon Your sons and they could not stand it; You brought bountifulness upon Your sons and they could not stand it. Rather, may it be desirable before You that You should bring easiness (רווחה).'" Accordingly, man can take neither God's bountifulness nor the evil he sends, not because they are "too much" (BT) but because they are directly from the divine. Thus, PT's reading of "'*Rather* [likewise some variants in BT] . . . bring easiness'" is to be understood as seeking not merely relief but an alternative to direct divine intervention, a more human mode, an "easiness."

12. רוב הטובה, literally, "too much goodness."

13. Following almost all the variants. The printed text reads, "Our Rabbis repeated". Cf. PT ibid. 3:12 (67a).

14. בני לשכת הגזית, literally, "those of the Chamber of Hewn Stone [in the Temple complex]," see M *Middot* 5:4.

15. Following Malter in the matter of scriptural quotation. In some variants, we have another example of the practice, on the part of scribes, of abbreviating such quotations.

16. Disregarding the printed reading alone, which would translate as a present, since the beginning of the sentence unanimously translates as a past.

17. דור ששח בעונו. The phrase שח עינים in the verse is not taken to mean simple humility ("humble person"); rather it is read literally as "one with lowered eyes," that is, one who is humble in his inability to look the other in the eye, suggesting a sense of guilt or shame. This understanding of the verse also is a result of the way in which its continuation is read, discussed later. Both *DDS* and Malter prefer the variants which read, עיניו שחות, "humble," without the notion of sin, because that makes the homily's connection to the verse more facile. However, the similarity of this homily with the targum to the verse in Job suggests that we should read it like the targum, as I have, while the homily in PT *Ta'aniot* 3:12 (67a), though in the same context, is a different version of our homily and not merely a variant reading of it.

18. Reading the phrase אי נקי in the verse as "him that is not innocent" rather than "him that is innocent." PT ibid. has, "I [God] said 'He delivereth him that is

innocent', while you [Honi] said 'He delivereth him though he is not innocent'. Yours prevailed while Mine did not."

19. Taking בר in the verse to mean "clarity of" rather than "cleanness of."

20. Following Malter who disregards the few variants that read "You delivered through your perspicuous actions" as influenced by the preceding portion. Accordingly, this last line may be seen as referring back to the entire homily and epitomizing it; and it is to be understood as perceiving Honi's praying, in its attitude, dramaturgy, and effect, as much more than praying, as doing. Also discussed later.

21. PT ibid.: "What does '. . . delivered through the cleanness of thy hands' mean? 'Through the clarity of thy hands.' Because of the deeds and good works which were yours from the beginning." We have here, apparently, two different understandings of *cleanness*, the former being similar to BT. But the latter, in referring to Honi's righteousness, is only "explaining" why Honi's circle drawing brought about the rain: His righteousness was there "from the beginning" but that was followed by the rain making drama, the latter bringing the rain even if it was the merit of the former. Thus, the second understanding of *cleanness* is a rationalization of the Honi story but does not change its scenario. It attempts to bring the story closer to rabbinism by moving it away from magical associations toward notions of meritoriousness. By itself, it refers to the fact of rain making and not to the deliverance of others through the value of one. Its very orthodoxy serves to underline the uniqueness of the original story, which centers around Honi's heroically dramatic success in making rain.

22. Following, with Malter, the variants, and thus retaining more manifestly the sense of this part of the *Baraitha* as being an addition to our Mishnah (or to a version similar to it); so that the following is *an* explanation but by no means necessarily the original explanation of Simeon's disapproval of Honi's behavior. R. Elijah Gaon goes so far as to read, "And moreover, if . . .". Cf. BT *Berakhot* 19a where the rabbinic displeasure with Honi is expressed by referring to him as "one who is impertinent towards Above".

23. See I Kings 17:1–18:45. Malter deletes "when the keys of rain were in the hands of Elijah" as a "late legend found in BT *Sanhedrin* 113a that also contradicts R. Johanan's statement in BT *Ta'anit* 2a" and so on. Actually, R. Johanan's same statement "Three keys are in the hands of the Holy One Blessed is He, which were not given over to a consignee, and they are the following: The key of the rains, the key of the woman who gives birth, and the key of resurrection" points up his knowledge of how much there is in the world that does not partake of that divine mercifulness with which man feels intimate in prayer (indeed R. Johanan was no stranger to the blind malice of suffering, cf. BT *Berakhot* 5b), and such knowledge certainly may have influenced rabbinic attitudes toward aspects of nature, making R. Johanan's statement a polemical one within the rabbinic circle itself. As for the Honi story, a statement by Simeon ben Shetah saying the possibility of the "keys of rain" being in "hands" other than God's would probably be quite an authentic

expression of a rabbinic attitude toward praying, where the latter is a standing before God in the midst of a world that defies the expectancy of the way of prayer and answer, of divine mercy in an earthly orderliness. Indeed, praying would be a standing before God that sets off the standing before the world as something quite different, even if man is called upon to do both and to work and hope for the comingling of both. That was the very point upon which Honi the rain maker could not agree, and his praying was something very different from the sage's.

24. Because then Honi's impertinence toward God, ending in a whimper, indeed would have been a mockery, not vindicated by successful rain making, which would be the only justification rooted in Honi's own terms, as the story is told here.

25. "When he says to him . . . he gives him" following Malter.

26. See the pertinent notes to the Mishnah.

27. See Numbers 25:1–15.

28. Attributing the death by plague of the twenty-four thousand (25:9), beyond the number executed before the incident with Zimri (25:5, and see PT *Sanhedrin* 10:2 [28d] on this verse), to the wickedness of Zimri alone. The complaint of the Sepphorians and R. Hanina's reaction is reminiscent of *Sifre* 131 (p. 172) and BT *Sanhedrin* 82a where it is said (on verse 5) that the tribe of Zimri, Simeon, complained to Zimri saying, "They are judging for the death punishment and you are sitting in silence!" If this association is intended then it underlines the sense of R. Hanina's annoyance with the people's desire for deliverance from the way of divine judgment itself (discussed later). And there, too, R. Isaac in the name of R. Eleazar attributes death by unnatural intervention to the sin of Zimri. And cf. 82b, "He [Phinehas] came and threw them down [Zimri and the Midianite woman Cozbi] before the Divine, saying before Him, 'Master of the World, for *these* should twenty-four thousand of Israel fall?'" And cf. PT ibid. (29a, top).

29. Cf. BT 25a (reading "R. Hanina bar Hama" rather than "R. Hama bar Hanina," see *DDS* and Malter). D. Sperber in *Roman Palestine 200–400, The Land* (Ramat Gan 1978), p. 75, correctly assumes PT to be "the fuller and more authentic version of this story." Also see p. 74, note 8.

30. BT *Ketubbot* 103b. According to PT *Ta'aniot* 4:2 (68a) R. Hanina willingly forfeited the position to still another rabbi in order to avoid controversy and only after the latter's death as well did R. Hanina finally become head.

31. See Hyman, *Toldoth*, p. 618, and Albeck, *Introduction*, pp. 245–46.

32. See Sperber, op. cit., pp. 190–92.

33. While both versions clearly contain the same story kernel neither is dependent on the other. This is evidenced by the following points among others: (1) the carob tree motif in BT and the destruction–rebuilding of the Temple in PT; (2) the significantly different use of the same verse in two versions; and (3) the very

interesting interpretation of the motif of light by each, PT telling it as an entering into the Temple court while for BT it takes place as an entering into the House of Learning. This parallelism of the two enterings is a conscious rabbinic perception; similarly, in some rabbinic practice a *ba'al keri* has to immerse himself ritually before studying the Law, just as he had to do before entering the Temple Mount. The practice was attributed to Ezra the Scribe (see BT *Bava Kamma* 82b and *Tosafot* ד"ה אתא, *Berakhot* 22a–b, *Hullin* 136b, *Pesahim* 67b–68a, and *Mishneh Le-Melekh* to Maimonides's·*Yad, Bi'at ha-Mikdash* 3:3). But it is unlikely that this should result here from the dependence of one version on the other—in any case, their independence is otherwise sufficiently evidenced. The two versions, then, are different retellings of a folk story. The various rabbinic tellings of the Honi stories constitute a crystallization around a traditional, interpretative sense of Honi's personality. That sense is, as I attempt to show here, an organic one, though it does not fully emerge in the *Talmudim* and survives there in its influence as drawing in, molding, and structuring material around the name of Honi ha-Me'aggel.

34. Cf. *Tosefta B.B.* 2:17 and BT *B.B.* 60b.

35. According to BT. But PT *Ta'aniot* 1:4 (64b) knows him only as "a *Hasid* of Kefar Yamma" (see PT *Megillah* 1:1 [70a]).

36. Following Malter.

37. Following Malter, in accordance with most variants. The printed text adds an allusion to the success of the husband's prayer as well even if that success is "belated."

38. Malter assumes "Or perhaps also concerning some delinquents" etc. to be a gloss influenced by BT *Berakhot* 10a, because it is missing in many variants. However, this motif is not uncommon (cf. BT *Sanhedrin* 37a) and, other than the inconclusive evidence of the variants (*Rashi*'s text did apparently contain the text, see Malter's comment to that effect), I see no reason to delete it. On the contrary the motif of repentance fits in with the personality of the penurious rain maker, as I show later on.

The printed version of our story begins: "Abba Hilkiah was the son of Honi ha-Me'aggel's son, and when the world was in need of rain the Rabbis would send to him [messengers] and he would beg mercy and the rain would come. Once . . .". This is a claim to a habitual relationship between the Rabbis and Abbah Hilkiah. The repetition of "to beg mercy so that the rain should come" [also see Malter] points up the literary independence of the story from the heading and, therefore, I have deleted it as Malter has, following almost all the variants. In any case, the following is to be noted.

First, There is no hint here of any attitude between the Rabbis and the rain maker that partakes of a pupil–teacher relationship. The Rabbis who come to him do not sit to learn from Abba Hilkiah, or anything of the sort, they only want an explanation for his seemingly strange behavior, finally shown to be not irrational though unfamiliar to them. He, in turn, neither attempts to show learning—

he presents his explanations as common sense—nor does he show any diffidence toward the Rabbis as learned. The Rabbis carefully refer to him as "sir" (*mar*) but it is this very correctness that underlines their total lack of turning to him as a bearer of learning. And, G. Vermes's assertion (*Jesus the Jew* [London 1973], p. 119) that here "*mar* is a title superior to that of *rabbanan*" (I have translated the latter as "the Rabbis"), serving "to underline the pre-eminence of a holy man over ordinary teachers" is baseless. Nor does the prefixing of *Abba* to Hilkiah's name imply his being learned; cf. BT *Berakhot* 16b, "*Tanya* . . ., Slaves and slave-girls are not referred to as 'Abba so and so' or 'Imma so and so' but those of *Rabban* Gamaliel were referred to as 'Abba so and so' or 'Imma so and so'." Also, cf. BT *Ta'anit* 23b where it is told about Hanan ha-Nehba, the "son of Honi ha-Me'aggel's daughter," that during droughts the Rabbis would send young school-children who would grab the tail of his cloak and say to him, "*Abba, Abba*, give us rain". He would pray to God asking Him to be indulgent with those who did not know which *abba* [father] really gives the rain. Not only does the Talmud itself not refer to Hanan as *Abba*, despite the popular appellation, but it would seem that the Rabbis, who did not approach the rain maker by themselves but rather sent the children, felt an uneasiness about the business—though they did give in to its attraction. And the children's antics give the term *Abba* in this scene a certain sense of derision.

Second, It emerges that there is a definite sense of alienness between Abba Hilkiah and the Rabbis. In fact, this is probably the whole mood of the popular tale behind our story: The strangeness and wonderment felt by the Rabbis upon meeting the unfamiliar, humble, peasant rain maker. Indeed, the latter is even able, in turn, to be unsure of the former's modesty, separating them from his wife upon entering his house!

39. See PT *Ta'aniot* 1:4 (64b,c) for the parallel. There, the Rabbis' visit is manifestly singular.

40. Translating פועל in the sense of a noun rather than of a verb, following the homily. This is a rabbinic usage. Cf. M *B.M.* 5:4 and 7:1, *Avot* 2:15 and BT *B.M.* 77a, among many others.

5. R. Hanina ben Dosa

1. חברבר. The *Tosefta* reads ערוד.

2. PT reads R. Hanina ben Dosa but I have here followed the *Tosefta*.

3. *Tosefta* 3:20, with some differences.

4. BT *Berakhot* 32b, and cf. PT 5:1 (8d): "The Rabbis repeated: The early *Hasidim* would linger for an hour and then pray for an hour and then linger again for an hour. But since they would linger nine hours a day for [the thrice-daily] prayer, how was their learning preserved and how was their labor accomplished? By their being *Hasidim* their learning was preserved and their labor was blessed."

5. למקום. Variant: "to their Father in Heaven," see *DDS*.

6. This is not the generally accepted rabbinic understanding of the Mishnah, cf. BT 32b and 33a.

7. אהבהו עד מצוי נפש. Also, cf. *Tosefta Berakhot* 7:7.

8. M *Berakhot* 9:5, *Tosefta* ibid., and BT 61a (in the name of R. Akiva). There is no interdependence.

9. See Finkelstein's comment.

10. Cf. *Tosefta Berakhot* 3:4: "Ben Azzai says: If one's body is harmed because of his learning, it is a good sign for him; [if] his learning [is harmed] because of his body, it is a bad sign for him. If one's mind becomes deranged because of his learning, it is a good sign for him; but if one's learning is deranged because of his mind, it is a bad sign for him."

But, if there is a martyrial tendency descernible in Ben Azzai that is not to equate him in that sense with R. Hanina ben Dosa. Ben Azzai's "*hassidut*" (cf. BT *Berakhot* 57b) is something of an asceticism rooted in a preoccupation with a personal need that draws him along a way that sublimates the energy of being toward his perceived spiritual goals and shirks the encumbrances that are needs (cf. BT *Yevamot* 63b, *Sotah* 4b, M *Sotah* 9:15, and BT *Berakhot* 6b): It is a love of God that is a "wringing out" of oneself through which man comes closer to Him. But R. Hanina ben Dosa's way is different, as we shall see. I have suggested a similarity only in their experience of the devotion to God as entailing self-sacrifice by the very intensity of that devotion.

11. The reading here is problematic, and see the reading in the *Arukh* under *havarbar*, and see Epstein's *Introduction to Amoraitic Literature* (Jerusalem 1962) [Hebrew], p. 358 and note 14. Also, see Kohut's comment in *Aruch Completum*, 2d ed. (Vienna 1926) [Hebrew], vol. 3, p. 342, note 5.

12. The opening of the poisonous lizard's burrow figures in both the PT-*Tosefta* version and the BT. In the former, the lizard is found dead there, whereas in the latter it dies there. This, together with the similar epithet that closes the stories, helps to justify my treatment of the two as versions of the same story, as literary remains that are expressions of an interpretative tradition that discernibly partakes of coherence and organicism beyond that presenting itself on the surface of those two tellings about R. Hanina.

13. The variants contain a different version, which Malter has followed, but I have followed the printed text with the emendations of the *BaH*. For our purposes the differences and their histories are not essential.

14. Some variants read, "pushed his head on the ground," see *DDS*. M. Jastrow in his *Dictionary*, p. 522b (טוח II) translates, "his head between his [the son's] knees." But the interpretation as a gesture of bending into oneself is borne out by BT *Avodah Zarah* 17a, where the same phrase describes the behavior of R. Eliezer ben Durdaya who put his head between his, undoubtedly, own knees, also in a prayer gesture.

15. Following the variants that read this question and answer as between the daughter and the Rabbi and not with "they," see *DDS*.

16. In some variants (*DDS*) the wording of Amos (7:14) is less manifest so that one cannot be sure whether any irony is meant here by quoting.

17. Uncertain, and should be read as *R.A.*, each variant deciphering in its own way.

18. Some read "daughter" (*DDS*).

19. In the Hebrew a play is made on the word נשערה ("stormeth") in the psalm and the word שערה ("hair"). But in my opinion this is merely a mnemonic device and the idea expressed is rooted deeply in the psalm, see my discussion later.

20. Most variants read: "R. Hanina" but this need not indicate the same R. Hanina who follows. In any case, neither of the men referred to in the story is meant.

21. Some variants, "let his bowels be thusly overlooked: But rather He is long suffering and collects His due" (also see *DDS*): Cf. PT later.

22. And *Yevamot* 121b, not including the last statement of R. Hanina, and with slight differences.

23. Or, "R. Eliezer".

24. Or, "R. Yose bar Avin." And see *DDS* to BT *B.K.* 50a for the reading, "Ravina," which *DDS* dismisses. PT *Bezah* 3:9 (62b) reads, "R. Yose *bei* R. Bun."

25. From "R. Haggai" to the end, also in PT *Demai* 1:3 (22a). For the beginning, see PT *Bezah* 3:9 (62b) and *Ta'aniot* 2:1 (65b).

26. Or, cf. Judges 5:10.

27. R. Hanina's statement concerning the unacceptability of the claim that God easily overlooks man's actions and the homilies of R. Aha and R. Yose also are found in PT *Bezah* 3:9 (62b), and R. Hanina's statement alone in PT *Ta'aniot* 2:1 (65b). However, that the material is drawn from the context of the ditch digger's tragedy to the other *sugyot* and not vice versa is borne out by the fact that, in PT *Shekalim*, there is no evident cause for quotation of the material and only the tradition behind the text, as it finds expression in BT *B.K.* 50a, explains the sequence. In PT *Bezah*, the presence of the material is explainable as being appended to the preceding material by association, and so, too, in PT *Ta'aniot*. Something similar to the homilies of R. Aha and R. Yose is found in *Mekhilta* to Exodus 15:11 (p. 143) but our material cannot be explained as originating there where it is anonymous and undifferentiated.

I, therefore, have interpreted the above material in the context of PT *Shekalim* and its parallel in BT *B.K.*.

28. Rather than, "mighty."

29. In PT and BT *B.K.*. In BT *Yevamot* the latter is "R. Abba," the former is

quoted as similar to R. Yose of PT—"R. Nehunya" (*not* the ditch digger) of BT B.K. The view attributed in PT and BT B.K. to "R. Hanina" does not appear in BT *Yevamot.*

30. R. Nehunya (*not* the ditch digger) in BT B.K. and R. Hanina (*not* ben Dosa) in BT *Yevamot.* The mixing up of names results both from their being written by copyists as abbreviations and through the influence of the names of the characters in the stories as well.

31. See I. A. Agus in *The World History of the Jewish People,* Second Series (Tel-Aviv 1966), vol. 2, pp. 191, 211, 213, 217, 220–22, and 230–33.

32. M in PT reads, "With the death of R. Hanina ben Dosa and Yose ben Kitunta *Hasidut* disappeared," while a *Baraitha* in PT :17 (24c) and *Tosefta* 15:5 read like the other versions of M.

6. *Nahum ish Gamzo and R. Hananiah ben Teradyon*

1. Both *DDS* and Malter follow the variants that do not read here "and he was lying in a shaky house." As the sentence appears in the continuation, it would seem to be redundant here; and indeed all texts read it only in one or the other, each sufficiently evidenced. However, as is common, our story actually is put together from literary fragments whose incompleteness becomes manifest when they are put together, uncovering a richer perception than they betray when taken in the illusionary completeness of isolation and literalness. So that the continuation ("Once . . .") does indeed overlap at the point of describing the sufferer's house, as evidence of the history of the entire pericope, and for this reason, the texts cannot agree on its place, here or in the continuation; both are correct.

2. The variants read "R. Akiva said to him," but they are influenced by PT, see the next note.

3. Cf. the parallel in PT *Shekalim* 5:6 (49b) and *Pe'ah* 8:9 (21b). The BT and PT versions are independent of one another, and Malter's claim (following Rapoport) that the BT version is a "later addition" in BT is wistful. And in any case, PT, too, contains what is germane to my argument here, though I have chosen BT because its richness is a genuine reflection of tradition's interpretive perception of Nahum.

4. Taking his name, which probably derives from Gimzo in central Israel, to mean "this too."

5. "The next day . . . 'This, too, is for the good'" appears only in the printed text, see Malter's comment. Also see the next note.

6. This sentence is missing in the printed text, also see the previous note. It is possible that Nahum's saying "This, too, is for the good" in the context of this story is indeed a later emendation, see discussion later.

7. See BT *Sanhedrin* 108b.

8. The Munich Ms and others do not read the attribution to Rav.

9. The Munich Ms reads with the sense of the latter ascription as denying the former, while another variant lacks the latter altogether. R. Meir was a student of R. Akiva and it is not unusual to have the two quoted as saying the same thing.

10. In the printed version, which I am following, this final quotation of the aphorism is in Hebrew, unlike the earlier texts, which are in Aramaic. This indicates a literary crystallization of the *Bet-Midrash*, thus stengthening an assumption of contiguity between the perception of R. Akiva here and other rabbinic thinking on the matter. The stressing in the Hebrew version of the ubiquity of the aphorism's application fits in with the more systematic nature of the view in its later setting, as will be discussed later.

11. PT *Ta'aniot* 4:8 (68d)

12. See, e.g., BT *Berakhot* 61b.

13. See M. S. Feldblum's *Dikduke Sopherim, Gittin* (New York 1966) [Hebrew].

14. Rav Joseph, a Babylonian amora of the fourth century, is quite possibly quoting a tannaitic tradition as he often does. In that case this would constitute a late tannaitic reinterpretation of an older Mishnah.

15. Deuteronomy 4:5, where Moses says to Israel, "Behold, I have taught you statutes and ordinances, even as the Lord my God commanded me."

16. Following Rashi's reading, (BT *Sanhedrin* 90a) and see *DDS* there.

17. Referring, probably, to one who denied the appropriateness of any relationship between the divine and the human spheres, in the mood of Epicureanism and gnosticism. This understanding of the term would place it together with the denial of revelation (which scorns the notion that God turns to man and man, at that calling, faces God) and the denial of bodily resurrection (which scorns man's yearning for his physical being in the world to stretch out to ever more than dust). It thus is a heresy that strikes contrary to some of the most vibrant chords in rabbinic Judaism. For later applications and interpretations of the term cf., e.g., BT *Sanhedrin* 99b–100a.

18. בספרים החיצוניים. See ibid., 100b, "In the writings of the sectarians." Also cf. *Tosefta Hagiga* 2:5 "כבר בן זומא מבחוץ," and BT *Hagigah* 15a.

19. If we take this as cynically intended, then it points toward a gnostic heresy, bringing us again to particular sectarianisms (see the previous two notes). It thus is not clear whether this is a continuation of R. Akiva's version of the Mishnah or of the previous sentences as it would fit into the context of both.

20. See the discussion later.

21. Our text contains only part of this Mishnah, but I have copied it out in its entirety (following the *Mishnayot* text) because of the implications of its context (see my notes).

22. Another possible interpretation is that the martyr's devoted wife is reiterating, with the intensity of tragedy, her life's way (fidelity to her husband) as God's way. Thus she is reasserting her partnership with God in the derision by brute circumstances. And cf. *Targum Jonathan*, "Moses the prophet said, 'When I went up on Mount Sinai I saw the Master of All the Worlds, God, dividing the day into four parts: For three hours He learned Torah, and for three [hours] He dealt with justice, and for three [hours] He [dealt with] the bringing together of man and woman and decreed to uplift and to humble, and for three [hours] he [dealt with] the sustaining of every creature.' For that is what is written, 'He ["The Rock"] is sturdy . . .' [i.e., the verse is made up of four sections, each referring to one of the four characteristics of His fourfold day; the third, 'A God of faithfulness . . .' corresponding to the 'bringing together of man and woman . . .']." Woman's faithfulness to her husband partakes of God's faithfulness to man, with all its tragedy; and God is the One Who, in His knowledge of faithfulness, brings man and woman together. If this is the proper interpretation then the fact that the homilies of both husband and wife are rooted in traditions gathered around the same verse (discussed later) and are yet essentially different—the former taking the thread of "perfect" (see discussion later) and the latter painting a mood of womanly faithfulness and tragedy—strengthens, in this part of the story, a depth of sensitivity to the realities of living out a religious life that is impressive.

23. Based on the Hebrew spellings.

24. Meaning each and every man, see continuation, also cf. M. *Rosh ha-Shanah* 1:2: It is God's working with the being of man that is perfect, not otherwise.

25. BT *A.Z.* 18a and b.

26. Cf. Rashi to BT *A.Z.* 17b (bottom) and Urbach, *The Sages*, p. 113.

27. See notes earlier on the heresies enumerated in the Mishnah.

28. Recognizable in its being anonymous and in Aramaic and in the fact that it manifestly does not flow with the material it purports to elucidate.

29. The Jewish Theological Seminary Ms, by S. Abramson (New York 1957), p. 31 (16a), line 15, reads "and" instead of "for."

30. Cf. BT *Sanhedrin* 98a and b.

31. קלצטונירי,see D. Sperber, *A Dictionary of Greek and Latin Legal Terms in Rabbinic Literature* (Jerusalem 1984), pp. 190–91.

32. ביום חתנתו.

33. Malter (p. 123) maintains that this homily is a later addition to the Mishnah and has its source in the *Seder Olam*, 15. This he concludes from having found no connection to the previous material, where R. Simeon ben Gamaliel describes an old custom in which the maidens of Jerusalem, on the fifteenth of Av and at the waning of the Day of Atonement, would "go out and dance in the vineyards" where the lads of Jerusalem would take notice of them and so Judea

would be joyous with marriage. However, there is no evidence that the homily is indigenous to the *Seder Olam*. Furthermore, the version in the latter sounds like a later version with its play on spellings to make its point. In the older version, as in the Mishnah, the connection between the "day of his espousals" and the "giving of the Torah" relies on the language of the Song of Songs as the Rabbis read it and that which is crystallized around it, see my discussion later. Moreover, there is a lucid continuity between R. Simeon ben Gamaliel's description of the old custom in the Mishnah and our homily. The boys are admonished by the girls "do not look at beauty, look at family" because the latter is supposed to ensure the roots of religiosity; and the perception of the "day of espousals" in the Song of Songs as the "giving of the Torah" is a perception of a sympathy between the yearnings behind the two moments so that, for the homilist, the religiosity of the boy and girl is truly to be a part of their love. Nevertheless, Malter is correct in accepting the possibility that the homily is not indigenous to the Mishnah, even if it does not ensue from the *Seder Olam*. As for the age of the homily, Malter also is correct in questioning the originality of the reading in most variants that ends our homily with the words, "may it [the Temple] be speedily rebuilt in our days." This leaves the age of the Mishnah open. As Malter points out, R. Simeon ben Gamaliel may be the first rather than the second since he is describing an undoubtedly ancient custom—and so the homily, too, may be of early origin. Inasmuch as the homily fits in with the mood of the Song of Songs as the Rabbis sang it (discussed later) and inasmuch as that strain is probably ancient, having to do with the very occurence of the Song of Songs in the tradition of Israel, we may conclude that R. Simeon ben Gamaliel, however we identify him, or the tanna of the Mishnah, is using material whose roots are considerably older.

34. Playing on the Hebrew spellings.

35. See Malter ibid. for the parallels.

36. See the context!

37. Translating in accordance with the homily that reads ולאמי instead of ולאומי.

38. And cf. *Exodus Rabbah* 46 (anonymously).

39. He died in prison, in 1293, having been incarcerated by Rudolph I, after the spring of 1286, for having attempted to leave Germany at the head of thousands of Jews. The Jews imposed upon themselves exile in opposition to Rudolph's reinterpretation of the *servi camerae* ("serfs of the treasury") status of the Jews to mean that they really were the slaves of the treasury of the empire. Rudolph's offer to accept a large ransom for the rabbi was refused since this would have been seen as an acquiescence of the Jews to the emporer's policies. See I. A. Agus, *Rabbi Meir of Rothenburg* (Philadelphia 1947), vol. 1, pp. 125–53.

40. Also quoted in BT *A.Z.* 10b and 17a, also in a context of martyrdom. It is quite possibly indigenous here, since it follows upon a previous statement made by

the sage in the context of our story. In any case, it describes his attitude concerning the auspiciousness of martyrdom.

41. Cf., e.g., R. E. Agus, *The Literary Sources of the Babylonian Talmud, Moed-Katan* (doctoral diss., Yeshiva University, New York, 1977), English summary, pp. 1–4, 16, 19–20, 21–22.

7. If I Am Here, All Are Here

1. "To the place . . . take me" is missing in several variants. Rashi insists on reading it, like the *Tosefta* (4:3), because only this explains the juxtaposition of the following material (discussed later).

2. Rashi and the *Tosafot* read this sentence as being attributed by Hillel to God, who says it to man. The *Tosafot* bear this out by the fact that the *Baraitha* continues with a quotation of Exodus 20:21, "in every place where I cause My name to be mentioned I will come unto thee and bless thee." However, even if the quotation is an original part of the tannaitic material, it does not show that Hillel did not say it. Hillel is not doubting the participation, as it were, of God but is saying that he "comes to His house" only in the certainty that He, too, will "come" (see later discussion). In any case, it is difficult not to read the material with its manifest meaning—the same holds true for the beginning of the *Baraitha*, see Rashi and *Tosafot*.

3. "It was he, too" etc., M *Avot* 2:6. Although the mention of Hillel there follows upon a chronological listing of sages ending with R. Gamaliel the son of R. Judah ha-Nasi (M 2), it is nevertheless Hillel the Elder who is meant. "Hillel says" in M 4 is the beginning of another listing which continues in M 8 with the student of Hillel the Elder, R. Johanan ben Zakkai. Cf. *Tosafot Yom Tov* to M 4.

4. מענה לשון, which should be taken to mean "the speaking of the tongue," cf. the *Targum*.

5. See note 3.

6. The similarity in form yet difference in meaning (discussed later), R. Johanan clearly not dependent on Hillel, means a change in the implication of a particular linguistic crystallization. This demonstrates, to me, a change in an underlying sensibility.

7. Some variants do not read "the Elder."

8. Cf. PT 9:5 (14b)

9. See note 3.

10. Shammai's statement could also be understood as "make your Torah fixed," in the sense of crystallizing its form or standardizing its content (see Bertinoro). However, in BT *Berakhot* 35b, R. Johanan in the name of the tanna R.

Judah bar Ilai (second century) uses the same phrase in clear contradistinction to one's other occupations, which were, "in earlier generations," only sporadic in comparison with their studying of Torah. Cf., also, BT *Yoma* 19b in the name of R. Aha, and *Be'urei ha-Gra* to *Avot*.

11. לכבוד שבת literally, "for the honor of the Sabbath." Some variants read בכבוד שבת (*DDS*), literally, "in the honor of the Sabbath." The latter reading is a "correction" of the original reading, the original sounding strange in its sense of eating during the week as an active preparation for the Sabbath (לכבוד שבת generally having this meaning); see the later discussion. One variant (see *DDS*) even reads "he was busy with the honor of the Sabbath" instead of "he ate."

12. See Deuteronomy 5:23 and Jeremiah 23:6 (in context!).

13. See Hyman, *Toldoth*, vol. 1, pp. 363–64.

8. If Not Now, When? Repentance

1. Also see Ezekiel 3:17–21, 33:1–20.

2. Cf. BT *Rosh ha-Shanah* 16b, "And R. Isaac also said: Four things" and ibid. 16a, also in the name of R. Isaac, "It is good for man to cry out."

3. The story of the great fish may be viewed as a retelling of the ancient myth of death (the descent into the monster's belly is the descent into Hades) and rebirth. Death now is the flight from God into deep despair, and the return from the depths is the rebirth of repentance.

4. *Tosefta* 1:14 reads "lost everything."

5. Ibid. reads, instead of "he . . . evilness," "God accepts him." BT's reading is sharper and echoes the break with the past as rooted in the psyche of the repenter. It also is a more sensitive inflection of the verse quoted. Cf. M *B.M.* 4:10 and BT *B.M.* 58b.

6. The *Targumim, Onkelos, Jonathan,* and *Neofiti,* understand אז ירצו את עונם as meaning rather that in their repentance Israel will embrace the suffering of their punishment.

7. מכניעים rather than the biblical יכנע. The shift of the same verb from the passive form to the active, transitive form smartly changes the mood of the verse, discussed later.

8. See note 6.

9. Playing on a reading of the Hebrew in accordance with Deuteronomy 21:4, "break the heifer's neck," rather than with Deuteronomy 33:28.

10. Exodus 32:9, 33:3, 5, 34:9; Deuteronomy 9:6, 13; Proverbs 29:1. For the sense of "breaking" see the previous note.

11. Cf. *Tosefta* 1:8 and BT 16a.

12. See M *Ta'anit* 1:1–7 (especially 4–7) and BT 15b.

13. Variants: "lest he will die—repentant. And concerning him Solomon," or "lest tomorrow he will die, he should repent tomorrow lest he will die the day after; and he will thus." Also see *Avot de-R. Nathan* 15 (ed. Schechter, p. 62, versions a and b, and notes).

14. Compare A. Heidel's version in his *The Gilgamesh Epic and Old Testament Parallels* (Chicago 1946), p. 70.

15. Cf. also the Egyptian "A Song of the Harper," *ANET* p. 467. The context of the Gilgamesh epic adds to these quoted portions a breadth and depth that, to me, is far more resonant to the mood of Kohelet, comparable only to the sense of the disconcertingness of death as expressed in some of the tombs where the Egyptian material is found. Although the Gilgamesh epic, to me, is clearly a critique of its contemporary temple beliefs, the Egyptian material only hints at some feeling of dissatisfaction with the priestly gospel. How much dare an artist express himself in the established religious domain?

16. See also 2:21–25, 3:12, 13, 4:9, 5:12–19, 6:2–6, 8:15, 9:7–10.

17. Cf., e.g., 9:12.

18. יפשפש, see Moreshet, *Lexicon*, pp. 298–9.

19. I.e., a different version.

20. ימשמש, literally, "caress," see ibid. p. 216. The *Arukh* (*Aruch Completum* vol. 6, p. 458b) and *Rashi* interpret the first version to mean a probing of one's past actions and the second version to mean a weighing of his as yet unperformed actions.

21. See Urbach, *The Sages*, pp. 224–26. The basic reasons for suspicion are (1) that, in subject, the pericope is too all-embracing to be yet so succinctly descriptive of an actual, defined controversy between the two houses; (2) that the possibility of delineating the duration of such a disagreement to "two and a half years" is highly unhistorical; and (3) that a decision by majority on such a matter would be totally foreign to what we know about rabbinic concepts of authority. A proper treatment of the *Baraitha*, therefore, is one that attends to it as an interpretative knowledge of the Bet Shammai–Bet Hillel confrontation and not as a chronicle. However, to deny the congruence of the "decision" with mainstream rabbinic thinking (see Urbach, ibid.) is wrong, I think. The notion that being *Homo sapiens* places upon man a burden of responsibility as great as the force and positivity of that being is decidedly rabbinic. Therefore, the irresistible, and thus wonderful, drive to be must be experienced as an equally huge effort of will to good, so that no matter how positive it is to live, man also may be allowed a sense of exhaustion, a yearning for rest, a prayer that he be spared that effort. In short, a true description of a rabbinic perception of man's responsibility is that he must

"probe" or "weigh his actions" with the sense that being is so vastly demanding that, from the point of view of will, it "were better for man had he not been created." Nor is this feeling mitigated by man's sense of his own uniqueness and superiority or of the goodness of God's ways and creation. On the contrary, these convictions only increase the sense of personal potential and, thus, burden. God's mercy alone can assuage the force of that which is rooted in the sense of being itself. As for that sense of being as a lonely sense, as yet ungraced by the experience of God's mercy, it is "better to be not": a sense of the burdened will and not a lacking in the ontology of man.

22. Although there is a contested tradition that Akavyah was excommunicated by other Rabbis, it would be because of a controversy over authority and not because of heresy, see M *Eduyyot* 5:6, 7 and BT *Sanhedrin* 88a.

23. H. Jonas, *The Gnostic Religion* (Boston 1963), p. 45.

24. See, e.g., Urbach, *The Sages*, pp. 415–418.

25. *The Nag Hammadi Library in English*, ed. J. M. Robinson (Leiden 1977), p. 114.

26. Ibid., pp. 115–16.

27. Ibid., p. 172.

28. Ibid., pp. 172–73. Also cf. "The Hypostasis of the Archons," II, 4 (89:4–30); ibid., pp. 154–55.

29. Ibid., p. 112.

30. Ibid., p. 168.

31. And *Sifre* to Deuteronomy 6:5 (p. 55), but as part of a different midrashic flow, and *Tosefta Berakhot* 7:7 in the name of R. Meir.

32. I.e., he is not only the maker of the immanent world order, he is the creator of the cosmos, too.

33. See Isaiah 1:18; Psalms 51:9; and Zechariah 3:4–5.

34. *Tosefta Kiddushin* 1:13, according to the Erfurt Ms. does not read with the meaning of "as if."

35. Reading וחוטא אחד in the verse to mean "a sinner of one [sin]."

36. Cf. the beginning of *Tosefta* ibid.

37. *Tosefta* ibid.:14. Ms Erfurt, reads, "R. Simeon ben Eleazar" [also second century] and Ms Vienna and the printed text read the same, adding "in the name of R. Meir"—who was his teacher. BT probably is influenced by the continuation that is in the name of R. Simeon ben Yohai.

38. *Tosefta* Ms Erfurt and the printed text add here "One should always see himself" etc., as in the first part of the *Baraitha*. In any case, the second tanna is clearly rereading the preceding pericope.

39. See note 37.

40. Variants do not read here "R.," but nonetheless do so later.

41. Some early prints "correct" to "he." The *Aggadot ha-Talmud* reads, "He heard an Echo saying"!

42. Taking the Hebrew ונקה לא ינקה to mean, "He clears [the guilty] He will not clear [the guilty]".

43. *Tosefta*, 5(4):6 reads, "R. Ishmael says: There are four categories of atonement." R. Eleazar ben Azariah here means that in only three of the categories can man be said to be atoned, for in the fourth, atonement is complete only with death, see later, "But one who."

44. See ibid., 5(4):5–9.

45. Ms Vienna and the printed text add "intentionally." This softens the implicit widening of the culpability for a sin that involves diminishing, as it were, the divine name's glorification in the happening of godliness beyond the dimension of individuality.

46. Following Ms Erfurt (reading as Ms Vienna did earlier).

47. Ms Vienna and printed texts do not read "the day of."

48. Ibid. add "together with sufferings."

49. Understanding מקוה as a "ritual bath," see Leviticus 11:36. In M *Mikva'ot*, מקוה alone has the meaning of "a gathering of water," specifically, a ritual bath (see, e.g., 1:1, 4, 7; 2:2, 4, 5,10; 3:1; also see M *Eduyyot* 1:3 and so on). The sense that this gives the verses in Jeremiah is borne out by the context of 14:7–8 and 17:13.

50. In one variant the Mishnah does not include from "The following" till the end. In another, R. Eleazar ben Azariah's statement ends on the note of "Sins . . . and God are atoned for by the Day of Atonement" and so too the Mishnah. In yet another variant, the Mishnah ends with "and ye shall be clean." Also see *DDS*. PT (end of *Yoma*, 45c) did read at least until "shall be clean." The rest is there, probably as a *Baraitha*, cf. *Pesikta de Rav Kahana* 24; *Shuvah*; ed. Mandelbaum, p. 350; *Yalkut Shimoni* to Ezekiel 36:25 (374) and to Psalms 4:5 (627), and *Midrash Tehillim* to ibid., but not in the name of R. Akiva.

51. Cf. the famous story of R. Amnon of Mainz, the alleged author of the beautiful prayer *U-Netanneh Tokef*, which is said on *Rosh ha-Shannah* and the Day of Atonement. The story connects the authorship of the prayer on *Rosh ha-Shannah* with the martyrdom of R. Amnon, *Or Zaru'a, Rosh ha-Shanah* 276.

9. Pangs of Messiah

1. The section "and . . . soar" is missing in Ms Munich; also see *Tosafot Yom Tov.*

2. Cf. Isaiah 59:15 and the entire chapter.

3. It is not clear whether this pericope was considered to be part of the Mishnah or was a *Baraitha* appended to the end of the mishnaic tractate, though Rashi does read it. BT *Sanhedrin* 97a quotes three different *Baraithot*, in the names of R. Judah, R. Nehorai, and R. Nehemiah, that together make up a close parallel to our pericope, but does not quote the latter; also cf. *Songs Rabbah* to 2:13. And see *Tosafot Yom Tov* to "R. Phinehas ben Jair says" preceding the material quoted here.

4. Taking "a paved work of sapphire stone" as meaning "whenever Israel are oppressed" and as indicating a certain opaqueness of texture compared to the azure "clearness" of heaven that signifies "when they are redeemed." *Targum Jonathan* says that the angel Gabriel made a "brick" out of a premature baby that was miscarried by a "delicate young woman" working on mortar, and placed it under the "footstool" of God's "seat" in order to remind Him of Israel's oppression. This is already a compound *midrash* that almost loses the point that God's perfection is hindered in Israel's suffering. The tannaitic source thus has preserved a more pristine version of the motif, adhering as it does to a starkness of theology underlined by a direct and seemingly simple use of a verse that in any case is theologically daring, whatever its history. The *Sifre* (discussed later) does not append any explanation to the verse. Perhaps, it understands the homilist as taking the verse's theophany as a presence of God in the exile of the wilderness.

5. Translating the verse in the way the homilist is reading it.

6. The homilist's point is brought home by a play on the Hebrew words so that he reads the verse as, "Was I [not] exiled to the house of thy father."

7. Translating in accordance with the homilist's reading.

8. See *Mekhilta* to 17:14 (p. 183, lines 1, 2).

9. From "And so you find that whenever Israel are oppressed" to "And it says, 'Come with me from Lebanon, my bride, With me from Lebanon,'" see *Sifre* to Numbers 10:35 (pp. 82–83); also see the context. From "Wherever Israel went to exile" till the end, cf. PT *Ta'aniot* 1:1 (64a) and BT *Megillah* 29a (discussed later; also see *DDS*). Also, cf. *Mekhilta* to 17:15 (p. 186).

10. The rich immanence of God that one often finds in certain trends of rabbinic religiosity means that the 'I' experience of Him is the content of the statement that God is. Therefore, in a true experience of the 'I', precisely because the 'I' leaves all else, except for the exceptional, as an 'it' centering around the being of the self; the knowledge that "God is," for the 'I' is always a statement of the omnipresence of God. The more personal the "God is" is, the more real is the

radiating out of His presence to that world which radiates out of the self to the world through the being of I–world. Only in the I–thou relationship does the "God is" become precarious because then another 'I' must be partner to it.

BT *Megillah* 29a, following on the *Baraitha* quoted in the name of *Rashbi* (discussed later) states: "Where [is the Divine Presence] in Babylon? Abbaye said: In the synagogue of Huzal and in the synagogue of *Shaf ve-Yativ* in Nehardea (see *Iggeret Rav Sherira Ga'on*, ed. Lewin, p. 72); and do not say that it is both here and there but rather it is sometimes here and at other times there." This means, to me, that happenings of salvation take place while yet in exile, that they happen, for Abbaye, in those synagogues, and that they are so fleeting (like sparks) that one dare not, if he appreciate the intense briefness of their flash, imagine them as bursting out for more than a moment in more than one place at a time.

11. A student of R. Akiva, cf. *Mekhilta* quoted earlier in the text.

12. And, similarly, in PT *Ta'aniot* 1:1 (64a).

13. In "mystic union" with God, he cannot be thought of as 'other' if the identity of the 'I' is to be retained. If religious man yearns for such togetherness, it is because in his knowledge of God he is asserting the "I am" of God in the fullest sense yet with a dwindling sense of His otherness. This is a rare flight, even for the most religious of men, and the religious experience that we are discussing runs the whole gamut from being "dust and ashes" before God to a mystical togetherness with God. Man's self-image as dust and ashes implies his unawareness of what believing in God involves psychically. But, paradoxically, it is precisely from this primal religious sense of smallness that the mystical flight to togetherness with the Sublime evolves, thus enabling man to have an awareness of his own sublimity.

Generally speaking, most trends in rabbinic Judaism are opposed to the notion of "mystic union with God," certainly if it entails the loss of personality. For the Jewish sensibility, personal responsibility is of greater moment than the ontological aspects of the hereafter. Hope for the mystic union with God is liable to draw away from the sharpness of personal responsibility, and that explains Judaism's shying away from the former notion. Nevertheless, I think that a God with whom one could imagine such a union, were one not committed to major rabbinic tendencies, would be a far more Jewish God than one described as ontologically foreign or 'other' to man's deepest experience of being. No doubt, this is a philosophically controversial point, but I am discussing rabbinic religiosity and not philosophy. Nor do I imply anything concerning other mysticisms.

At this point, a basic methodological distinction must be made. It is valid to attempt to retrace the psychic journey travelled by man in building his religious perceptions. But, one who would take those perceptions seriously, as I hope I have done, must know that religious truths are always far more than the sum of their parts. Reductionism, even of an existential nature, is not a serious mode of understanding if it is the religious phenomenology that rivets our attention. In the present case, a phenomenological understanding must realize that, as I have pointed out, in most trends in Judaism, God remains a "before whom" man stands. I have described a psychic road to the belief in God, one that may culminate in "mystic union" with him, in order to grasp the "whatness" of God as part of religious experience. But, for religious man, that experience is far more than its description; and in general, as I have said, Jewish or at least rabbinic sensibilities are against a recognition of a reality of mystic union with God. Furthermore, in the actuality of religious experience, the events of awe before and intimacy with Him, which alternate dialectically in moments of religious intensity and thus truth, are far more important than the ontology of man or God. It would be *unreal*, therefore, to use terms such as *mystic union*, or *I–thou*, or *totally other* in order to describe that experience. I have used such terms, albeit as a model only, in order to emphasize an aspect of rabbinic thinking germane to my argument at the present juncture and to delineate a distinction between Judaism and Christianity.

14. Translating the verse according to its homily, also see the verse's context.

15. See the discussion later.

16. Similarly in BT *Sanhedrin* 97b ("the Holy One Blessed is He will raise up over them a ruler. . ." should be read as being said by R. Eliezer, and see *DDS*) to 98a, ending with, ". . .and R. Eliezer was silent".

17. As R. Eliezer reads it.

18. This interpretation of the controversy between R. Eliezer ben Hyrcanus and R. Joshua assumes the correctness of the PT version over that of BT (*Sanhedrin* 97b–98a)—unless we accept the reading of the Florence manuscript and the Constantinople edition of the *Menorat haMa'or* (*DDS*), which as it agrees with PT is probably correct, its difficulty in the linguistic context of the *sugya* only heightens the probability. Urbach's preference for the reading in the printed editions of BT and his correction of PT to agree with it (*The Sages*, p. 601 and note 63) is unfounded as well as unlikely. My interpretation of R. Joshua's words, as saying the coming of redemption "in its time" only, is supported by the *sugya* in PT. The *sugya* states that the controversy between R. Eliezer and R. Joshua in the first Mishnah of *Ta'anit* is "reversed" in the controversy concerning redemption. In the Mishnah, R. Eliezer says that one "mentions the rains" in the *Amidah* from the beginning of *Sukkot*, while R. Joshua says this is done only from the end (meaning, probably, *Shemini Azeret*, see the note in the *Tifferet Yisrael*) because *Sukkot* is "not the time of rains." The *sugya* assumes, apparently, that it would make more sense if R. Joshua, who speaks of a redemption "in its time" only and nevertheless agrees to the mention of resurrection in the daily *Amidah*, should allow the mentioning of rain as well, even when it is not "in its time" (i.e., from the beginning of *Sukkot*); whereas it would suit R. Eliezer's view quite well to mention rain only "in its time" (i.e., at the end of *Sukkot*), because for him the mentioning of resurrection is *always* "in its time" of the present. Contrast, however, the interpretation of the *Penei Moshe*, which, to my mind, is forced.

19. Cf., e.g., Ezekiel 7:2, 3, 6; Habakkuk 2:3; Daniel 8:17, 19; 11:27, 35, 40; 12:4, 6, 9, 13.

20. Variants do not read "and good deeds".

21. Variants: R. Joshua ben Levi.

22. On R. Eliezer's confrontations with his colleagues due to his advocation of the old *Halakha* see Y. D. Gilat, *The Teachings of R. Eliezer Ben Hyrcanus, and Their Position in the History of the Halakha*, Tel-Aviv 1968 (Hebrew) pp. 7–35.

10. The Binding of Messiah: Messiah ben Joseph

1. J. Klausner in his *Ha-Ra'ayon ha-Meshihi be-Yisrael* (Tel-Aviv 1950), pp. 294–95, tries to date this R. Dosa as late as possible, as part of an attempt to handle the material referring to Messiah ben Joseph in this pericope as "late." However, he points out that the notion of such a Messiah and his death is already assumed in a *Baraitha* (BT *Sukkah* 52a, discussed later) to be common knowledge (p. 293). Also cf. Urbach, *The Sages*, pp. 618–19 and note 43. On R. Dosa ben Harkinas, see Hyman, *Toldoth*, vol. I, pp. 323a–24b. In the following discussion, I try to show that the subject of this pericope is part of a developed rabbinic motif. The fact that such a motif is expressed only fragmentarily in the tannaitic and amoraic–talmudic sources, to the point that in our pericope it is not known which disputant holds which view, indicates, probably, that we are dealing with a notion that was partially suppressed but survived as it did because of its old roots. For this reason, the *Baraitha* mentioned earlier assumes a currency of knowledge that is not readily transparent to us either in its currency or its meaning.

2. Ms Munich adds, "in the West" [Palestine], and *DDS* corrects that to "R. Judah *bar Ma'arava* [West] expounded." Other variants read the name as "R. Judah ben R. Ilai," a mid-second century tanna.

3. Ms Munich and others: "to cut off." The Venice edition of 1526 reads "suffer" instead of "conquer" in both instances.

4. So, too, in *Pesikta de Rav Kahana, ha-Ḥodesh*, ed. Mandelbaum p. 98, but in the name of R. Johanan; and in *Pesikta Rabbati, ha-Ḥodesh*, ed. Friedman p. 75b, also in the name of R Johanan. The reading of the *Tanna de-Vei Eliyahu Zutta*, ed. Friedmann p. 11, is taken from BT; see Friedmann's note.

5. That the millennium is to be ushered in by cataclysmic events is an ancient eschatological notion with roots running down through Ezekiel's "Gog" and "Magog" (Chapters 38 and 39) and earlier; see for instance BT *Sanhedrin* 97a, "The Rabbis repeated: The seven [year period] during which the son of David comes." But I have carefully selected a small set of sources that point to something unique, personal martyrdom. I see this driving to a salvational event whose truth is in that very dimension in which it happens, as I show below. This is, to me, the meaning of the Messiah ben Joseph events and in the light of this I have selected and interpreted my sources. But, rabbinic sources on eschatology are sometimes kaleidoscopic (at least in the form in which they have come down to us), and one may find different patterns broken up into each other. The perception of structure that I develop here, I believe, is justified by being part of a structure that manifests itself in the story that threads through this work as a whole.

6. In BT *Yoma* 69b, there is an unusually concrete personification of the evil inclination. However, it is told as part of a "historically" unique happening and not as a currently meaningful theology. Furthermore, the distinction between a historically rooted phenomenon, the "inclination to paganism," and the existential "inclination to sin" is firmly perceived, so that the historical waning of the former is possible as a final victory over that inclination, while a threat to the continuity of the latter is seen as a threat to the continuity of the entire world. Although we are tempted to categorize the imagery there as subsisting on the periphery of the *Bet ha-Midrash*, its usage there does not lose its grasp on the phenomenon of human wickedness as grounded in the very workings of nature, as understandable in terms of an integrated human psychology, and as occurring within the unfolding that is history, where only God is seen to be partner to humanity.

7. The homilist interprets the verse on the basis of its parallelism: "the sacrifice of thanksgiving" is the "ordering of his way aright." The latter is a "confessing" of sins in the sense that it is a repentance meaning a clarification and ordering of one's deeds: a clear identification of his sins (i.e., confession) and a consequent reordering of his way of life. (Compare BT *Mo'ed-Katan* 5a, where R. Joshua ben Levi's homily is explained by reading the verse to say, "And to him that *weigheth* his way will"; this, however, is probably a saboraic, and thus later, explanation that adds an unnecessary element but faithfully clarifies the homilist's meaning. Also cf. there Ravina's interpretation of the verse where it is understood to mean, "And to him that *pointeth out* the [wrong] way will" [i.e., in warning]). And conversely, to the homilist repentance, the "ordering of his way aright", is a "sacrifice," a veritable "slaughtering" of the evil inclination. This is an honoring of God in both worlds, an immolation of part of the self, as opposed to a Temple sacrifice that is an honoring of him in "this world." For this, he will "show the salvation of God" that is for man as saved from death, because in that dimension this honor of God occurs, in the dimension where self-sacrifice saves; that is, never an imperfect world but rather a "coming world" because martyrdom is a yearning for perfection.

The *Targum* to this verse reads, "who so slaughters the evil inclination it will be considered for him like a thanksgiving sacrifice." This clearly is dependent on both this statement of R. Joshua ben Levi and on the following, without a clear sense of the sage's treatment of this verse. The continuation of the *Targum* is similar to Ravina's treatment of the verse (discussed earlier). So that either these amoraim are expressing older traditions or this portion of the *Targum* is late, that is, posttalmudic. Cf. P. Churgin, *The Targum to Hagiographa* (New York 1945) [Hebrew], pp. 59–60 and p. 55.

8. Also cf. BT *Sotah* 5b, but the *Sanhedrin* text is independent. For the context here, see *DDS*.

9. Cf. *Tosefta Yom ha-Kippurim* 5(4):14–15(13–15); PT *Yoma* 8:9 (45c); BT 86b, 87b; *Ta'anit* 16a; Maimonides, *Yad*, *Teshuvah* 2:2–3. Also see note 7.

10. Following the variants that read "R. Eliezer" rather than "R. Eleazar," see *DDS*. This identification is borne out by the *Mekhilta* (discussed later), which quotes a similar tradition in his name (see note 11, below).

11. His contemporaries also are quoted by the *Mekhilta* here in the same context. The *Mekhilta of R. Simeon ben Yohai* reads "R. Joshua," the colleague of R. Eliezer ben Hyrcanus, but the reading of the *Mekhilta* and BT *Sanhedrin* 98b (mentioned earlier) support each other.

12. *Mekhilta of R. Simeon ben Yohai*, ed. Epstein-Melamed, p. 113, with variations.

13. This story is brought in connection with R. Akiva's distinction between one who practices magic and is accountable according to Exodus 22:17, Leviticus 20:27, and Deuteronomy 18:10–11, and one who merely creates an illusion (M *Sanhedrin* 7:11, BT 67a). But the anonymous material in BT 68a (bottom) assumes that R. Eliezer showed R. Akiva magic and not a mere illusion.

14. See M *Kelim* 23:1 and 26:4; and *Tosefta Kelim* B.B. 4:3,7.

15. Also see 101a, b.

16. PT *Mo'ed-Katan* 3:1 (81c,d) and BT *B.M.* 59b.

17. See Hyman, *Toldoth*, vol. 1, p. 175.

18. *Tosefta* 15:3, Ms Erfurt, reads, "the Scroll of the Law was made void." Ms Vienna and the printed text read, "the honor of the Law was made void," but that is probably a softening of the original reading. PT *Sotah* 9:17 (24c) reads, "the book of wisdom was hidden away," using the definite article. Therefore, I have translated it in such a way that the sage's death is perceived as meaningful beyond the confines of a particular event. Not merely "a Scroll" but "the Scroll." This is also in keeping with the contextual meaning of all the sources. Cf. also BT *Sanhedrin* 101a–b.

19. BT *Berakhot* 28b reads the same for "clear . . . Judah," adding, in the printed text, "who is coming" (or "who has come"). But Ms Munich does not add this.

20. Hyman, *Toldoth*, vol. 2, p. 681a.

21. R. David Luria in his introduction to the *Pirkei de R. Eliezer*, "Beit Zaddik," 1, and Hyman *Toldoth*, vol. 1, pp. 162b–163a.

22. Cf., e.g., M *Demai* 2:3 and *Tosefta* 2:2–5; M *Hagigah* 2:7 and BT 20a; BT *B.M.* 87a in the name of R. Meir and *Bekhorot* 30b. Also, discussed later. G. Alon in *Studies in Jewish History* (Tel-Aviv 1957) [Hebrew], vol. 1, p. 158, note 44, suggests that perhaps R. Johanan ben Zakkai and R. Eliezer ben Hyrcanus were such, on the basis of our pericope. But that is not in the least conclusive, even if they were not priests, discussed later. Alon, however, makes a case for his claim that the practice was more widespread among the rabbis than is generally assumed, up to a certain time; see ibid. pp. 159–69, also see note 27 of this chapter.

23. Translating literally, but in the singular, in keeping, I think with the original homily. The final sentence of this pericope, "these wounds" etc., implies

that the homilist is reading rather, "the house where they caused me to be loved." But I have taken this as the editor's elucidation and thus allowed a different intonation.

24. See *Mekhilta de-Rashbi* to Exodus 6:2 (ed. Epstein-Melamed, p. 6, line 21); BT *Hagigah* 16a; *Shabbat* 12b; and cf. ibid. 40b and *Sotah* 49b.

25. That is to say, laws of ritual cleanliness that parallel the laws dictating the ritual cleanliness necessary for entrance into the Temple; also see note 27.

26. Cf. M *Berakhot* 2:2; BT 13b; and *Pesahim* 56a.

27. G. Alon in his important monograph on the "Boundaries of the Laws of Ritual Cleanliness" (op. cit., pp. 148–76, and see also pp. 121–47) shows that many of the laws of ritual cleanliness pertaining mainly to the priests and the Temple were understood, during the second Temple period and afterwards, as pertaining to nonpriests outside the Temple as well. Taking this phenomenon as an organic whole it means that (1) priestliness becomes viewed not only as a function of an aristocracy identifiable through its heredity and its Temple functions but rather as a behavior pattern and attitude of personal sanctity; (2) entering the Temple becomes viewed not merely as an entrance into the concrete Temple buildings but rather as an entrance, in an attitude and state of sanctity, into those realms, those happenings rather, where sanctity "makes sense" in the concomitant view of things. Religiosity increasingly centers around the personal as holy inasmuch as it partakes of learning, performing the Law, and praying (though the stress placed on the latter may have varied among the various proto-rabbinic and rabbinic groups) rather than around an "objective" holiness identifiable in terms of absolute place and time in the geographic sense as well as the social. These two trends are actually one; they constitute a reinterpretation of "where" holiness happens (a reinterpretation that already finds expression in the Bible; for example, see my discussion of Psalms 84 and 122 in the next chapter). Hence, it is correct to say that the eating of meals in ritual cleanliness (like priests) and particularly a preoccupation with the laws thereof (which parallel those of Temple entrance) in the context of a deathbed scene, has to do with the whole structure of holiness as perceived by the Sages. This conjures up, as I have pointed out, messianic yearnings that ask What is to be with the place that is destroyed—God's land, his city, his temple served by his priesthood? and What is to be with the time that is no longer and refuses to come? It is a turning in the very same direction of the reinterpretation of the holy discussed earlier, it is a stretching out to "another" happening of holiness, of the kingdom of God, which deprecates destruction and exile. Similarly, Ezekiel saw the heavenly Temple when the first one lay in ruin (Ezekiel 40–44:4). All this has implications not only for "what" the messiah but for "when" the messiah as well, see the next chapter.

However, Alon's point that observance of laws of ritual cleanliness was not confined to a few individuals is not to be misinterpreted. It remains nevertheless a "priestly" preoccupation in the sense that it was still an elitistic one. The Rabbis viewed it as a mark of one of their own circle, indeed as a mark of a *Haver*, an initiate (cf. e.g., M Demai 2:3 and Tosefta 2:2–5, and BT Bekhorot 30b), while there were some who insisted that not to do so placed one outside the Rabbinic circle, not only outside of the *Haverim* cf. e.g. Tosefta A.Z. 3(4):10 and BT Gittin 61b). See also Ch. Rabin's fascinating *Qumram Studies*, New York 1975, especially pp. 11–21, and 37–52.

28. See also BT *Sanhedrin* 94a–b, where several messianic passages in Isaiah are applied to Hezekiah (Urbach, *The Sages*, pp. 600–601). And cf. J. Neussner, *A Life of Rabban Yohanan ben Zakkai* (Leiden 1962), pp. 172 ff.

29. PT continues with yet another story, where a certain scholar was sought for marriage into an important family but refused because he did not want "to embarrass them." Before his death, he, too, said, "Clear out the entire enclosure because of the ritual uncleanliness," but added "and prepare a chair for Jehoshaphat king of Judah. It was said: Let him who pursued honor come for this one who fled from honor." This is probably a reference to what is described in BT *Makkot* 24a. "Jehoshaphat . . . when he would see a student of the Sages he would stand up and hug him and kiss him and call him rabbi." The relationship between the three deathbed scenes in PT, R. Johanan ben Zakkai, R. Eliezer ben Hyrcanus, and the humble scholar thus is as follows: (1) "Clear out . . . cleanliness" is, as we have seen, so congruous with the parallel material in BT yet not dependent upon it, that we can conclude its being essentially rooted in a common structure of meaning that tradition perceives around R. Eliezer's deathbed scene. So that, even if the literary formulation in PT is influenced by R. Johanan's saying, it remains, in content, totally true to the context of R. Eliezer. In fact, if one wishes to identify a source it probably would be the reverse, the description of the older sage's initial sentence being influenced by his student's. (2) The request for "preparation of a chair" points back to the first deathbed scene. R. Eliezer's call is seen, as I pointed out, as referring back to the meaning inherent in his teacher's deathbed scene but is certainly not a mere borrowing; it deliberately points to a meaning that is appropriate to the student as well, but in his own terms. This is seen in the fact that neither version of R. Eliezer's second sentence is merely a copy of R. Johanan's words. (3) The initial sentence said by the humble scholar may be a mere borrowing from the previous two scenes. But his reference to Jehoshaphat, king of Judah, expresses a meaning that pertains uniquely to his own story. In fact, its setting against an already formulistic backdrop serves to heighten the pathos of that scholar's unusual humility.

30. Cf., e.g., BT *Sukkah* 52b; *Pseudo-Jonathan* to Exodus 40:4–11; and the *Targum* to the Song of Songs 4:5.

11. When the Messiah

1. BT *Sanhedrin* 100a reads, instead, in the name of Rabbah (or Rava, see DDS) bar Mari. But he is known to quote R. Joshua ben Levi, see BT *Berakhot* 42b and 44a, and in BT *Yoma* 78a he describes the earlier sage's behavior (C. Albeck, *Introduction to the Talmud*, p. 377). Also see note 3.

2. The number *310* is arrived at through the numerical value of the Hebrew word.

3. On the inclusion of R. Joshua ben Levi in a Mishnah, see the end of the *Tosafot Yom Tov* and see M *Avot* 6(a *Baraitha*):2.

4. PT *Ta'aniot* 1:1 (63d).

5. II Samuel 20:1–22. This *Baraitha,* in PT, is followed by a controversy between R. Simeon ben Lakish and R. Johanan as to whether the identified individual must be "deserving of death like Sheba" in order to justify surrendering him. R. Joshua ben Levi's dilemma as will be related, however, is not an uncertainty concerning that controversy since even "Elijah" agrees that the law of the "Mishnah" was followed.

6. *Tosefta* Terumot 7:20. There it reads, "like Sheba the son of Bichri was picked out" thus enabling the opinion (see the previous note) that the victim need not be actually deserving of death, the similarity to the case of Sheba being in form not essence. Also see the continuation there.

7. Referring, perhaps, to M *Terummot* 8:12, or else to the *Baraitha* mentioned earlier, a Mishnah *ḥizonit,* a Mishnah not included in the universally accepted compilation "of R. Judah ha-Nasi."

8. See the material preceding this in the Talmud, where only drastic and dangerous treatment is considered to hold out hope for such sufferers.

9. The context of this verse is devoted attendance to the Law and it is in light of this that R. Johanan, in the continuation, adjusts, but does not abandon, his initial wry remark; see the discussion later.

10. The Hebrew is taken by the homilist to mean, literally, "something attached to" or "accompanying."

11. Cf. PT *Berakhot* 2:1 (4b) and BT *Shabbat* 30a (bottom).

12. משכנותיך.

13. דרור, *swallow* of verse 4, means "freedom" in Leviticus 25:10; Isaiah 61:1; Jeremiah 34:8, 15, 17; and Ezra 46:17.

14. See *DDS.*

15. Cf. BT *Berakhot* in the name of Rav Hisda on Psalm 87 (also a psalm of the "sons of Korah," like 84!):2.

16. From the variants (see *DDS*) it emerges that the reading "R. Joshua ben Levi" is incorrect. This reading results from the continuation where R. Joshua ben Levi comments on his son's experience in the same vein in which the homily here is related. Thus, in its error, this reading bears out the reading "Joseph ben R. Joshua ben Levi" later, see note 18. That the following story is told here within the context of the homily on Zechariah 14:6 remains clear; see note 18.

17. Reading the verse with the meaning that the "heavy," that is, the dear, will become light, insignificant (not "thick" as in Exodus 15:8, but rather as in M *Terumot* 4:11, see Moreshet, *A Lexicon of the New Verbs,* pp. 332–33).

18. The *Aggadot ha-Talmud* here does not read "ben Levi" (and the same reading was before the *Sefer Yuhasin,* see *DDS*), and so too BT *B.B.* 10b according to the printed text and some variants. However, the great majority of variants (see *DDS* here and in *B.B.*) do read "ben Levi" and this reading is borne out by the reading "R. Joshua ben Levi" in the beginning of the pericope, whether that be in error or not. If in error it must be influenced by the reading here (see note 16), and if it is correct then the parallel in content between the comment of Joseph's father (discussed later) and this homily make it likely that the same homilist is referred to. That R. Joshua ben Levi had a son named Joseph; see, e.g., PT *Ta'aniot* 1:6 (64c), BT *Yoma* 78a and *Hullin* 56b.

19. "Happy . . . intact," see BT *Mo'ed Katan* 28a and *Ketubbot* 77b, if borrowed then probably from here.

20. The story about the son, until ". . . Lydda", BT *B.B.* 10b, but not borrowed from there as here the context is much closer.

21. Cf. BT *Sanhedrin* 43b and see my discussion of that in Chapter 10, p. 236.

22. פגעת.

23. שושביניה, apparently to be taken metaphorically in the context of his desire to emulate R. Joshua ben Levi, his "friend," as related in the continuation, and not in the sense of his being a contemporary, if he is the R. Hanina bar Papa of the turn of the fourth century, Palestine, (see Hyman, *Toldoth,* vol. 2, pp. 494b–95a). Rashi's explanation that his "friend" here is the angel of death fits in with the aura around him as it emerges from PT *Pe'ah* 8:9 (21b).

24. Literally, "that he is all of him full of eyes," and see Ezekiel 1:18 and 10:12.

25. M *Nedarim* 9:1–9, BT 64a–66a; *Shevu'ot* 27b; *Yad, Shevu'ot* 6:1ff.

26. Some variants (see *DDS*) include R. Simeon ben Yohai as a participant in the following conversation, speaking Elijah's words together with him, while they all stand at "the entrace to the Garden of Eden." Also see the next note.

27. Literally, "Two, I saw," and this is probably the source of the reading mentioned in the previous note. Rashi also had that reading and he therefore identifies the "voice" as that of God, but this seems unlikely. The most likely reading, therefore, seems to be that of the printed text (as I translate it) with the addition that R. Simeon ben Yohai's *voice* was heard as well, and this is indeed the reading of Ms Florence as copied in *DDS*. On the connection between R. Simeon ben Yohai and R. Joshua ben Levi see later, but this is a subject that must be studied profoundly within the further context of R. Simeon's own ways and thoughts as seen through tradition.

28. Following the uncensored reading.

29. Ms Florence reads instead, "Peace upon you Sir" (*DDS*).

30. The variants reverse the order, having the sage report first "Peace upon you . . ." and Elijah answering that followed by the reporting of the answer to the question "When" together with the sage's pained comment and Elijah's explanation.

31. Identified by the Rabbis as referring to Rome: "In R. Meir's copy of Scripture it was written, 'The burden of Dumah (Isaiah ibid.)—The burden of Rome'" (as the text should read, PT preceding our pericope), and see *Pseudo-Jonathan* to Genesis 36:43 (the reading in ed. Ginsburger [Berlin 1903], p. 68; also see note) followed by Rashi.

32. See my discussion in Chapter 9.

33. Cf. *Gen. Rabbah* 35 (pp. 328–29, also see notes).

34. Apparently, this is a combination of two versions (see BT *Berakhot* 59a and *DDS*) but see also *Tosefta* 7:5. "Faithful in His covenant" implies that God is faithful in the very making of the covenant; i.e., in so doing he faithfully ensured that in the future there would never be another world-destroying flood, cf. Genesis 8:22. "Who remembers the covenant" implies that God's attitude toward man as expressed in the fact of such a covenant (cf. ibid.:21) remains unchanged now and always. The former thus is a turning to God as the lord of nature, whereas the latter speaks of him in his stance, as it were, vis-à-vis man.

35. Cf. BT *Sukkah* 45b.

36. Cf. ibid., and *Gen. Rabbah* ibid. (pp. 329–30). On the subject of the rainbow, see also BT *Hagigah* 16a and *Berakhot* 59a.

37.   Behold, I will send you
        Elijah the prophet
        Before the coming
        Of the great and terrible day of the Lord.
        And he shall turn the heart of the fathers to the children,
        And the heart of the children to their fathers; (Malachi 3:23–24)

Bibliography of Primary Sources

Translations of biblical passages are from the translation of the Bible published by The Jewish Publication Society of America, Philadelphia, 1917, unless otherwise noted.

ANET (*Ancient Near Eastern Texts Relating to the Old Testament*), ed. J. B. Pritchard, 3rd ed., Princeton, 1969.

Avot de-Rabbi Nathan, S. Schechter, Vienna, 1887 (N.Y., 1967)

Exodus Rabbah, 1–14; A. Shinan, Jerusalem, 1984.

Genesis Rabbah, J. Theodor and C. Albeck, Berlin 1903–1936; republished Jerusalem 1965.

Ginze Midrash, Z. M. Rabinovitz, Tel Aviv 1976.

Lamentations Rabbah, S. Buber, Vilna 1899.

Leviticus Rabbah, M. Margulies, Jerusalem 1953–1960.

Mekhilta (de-Rabbi Ishmael), H. S. Horovitz and I. A. Rabin, Frankfort 1931; republished Jerusalem 1960.

Mekhilta de-Rabbi Simeon ben Yohai, J. N. Epstein and E. Z. Melamed, Jerusalem 1955.

Midrash Lekah Tov, S. Buber, Lemberg 1884; republished Jerusalem 1960.

Midrash Rabbah (on the Pentateuch and Five Megillot), Vilna 1878.

Midrash Tannaim, D. Z. Hoffmann, Berlin 1909.

Midrash Tehillim (Psalms)—Shoher Tov, S. Buber, Vilna 1891.

Midrash Zuta, S. Buber, Berlin 1894.

Mishnah

Pesikta de-Rav Kahana, B. Mandelbaum, New York 1962.

Pesikta Rabbati, M. Friedmann, Vienna 1880.

Seder Eliyahu Rabba, M. Friedmann, Vienna 1902; republished Jerusalem, 1969.

Seder Eliyahu Zuta, M. Friedmann, Vienna 1902–1904; republished Jerusalem, 1969.

Seder Olam, The Order of the World, A. Neubauer, Oxford 1895; republished Jerusalem, 1967.

Semahot, Tractate, M. Higger, New York 1932; republished Jerusalem, 1970.

The Tractate "Mourning", D. Zlotnick, New Haven 1966.

Sifra, A. H. Weiss, Vienna 1862.

Sifre—Deuteronomy, L. Finkelstein, Berlin 1940; republished New York, 1969.

Sifre—Numbers, H. S. Horovitz, Leipzig 1917; republished Jerusalem, 1966.

Ta'anit, Tractate, H. Malter, New York 1930; republished Jerusalem, 1973.

Talmud, Babylonian, Romm, Vilna 1880–1886.

Talmud, Palestinian, Venice 1523; Krotoschin 1866.

Targumim:

  (Pseudo) Jonathan, M. Ginsburger, Berlin 1903.

  Yerushalmi; Das Fragmententhargum, M. Ginsburger, Berlin 1899.

  Neofiti; Codex Vatican, Neofiti 1, Jerusalem 1970

  Jonathan to the Prophets, A. Sperber, Leiden 1959, 1962.

  Jonathan to the Writings, A. Sperber, Leiden 1968.

Tosefta, M. S. Zuckermandel, Jerusalem 1937.

Yalkut Shimoni, Salonika 1521, 1526; Warsaw 1876–1877; A. Hyman, I. N. Lerner, I. Shiloni, Jerusalem 1973–.

General Index

This index does not include references that appear in the table of contents or that are an integral part of the book as a whole.

Index of Sages

References are to pages where the sages appear in quoted texts only.

Index of Biblical Sources

References are to pages where the verses are quoted only.

Index of Rabbinic Sources

Only sources actually quoted or discussed are cited. In the case of the former the references are to the page where the source is quoted only.

Mishnah

Berakhot
2:2 292
4:3 53
4:4 53
4:5 53
5:1 89
9:2 95
9:5 95, 174, 268, 275

Demai
2:3 292

Terumot
8:12 294

Shekalim
5:1 93, 94, 106

Yoma
5:1 92
8:9 184

Rosh ha-Shanah
1:2 279

Ta'anit
1:5 35
2:1 35, 161
2:2 36, 85
2:4 36
3:5 36
3:6 36
3:7 36
3:8 36, 70
4:8 128, 129

Megillah
1:3 258
1:4 258

Sotah
9:12 55
9:15 114, 189–190, 275, 277

Gittin
3:4 121

Bava Meẓia
4:10 282

< LONG